P9-ASJ-304

A GRAMMAR
OF THE
ENGLISH LANGUAGE

Volume I
PARTS OF SPEECH

A GRAMMAR OF THE
ENGLISH LANGUAGE

IN TWO VOLUMES

by George O. Curme, Ph.D., Litt.D.

Volume I: Parts of Speech
Volume II: Syntax

REPUBLICATION BY

VERBATIM

Essex, Connecticut

PARTS OF SPEECH

by

GEORGE O. CURME

Ph.D., Litt.D.

A

VERBATIM

BOOK

Reprinted 1977 by VERBATIM, Essex, Ct. 06426
Second VERBATIM printing May 1978.
Third VERBATIM printing June 1979.
Fourth VERBATIM printing June 1981.
Fifth VERBATIM printing June 1983.
Sixth VERBATIM printing August 1986.

#

ISBN: 0-930454-02-2 (Volume I)
ISBN: 0-930454-03-0 (Set)
L. C. catalog card number: 77-87423

PRINTED IN THE UNITED STATES OF AMERICA

PREFACE

This volume of the *Grammar* contains *Parts of Speech* and *Accidence.* The two subjects are closely related and are here treated together. The purpose of the treatise is to describe fully the parts of English speech and their changes of form to express thought. The word 'form' does not mean today what it did in the Old English period. It was then associated with the idea of a change of endings to express thought. Most of the old endings have disappeared. The old syntactical framework remains intact, but the grammatical forms, case and verbal endings, have been greatly reduced. This was effected by employing simpler means of expression. For instance, today we often express a change of thought, not by changing the endings, but by changing the position of the words: '*The hunter* (subject) killed *the bear*' (object), but '*The bear* (subject) killed *the hunter*' (object). Thus position is an important modern English grammatical form. Often, however, we now express our thought without the aid of a grammatical form: I *go*, you *go*, we *go*, they *go*. The verb here does not express person or number. We feel that the context makes our thought clear. Thus context plays a rôle in our modern English. In this volume the author has tried very hard to gather together and put into orderly shape everything known to him about English grammatical form or English lack of it.

Form now plays a much less important part in the language than in Old English, but it is playing a greater rôle than in early Modern English. The simplification of our English, our most precious heritage, was carried a little too far in older English, and it was later found necessary to add more forms, and in the present interesting period of development still more are being created. This will become evident from the study of the Parts of Speech and Accidence presented in this volume. The loss of inflection in the adjective in Middle English made it impossible to make from adjectives distinctive pronominal forms, so that it became necessary to create a new grammatical form, namely, 'one,' to indicate the pronominal relation: '*every* child,' but '*every one* (in older

English simple *every*) of the children.' This construction first appeared in the thirteenth century, but it is in the modern period that it has done most of its growing. Moreover, it is still growing. In this book there is a good deal said of this 'one.' But the most marked feature in the growth of modern English forms is the amazing activity in the field of the verb, which is carefully described in *Accidence.* Not only entirely new structures have been reared but new life has been injected into older creations that were living but feebly. In the modern period the English people has shown its love of activity not only by establishing empires all over the world but also by creating new forms of the verb so that it can talk about the things that it is conceiving and doing. And the marvel of it all is the simplicity of these new forms of expression. In order that the reader might get a clear idea of the importance attached to form in the different periods of English, an outline of the Old English and Middle English inflections of nouns, pronouns, adjectives, and verbs has been given, also an insight into the reduced condition of adjectival and pronominal forms in early Modern English and their later gradual increase.

In *Accidence* there has been presented a rather full view of the great fluctuation in the use of our verbal forms earlier in the present period. In a number of cases there is still fluctuation here, and in some words it will be a long while before final results are reached and a uniform usage is attained. The English-speaking peoples have never planned and regulated the development of their language as they do their economic development. They wisely muddle along to greater stability and accuracy of expression. There is in fact here a very fine natural regulation — the survival of the fittest. Aptness of expression has a strong appeal, spreads, and finally becomes fixed in the language. But also caprice plays a rôle here. At a few points the choice of a final form from different competing rivals has fallen out differently in England and America. Moreover, American English sometimes preserves older forms, while British English abandons them for newer ones. In spite, however, of the considerable fluctuation in present usage in the best literature and the many variations in different countries and different social strata, there is much to rejoice over. Looking backward at early Modern English as described in this book, we can plainly see what tremendous gains have been made in the direction of uniformity of usage. There has been much progress also toward greater accuracy of expression. For a long while the trend has been toward better things.

As an individual grows from childhood to maturity, he has to enlarge his apparel. In the same manner the language of an individual grows with his developing mental power. Similarly, the language of a people unfolds with its developing intellectual strength. Each generation embodies in its speech its own growth and bequeaths the improved means of expression to the next generation for further improvement. Any attempt to check the development of the language and give it a fixed, permanent form is misdirected energy, and, moreover, as foolish as to attempt to arrest physical or mental growth. The great principle of life is growth and development.

Hence, the formulations of usage in *Parts of Speech*, *Accidence*, and *Syntax* are presented, not as fixed rules but as the description of the means employed by English-speaking people to express their thought and feeling. These means are not represented as fixed but as ever changing and developing as the result of the long struggles of the English mind in its unfolding intellectual life to express itself more fully and more simply. Glimpses of important older developments are given here and there throughout the *Grammar* in order that the reader may obtain an insight into the forces that have been at work shaping English. A careful study of these older developments will enable him to understand his heritage better and will give him a clearer idea of his own relation to it. The story of these older struggles for more complete or more simple expression should be of especial interest to those who are now forming their habits of expression, for this struggle has now become theirs, and the further shaping of the language will soon lie in their hands.

The author has, perhaps, stressed too strongly the conception of English as a development reflecting our inner life and struggles. We are not free to replace older formations by newer ones that express our thought and feeling more fully. It is widely felt as sacrilege to tamper with this inheritance. To countless thousands an inexpressive older type of expression is better than an expressive new one. Fortunately, there are always many who yield to the urge to say just what they think and feel, also many who recognize the charm of well-spoken words. Those who are acquainted with the history of our language know that forceful and accurate expression, though frequently gaining ground only slowly against prejudice and unwise conservatism, often in the course of the centuries wins recognition.

It is hoped that the many glimpses of older English presented in this book will help to divest our inherited speech of its mystic character. These glimpses will reveal our forefathers, not as demigods but as human beings like ourselves, often vacillating, sometimes blundering, even the best of them, but in the main trying to say what they thought and felt, employing the best means at hand, at times in their endeavor to attain to greater accuracy or simplicity daring even to make radical changes in their inherited means of expression, more radical than any we have ever dreamed of.

Everywhere throughout this book the American and the British literary usage of the immediate present have been put into the foreground as the principal objects of study, but the usage of the earlier parts of the Modern English period has been treated with considerable care, as the great masterpieces of these centuries are still read and thus belong to our world. English before the sixteenth century is only occasionally introduced, to throw light upon present usage or to give an insight into the forces that have shaped our language. In older English there were two literary standards — the southern and the northern British standard. Northern British no longer exists as a common literary language, but before disappearing it influenced southern British, which was to become the common British standard. The old northern standard survives also in many respects in current northern British dialects and in a considerable body of dialectic literature of permanent value. Earlier in the present period northern British influenced our American English through immigrants from the northern part of Ireland and Great Britain.

The present language of the common people — here called popular speech — is often treated in this book as presenting interesting features of current English, having on its conservative side relations with our older literary language and in its newer developments influencing our present colloquial and literary English. Considerable attention has been given also to colloquial speech, which in its place is as good English as the literary language is in its place. Our expression should vary according to the occasion, just as our dress varies according to the occasion. Many teachers would replace colloquial speech by the literary standard. If this should ever take place there would be no distinctive literary form for higher purposes, which would be the greatest calamity that could befall us.

The author's heavy indebtedness to others in the preparation of *Parts of Speech* and *Accidence* is the same as for his work *Syntax*, and is described in the preface to *Syntax*, but, moved by a feeling of profound gratitude, he desires to reacknowledge here his heavy indebtedness to the great *Oxford Dictionary* and the large English Grammars of Jespersen, Poutsma, and Kruisinga. As the present volume rests upon fact it was necessary for its author during the long period of its construction to be constantly drawing upon these great stores of fact. For a long period he has himself been diligently reading in the literature of England and America to get a clear, independent view of present English usage and its historical development, but he could not have written this book without the aid of these great European scholars. Of course, he is indebted also to other scholars, both European and American. The growing interest in American English among American scholars has been a great help in the preparation of this book. Moreover, the author owes much to his associates and friends, especially Professor Leopold and Dr. Goedsche of Northwestern University, with whom he has discussed, over and over again, the difficult problems of this volume.

The author desires here to thank those who have helped him with the various proofs. He feels especially indebted to Professor McCorkle of the University of Southern California, and to Mrs. Georgia Curme of Claremont, California.

George O. Curme

University of Southern California
Los Angeles

TABLE OF CONTENTS

See analysis of contents at the head of each chapter

PARTS OF SPEECH

ACCIDENCE

PARTS OF SPEECH

CHAPTER I

THE PARTS OF SPEECH

1. There are eight parts of speech: noun, pronoun, adjective, verb, adverb, preposition, conjunction, interjection.

THE NOUN

2. Definition. A noun, or substantive, is a word used as the name of a living being or lifeless thing: *Mary, John, horse, cow, dog; hat, house, tree; London, Chicago; virtue.*

3. Classification. There are different classes of nouns:

1. *Common Nouns.* A common noun is a name that can be applied to any one of a class of living beings or lifeless things: *teacher, student, mayor, president, king, man, lion, tiger, cow; house, tree, city, country,* etc. Such nouns are called also class nouns. These nouns usually have a plural.

To emphasize nouns, especially common nouns, and impart feeling to the statement, we often, in colloquial speech, place before the noun some intensive adjective, such as *blessĕd, blooming, deuced, confounded, darn* (or *darned*), or in stronger language *damned:* 'Not a *bléssed égg* was fresh,' or 'Every *bléssed égg* was rotten.' 'She is a *déuced déal* cleverer than lots of men.' 'He's a *confóunded blóckhead.*' 'He's a *dámned fóol.*'

2. *Proper Nouns.* A proper noun is the name of a particular living being or lifeless thing: *Mary, John, Longfellow, Shakespeare,*

Carlo (name of a dog); *Chicago, London, England, Pennsylvania, January, Friday, Christmas, Macbeth* (name of a general), 'Macbeth' or *Macbeth* (name of a drama), *Hamlet* (name of a prince), 'Hamlet' or *Hamlet* (name of a drama), etc. '*The Woods* (members of the Wood family) are our best friends.' '*The Cummingses* (the members of the Cummings family) will give a reception this evening.' '*The Greeks* have contributed much to the civilization of the world.' '*The Germans* are industrious.'

In the last four examples the proper nouns are in the plural, but they are not on that account common nouns, as claimed by some grammarians. The use of the definite article is significant. It indicates a distinct group in its entirety. In the general class of man each of these groups is a particular group representing something single in kind, a particular family or a particular nation. The members of a particular group are each single in kind, hence not marked by common characteristics. Also 'the rich' and 'the poor' represent distinct groups, but they are not particular groups, for the members of each group are gathered together on the basis of common characteristics.

As described in **5** below, however, proper nouns are often used as common nouns: *a Packard* (car), *a Shakespeare* (a great dramatist). Such nouns are common nouns, for we regularly, as in the case of common nouns, drop the article before the plural form when we desire to generalize: '*Packards* stand a good deal of rough usage.' '*Shakespeares* are not common in every generation.'

We employ the definite article with proper noun plurals when we desire to generalize: '*The Cummingses* are always on the side of good government.' '*The Negroes* have made a good deal of progress since their emancipation.' 'In earlier centuries *the Christians* were much persecuted.' When, however, the idea of class, i.e. a division upon the basis of common characteristics, enters into these plurals, the article is dropped, as in common nouns: '*Christians* shouldn't do such things.' The definite article with proper noun plurals, often, merely denotes totality: '*The Cummingses* have left town for their summer home.' We express the partitive idea by dropping the definite article: 'You will find *Cummingses* active in the various benevolent activities of our city.' The indefinite article is used for an indefinite reference to one member of a particular group: 'I never knew *a Cummings* to stand in the way of progress.' But in 'He is *a Cummings* through and through' *Cummings* is a common noun, for it represents a person as assigned to a class upon the basis of his having the common characteristics of the class.

Proper noun plurals often represent not particular groups but particular individuals: *the Carolinas* (North Carolina and South Carolina). 'There were three *Johns* and four *Maries* in our party.'

There are proper noun plurals that have no singular form: *the Alps, the Alleghenies, the Rockies, the Hebrides.* They represent definite groups.

Many proper nouns were originally common nouns: *Baker, Taylor, Smith, Fisher,* etc.

3. *Mass Nouns.* A noun may be not only the name of a thing with a definite form but also the name of a formless mass, a material, here called a mass noun: *tea, wheat, sand, water, iron, gold, paper* (but with a different meaning in 'this morning's *paper*'). In 'a pretty *lamb*' *lamb* is the name of a definite thing, but in 'We had *lamb* for dinner' it is a mass noun. Mass nouns do not usually have a plural, but with changed meaning they often have a plural form. See *Syntax,* **59** 4.

4. *Collective Nouns.* A noun may be the name of a collection of living beings or lifeless things, here called a collective noun: *nation, army, crowd,* 'a *herd* of cattle,' 'a *row* of trees,' 'a *chain* of mountains,' etc. For the use and the meaning of the singular and the plural of this class of nouns see *Syntax,* **59** 1.

A collective noun may by a change in meaning become a common class noun: 'The principal has a very fine *library*' (collective noun), but 'The principal discussed the question with the committee in his *library*' (common noun). On the other hand, a common noun may by a change in meaning become a collective noun: 'A foreign *body* (common noun) in the ear may be very dangerous' (Grattan, *Our Living Language,* p. 111), but 'What a fine *body* (collective noun) of men!' (*ib.*).

5. *Abstract Nouns.* A noun may be the name of a quality, state, action, or general idea, here called an abstract noun: *force, peace; hardness, kindness,* formed from the adjectives *hard, kind* by the addition of the suffix *-ness; warmth* (*warm* + *-th*); *youth* (*young* + *-th* = young state), but a concrete common noun in *a youth* and a collective noun in 'the *youth* of the land'; *friendship* (*friend* + *-ship*), *manhood, bondage, serfdom, slavery, hatred, fraternity* (but a concrete collective noun in 'the members of *this fraternity*'), formed from nouns; *stroke* (from *strike*), *throw, growth, growing, singing, scolding, increase, decrease,* formed from verbs; many names of general ideas: *music, art, chemistry* (but concrete in 'the *chemistry* lying upon the table'), *grammar* (but concrete in 'the *grammar* lying upon the table'). Abstract nouns do not usually have a plural, but with changed meaning they often have a plural form: 'The enemy brought up fresh *forces*' (= *troops*). For fuller treatment see *Syntax,* **59** 5.

4. Common Noun Used as a Proper Noun. A common noun is often employed as a proper noun: 'We live at *the Eagle*' (name of a hotel). 'Ask *Father* whether we may go.' 'He is a *Wrangler*' (member of the society called 'Wranglers'). 'They are both *Wranglers*.' 'He is a *Democrat*' (member of the Democratic party), but 'He is a *democrat*' (an adherent of democracy). A common noun often becomes a proper noun through personification: 'Speak, O *Star*, thy secrets old.'

5. Proper Noun Used as a Common Noun. A proper noun may often be employed as a common noun: 'Virgil was the *Homer* (i.e. great epic poet) of the Romans.' 'He was a *Napoleon* of finance.' 'She was a regular *Xantippe*' (an ill-tempered woman, originally the name of Socrates' wife). 'Lend me your *Webster*' (dictionary). 'He bought a *Packard* (automobile) yesterday.' 'He has just sold two *Packards*.' Compare **3** 2 above.

6. Compound Nouns. In the case of both common and proper nouns a group of two or more nouns often forms a unit, a compound: *toothpick, tablecloth, sidewalk; George Washington, the Black Sea, James Russell Lowell; the White House, the Northshore Hotel,* 'Vanity Fair' or *Vanity Fair* (novel by Thackeray), etc. Notice that we do not always write real compounds as one word.

A long stem vowel in the first component of a compound is shortened in a few words where the first component is a monosyllable: *bŏnfire* (*bōne* + *fire*), *breakfast* (*brĕkfast* = *break* + *fast*), *fŏrehead* (*fōre* + *head*), *shĕpherd* (*sheep* + *herd*), etc. This principle was once more active in our language than now. There are also elsewhere traces of it. Compare *a* below, 2nd par.

The formation of compound nouns is treated at considerable length in *Syntax*, **63** under the head of Group-Words and again in *Word-Formation*.

a. Derivative Nouns. Similar to compound nouns are derivative nouns, i.e. nouns formed by adding to a common or proper noun, an adjective, or a verb, a suffix which in many cases was originally an independent word. These suffixes are: *–ness, –ship, –dom, –th, –er, –ing* (suffix of gerund; see **56** 3 *c*), *–ess* (**28**), etc.; the diminutive endings *–kin, –ling, –ette, –let, –ie, –y,* which are also much used to express endearment: dark*ness*, friend*ship*, wis*dom*, Christen*dom*, warm*th*, find*er*, writ*ing*, heir*ess*; lamb*kin*, gos*ling*, kitchen*ette*, rivu*let*, kitt*y*, Kitt*y*, Kat*ie*, Bird*ie*, etc.

A long vowel in a monosyllabic stem is shortened in a few of these derivatives: *knŏwledge* (*knōw* + *–ledge*), *wĭdth* (*wīde* + *–th*), *wĭsdom* (*wīse* + *–dom*), etc. This principle of shortening a long vowel in the stem syllable when another element is added has been illustrated also in **6** (2nd par.). It is most active in verbs: *keep,* *kĕpt, kĕpt.* Compare **59** 2 B *c.* On the other hand, the long vowel of a monosyllabic word may become short under the influence of a derivative with shortened vowel. In the eighteenth century the noun *wind* was still pronounced *wīnd.* A common derivative of this word was *wĭndy* with shortened vowel. Under the influence of *wĭndy* 'wīnd' has become 'wĭnd.' The old long form survives in the verb *wīnd* ('*wīnd* a horn'). Compare *wind* in **63.**

The formation of derivative nouns is treated at considerable length in *Word-Formation.*

CHAPTER II

THE PRONOUN

7. Definition and Classification. A pronoun is a word used instead of a noun. As a pronoun always has the same syntactical functions as a noun some grammarians say it is not a distinct part of speech. But as it often has a marked distinctiveness of form and usually shows peculiarities of usage it is quite clear that it is a distinct part of speech. Although it is never the name of a person or thing, as is a noun, yet it has to do with nouns in that it is used instead of a noun that is used elsewhere or is suggested by the context. Thus it permits us to avoid the unpleasant repetition of a noun or the unnecessary naming of a person that is already known. It is a formal convenience of great importance.

There are seven classes of pronouns, two of them with subdivisions.

I. PERSONAL PRONOUNS

These pronouns are: *I, me, thou, thee, he, him, she, her, it; we, us, ye, you, they, them.* For politeness' sake the pronoun of the first person stands last when used in connection with other pronouns: '*He, you,* and *I* had better do it.' 'It is important for *you* and *me* to be there.'

The speaker employs *I* or *me* instead of his own name, or, when he includes others, he uses *we* or *us:* '*I* know it.' 'He knows *me.*' '*We* know it.' 'He knows *us.*'

You is used in direct address instead of the name of the person spoken to: '*You* know it.'

He, she, it, they, them, are used instead of nouns that have been previously mentioned: 'I shall talk with *Henry* about the *matter* this evening and shall discuss *it* (referring to the antecedent *matter*) with *him*' (referring to the antecedent *Henry*). '*Henry* found that *he* (referring to the antecedent *Henry*) was mistaken.' '*Henry* and *James* found that *they* (referring to the antecedents *Henry* and *James*) were mistaken.' 'John said *that he didn't do it,* and I believe *it*' (referring to the antecedent *that he didn't do it*). These pronouns always have an antecedent, i.e. a noun, pronoun, clause, or sentence to which they refer. Sometimes *such* is used with the force of *it, they,* or *them.* See **7** VII *c aa.* Sometimes *it* refers to a person: 'Would you like to marry Malcolm? Fancy being owned by that! Fancy seeing *it* every day!' See **33** *b.* Sometimes, like the relative *which* (**7** IV *a bb*), *it* is used to denote a quality, state, rank, dignity: 'She is a queen and looks *it.*' Compare **33** *b.*

My, mine, thy, thine, his, hers, its, our, ours, your, yours, their, theirs, were once used as personal pronouns, as the genitive forms to *I, thou, he, she, it, we, you, they,* and are sometimes still so used. See *Syntax,* **10** II 2 D (last par.), and *Syntax,* **57** 5 *a.* They are now usually possessive adjectives (**10** 1) and possessive pronouns (**7** VII *e*). For fuller information see *Syntax,* **57** 5 *a.*

a. Demonstrative 'The Same' Used as Personal Pronoun. In older English the demonstrative *the same* (**7** VII *b*) was often used as the equivalent of a personal pronoun — *he, she, it, they:* 'But he who shall endure unto the end, *the same* (= *he*) shall be saved' (*Matthew,* XXIV, 13). 'The natives, thinking we were determined to pay not the least consideration, at length ceased to apply for *the same*' (*Cook's Voyage,* V. 1755, A.D. 1772–1784), now *it.* This usage survives in legal and commercial language.

b. Adverb Used instead of Personal Pronoun. Where the reference was to things it was common in Old, Middle, and early Modern English to employ a compound adverb instead of a personal pronoun preceded by a preposition: 'Mr. Sherleys letters were very breefe in answer of theirs this year. I will forbear to coppy any part *theróf*' (Bradford, *History of Plymouth Plantation,* p. 303, A.D. 1630–1648). Similarly: *therewíth, therefór, thereón, thereupón,* etc. *Thérefore* (= *on account of that*) has become differentiated from *therefór* in spelling, pronunciation, and meaning, hence has been retained as a useful new word, but the other compounds, apart from legal and poetical language, are now little used. We feel the pronominal forms as clearer and more concrete. For instance, in the example from Bradford the adverbial form *therof,* as adverbs in general, cannot express the plural idea contained in the context and is much more abstract than the pronominal form *of them,* which impresses us today as delightfully concrete as against the vague *thereof.*

In older English, *hence* or *from hence* and *thence* or *from thence* often had the force of *from it, them,* and in literary style are sometimes still so used: 'My Flora was my sun . . . All other faces borrowed *hence* Their light and grace' (Suckling, *Love's World,* II, A.D. 1641). 'They went into one tent and carried *thence* silver and gold and raiment' (II *Kings,* VII, 8). 'A leopard shall watch over their cities: everyone that goeth out *thence* shall be torn in pieces' (*Jeremiah,* V, 6).

c. Forms Used for Reference to Preceding Idea. When the reference is to the general idea contained in a preceding word, clause, or sentence, the pronoun employed is *it,* or where there is more or less emphasis to be conveyed the demonstrative pronouns (**7** VII *b*) *this, that,* or sometimes still as in older English, *such,* which are used as emphatic personal pronouns: 'I have more than once had the pleasure of *meeting him*, but he has doubtless forgotten *it*.' 'Do thou grant, Lord, That, *when wrongs are to be redressed, such* (or now more commonly *it* or *this*) may be done with mildness' (Bailey, *Festus*, 77, A.D. 1845). 'Many were accordingly of the opinion that the army should take this course and abandon the original destination to Caxamalca. But *súch* (now more commonly *this*) was not the decision of Pizarro' (Prescott, *The Conquest of Peru*, Book III, Ch. III). 'Both Edith and I were delighted to hear *that the trip had already done you and Nannie good*. I was sure that *such* (more commonly *this*) would be the case' (Theodore Roosevelt, *Letter to Henry Cabot Lodge*, Aug. 8, 1908). 'I would be entirely willing *to be presented privately at court*, or *call on the leading public men in the different countries*, if *this* did not involve foolish and elaborate functions' (*ib.*). 'I may have offended, but *thát* (or sometimes *súch*) was not my intention.' 'He does stare dreadfully, though, but I suppose all artists do *thát*.' Compare *Syntax*, **7** C. If there are two references in the sentence to something that precedes and the idea is felt as important, *this* is used for the first reference and *it* is employed for the second since the idea has already been represented as important: 'He could not tell even his daughter that after such a life as this, after more than fifty years spent in the ministration of his darling cathedral, it especially behoved him to die — as he had lived — at Barchester. He could not say *this* to his eldest daughter; but had his Eleanor been at home, he could have said *it* to her' (Trollope, *Last Chronicle*, Ch. XLIX).

In the predicate relation, the adverb *so* competes here with *that*, *it*, and sometimes *such*: '*How the conversation took that particular turn* I do not know, but *só* (or sometimes *such*) it was.' 'He is discouraged, and *só* am I.' 'M. Caillaux's return to the scene as the director of the financial affairs of his country was marked yesterday by the dismissal (for *súch* it was) of M. Robineau, Governor of the Bank of France' (*The New York Times*, June 28, 1926). Sometimes both *so* and *that* or *so* and *it* are put to good use in the same sentence: 'Listen, friend — dear, dear friend . . . I may call you *so*, for you have béen *that* to me.' 'She is shy, but it is a peculiarity of hers that she never looks *it* and yet is intensely *so*.' Similarly, *so* is often used as objective predicate, i.e. is predicated of an object: 'She made life interesting just because she found *it so*.' Compare *Syntax*, **7** C.

With reference to the thought contained in a preceding statement both *it* and *so* are used in the object relation, but *it* is positive and definite, while *so* lacks definiteness and is quite vague: 'He said she must go, and he said *it* with a peculiar look of determination in his eyes,' but in answering the question 'Is he going?' we may say: 'He says *so*,' 'I think *so*,' 'I suppose *so*.' *So* is largely associated with certain verbs — *be afraid, fear, believe, hear, hope, say, suspect, tell, think, trust*, etc.: 'Are you going to come home late today?' 'I fear *so*.' *So* is very common after the pro-verb *do*, i.e. the *do* that is employed to avoid the repetition of a verb that has just been used: 'I haven't called on him yet, but I hope to *do so* soon.' Sometimes the statement referred to by *so* follows it: 'I have never, when I could have done *so*, taken the trouble to read original reviews of this little book' (Saintsbury, *Essays*, quoted from Kruisinga's *Handbook of Present-Day English*, II, p. 229). Compare *Syntax*, **11** 2 *b*.

The adverbs or adverbial phrases *hence* or *from hence* and *thence* or *from thence* were once widely used, and in literary style are sometimes still used, instead of *it, this*, or *that* dependent upon a preposition: 'Learn courage *hence!*' (Pope, *Odyssey*, XII, 251, A.D. 1725) now usually *from it, from this*. 'They could present to Parliament everything which favored their own purposes, keep back everything which opposed them; and *thence* (now usually *on account of that*) more effectually deceive the nation' (James Mill, *British India*, II, v, ix, 702, A.D. 1817).

II. REFLEXIVE PRONOUNS

These pronouns are: *myself, ourself* (= *myself;* see **36** *a*), *thyself, yourself, himself, herself, itself, ourselves, yourselves, themselves*. They refer to the subject of the proposition in which they stand, indicating that the action performed by the doer passes back to him, or is associated with him: 'He is worrying *himself* to death.' 'I am sitting by *myself*.' For the older forms, *me, you*, etc., which are still sometimes used here, see **36** and **36** *a*. In the seventeenth and eighteenth centuries *its self* was sometimes used instead of *itself*. In early Modern English, the older plural forms *our self, your self, them self* were still lingering, but were a little later replaced by *ourselves, yourselves, themselves*. Compare **36** *a*.

The reflexive form can refer only to the subject of the proposition or clause in which it stands: 'I know that *he* blames Hóward, not *himsélf*.' Hence, if the pronoun in the subordinate clause refers to the subject of the principal proposition, a personal pronoun is used: '*He* knew that she despised *him*.' This usage has become well established in English, but it is sometimes disregarded: '*He* judged they knew Hóward and not *himsélf*' (H. G. Wells, *The Sleeper Awakes*), instead of *hím*. It is probable, however, that the author, Mr. Wells, uses *himself* here as short for *hím himsélf* (**10** 2); but the stress is not so strong but that a stressed simple *him* would suffice. This emphatic form in *-self* is older usage, but it is still quite common: 'Professor Ogburn denied that there had been a feud between *himsélf* and the cháirman of the consumers' board' (*The New York Times*, Aug. 15, 1933). The more natural form in present usage is a simple personal pronoun. Notice in the subordinate clause of the following sentence the use of both personal pronoun and reflexive, each employed properly: 'When youth desired to become personal, or middle age showed a tendency to grow silly, she chilled them alike, and had the art to leave them not angry with *hér*, but with *themsélves*' (Phillpotts, *Beacon*, I, Ch. I). Compare *Syntax*, **11** 2 *c*.

With these reflexives the reference is definite. For indefinite reference we employ *oneself* or *one's self*, which are treated in **7** VII *c*.

III. RECIPROCAL PRONOUNS

These pronouns are: *each other*, *one another*. They express mutual action or relation on the part of the persons indicated by the subject: 'These two never weary of *each other*.' For a more detailed treatment see **37.** In early Modern English, *either other* was sometimes used instead of *each other*. See **37** *b*. For older forms which are still sometimes used here see **37** and **37** *a*.

IV. RELATIVE PRONOUNS

There are two groups:

a. **Relative Pronouns with Antecedent.** The relative pronouns of this group, like the personal pronouns in I. above, have an antecedent, but they differ from them in two points. The personal pronouns may stand in either a principal or a subordinate clause, but these relative pronouns always stand in a subordinate adjective clause, where they have two offices to fill. They not only perform the function of a pronoun, referring back to the antecedent noun or pronoun, but they have also the function of a conjunction, i.e. they have conjunctive force, linking the subordinate clause to the principal clause. These relative pronouns are *who, which, that, as, but, but that, but what* (colloquial), the indefinites *whoever*, *whatever*, and *whichever*, and other less common forms enumerated in *Syntax*, **23** II 5: '*He* makes no friend *who* never made a foe.' 'I have read the *book which* you lent me.' 'I met a *man that* I knew.' 'I had *the same trouble as* you [had].' 'He has not *such a large fortune as* my brother [has].' 'Not a *soul* in the auditorium or on the stage *but what* (or *but* or *but that*) lived consummately in those minutes' (Arnold Bennett, *Leonora,* Ch. VI). '*Someone* in the crowd, *whoever* it was, demanded fair play.' 'He stumbled over something, *whatever* it was, and fell.' 'I'll send you one of my boys, *whichever of them* (or *whichever one*) you prefer.' 'You may use either of the expressions, *whichever* sounds best to you.' The antecedent is often the idea contained in some preceding word or words: 'He is *rich, which* I unfortunately am not.' 'I said nothing, *which* made him still more furious.' 'The rain washed away the tracks, *which* prevented the trains from running.' 'He has a very fine auto, *which* accounts for his popularity among the girls.' Compare **8** *b* (last par.). Where the reference is indefinite, *whatever* or *whichever* must be used: 'He is one of *the moderns, whatever* that may mean.' 'The leper *looked* or *listened, whichever* he was doing, for some time.' Compare *Syntax,* **23** II 5.

aa. Older Relative Forms. In Middle English *who that* was often used for simple *who,* and *the which, which that* for simple *which.* For detailed discussion of these forms see *Syntax,* **23** II 1, 2, 3. In early Modern English, *the who* was sometimes used for simple *who,* as in Shakespeare's *Winter's Tale,* IV, IV, 537, and *the which* for simple *which,* and indeed is sometimes still so used. See *Syntax,* **23** II 6 (4th and 6th parr.).

bb. 'Which' Used for Reference to Persons. In older English definite *which,* i.e. *which* with a definite antecedent, referred to both persons and things. In early Modern English this *which* could still refer to persons: 'Our Father *which* art in heaven' (*Matthew,* V, 9). 'A couple of women, one of *which* leaned on the other's shoulder' (Goldsmith). This *which* now always refers to things. It often refers to a noun denoting a person, but the reference is not to a concrete person but to some quality in him, so that the reference is in reality to a thing: 'He is exactly the man *which* such an education was most likely to form' (Trollope). Compare *Syntax,* **23** II 7 (4th par.). On the other hand, the indefinite *which* in *b* below may refer to concrete persons. Compare *b* (last par.).

cc. Relative Adverbs instead of Relative Pronouns. We often use the relative adverbs *where, whence* (in choice language; in plain prose replaced by *from which*), *whither* (in choice language; in plain prose replaced by *to which*), *when, why,* and in older English also *how* (now replaced by *in which*) instead of the relative pronoun *which* preceded by a preposition: 'We shall soon come to the house *where* (= *in which*) I live.' 'The old home is a place *whither* (in choice language; in plain prose *to which*) in thought I often go.' 'It is difficult to discover the source *whence* (in choice language;

in plain prose *from which*) these evils spring.' 'There are times *when* (= *at which*) he is very much discouraged.' 'I do not know the reason *why* (= *for which*) he did it.' 'We perceive not the ways and manner *how* (now *in which*) they are produc'd' (Locke, *Human Understanding*, A.D. 1690). In older English, *there*, *there as*, and *where as* were often used instead of *where*. See *Syntax*, **23** II 5 (near end, p. 223). *When* is used with reference to a preceding statement: 'The whole nation was jubilant, *when*, like a bolt from the blue, news arrived of a serious reverse.' 'I saw him a month ago, since *when* I haven't seen anything of him.' In early Modern English, *whether* was often employed instead of *whither*. In older English, where the reference was to things, *where* often entered into compounds with prepositions — *wherewith*, *whereon*, *whereupon*, *whereof*, etc.: 'the bed *whereon* (now *on which*) he lay'; 'the condition *whereof* (now *of which*) I spake.' Only one of these compounds is a living form, namely, *whereupon*, which is still used in narrative where the reference is to a preceding statement: 'He refused to act with them, *whereupon* they ejected him from the room.' The other adverbial forms, apart from legal and poetical language, are now little used. Notice that in all these examples the reference is definite.

The relative adverbs *when*, *where*, *whither*, came into common use here for definite reference in the Middle English period. *When*, *where*, *whither*, could not usually be so used in Old English since they at that time still had only indefinite or general force. As they, toward the end of the Old English period, gradually acquired more definite force, they became available for definite reference. In Old English, however, it was not uncommon to employ determinative adverbs instead of relative pronouns where there was a reference to definite persons or things. The determinative adverb *þær* was used where we now use *where:* 'on þære byrig *þær* se cyning ofslægen læg' (*Old English Chronicle*, A.D. 800) = 'in the town *where* the King lay slain,' originally 'in the town, *there:* the King lay slain,' the determinative *þær* pointing forward, like an index finger, to the following explanatory clause. In wide use was the determinative adverb *þe*, pointing forward to a following explanatory clause. If there was a preposition used, it stood immediately before the verb: 'mid *þæm* folce *þe* he *ofer* wæs' = 'with the people that he was placed over, had the command of,' originally 'with the people, *those:* he was placed over,' the *þe* pointing forward, like an index finger, to the following explanatory clause. Compare **39**.

dd. *Relative Clause without Relative Pronoun.* It is quite common in English to dispense with the relative forms altogether:

'Here is the book *you lent me.*' In fact, however, such clauses are not without a connective. In this sentence the definite article before *book* is a determinative that, like an index finger, points to the following explanatory clause. For fuller discussion see *Syntax*, **23** II.

b. **Indefinite and General Relative Pronouns.** The meaning here is always indefinite or general, hence there can be no reference to a definite antecedent; but these pronouns have the same conjunctive force as the relatives in *a*, linking the subordinate clause in which they stand to the rest of the sentence. These pronouns are: *who, whoever, whosoever, whoso* (archaic), *what, whatever, whatsoever, whatso* (archaic); *what, what one, what ones, what(so)ever one(s), which, which one, which ones, which(so)ever one(s)*, indefinite relative adjectives (**10** 5 *b*) used as indefinite relative pronouns. These pronouns are most common in substantive clauses, i.e. in subject clauses and object clauses. The subject clause is the subject of the principal verb. The object clause is the object of the principal verb or the object of a preposition. Subject clause: 'It is not known to me *who did it.*' Object clause, object of the principal verb: 'I did not see *whom he struck.*' 'I do not know *to whom he gave it.*' 'He knows *what I said.*' 'But I never touched the cards, I took *what were given me.*' 'I told him *which of the books I wanted.*' 'Here are my roses. Pick *whichever one(s) you like best.*' Object clause, object of a preposition, preposition and object forming a unit called prepositional clause: 'I am glad to get these books, and I shall be grateful *for whatever ones you may give me in the future.*' A few additional examples follow, illustrating these constructions: '*Whatever is worth doing at all* is worth doing well.' 'The two boys are equally bright, so that it is impossible for me to tell *which of them is more promising.*' 'The boys in our group are all such fine fellows that I can't tell you *which one* (or *which ones*) *I like most.*' 'I think that all the girls would dance with you, so that you may select *whichever of them pleases you most.*' 'I think that all the girls would dance with you, so that you may select from among them *whichever one* (or *whichever ones*) *you like most.*' 'As I have not read all the new books, I cannot tell you *which* (or more accurately *which one* or *which ones*) *I like most.*' 'Here are some new books. You may have *whichever one* (or *whichever ones*) *you choose.*' For other examples see **38** *b*. Indefinite and general relative pronouns are treated at still greater length in *Syntax*, **21** (2nd, 3rd, 4th parr.), **23** I, **24** III (3rd par.).

The pronouns in *-ever* are used also in adverbial concessive clauses: 'I am going *whatever he may say.*' 'He will find difficulties *whichever of these ways he may take.*' 'The task will be difficult *whichever of the brothers may undertake it.*' Compare **10** 5 *b*, **15** 2 *i*, **18** B 5.

In contrast to usage in *a*, *which* and *whichever* refer here to either a person or a thing — a survival of once universal usage. Compare *a bb*.

aa. Older Use of '*Whether*.' In older English, *whether* was much used as an indefinite relative pronoun referring to two persons or things, sometimes with reference to three, and this older usage lingers on in archaic prose and in poetry: '*Whether* (now usually *which*) of the two was the stronger and the fiercer it would be hard to tell' (Kingsley, *The Heroes*, II, II, 122, A.D. 1856). 'We came in full View of a great Island or Continent (for we knew not *whether*)' (Swift, *Gulliver's Travels*, II, I, A.D. 1726), now 'we knew not *which*.' The form *whether* is now usually a conjunction. See **18** B 1, 2, 3, 4 *a*, **15** 2 i.

V. INDEFINITE PRONOUNS

When we desire to convey an indefinite or general impression, we often avoid the use of a noun and employ instead of it an indefinite pronoun. The following are the most common: *somebody, anybody, everybody, nobody; something, somewhat, anything, everything, aught, nothing, naught* or *nought; a body* (now little used, though once common), *a person, a man, a fellow* (colloquial), *a chap* (colloquial), all with the force of the indefinite pronoun *one; a party*, with the force of *somebody, a person*, originally a technical legal term, which later came into more general literary use with this broader meaning, now confined to employment in popular or jocular language; *every man* = *everybody; no man* = *nobody*; *men; people; folks*, in England *folk*, both now less common than formerly, giving place to *people;* the personal pronouns, *we, you, they*, as described in **33** *g; a thing, things; whatever* (see *f* below); *muchwhat* = *many matters; a whit; a bit, a little bit, a good bit; a good deal; plenty*, sometimes in American English and British dialect *a plenty*, a survival of older British usage; *a host* (literary); *a number, a small number, a good number, a large number, any number* (stronger than *a good number*), *numbers, immense numbers; a lot* or *lots* (colloquial); *a heap* or *heaps* (colloquial); *no end; a world* or *worlds* (colloquial); *oceans; a sight* (colloquial) = *a lot; a heap sight* (popular American English); *a jolly sight* (colloquial British); *a smart chance, a smart, a right smart*, or *right smart*, in American dialect = *a considerable quantity* or *part; a hell* (colloquial) expressing feeling = *considerable; a power*, once literary, now popular = *a lot; a couple*, usually *two*, but in loose colloquial speech sometimes = *a small number*. In slang and dialect there are many others: *oodles, scads, stacks,* etc. = *lots*. In the literary language there are a number of pronouns associated with the negative form of statement: 'He hasn't *the shadow* of a claim, *the ghost* of a chance.' 'There's not *a shred* of evidence.' 'It doesn't make *a particle* of difference.' Of course, some of the pronouns given above may be used after a negative: 'He hasn't *a blessed* (or *single*) *bit* of modesty.' Many of these pronouns, or in the case of compounds their basal components, are old nouns that have in large measure lost their original concrete meaning.

Examples:

There was *somebody* here this morning to see you.
I'll offer to go if *anybody* else will.
Everybody knows that.
The effort to please *everybody* usually results in pleasing *nobody*.
He has generally seen *something* of foreign countries.
There was *something* of bustle as well as of sorrow all over the house.
He liked to hear of their births, marriages, and deaths, and had *something* of a royal memory for faces.
He was *something* of a humorist and dry joker.
I must get you into bed at once — instantly or I shall have you down with pneumonia or *something* tomorrow.
He broke his leg or *something* (i.e. some other part).
I have *something* important (or 'of importance') to announce.
He is *something* of a philosopher.
Is there *anything* I can do for you?
Has *anything* important (or 'of importance') happened lately?
Have you seen *anything* of John lately?
She is *anything but* (**42** *c aa*) strong.
Everything depends upon that.
Pace is *everything*.
The book did *everything* but sell.
I know *nothing* about it.
I have seen *nothing* of him recently.
I have *nothing* important (or 'of importance') to report.
The fire is too hot for *a body* to kneel over (Charles Reade, *The Cloister and the Hearth*, Ch. II).
If *a person* can't afford a thing, he must do without it.
A man's religion is the chief fact about him (Carlyle).
In such a case what is *a man* to do?
A fellow feels queer under such circumstances.
You might give *a chap* (referring to the speaker, spoken of as representing people in general) a civil answer.
There was *a party* (popular = *somebody*) here last evening to see you.
What is *every man's* business is *no man's* business.

Men are blind to their own faults.

People may get a little impatient when their toes are trodden on.

That's what *folks* say.

How *folk* put up with such a din was a mystery (J. B. Priestley, *The Good Companions*, Ch. VI).

In ordinary life *we* use a great many words with a total disregard of logical precision (Jevons).

You can talk a mob into anything (Ruskin).

They say there is no danger.

In Germany *they* manage things better.

If she says *a thing* (= *something*), it must be done (Thackeray, *The Virginians*, Ch. II).

Things are going better now.

I gave him *a bit* of my mind.

The question is attracting *a good deal* of attention.

He has *plenty* of money.

Remember to let it have *a plenty* of gravel in the bottom of its cage (Longfellow, *Kavanagh*, Ch. XV).

He was *a host* of debaters in himself.

'There are *a large number* of things that I want to say,' or instead of *a large number* we may repeat the noun: 'The entrance to the floor given to executive offices was like the lobby of a pretentious hotel — waiting room in brocade and tapestry; then something like an acre of little tables with *typists and typists and typists*, very busy, and *clerks and clerks and clerks* with rattling papers' (Sinclair Lewis, *Dodsworth*, Ch. II).

There are *any number* of people who believe that.

Numbers of people from New England and elsewhere have traveled this way (Richard Smith, *A Tour of Four Great Rivers*, I, p. 23, A.D. 1769).

Numbers of Pen's friends frequented this very merry meeting (Thackeray, *Pendennis*, I, Ch. XXX).

There were *a large number* there.

There were only *a small number* there.

There is *a lot* (or *lots*) of time.

We had *a lot* (or *lots*) of fun yesterday, and we shall have *a lot* (or *lots*) today.

There are *a lot* (or *lots*) of men who can do that.

He has had *a heap* (or *heaps*) of trouble.

I have had *no end* of trouble.

There are *no end* of people here that I don't know (George Eliot).

My opponent has made *no end* of charges.

It will do you *a world* (or *worlds*) of good.

He has *oceans* of money.

It done him *a sight* of good (*Dialect Notes*, I, p. 393).

There was *a sight* of folks at meetin' today (*ib.*, III, p. 369).

There will be *a smart chance* of peaches this season (*ib.*, II, p. 330).

There was *a smart* of things you were doing, too (Hergesheimer, *Lonely Valleys*, V).

He raises *a right smart* of cotton (*Dialect Notes*, III, p. 398).

Directing the work, and Yankee-like, doing *right smart* of it himself (Tourgee, *Fool's Errand*, p. 88).

Right smart o' (of) fish up there (R. H. Barbour, *Pud Pringle Pirate*, Ch. XII).

They were making such *a hell* of a noise that I couldn't study.

'But *a hell* of a lot of good it did me' (Anderson and Stallings, *Three American Plays*, p. 75) (ironical).

I've *a power* of things to do at home (Mrs. H. Wood, *Dene Hollow*, Ch. IV).

'I lost *a couple* of dollars' or in loose colloquial speech '*a couple* (treated as an adjective) dollars.'

Besides these indefinite pronouns there is another group, given in VII *c* below as they are of different origin. The two groups of indefinite pronouns compete with each other, some of them without a difference of meaning, as in the case of *somebody* or *someone*, some of them with differentiated meaning, as in the case of *some* (a fair amount) and *something* (a small amount, a slight trace): 'I should like to have *some* of his patience.' 'She has *something* of her mother's sweetness.' On the other hand, *something* sometimes means *something of value:* 'There is *something* in what you say.'

a. Compounds with 'Thing' and 'Body.' Of the forms given above, the compounds with *thing* arose in the eleventh century and those with *body* in the fourteenth century, at a time when *body* was an exact equivalent of *person*, hence before it developed the tinge of compassion, as in 'She is a poor, feeble, fragile old *body*.' The old meaning of *person* still occurs occasionally in the literary language: 'The little children of both sexes were nearly always nice enough to take into *a body's* lap' (Mark Twain, *A Tramp Abroad*, 2). 'Life was, indeed, a strange thing, and would *a body* comprehend it, then must *a body* sit staring into the fire, thinking very hard, unheedful of all idle chatter' (J. K. Jerome, *Paul Kelver*, I, Ch. I). It survives chiefly in dialect, especially Scotch: 'Gin (= if) *a body* meet *a body* — coming through the rye, Gin *a body* kiss *a body* — Need *a body* cry?' (R. Burns). It was the concrete meaning of *thing* and *body* that at first brought these compounds into use and established them in the language. They distinguished life from the lifeless and were thus more concrete than older *some*, which competed in part with them. Similarly, the adverbial accusatives (*c* below) *any place, some place, no place*, etc., by reason of the concrete force of *place* are often used in popular speech instead of the literary compound adverbs *anywhere, somewhere, nowhere*, etc.: 'I can't find it *any place*.' 'I am going *some place* today.' The common people employ also compound adverbs here, but they use the more concrete genitive forms *anywheres, somewheres, nowheres,* instead of the literary uninflected forms *anywhere, somewhere, nowhere.*

b. 'Somewhat,' 'Aught,' 'Naught,' 'Nought.' Of the indefinite pronouns in this group *somewhat, aught, naught* or *nought,* are in plain prose not now so common as they once were, being now largely confined to archaic or poetic language. As pronouns *aught* and *naught* still have a limited field of usefulness in rather choice language: 'for *aught* (or more commonly *anything* or *all*) I know.' 'Their plans will come to *naught*' (or more commonly *nothing*). 'Religion was a part of men's daily lives, but the principles of Christianity were set at *naught* at the first bidding of expediency' (Beerbohm Tree, *Henry VIII,* 12), in this set expression still common, although *nothing* is sometimes used in its stead. As a pronoun *naught* is now more common than *nought,* but as a noun, used as the name of the figure *0, nought* is the usual form. *Somewhat* is now usually replaced by *something, aught* by *anything, naught* by *nothing.*

c. Neuter Accusative Used as an Adverb. The neuter accusative singular or plural of a number of these pronouns is employed also as an adverb. *Somewhat* is used both as pronoun and as adverb: 'This argument has lost *somewhat* (pronoun) of its force.' 'He is *somewhat* (adverb) better this morning.' The pronoun *muchwhat* (= *many matters*) has not been used in the present period, but the adverb *muchwhat* formed from it was very common in the seventeenth century: 'God's dealings are *muchwhat* (now replaced by *pretty much*) the same with all his servants' (Richard Baxter, *Autobiography,* Ch. X, A.D. 1698). Also *nothing* is used as both a pronoun and an adverb: 'He has *nothing* (pronoun) in him.' '*Nothing* (adverb) daunted, he began again.' 'It helps us *nothing* (adverb) in such a difficulty to say that,' etc. In older English, *nothing* was much more widely used as an adverb than now, often where now some other word or expression must be used: 'For the Indians used then to have *nothing* so much corne' (Bradford, *History of Plymouth Plantation,* p. 118, A.D. 1630–1648), now 'For the Indians then didn't use to have *nearly* so much corn.' *Something, anything, aught, naught,* are now little used as adverbs, although this usage was in older English not uncommon. *Something* still lingers as an adverb in certain expressions: 'It was shaped *sómething* like a cigar.' 'He walks *sómething* like his father.' *Something líke, anything líke, nothing líke,* are employed as compound adverbs: 'He has given the institution *something líke* (= *about*) $10,000.' 'The $10,000 he has given the institution is not *anything líke* (= *nearly*) adequate to its present needs.'

'This cloth is *nothing like* as good' (*not nearly so* good). *A whit, a bit, a good bit, a lot* or *lots* (colloquial), *a heap* or *heaps* (colloquial), *a sight* (colloquial and popular), *a heap sight, a good sight, right smart* (dialect), *plenty, no end,* etc., are much used adverbially: 'I don't care *a whit* for what he thinks of me.' 'Wait *a bit.*' 'I think *a good deal* of him.' 'He is *a lot* (or *lots,* or *a good deal*) better.' 'He is *heaps* better.' 'I'd *a sight* rather not do it' (*Dialect Notes,* III, p. 369). 'It will cost *a sight* of money' (*Concise Oxford Dictionary*). 'Smallpox is *a heap sight* worse than measles' (*Dialect Notes,* III, p. 398). 'He knows it *a good sight* better than you.' 'He said the water had been on the rise *right smart* of time already.' 'That is *plenty* good enough for me.' 'You are *no end* cleverer and stronger' (Farrar, *Eric,* 55). 'I heard you rummaging around in there *no end*' (Albert Payson Terhune, *Treasure,* Ch. V).

d. Indefinite Pronouns Used as Nouns. Some of the indefinite pronouns in this group are used as nouns: 'They are *nobodies, somebodies*' (plural nouns). 'She then proceeded to relate the little *nothings* that had passed since the winter.' 'There was an indefinite *something* about his manner that always attracted my attention.' *Something* is often employed as a substitute for a word that is not remembered: 'I just caught the five *something* train.'

e. 'Else' after Indefinite Pronouns. Some of the indefinite pronouns in this group, though themselves compounds, enter into a close relation to the adverb *else,* which often follows them, forming with it new compound pronouns: '*somebody else's* child,' '*nobody else's* business.' Compare **40** (3rd par.). *Somebody* and *something* enter into a close relation to the indefinite adjective *other,* forming with it a compound pronoun with pronounced indefinite force: '*Somebody or other* will find something to criticize about it.' 'There is *something or other* about him that is unpleasant.'

f. 'Whatever.' In Old English, simple *what* was used as an indefinite pronoun with the force of *something, anything.* In composition with *ever* it is sometimes still used, in its strengthened form with the force of *anything,* usually followed by *else:* 'The torrent bursts in on me and pours over my wasted bulwarks, resolves high aims and *whatever else*' (M. Dods, *Gosp. John,* II, XIV, 218, A.D. 1892). Though this *whatever* is not much used as an indefinite pronoun, its accusative is widely employed as an adverb with the force of *at all:* 'I feel no anxiety *whatever.*' 'I'll agree to anything *whatever.*' 'I'll support my claim against any man *whatever.*' This adverbial *whatever* is much less widely used in the sense of *at any rate:* 'Thank the Lord you are not a coward, *whatever*' (Ralph Connor, *Glengarry School Days*, Ch. VI). 'Your face and breast seem very badly bruised and cut.' — 'Aye, yes,' said Macdonald, 'the breast is bad *whatever*' (*id.*, *The Man from Glengarry*, Ch. V).

VI. INTERROGATIVE PRONOUNS

When the situation is so indefinite that we are aroused to inquire after the exact state of things, we do not use nouns at all but employ certain indefinite pronouns, which we now call interrogative pronouns, since by giving them a peculiar intonation we indicate that they are intended to ask for an explanation of the indefinite situation and that we are expecting an answer. These pronouns are *who* (*whose, whom*), *what, what one*(*s*), *which, which one*(*s*), the last three of which are interrogative adjectives used as pronouns: '*Who* did it?' '*What* did he want?' 'Here are the books. *Which one* is yours?' or '*Which* are yours?' For fuller treatment and illustration see **41.**

In older English, *whether* was much used as an interrogative pronoun referring to two persons or things, sometimes with reference to three: '*Whether* (now *which*) of them twain did the will of his father?' (*Matthew*, XXI, 31). '*Whether* (now *which of the two*) would you advise me, to purchase some post by which I may rise in the state, or lay out my wife's fortune in land?' (Smollett, *Roderick Random*, Ch. XVI, A.D. 1748). This old pronoun survives in poetry and in archaic prose: '*Whether* (now in plain prose *which of the two*) would ye? gold or field?' (Tennyson, *Gareth and Lynette*, 333). *Whether* is now usually a conjunction. See **18** B 1, 2, 3, 4 *a*, **15** 2 *i*.

a. Interrogatives in Rhetorical Questions. Interrogative pronouns are used also in rhetorical questions, i.e. questions which do not expect an answer but express the indefiniteness or uncertainty present in the mind of the speaker: 'Well, *what* in the world will happen now?' Such a question, however, often has the force of a negative statement: '*What is the use?*' = '*There is no use.*' Compare *Syntax*, **16** 3 *b*.

b. Indirect Questions. The usual interrogative pronouns are used also in indirect questions, i.e. indirect ways of asking a question, or indirect reports of them: 'Tell me *who did it*,' indirect form instead of 'Who did it?' 'Tell me *what he wanted*,' an indirect form instead of 'What did he want?' 'Take these hats to John and ask him *which one is his*,' an indirect way of asking a question through another person. 'I asked him *to whom he gave it*,' an indirect report of the question '*To whom did you give it?*' 'After my talk on juvenile books he asked me *what ones I would recommend for the new town library*,' an indirect report of the question: '*What ones would you recommend for the new town library?*' Such interrogatives are interrogative conjunctive pronouns (**18** B), i.e. they bind the clause to the principal proposition.

c. Origin of Interrogative Pronouns. Notice that the interrogative pronouns *who, what, which,* are identical in form with the indefinites *who, what, which,* in IV *b* above. The interrogatives have developed out of the indefinites and are still indefinites, differing only in that they, by means of a peculiar intonation, indicate that the speaker is asking for an explanation of the indefinite situation and is expecting an answer. Compare *Syntax*, p. 211.

VII. LIMITING ADJECTIVES USED AS PRONOUNS

In this class there is a tendency for the substantive (**43** 1, 2nd par.) form of limiting (**8**) adjectives to develop into pronouns. The reciprocal pronouns in **7** III above were once the substantive forms of limiting adjectives used as pronouns, but they have further developed into real pronouns. The substantive forms of a number of limiting adjectives are used as pronouns. Compare **43** 1 and *Syntax* **57** 2, 3.

There are seven groups:

a. **Intensifying Adjectives Used as Personal Pronouns.** The intensifying adjectives *myself, ourself* (= *myself;* see **10** 2), *thyself, yourself, himself, herself, ourselves, yourselves, themselves,* are often used for emphasis instead of the personal pronouns in **7** I above: 'Did you ever know a woman to pardon another for being handsomer than *herself*' (= *she herself is*)? 'Most people do not realize how closely the mute creatures of God resemble *ourselves* in their pains and griefs.' 'You are not *yourself* today.' For fuller treatment see **10** 2 *b*. With all these pronouns the reference is definite.

The intensifying adjective *oneself* or *one's self* is often used as an emphatic indefinite pronoun: 'One is often not *oneself*' (or *one's self*). 'If it were said to *oneself* (or *one's self*) one would resent it' (*Oxford Dictionary*). Other examples are given in *c* (pp. 32–33).

b. **Demonstrative Adjectives Used as Demonstrative Pronouns.** These pronouns point out in various ways living beings and lifeless things. The reference often becomes clear with the help of a gesture or the situation or context. These pronouns frequently point of themselves backward or forward to individuals already mentioned or to be mentioned or described, or point backward to the idea contained in some word or group of words or in an entire sentence. Some of these pronouns indicate the individual by giving his place in a series or by including each individual in the series. In this important category we employ the substantive forms of the demonstrative adjectives, namely: *this, this one, these; that, that one, those; them,* once frequently used instead of *those* in literary language, still common in popular speech; *whose* (in literary style) = *that one's; the one, the ones; such, such a one* (in older English *such one*), *such* (pl.) or *such ones;* in older English *such* (pl.) or *suchlike* (pl.), now *the like; the same, the same one* (or *ones*); *the identical one* (or *ones*); *the very one* (or *ones*); *one and the same; the former, the latter; the first* (*one*), *the second* (*one*), etc.; *the last* (*one*); *both; either; neither; one — one* or more commonly *the one — the other, t'other* (in older English; see **44** C 1), *the other one,* in older English often simple *other* instead of *the other* or *the other one;* in older English sometimes *another* with the force of *the other,* as *an* once sometimes had definite force; *the other ones,* always referring to a preceding noun and emphasizing the idea of individual units; *the others,* sometimes referring to a preceding noun and emphasizing the idea of a definite group, sometimes used absolutely without reference to a preceding noun; *each, each one, one and all, each and all; every one* (or earlier in the period simple *every*), in early Modern English also with the forms *euerich, euerichone; every soul, every man jack, every mother's son* — all = *every one* but with more concrete force; *all; half.* Compare *Syntax,* **57** 1, 2, 3.

In older English, *either* had two quite different meanings — the older with the force of *each of two, both,* now on account of its ambiguity much less used than formerly, the younger meaning with the force of *the one or the other of two,* now the common meaning. Examples are given under **Examples** below.

In older English, *each* and *every* had the same meaning, as they were originally forms of the same word, *every* (a reduction of *ever each*) being a strengthened form of *each.* They both originally had individualizing and totalizing force. Now *each* individualizes, while *every* totalizes, a fine differentiation as the result of a long development: '*Each* (or *each one*) in the class should bring a friend along, and *every one* must be at the station by six.' In older undifferentiated usage *each* was often used where we now employ *every,* and *every* was used where we now employ *each.* As *every* totalizes, it is not used of low numbers: '*each* of the two brothers,' but '*every one* in the big class.' There are two *every's,* the definite *every* of this group and the indefinite one in *c* (p. 30): 'We arrived at home at six in the evening, *every one* as happy as he could be,' but '*Everyone* (general and indefinite) has his troubles.' The parts of definite *every one* are usually separated, while they are written together in indefinite *everyone*. In *every one* and *each one* there is often double stress for especial emphasis: 'I want *évery óne* of you to come.' 'I see new developments in art and life, *éach óne* of which is a fresh mode of perfection' (Wilde, *De Profundis*, 49). Compare *Syntax*, **57** 1 (6th par.). But when the stress upon *one* is stronger than that upon the preceding *every*, *one* is a numeral pronoun, and *every* is an adherent (**8**, 3rd par.) adjective: 'We shall have to go on quietly building ships — two to Germany's *every óne*' (*English Review*, March, 1912, p. 682).

Examples:

This is the picture of my wife and *that* the picture of her mother.

This picture is more beautiful than *that one*.

Is *this* (= Are you) Mrs. Smith? (addressing a lady).

This is (= I, the speaker, am) Mr. Smith (at the telephone).

That picture is more beautiful than *this one*.

These pictures are more beautiful than *those* (or in popular speech *them there*).

Those (or in popular speech *them*) are the girls I meant.

This boy and *that one* coming towards us are brothers.

I have spoken briefly of three scholars. I now desire to direct your attention to another. *This one*, Henry Sweet, I shall treat at some length.

This is the place our club meets in.

This is a friend of mine, Mr. Smith.

Fold it like *this*.

This is not fair.

Who is *that* just came in?

Who is *that* standing by the window?

Can any of you show me a woman like *that?*

Don't roll your eyes like *that!*

I wouldn't give *that* (a finger-snap) for it!

He talked about responsibilities and all *that* (similar commonplaces).

It was necessary to act and *that* promptly.

Would you like to marry Malcolm? Fancy being owned by *that!* (see **28**, 2nd par., **33** *b*).

He thinks highly of you. *This* I know.

They would like the present to be like the past; but the present, if it is alive, can never be *that*.

John, run over to the grocery and get a loaf of bread, *that's* a good boy.

I never bargained for *this*. He knows *that* very well.

Human pride and envy, human ambition and emulation, the desire to shine in the world — *these* are the main causes of the war.

Our schools are better than *those* of a generation ago.

This butter is better than *that* [which] we bought yesterday.

The most triumphant death is *that* of the hero in the hour of victory.

The face before me was *that* of a young man of thirty years.

Vengeance is his or *whose* (= *that one's*) he sole appoints (Milton, *Paradise Lost*, V, 808).

This book is more interesting than *the one* I lent you last time.

These books are more interesting than *the ones* I lent you last time.

His condition is about *the same* this morning as it was last evening.

Instead of getting into separate beds as they thought they were doing, they both climbed into *the same one* (Jerome, *Three Men in a Boat*, Ch. X).

The same individuals who in 1888 read *Robert Elsmere* with dismay are *the same ones* who now worship what they once denounced (W. L. Phelps, *Essays on Modern Novelists*, Ch. X).

'Are you sure it is the same hat?' — 'Yes, it is *the identical* (or *very*) *one*.'

These girls are *the very ones* we met yesterday.

The universe is *one and the same* throughout (Leonard Huxley, *Life and Letters of Thomas Henry Huxley*, I, Ch. XVI).

He never tired in the service of the community. The death of *such a one* is a great loss.

Look at these two fine large pears! *Such ones* you don't often get to see around here.

'He keeps rats, mice, rabbits, and *such*, or *suchlike*, in cages' (current popular English preserving older literary usage, in literary English now replaced in both cases by *the like*).

Both of them are good men.

John and *William* are both hard-working students. *The former* excels in mathematics, *the latter* in history.

He married her and took her away, *the latter* greatly to my relief (Pinero, *The Second Mrs. Tanqueray*, 22).

'Which of these modes of expression is correct?' — '*Either is* (or *Both are*) correct.'

I don't know *either* of these gentlemen (= Both of these gentlemen are unknown to me).

There are also in this Islande two famous Universities, *the one* Oxforde, *the other* Cambridge. I was my selfe in *either* (now *both*) of them (John Lyly, *Works*, II, p. 293, A.D. 1580).

They are both fine houses. I should like to have *either* (= *the one or the other*) of them.

Just above the feet at *either* (now *each*) of the three corners is an exquisite female bust (Howells, *Italian Journey*, p. 228).

You may have *either* (or *either one*) of these (two) books.

You may have *either* (now usually *any one*) of these four books.

I have seen *neither* of the (two) boys.

'She has style, talent, and money, and in the strict sense of these words Phillis has *neither*' (Hocking, *Awakening of Anthony Weir*, Ch. XI). *Neither* often, on account of its great convenience, is used thus loosely with reference to more than two, but in choice language we avoid it and use *none*, in the present instance saying *none of these things*.

These were subjects on which *neither* ever touched to *the other*.

Some words, like *envelope* and *avalanche*, have two pronunciations, *one* English and *one* as nearly French as possible.

The twins were both so exactly alike that it was impossible to distinguish *the one* from *the other*.

'Eche of them fersly regardyd *other*' (Lord Berners, *Huon*, I, p. 41, A.D. 1534), now *the other*.

'So aprochyd eche to *other* (now *the other*) and so fought eche with *another*' (*ib.*, p. 42), now *the other*.

'And now let's go hand in hand, not one before *another*' (Shakespeare, *The Comedy of Errors*, V, I, 425), now *the other*.

These apples are not good; *the other ones* are better.

Take this book and put it in on the shelf with *the others*.

I remained in the hotel; *the others* went to the lake.

The problem has exercised the minds of the two brothers, and *each* has solved it according to his temperament.

Each (or *each one*) of us here has just claims.

The whole conversation ran on the breakfast, which *one and all* abused roundly.

They seemed joyous *each and all* (Byron, *Prisoner of Chillon*).

'The fairest children of the blood royal Of Izrael he leet do gelde anoon, And maked *ech* (*each*) of hem to been his thral' (Chaucer, *The Monkes Tale*, 161), now 'He (Nebuchadnezzar) soon had the fairest children of Israel's royal blood delivered up to him, and made *them all his slaves* or *every one of them his slave*.'

'There are in this Isle two and twenty Byshops, which are as it were superintendents ouer the church, appoynting godlye and learned Ministers in *euery* (now *each*) of their Seas,' etc. (John Lyly, *Works*, II, p. 192).

I want *évery óne* of you to come.

Évery (now *évery óne*) of this happy number That have (now *has*) endur'd shrewd days and nights with us Shall share the good of our returned fortune (Shakespeare, *As You Like It*, V, v, 178).

Go to bed, *évery sóul* (or *évery mán jáck*) of you, instantly! (Thomas Holcroft, *Road to Ruin*, I, 2).

Évery móther's són of them wishes to be considered Samson and Solomon rolled into one (Mrs. Gaskell, *Cranford*, Ch. X).

So I went in and saw . . . all the Idols and abominacions of the house off Izrael paynted, *euerychone* (now *every one of them*), rounde aboute the wall (Coverdale, *Bible*, *Ezechiel*, VIII, 10, A.D. 1535).

She invited her *Sunday-school class*, and *all* came.

Half of the speech was good, *half* of it was very bad.

Half of the speeches were bad.

aa. 'Each' Used as Predicate Appositive. We should carefully distinguish between *each* employed as predicate appositive (**8**, 5th par.) and *each* employed as subject in an elliptical proposition: 'They *each* (predicate appositive) have, *in their several ways*, done fine service to the community,' or 'They have done fine service to the community, *each* [has done it] *in his own way,*' or 'We *each* (predicate appositive) have, *in our several ways*, been trying to serve the community,' or 'We have been trying to serve the community, *each* [has been trying to do it] *in his own way.*' *Each*, when used as subject, requires the possessive *his* (or *her*), as the reference is always to a singular subject in the third person, while predicate appositive *each* is often associated with *their* or *our*, for it is a part of the predicate, not the subject, hence has nothing to do with the choice of the possessive. These two constructions should not be blended, as in 'You will go *each your own way*' (instead of the correct *each his own way*). Mr. Fowler in his *Modern English Usage* calls attention to such a blending in a hymn: 'Soon will you and I be lying *each within our* (instead of the correct *his*) *narrow bed.*' He remarks facetiously that the author of this blending has failed to observe that he has restricted the application to married couples.

bb. Determinatives. A demonstrative pronoun points out a person or thing in various ways. Often it is accompanied by a gesture; often it refers to a preceding word called antecedent. These uses have been amply illustrated in the preceding paragraphs. There is another kind of demonstrative — the determinative pronoun. It points to a following genitive, prepositional phrase, or relative clause. There are two classes of such pronouns.

The determinative has no antecedent: 'In life I admire most *those* of a simple contented mind.' 'There was no time, no opportunity for *those* on board to save themselves.' '*Those* (or sometimes *they*, as in older English; in popular speech *them*, as in older literary English) who do such things cannot be trusted.' 'Blessed be *them* (now *those*) that hath brought that about' (Lord Berners, *Arthur of Lytell Bretayne*, 393, A.D. 1530). 'But on *those* of us who are not soldiers the influence of the war broods like the memory of a nightmare.' 'His mother parted her lips to begin some other vehement truth, but on looking at him she saw *that* in his face which led her to leave the words unsaid.' '*That one* of us who is first called away knows the survivor will follow ere long' (Thackeray, *The Virginians*, Ch. LXXV). In the singular the personal pronouns may be used as determinatives: '*He* (or *she*) who does such things cannot be trusted,' or in colloquial speech '*A man* (or *a woman*) who does such things cannot be trusted.' Similarly before a prepositional phrase: '*She* (or more commonly *the girl*) with the auburn hair.'

The determinative often has an antecedent: 'this hat and *that* of John's'; 'this book and *that one* upon the table'; 'this book and *that one* which you hold in your hand.' 'These books and *those* which you hold in your hand.' In Modern English, *that* (*those*) is often replaced by *the one*(*s*) except before a genitive: 'this hat and *that* of John's' rather than 'this hat and *the one* of John's,' or still more commonly 'this hat and *John's*'; 'this book and *the one* (or *that one*) upon the table'; 'this book and *the one* (or *that one*) which you hold in your hand'; 'these books and *the ones* (or *those*) which you hold in your hand.' 'Of all my nephews and nieces you are *the one* whose conduct in life has most pleased me.' 'Of all my nephews and nieces you and your brother are *the ones* whose conduct in life has most pleased me.' 'These boys are *the* very *ones* I saw yesterday in the act of robbing a pheasant's nest.' But *the one* differs from *that* in that it refers only to class nouns, hence cannot be used at all for reference to mass nouns and abstract nouns: 'This tea is better than *that* (not *the one*) we bought last week.' 'The depth of feeling in this book surpasses *that* (not *the one*) which I have observed in his other works.' The determinative *the one* is usually followed by a prepositional phrase or relative clause, but the construction is sometimes elliptical: 'Hand me his letter.' — 'This one?' — 'Yes, that's *the one* [I want].' Compare **10** 3 *e*.

When there is present the idea of kind, quality, we often employ the qualitative determinative *such:* 'Associate with *such* as will improve your mind and manners.' 'The studios think lightly of *such* of their men models as are able to offer nothing but curly hair, good teeth, and a sweet smile' (Beecher Edwards, 'Faces That Haunt You' in *Liberty*, May 22, 1926). 'I have had some good teachers, but never *such a one* as [is] Professor Jones.' '*Such* as I [am] are free in spirit when our limbs are chained' (Scott, *Quentin Durward*, Ch. XVI). When a restrictive clause follows, *those* is often in colloquial speech used as a qualitative determinative instead of *such*, since the restrictive clause is felt as indicating with sufficient clearness the idea of quality, and *such* is avoided as a literary word: 'Mention especially the intelligent and *those who* (or in more exact formal language *such as*) want to study literature as an end, not as a means' (Sir Walter Raleigh, *Letter to Percy Simpson*, Dec. 13, 1913). Where there is no preceding noun to which it can refer, the singular determinative *such a one* is a distinctively literary form, replaced in simple prose by *someone* or *a man* (*woman, boy, girl*): 'Associate with *such a one* as you can look up to,' or 'Associate with *someone*, or *a man* (*woman, boy, girl*), that you can look up to.'

In older English, *such* often lost the idea of a particular kind, and pointed, as described for adjective function in **10** 3 *f*, to definite persons or things, just like *those:* 'I See no Right the Indians have to make such a Demand, as those Posts have never been put to a Bad Use against them; but on the Contrary are for their Security as well as Ours: *Such as* (now *those which*) have been Destroyed in the upper Country shall be Re Established' (Sir Jeffery Amherst, *Letter*, written at New York, Sept. 10, 1763). In older English, *such* was also used referring to a single individual but with indefinite reference: 'I must desire that you will give Orders to *such one of the Captains as* (now *one, the one*, or *that one of the captains whom*) you think most fit to continue after the first of May' (Cadwallader Golden, *Letter to Sir William Johnson*, written at New York, Apr. 22, 1764). *Such* is still used with indefinite reference to a preceding abstract noun, where, however, it is now often more common to employ *it:* 'An appeal to philanthropy is hardly necessary, the grounds for *such* (or *it*) being so self-evident.' Compare **7** VII *c aa*. In older English, the neuter singular *such* was much used referring back to the thought contained in a preceding sentence, clause, or word, and this old usage still lingers. See **7** I *c*. The plural determinative *such* was once widely used for general reference: 'Let *such as* (now in plain prose usually *those who*) would with Wisdom dwell frequent the house of woe' (W. Cameron in *Trans. & Paraphr. Ch. Scott.*, XIV, I, A.D. 1777). When we desire to use a singular determinative form with general reference, we employ in literary style *he* (*she*) and in colloquial language *a man* (*woman, boy, girl*): '*He* (*she*), or *a man* (*woman, boy, girl*), who would do such a thing is not worthy of confidence.' At one point the old determinative *such* has been retained alongside of the determinative *those*, namely, where there is a desire to point, somewhat indefinitely without stating the exact relations, to a definite group of persons or things mentioned either in a following modifying phrase or in a noun or pronoun previously mentioned: 'It seems to have cooled the ardor of *such of the Bishops as* (or *those of the Bishops who*) at first tended to favor Sinn Fein as a means of smashing the Irish party' (*London Times*, Educational Supplement, Nov. 18, 1918). 'The number of those who were thus butchered cannot now be ascertained. Nine were entered in the parish registers of Taunton; but those registers contain the names of *such only as* (or *only those who*) had Christian burial' (Macaulay, *History*, II, Ch. V). The force of *such* here is often felt as more indefinite than that of *those*, which leads some to use it to convey greater indefiniteness and has thus preserved it. Similarly, *such others* is sometimes preferred to *the others* when it is desired to emphasize the idea of indefiniteness: 'Your Lordship and *such others as* (or *the others that*) you may please to consult on the matter, will at once see that my resignation of the wardenship need not offer the slightest bar to its occupation by another person' (Trollope, *The Warden*, Ch. XIX). Some use this indefinite *such* instead of the usual *they* or *them* when there is an indefinite reference to things that have just been mentioned: 'Those who have left parcels can recover *such* (usually *them*) on application.'

c. **Indefinite Limiting Adjectives Used as Indefinite Pronouns.** When we desire to convey an indefinite or general impression, we often avoid the use of a noun and employ instead of it an indefinite limiting adjective, treating it as an indefinite pronoun. Indefinite pronouns of a different origin have been treated in **7** V above. The indefinite pronouns made from indefinite limiting adjectives are: *all, any* (sing. or pl.); *anyone* (or earlier in the period simple *any*) = *anybody; any one*, an indefinite reference to a member of a group of individuals, persons or things; *ary one* (popular contraction of *e'er a one*) = *one, any one, either one; this and* (or *or*) *that* = *one thing and* (or *or*) *another; this one and that*, or *this and that one*, or *this one and that one; this, that, and the other; this, that, and the other one; everyone* (in older English simple *every* or in its older form *euerich*), an indefinite reference = *everybody*, but *every one* (**7** VII *b*, 3rd par.), a definite reference to every member of a group; *each* or *each one; someone* = *somebody; some one*, an indefinite reference to a particular person or to a member of a group of individuals, persons or things; *some* = *a fair amount* and *some people*, earlier in the period also with the meaning of *someone;* in older English, *some other*, now *someone else; someone or other; one or another* or *one or other*, usually referring indefinitely to one in a group of more than two; *one or the other*, referring indefinitely to one in a group of two; *one and another*, i.e. two or more in succession; *such* (sing. or pl.); *such and such a one; such and such ones; such and such* = *such and such persons, such and such a thing; so and so* = *such and such a person, such and such a thing; several; many; many a one; a one; a many*, once a literary form, now confined to popular speech; *a great many; the many; numerous* and *various*, both forms usually employed as adjectives, but in recent literature manifesting a tendency to become pronouns after the analogy of *many* and *several; one*, in early Modern English used with the force of *somebody; one*, referring indefinitely to an antecedent or a following modifying phrase or clause; *one*, an absolute indefinite pronoun without reference to an antecedent or a following modifying phrase or clause; *oneself* or *one's self* (**7** VII *a*, 2nd par.), both in use, the latter the older form and still often used in America, the former the newer but now more common form, used in the accusative after a verb or a preposition as the reflexive forms of absolute *one*, used also in the nominative or the accusative as emphatic forms of absolute *one; one's own*, used as an emphatic genitive of absolute *one; none* (sing. or pl.), negative form of *one*, referring to an antecedent or a following modifying phrase or clause; *not óne* (numeral), more emphatic than *none;* in popular speech *nary one, nary a one*, emphatic negative forms of *none; none* or *nó one*, negative forms of absolute *one*, the former a singular or a plural, more commonly, however, a plural, the latter always a singular, more common than singular *none; none*, sometimes a neuter singular ('I want *none* of your impudence'); *other* or *other one, another, others* or sometimes still as in older English *other* (pl.); *one — another; some — others; a certain one, certain ones, certain* (pl.); *sundry* (archaic); *all and sundry* (archaic); *considerable* (colloquial American); *much; more* or, in older English where the reference is to number, *mo* or *moe* (Old English *mā*); *a little, little; less; few; a few; enough; sufficient.*

Examples:

All is not gold that glitters.

I know *all* about him.

All who have studied this question have come to the same conclusion.

Doth *any* (now *ányone*) here know me? (Shakespeare, *King Lear*, I, IV, 246).

Ányone could do that.

Ány óne of my boys could have told you where to find him.

Do *any* of you know him?

Is there among the new books *ány óne* that would interest a boy?

Are there among the new books *any* (plural) that would interest a boy?

Age has not yet dimmed *ány óne* (singular), or *any* (plural), of his senses.

He hasn't *any* of his father's ability.

Amy and Virginny is the deceivingest in their looks ever you seed, and don't *ary one* of 'em look hardly twenty (Lucy Furman, *The Quare Women*, Ch. V).

I chatted with *this and that one.*

We talked about *this, that, and the other.*

Euerich (an older form of *every*, now *everyone*) hadde well eten and dronken raysonably (Caxton, *Jason*, p. 8, A.D. 1475).

Everyone says so.

I want *every one* in the class to come.

Each (*one*) *of us* (general and indefinite reference) has his several ideal.

I thought I heard *some* (now *someone*) stirring in her chamber (Vanbrugh, *False Friend*, V, I, 411, A.D. 1702).

I heard *someone* coming up the stairs.

I know *some one* from whose gentle lips there only fall pure pearls and diamonds (Thackeray, *The Virginians*, Ch. LXX).

I don't know who did it, but it was *some one* in the class.

I shall not have time tomorrow to treat all of these questions, but I hope to be able to discuss *some one* (singular), or *some* (plural), of them.

'I would she had receaved her punishment by *some other*' (Sir Philip Sidney, *Arcadia*, Book III, Ch. 24, A.D. 1590), now *someone else* (**42** *c bb*).

Some were captured, *others* were killed.

I should like to have *some* of his patience.

Someone or other is meddling in things that do not concern him.

One or another, or *one or other*, or *some one* of us (three or more) has to do it.

One or the other of us (two) has to do it.

I have heard it from *one and another* during the week.

Ernestine had already ventured upon several screen tests in *one and another* of the new studios in New York (Theodore Dreiser, *Bookman*, Sept., 1927, p. 5).

The stranger is welcome as *such*.

Strangers are welcome as *such*.

If you want to know who *such and such a one*, or *so and so*, is, just ask Jones.

If you review in your mind your favorite friends and your favorite books, you will find that *such and such a one* stands nearer to you, or *such and such ones* stand nearer to you.

Don't listen to everything that *such and such* say to you.

He is always ordering me about and telling me to do *such and such*, or *so and so*.

Several, *many*, of the books were damaged.

Several, *many*, have inquired after you.

While *a many* (popular for *many*) of the first settlers had been knowledgeable men with larning, their offsprings growed up in the wilderness without none (Lucy Furman, *The Quare Women*, Ch. III).

A great many were injured.

To *the many* who know him the news of his recovery will bring great joy.

Mr. Mick came to and fro from the regiment, and brought *numerous* of his comrades with him (Thackeray, *Barry Lyndon*, Ch. I).

The Queen has caused large hampers of the choicest blooms to be forwarded to *various* of the hospitals (quoted from Fowler's *Modern English Usage*, where a number of other examples are given).

Hark! hark! *one* (now *somebody*) knocks (Shakespeare, *Julius Caesar*, II, I, 302).

I lose a neighbor and you gain *one*.

However, there were serious complications in the case and *ones* which were quite unforeseen by either the British or the Irish government (G. W. Powell, *Donovan's Island*, Ch. XV).

He recommended him as *one* (literary, replaced in colloquial speech by *a man*) on whom I could depend.

If *one* cuts off *one's* (genitive of *one*) nose, *one* hurts only *oneself* (or *one's self;* reflexive accusatives of *one*).

One might do that for another, but not for *oneself* (or *one's self;* reflexive accusatives of *one*).

Oneself (or *one's self;* nominatives, emphatic forms of *one*) is the last person upon whom *one* turns the light of comedy (J. W. Beach, *The Comic Spirit in G. Meredith*, Ch. I, p. 10).

One is not always *oneself* (or *one's self;* nominatives, emphatic forms of *one*).

If it were said to *oneself* (or *one's self;* accusatives, emphatic forms of *one*), *one* would resent it.

It is narrowing to be always occupied with *oneself* (or *one's self;* reflexive forms of *one*) and *one's own* (emphatic form of *one's*) affairs.

'Lend me your pencil.' — 'I have *none*' or 'I haven't *any*.'

You have money and I have *none*.

He is *none* of my friends (*Concise Oxford Dictionary*).

He is *none* of your canting hypocrites.

None (singular; or more emphatically *not óne*), of his hopes has been realized.

None (plural) of his hopes have been realized.

I ain't goin' to *nary one* (or *nary a one*) of them places.

None (or more commonly *nó one*) has beat that.

None (plural) are so deaf as those that will not hear.

It is *none* of my business.

You may have this book or any *other* (or *other one*) you may select.

In these financial difficulties Mr. Broadwood and *others* of her old friends came to her aid.

The rest of the boys were accommodated at the houses of *other* (now more commonly *others*) of the masters (Mrs. Henry Wood, *Orville College*, Ch. I).

One may like it, *another* may dislike it.

'*One* hates *his* enemies and *another* forgives them,' but absolute *one*, differing from this *one*, which has *another* as a correlative, takes the possessive *one's* instead of *his:* '*One* hates *one's* enemies and loves *one's* friends.'

One man's (the regular possessive of the *one* that has *another* as a correlative) misfortune is often *another man's* fortune.

Some like it, *others* dislike it.

And *some* (seeds) fell among thorns . . . But *other* (now *others*) fell into good ground (*Matthew*, XIII, 8).

Among the students who pass our house every evening there is *a certain one that always attracts* (or 'there are *certain ones that always attract*') my attention.

Certain of the boys were honest enough to tell the truth about the matter.

Most of these books are worthless, but *certain ones* among them, which I desire here to mention, are worth reading.

'*Sundry* of the modern languages' (Whitney, *The Life and Growth of Language*, Ch. VII, p. 115), more commonly *several*.

'When you see the postman coming up the street with the morning's crop of bills and *sundry*,' etc. (*San Francisco Bulletin*, July 26, 1927), i.e. *various other things*.

'He has essayed to make his poet (Browning) comprehensible to *all and sundry*' (*Literary World*, 1892), more commonly *one and all*.

There is *considerable* to do.

After *considerable* of a row order was restored.

The book is very large, and *considerable* of it has been hastily written.

There is *much* to do today, and there will be *more* to do tomorrow.

There were *more* present today than yesterday.

Of these valiant beggers there be in euery place *mo* (now *more*) then (now *than*) a great meny (Langley, *Pol. Verg. De Invent.*, VII, VI, 144, A.D. 1546).

'Unto life many implements are necessary; *moe* (now *more*) if we seek such a life as,' etc. (Hooker, *Ecclesiastical Polity*, I, x, 2, A.D. 1594).

There is *enough* to do.

Here was *sufficient* to tax the energies of any man.

That young man was able to depart for the west with *sufficient* of money to insure the completion of his monumental work (Clarence Buddington Kelland in *Saturday Evening Post*, July, 5, 1930, p. 36).

aa. Indefinite 'One' Referring Backward or Forward. Indefinite reference is now in the singular expressed by *one* if it is desired to refer back to a noun that has just been mentioned, but, as in older English, *such* is sometimes still used here: 'He is a friend, and I treat him as *one*.' 'Two or three low broad steps led to a platform in front of the altar, or what resembled *such*' (Scott, *Aunt Marg. Mirror*, II), or now more commonly *one*. When the indefinite article *a* precedes the noun immediately, *a one* is often used instead of *one*: 'It was too good *a chance* to be lost,' or 'The chance was too good *a one* to be lost.' 'I had only half *a piece*,' or 'He had a whole piece, but I had only half *a one*.' Compare *Syntax*, **57** 5 *b* (8th par.). Of course, *one* cannot be used with indefinite reference to an abstract or general conception contained in a preceding noun. Here we use *such* or now often more commonly the personal pronoun *it*: 'An appeal to philanthropy is hardly necessary, the grounds for *such* (or *it*) being so self-evident.' *It*, however, cannot be used when the idea of specific character or capacity is prominent: 'Insolence in a child should always be treated as *such*, and the child should be punished for *it*.' 'It is difficult for me to appreciate in him the scholar as *such* apart from the man.' As indefinite *one* usually has no plural, we still employ here *such* or now often more commonly a personal pronoun: 'I should like to have some more examples of this construction if *such* (or perhaps more commonly *they*) can be found.' *Such*, however, is used if the idea of specific character or capacity is prominent: 'They are my friends, and I treat them as *such.*' But *one* is freely used, in the singular or the plural, if it is employed as a determinative pointing to a following modifying word, phrase, or clause: 'He behaves like *one* frenzied.' 'However, there were serious complications in the case and *ones* which were quite unforeseen by either the British or the Irish government' (G. H. Powell, *Donovan's Island*, Ch. XV). This determinative is especially common when it has qualitative force: 'When you get a new *pen* (new *pens*), get *one* (*ones*) with a sharper point (sharper points).' 'Are not the suggested improvements *ones that* (or *such as*) would be accepted nowadays in any design?' (*Punch*, 1893, p. 165). 'The step you have just taken is *one* of great importance.' See **7** VII *b bb* (4th par.).

There is another determinative *one*, which is always in the singular and always refers to a person: 'It lost you the love of *one* who would have followed you in beggary' (Sheridan, *The Rivals*, V, I). 'For *one* who can read between the lines there is much that is melancholy in Mr. Tozer's Chronicle.' In the plural, *one* is replaced by *those:* 'For *those* who can read between the lines,' etc. The plural form *those* is common, but the singular form *one* is in general literary, replaced in colloquial language by *a man, a woman*, etc.: 'She was *one* (more commonly *a woman*) on whom such incidents were not lost.'

bb. Absolute Indefinite 'One.' The reference here is quite indefinite and general: 'It hurts *one* to be told *one* is not wanted.' Other examples are given in *c* (p. 33). Attention is called to the fact that English *one* has a meaning somewhat different from that of the corresponding indefinite in other languages, such as German *man*, French *on*, etc. The force of English *one* is more indefinite. In German and French, *man* and *on* are often used to refer indefinitely to a definite person or definite persons. These German and French forms are very convenient expressions, for they make it possible to refer to a definite person or definite persons without taking the time or the trouble to name or describe the person or persons: '*Man* hat viel über diesen Gegenstand geschrieben' = 'Much *has been written* on this subject.' As we have no appropriate indefinite pronoun we have to translate the German statement by employing the passive form of the verb. Thus on account of the lack of an appropriate indefinite pronoun the passive has become a favorite form of expression in English.

cc. Accusative of Indefinite Pronouns Used Adverbially. The accusative of a number of these pronouns is used adverbially: 'He is *much* better today.' 'I can't go *any* faster.' 'He has a zeal *little* tempered by humanity or by common sense.' 'I am *none* the less obliged to you.' Compare **42** *c aa.* Feeling may be imparted to the statement by placing *ever so* before the adverbial accusative: 'It's *ever so much* better to face things cheerfully.'

For fuller treatment of this important accusative see **71** 1 *a*.

dd. Indefinite Pronouns Used as Nouns. A number of indefinite pronouns are used as nouns: 'He lost his *all* (or 'his little *all*') in the fire.' 'My father bid me pack up my *alls* (now usually singular) and immediately prepare to leave his house' (Fielding, *Amelia*, VII, III, A.D. 1752). 'He was a small grocer and dealer in *sundries*.' 'He is apt to boast of the *little* he has done, while he utterly forgets the *much* that he has left undone.' 'His *little* is more than my *much*.' On the other hand, such a noun may become a pronoun or an adjective: 'I should like to have *a little* (a pronoun = *some*) of his money.' '*A little* (an adjective) learning is a dangerous thing.'

ee. 'One' with the Force of 'I.' There is a tendency in the present period from the feeling of modesty to employ *one* instead of the sharply precise *I* or *me:* 'I think I should like to have been with them — for it was very close in the room with that great Mrs. Roundhand squeezing up to *one* (for *me*) on the sofa' (Thackeray, *Samuel Titmarsh*, Ch. IV). 'His later poems have their great limitations, as *one will* (for *I shall*) presently suggest, but they are extraordinarily powerful.' The present extensive use of *one* here is justly criticized by some grammarians. It is least objectionable where *one* may refer to others as well as to the speaker and has thus general force: '*One* doesn't like to be told *one's* faults' (retort of the speaker to his tormentor). Compare **33** *g*.

d. **Numeral Adjectives Used as Pronouns:**

aa. Cardinal Numeral Adjectives Used as Pronouns: 'There is only *one* of the four brothers alive.' 'There are many new houses going up in our town this year. *Two, three,* were started in our neighborhood today.' 'The cake was cut in *two*.' 'The nation was severed in *twain* by religious faction' (Buckle, *Miscellaneous Works*, I, p. 84, A.D. 1862). 'She made *one* too many in the omnibus' (*one* who could not be accommodated). 'He was *one* too many' (*one* who was not wanted). 'He was *one* too many for us' (outwitted us). 'They came in *one* by *one*.' 'Some *óne* of you must be responsible for this.' 'No *óne* of you is equal to this.' 'You may select any *twó* of these apples.' Other examples are given in **42** *d aa*. Compare '*Nó one* (indefinite pronoun) can do it' with '*No óne* (numeral pronoun) of you can do it.' *One* is often used as a pronoun although there is no noun present to which it can refer, the speaker trusting to the situation to make the reference clear: 'I gave him *one* (i.e. a blow) in the eye.' 'I owe him *one.*' 'The man who wishes to curry favor goes *one* better on the title.' *Hundred, thousand,* and *million* are distinguished as pronouns from nouns of the same form by the lack of inflection: '*A hundred* (or emphatically *óne húndred*) of these men were arrested.' '*Two hundred* (*two thousand*) of the men struck for higher wages.' 'He lost *five thousand* of his men.' 'There were *five hundred* present.'

The cardinals are used also as nouns: 'The people dispersed in *twos* and *threes.*' 'The business was over in two *twos*' (Stevenson, *New Arabian Nights,* II, p. 112), colloquial for *in a very short time.* 'Please give me five *tens* (ten-dollar bills) and ten *fives* (five-dollar bills) for this *hundred* (hundred-dollar bill).' 'To bless this *twain* that they may prosperous be' (Shakespeare, *The Tempest,* IV, I, 104). 'His wife was a slender sweet-voiced woman in the early *thirties.*' 'I made a shift to creep on all *fours*' (in older English *four*). Pronouns represent separate units, while nouns represent groups: 'He cut the cake in *two*' (pronoun). '*Two* and *two* (pronouns) is (or 'are') four.' 'These *two* (pronoun) are the best students in the class.' 'They wandered off in *twos*' (noun representing groups of two). *Hundred, thousand,* and *million* were originally nouns, but now under the influence of the smaller numbers are felt as pronouns as shown by their lack of inflection: 'The garrison is not *two hundred* strong.' '*Three hundred, three thousand* saw it.' 'He gave *seventy-five thousand* to the university for scholarships.' 'STATE AID QUOTA OF 150 *MILLION* SET FOR JOBLESS' (headline in *New York Herald-Tribune,* Sept. 6, 1932). *Million,* however, differs from *hundred* and *thousand* in that with reference to money it is still often felt as a noun and takes a plural in *-s:* 'a state aid quota of 150 *millions* set for the jobless.' All three words — *hundred, thousand,* and *million* — are used as nouns with a plural in *-s* when employed in the indefinite sense of *a large number:* '*Hundreds, thousands, many thousands, millions* have felt the truth of it.' Of course these three words are always uninflected when used as adjectives: 'Two *hundred* copies, two *thousand* copies, two *million* copies of the book have been sold.'

bb. Ordinal Numeral Adjectives Used as Pronouns: 'The book has four volumes, of which *the third* and *the fourth* are much larger than *the first* and *the second.*' 'Of the speakers *the first* (or *the first one*) was the best.' 'Here comes another visitor, and I hope it is *the last one* today.' '*The last* of the speakers was my brother.'

Many of these forms are used also as nouns: '*one third* of the books,' '*two thirds* of the boys.' 'I was interested from *the first.*'

e. **Possessive Adjectives Used as Pronouns.** The substantive forms of the possessive adjectives *my, thy, his, her, its, our, your, their,* are *mine, thine, his, hers, its, ours, yours, theirs,* two of them, *his* and *its,* remaining unchanged in the substantive relation. These substantive forms, though originally the genitives of the personal pronouns and sometimes still used as such, are now usually employed as possessive pronouns, standing in any case relation required by the construction of the sentence. Nominative: 'Her pencil is longer than *mine* [is].' '*Hers* is a sad fate.' 'The children's health is poor except the baby's and *its* is perfect.' 'These books are *ours'* (predicate nominative). 'Women take to a thing, anything, and go (= let them go) deep enough, and they're *its* (predicate nominative); they never, never will get away from it' (A. S. M. Hutchinson, *This Freedom,* p. 253). Genitive: 'I gave him the titles of my books, but I couldn't recall all the titles *of yours.*' Dative: 'I think you know that I lend my books freely to my friends and *to yours.*' Accusative object of verbs: 'As she didn't have any pencil I lent her *mine.*' 'But the body has its function also, without which the soul could not fulfil *its.*' Object of preposition: 'Yesterday we played in our yard, but today we are going to play in *theirs.*'

This group of words has become very productive. After the analogy of the possessive pronouns in *-s* any noun, common or proper, may become a possessive pronoun by assuming the ending *-s:* 'Her hair is lighter than *her brother's* (subject nominative) [is].' '*Mary's* (subject nominative) is a sad fate.' 'Of the three autos I like *John's* (accusative, object of verb) most.' 'I am better pleased with Mary's work than with *her sister's'* (accusative, object of the preposition *with*). Similarly, a number of pronouns become possessive pronouns by the addition of *-s.* These new formations, like the original group of possessive pronouns, are freely used as subject, predicate, object of verb or preposition: 'His achievements have never measured up to his aims, but then *whose* (subject nominative) have?' (Barrett H. Clark, *Eugene O'Neill,* p. 197). 'Both boys have a good record, but *the younger one's* (subject nominative) is a little better.' 'One of the boys has left his hat here. I think it is *the younger one's'* (predicate nominative). 'Both John and Henry are doing good work, but I regard *the latter's* (accusative, object of verb) as a little better.' 'The same word may be "popular" in one man's vocabulary and "learned" in *another's'* (Greenough and Kittredge, *Words and Their Ways,* p. 21). In the last example *another's* is a possessive pronoun in the accusative, object of the preposition *in.* This construction is one of the finest illustrations of English terseness and is one of the characteristic features of our language. Compare **42** *e.*

Originally the old group of possessive pronouns were the genitives of the personal pronouns. They gradually developed into possessive adjectives and pronouns. The present difference of form for the two functions is the result of a long development described in *Syntax*, **57** 5 *a*. The pronominal forms here are peculiar. Elsewhere the common way to make a pronominal form is to add *one* to the adjective form. In England *one* is actually coming into use also here: 'Leaning back in *his one* of the two Chippendale armchairs in which they sat' (Juliana Ewing, *Jackanapes*, p. 26). *One* is coming into use also after the newer group of possessive pronouns: 'Her parasol is fine, but *her sister's one* is finer' (heard by Jespersen from an English gentleman). The use of *one* here is an absolute proof that these new formations in *-s* are now felt as pronouns. For fuller treatment see **42** *e* (2nd par.).

aa. Origin of Possessive Pronouns and Adjectives. Mine and *thine* developed out of the genitive of the personal pronouns *I* and *thou*. At first both forms were used as possessive adjectives and possessive pronouns. In the twelfth century they began in adjective function to lose their *-n* before consonants: '*min* arm,' but '*mi* fot' (foot). Gradually *my, thy*, became established as the adjective form before vowels and consonants and *mine* and *thine* were restricted to pronominal use.

Also *his, her, our, your, their*, were originally genitive forms, the genitives of *he, she, we, you, they*. They were at first used as possessive adjectives and possessive pronouns. About 1300 *-s* began to be added to these forms so that *hers, ours, yours, theirs*, began to be used alongside of the older shorter forms. No *-s* was added to *his* as it already ended in *-s*. Gradually the two forms began to be differentiated, so that *her, our, your, their*, were employed as adjectives and *hers, ours, yours, theirs*, as pronouns. *His* was used for both functions.

His at first referred not only to persons but also to things. *His* could refer to things until towards the close of the sixteenth century, when *its* (in older English often with the apostrophe, *it's*) began to replace it here: 'Ye are the salt of the earth: but if the salt have lost *his* (now *its*) savor,' etc. (*Matthew*, V, 13). This old usage lingered on until the close of the seventeenth century. The new form *its* developed out of the old possessive *it*, which about 1600 began to be common. A little before this date its new form *its* came into use, which by reason of its distinctive genitive ending soon gained favor and supplanted older *it* and still older *his*. The older form *it* occurs in the Bible of 1611: 'of *it* own accord' (*Leviticus*, XXV, 5; changed to *its* in the edition of 1660).

The possessive forms in *-s* were originally northern English, which later spread southward. In the South and Midland the possessive forms originally followed the analogy of *my* (adjective), *mine* (pronoun): *my, mine; thy, thine; his, hisn; her, hern; our, ourn; your, yourn; their, theirn.* These forms survive in British and American dialect, and *whosen* has been added to the list: 'If it ain't *hisn,* then *whosen* is it?'

bb. Possessive Pronouns Used as Nouns. The possessive pronouns are used also as nouns: '*Yours* (= *your letter*) of the 18th has just reached me.' 'Kind regards to you and *yours*' (= *your family*). Compare *Syntax,* **57** 5 *a.*

f. **Indefinite Relative Adjectives Used as Pronouns.** These pronouns are treated in **7** IV *b* and **38** *b.*

g. **Interrogative Adjectives Used as Pronouns.** These pronouns are treated in **7** VI and **41.**

CHAPTER III

THE ADJECTIVE

8. Definition, Classification, and Function. An adjective is a word that modifies a noun or pronoun, i.e. a word that is used with a noun or pronoun to describe or point out the living being or lifeless thing designated by the noun or pronoun: a *little* boy, *that* boy, *this* boy, a *little* house. There are two classes, descriptive and limiting. A descriptive adjective expresses either the *kind* or *condition* or *state* of the living being or lifeless thing spoken of: a *good* boy, a *bright* dog, a *tall* tree; a *sick* boy, a *lame* dog. The participles of verbs in adjective function are all descriptive adjectives, since they indicate either an active or passive state: *running* water, a *dying* soldier, a *broken* chair.

A limiting adjective, without expressing any idea of kind or condition, limits the application of the idea expressed by the noun to one or more individuals of the class, or to one or more parts of a whole, i.e. points out persons or things: *this* boy, *this* book, *these* boys, *these* books, *my* house, *each* house, *many* books; *this* part of the city, *his* share of the expense, etc.

In all the examples given above, the adjective stands before the noun. The adjective in this position is called an adherent adjective (*Syntax*, **10** I 1). In this position a descriptive adjective has less stress than the noun when it is desired to describe: 'this *little bóy*.' When we desire to distinguish or classify we stress the descriptive adjective more than the noun: 'the *líttle boy*, not the *bíg one*' (distinguishing stress); '*Bíg words* seldom go with *góod deeds*' (classifying stress). But when we desire to stress a descriptive adjective and at the same time impart to it descriptive force we place it after the noun: 'a laugh *músical but malícious*.' In this position the adjective is called an appositive adjective. For fuller treatment see *Syntax*, **10** I 1.

In all of the examples given above, the adjectives are used attributively, i.e. are attributive adjectives, i.e. they stand before the noun or after it in direct connection with it; but the adjective can stand also after a linking (**12** 3) verb as a predicate, i.e. a word which says something of the subject: 'The *tree* is *tall*.' Here the adjective can be used also with a pronoun: 'John isn't here today; he is *sick*.' The predicate adjective stands also after the passive form of certain transitive verbs: 'He was found *sick*.' 'He is reported *sick*.' The predicative use of the adjective is discussed in *Syntax*, **7** B. As explained in **12** 3, the linking verb is lacking when the adjective or participle predicates something of an object:

'I found him *sick.*' 'She boiled the egg *hard.*' 'I started the clock *going.*' 'I have some money *coming* to me yet.' 'They caught him *cheating.*' 'He kept me *waiting.*' 'I at last got the machine *running.*' 'I got my work *dóne* before six,' but with a different meaning with a change of accent: 'We gét (or háve) our work *done.*' 'I had (or got) my leg *húrt* in an accident,' but 'I hád (or gót) a new suit *made.*' 'I consider the matter *séttled.*' The predicate here can be also an adverb or a prepositional phrase with the force of a predicate adjective: 'She wished *him here.*' 'She wished *him in better circumstances.*' In all these examples the adjective, participle, adverb, or prepositional phrase is called an objective predicate. The subject of such a predicate is the preceding object. The objective predicate is now sometimes joined to its subject by a linking verb: 'She wished *him to be here.*' 'She found *him sick*' (or *him to be sick*). Compare **47** 5 *a* (8th par.). In the passive the object becomes subject and the objective predicate becomes predicate: '*He* was found *sick.*' '*He* was caught *cheating.*'

A predicate adjective is often used as an appositive to a predicate noun — the predicate appositive: 'He is a good neighbor, always *ready* to lend a helping hand.' The predicate appositive is frequently joined to a verb of complete predication as a supplementary, modifying predication: 'I came home *tired.*' 'She ran into the house *crying.*' 'He was drowned *bathing* in the river.' The predicate appositive adjectives *tired, crying, bathing,* modify the verb of the sentence in which they stand and are thus adverbial elements. An adjective does not usually modify a verb, but a predicate adjective in this very common construction regularly does so, for one predication can modify another. In two of these three examples the predicate appositive is an adjective participle. The exceedingly frequent use of adjective participles as predicate appositive alongside of a verb of complete predication, as in the preceding examples, is one of the most conspicuous features of our language. Compare **47** 4 and **15** 2 (2nd par.).

An adjective or participle is often used as a noun: 'the *dead* and *dying.*' For fuller treatment see **43** 3.

a. Noun, Adverb, Phrase, or Sentence Used as an Adjective. A noun, an adverb, a phrase, or a sentence is often used as an adjective: 'a *stone* (noun used as an adjective) bridge'; 'obvious *printer's* (or *printers';* genitive of a noun used as an adjective) errors'; 'the *above* (adverb used as an adjective) remark'; 'the *then* prime minister' (Trollope, *Barchester Towers,* I) (adverb used as an adjective); 'an *up-to-date* (prepositional phrase used as an adjective) dictionary'; 'a *go-ahead* (sentence used as an adjective) little city.' The use of a noun, a prepositional phrase, or an adverb as an adjective is especially common in the predicate: 'He was *fool* enough to marry her.' 'He turned *traitor.*' 'The car is *in good condition.*' 'I am *in favor* of the measure.' 'He is always *at strife* with the world.' 'He was quite *at ease.*' 'He is not *in.*' 'The secret is *out.*' '*How* are you today?' 'The struggle is *over.*' 'He is already *up.*' 'He is *about* (*at the point, ready*) to take the step.' 'How could it be *otherwise?*' 'She has her faults, but I should not wish her *otherwise*' (objective predicate). 'No further threats, [whether they be] economic or *otherwise*, have been made.' Compare *Syntax*, **7** A *e*, **7** B *a aa*, **7** F, **10** I 2, II 2 F *a*, *b*. Expressions like 'thoughts [which are] *wise or otherwise*' have led to incorrect expressions like 'the financial *wisdom or otherwise* of such undertakings,' 'the *truth or otherwise* of the statements.' We should say here: '*the wisdom or unwisdom* of such undertakings,' '*the truth or untruth* of the statements.' Also after passive verbs these forms are used as predicate adjectives: 'The car was found *in good condition.*'

There is a strong tendency for a predicate *of*-genitive modified by an adjective to drop its *of*, as noun and adjective are felt as a group of words with the force of an adjective: 'We are [*of*] *the same age, the same size.*' 'The door was [*of*] *a dark brown.*' 'The ring is [*of*] *a pretty shade.*' 'It's [*of*] *no use* to fret about it.' '*What price* are potatoes today?' Likewise in the objective predicate relation: 'He made the two planks [*of*] *the same width.*' 'He painted the door [*of*] *a green color.*'

The use of nouns, adverbs, phrases, or sentences as adjectives has brought a large number of new, often very expressive, adjectives into the language: 'a *baby* boy,' 'a *cat-and-dog* life,' 'an *up-to-date* dictionary,' 'a *dry-as-dust* study,' 'a *pay-as-you-go* policy,' etc. Sometimes the new adjective is used alongside of an older adjective but with a different meaning. The new adjective is concrete, the older form abstract: 'a *girl* cashier,' but '*girlish* ways'; 'a *boy* actor,' but 'a *boyish* trait'; 'a *winter* day,' but 'a *wintry* day'; 'Milton's *prose* works,' but 'a *prosy* talker' and 'a *prosaic* life'; 'a *gold* watch,' but 'a *golden* opportunity' and, in accordance with older usage, 'the hen that laid the *golden* (now *gold*) eggs.' Sometimes the two forms are differentiated in other ways: 'a *stone* bridge,' but 'a *stony* farm.' Sometimes there is no difference of meaning between the two forms — *adjective* or *adjectival; substantive* or *substantival:* '*adjective*, or *adjectival*, elements.' In this last category the adjective with the distinctive adjective ending *-al* is the newer of the two forms, and often has not become thoroughly established yet. In a number of cases, however, the form with the distinctive adjective ending has become established: 'the *adverbial* (more common than *adverb*) suffix *-ly*,' 'a *prepositional* phrase,' 'the *verbal* ending,' etc. We usually say '*autumn* woods,' etc., but '*autumnal* equinox.' Adjectives in *-en* are often used when the stem is simple, while the noun form is employed if the adjective is a compound or is modified: '*wooden* chairs,' but 'maple-*wood* chairs'; '*woollen* shawls,' but 'Shetland *wool* shawls.' We use *beech, flax, hemp, lead, leather, oak*, etc., as adjectives, or in more formal language we may employ the form in *-en; beechen, flaxen*, etc.

b. Adjective Elements. Although a genitive or an appositive prepositional phrase may have adjective force, they are not adjectives in a formal sense, for they have marked peculiarities of form, or they do not have the usual position of an adjective. In '*John's* book' *John's*, though formally the genitive of a noun, has the force of a limiting adjective. The fact that *John's* has an ending shows that it is not an adjective, for adjectives do not take endings. In 'a boy *of the same age*' *of the same age*, though formally an *of*-genitive, has the force of a descriptive adjective; it has neither the form nor the usual position of a descriptive adjective. When *of the same age* becomes formally a predicate adjective it drops *of:* 'We are *the same age*.' Similarly, an adverb and a prepositional phrase often have the force of adjectives, though formally they are not adjectives, as is revealed by their position after the governing noun: 'the room *above*,' 'the book *on the table*.' Here *above* and *on the table* have the force of limiting adjectives, but their position shows that formally they are not adjectives. An infinitive often modifies a noun with the force of a descriptive adjective: 'An opportunity *to advance* came.'

A relative clause, though it has a peculiar grammatical structure of its own, modifies, like an adjective, a noun or pronoun, pointing out or describing some person or thing: 'The boy *who is leaning on the fence* is my brother.' 'He is a boy *who loves play and hates work*.' The relative clause with a finite verb, as in these examples, is often replaced by a participial or infinitival relative clause: 'The circus was all one family — parents and five children — *performing* (= *who performed*) *in the open air*.' 'He is not a man *to be trifled with*' (= *who can be trifled with*). Also a conjunctional clause may modify a noun with the force of an adjective: 'The day *after* (or *before*) *he came* was very beautiful.'

There is adjective force also in an appositive noun or clause: 'And these footsteps dying on the stairs were Charley's, *his old friend* of so many years.' 'These words were Cicero's, *the most eloquent* of men.' 'I bought the book at Smith's, *the bookseller* and *stationer*.' 'I bought the book at Smith's, *the bookseller* on Main

Street.' 'I bought the book at Smith's, *the bookseller's* [store].' 'I bought the book at Smith's *the bookseller.*' 'We stopped at Mr. Barton *the clergyman's* house for a drink of water.' Similarly a whole clause may be an appositive: 'The thought *that we shall live on after death in a better world* is a solace to many.' An appositive clause of the nature of a loose comment upon some idea contained in a preceding word or group of words is now introduced by the indefinite relative pronoun *what,* earlier in the period by *which:* '*To know* a thing, *what we can call knowing,* a man must first love the thing' (Carlyle). 'Brown has always envied *the creative life force* in Dion — *what he himself lacks*' (Barrett H. Clark, *Eugene O'Neill,* p. 161). The appositive may precede its head-clause or be embedded in it: '*What was very unusual with him,* he arrived on time.' 'She would never change unless, *what was absurd,* he changed first.' 'And, *which* (now *what*) *is worse,* all you have done Hath been but for a wayward son' (Shakespeare, *Macbeth,* III, v, 10). Compare **7** IV *a.* On the other hand, a modified noun may serve as an appositive to a preceding statement: 'I, like many another, am apt to judge my fellow men in comparison with myself, *a wrong and foolish thing to do.*'

9. Compound Adjectives. On account of the loss of its endings the modern English adjective has acquired a great facility to form compounds: 'an *up-to-date* dictionary,' 'a *cut-and-dried* affair,' 'a *plain-clothes* policeman,' 'my *next-door* neighbor,' 'a *large-scale* map,' 'the *quarter-past-seven* train,' '*this, that, and the other* newspaper.' Notice that English compounds are not always written together as one word. Compare **8** *a* and *Syntax,* **10** I 2.

a. Derivative Adjectives. Similar to compound adjectives are derivative adjectives, i.e. adjectives formed by adding to a noun, an adjective, or a verbal stem a suffix, which in most cases was originally an independent word. These suffixes are: *-en, -fold, -ful, -ish, -less, -ly, -some, -y, -able,* etc.: wood*en,* mani*fold,* hope*ful,* child*ish,* friend*less,* man*ly,* lone*some,* ston*y,* bear*able,* etc.

The formation of derivative adjectives is treated in detail in *Word-Formation.*

10. Classes of Limiting Adjectives. Descriptive adjectives are so simple in nature that they do not form classes. Limiting adjectives, on the other hand, form distinct groups:

1. *Possessive Adjectives.* They are: *my* (in older English *mine* before a vowel), *thy* (in older English *thine* before a vowel), *his, her, its* (in older English *it* and in still older English *his*), *our, your, their.* Examples: *my* book, *my* books; *thy* kindness to us, O Lord; *his* book, *his* books; *her* book, *her* books; the little baby and *its* mother; *our* book (one book owned by two or more per-

sons), *our* books (the books owned in common or those owned separately); *your* book (one book owned by the person addressed); *your* book (one book owned by the two or more persons addressed); *your* books (the books owned in common by the two or more persons addressed, or the books owned by them separately); *their* book (one book owned by the two or more persons spoken of); *their* books (the books owned in common or the books owned separately). Examples of older usage: 'Shall I not take *mine* (now *my*) ease in *mine* (now *my*) inn?' (Shakespeare, I *Henry the Fourth*, III, III, 93). 'It had *it* (now *its*) head bit off by *it* (now *its*) young' (*id.*, *King Lear*, I, IV, 236). 'Ye are the salt of the earth: but if the salt have lost *his* (still lingering in the seventeenth century, though older than *it;* both later replaced by *its*) savor,' etc. (*Matthew*, V, 13, edition of 1611). For the history of the possessive adjectives see **7** VII *e aa.*

a. LIVELY TONE IN POSSESSIVE ADJECTIVES. Possessive adjectives are often employed, not to express possession, but to convey the idea of appreciation or depreciation: 'He knows *his* Shakespeare.' 'The boy has just broken *his* third glass.' '*Your* true rustic turns his back upon his interlocutor' (George Eliot). The writer or speaker often employs *your* to direct the attention of his readers or hearers to his own view: 'I should like to believe it (i.e. that the greatest writers have never written anything); but I find it hard. *Your* great writer is possessed of a devil over which he has very little control' (Huxley, *Vulgarity*, p. 7). *Our* often denotes a lively interest present in writer or speaker or to be evoked in reader or listener: '*our* hero,' '*our* young friend,' '*our* young scapegrace.' 'We must now introduce *our* reader to the interior of the fisher's cottage' (Scott, *The Antiquary*, Ch. XXVI, A.D. 1816).

b. PERSONAL PRONOUN INSTEAD OF POSSESSIVE ADJECTIVE. In the language of American Quakers *thee* is often used instead of *thy:* 'Look, Margaret, thee's (**33** *f*, last par., and **54,** close of 2nd par.) tearing the skirt of *thee* dress' (*American Speech*, Jan., 1926, p. 118). The use of a personal pronoun instead of a possessive adjective is common in southern American dialect: 'He roll *he* (= *his*) eyeballs "roun"' (Joel Chandler Harris, *Nights with Uncle Remus*, p. 69). Similarly, *who* for *whose:* 'SCIPIO. "I been to de trial." VOICE. "*Who* trial?"' (Edward C. L. Adams, *Congree Sketches*, p. 4). Of course also in British dialect, for our dialect was brought here by early British settlers: 'arter *we* horses' (Gepp, *Essex Dialect Dictionary*, p. 131) = *after our horses;* 'at *us* (= *our*) own fireside' (Lancashire).

c. USE OF POSSESSIVE ADJECTIVES AND PRONOUNS WITH IN-

DEFINITES. *He, his, him,* correspond to the numeral *one,* to *one — another,* and to *no one, someone, everyone, anyone:* '*One* of these men hates *his* enemies.' '*One* hates *his* enemies and *another* forgives *his.*' 'If *someone* (or *anyone*) should lose *his* purse, *he* should apply to the Lost Property Office.' '*No one* likes what doesn't interest *him.*' The corresponding reflexive is *himself:* '*One* of the boys fell and hurt *himself.*' '*No one* can interest *himself* in everything.'

On the other hand, the possessive corresponding to absolute indefinite *one* (7 VII *c bb*) is *one's:* '*One* never realizes *one's* blessings while *one* enjoys them.' The corresponding reflexive is *oneself* or *one's self:* '*One* cannot interest *oneself* (or *one's self*) in everything.' We often, however, hear *himself* instead of *oneself* or *one's self,* as in older English: '*One* might fall and hurt *himself*' (instead of *oneself* or *one's self*).

2. *Intensifying Adjectives.* They are: *myself, ourself* (= *myself*), *thyself, yourself, himself* (in dialect *hisself*), *herself, itself* (in seventeenth and eighteenth centuries *its self*), *ourselves* (in older English *ourself*), *yourselves* (in older English *yourself*), *themselves* (in older English *themself;* in current dialect *theirselves*), *oneself* or *one's self* (the latter the older form and still often used in America, the former now the more common form). They intensify the force of a preceding noun or pronoun, making it emphatic: 'Father *himself* admits it.' 'I saw it *myself.*' 'We think we have hinted elsewhere that Mr. Benjamin Allen had a way of becoming sentimental after brandy. The case is not a peculiar one as we *ourself* can testify' (Dickens, *Pickwick*, Ch. XXXVIII). 'I heard it from a lady who *herself* was present.' 'They admit it *themselves.*' 'One must decide such things *oneself*' (or *one's self*). 'That one should do right *oneself* (or *one's self*) is the great thing.' *Oneself* or *one's self* intensifies the force of indefinite *one.* In infinitive clauses an indefinite subject is never expressed. Here indefiniteness is indicated merely by the suppression of the subject. Thus in such clauses intensifying *oneself* or *one's self* stands alone without a preceding *one:* 'To do right *oneself* (or *one's self*) is the great thing.'

In case the governing word is a noun, we often use *very* instead of these adjectives, but it always precedes the noun: 'He drew me out of the *very* jaws of perdition.' To increase the intensity here we put *very* in the superlative: 'You have bought the *veriest* rubbish.' We always use *very* when we desire not only to intensify the force of the word but also to emphasize the idea of identity or coincidence: 'You are the *very* man I am looking for.'

a. ORIGIN OF INTENSIFYING ADJECTIVES. Originally, as explained more fully in *Syntax*, **56** D, the *him* in *himself* and *her* in *herself* were datives: 'He saw it *himself*,' literally *for himself*, *on his own account*. In 'She saw it *herself*' *her* was originally a dative, like *him* in *himself*, but it was construed as a possessive adjective modifying the noun *self*. Other intensifying adjectives assumed a form to conform to this new conception: *myself*, *ourself*, *thyself*, *yourself*, *yourselves*, *one's self*, in the seventeenth and eighteenth centuries *its self*, and in dialect *hisself*, *theirselves*. *Himself*, *itself*, *oneself*, *themselves*, follow the older type, in fact also *herself*, although we now feel it as belonging to the younger type. In this struggle between the two types *its self* has disappeared and *hisself* and *theirselves* have thrived only in dialect. *One's self* is still often used in America, but it has yielded in England to the younger form *oneself*, which, however, is formed according to the old type. The younger form is now getting the upper hand also in America.

Although these adjectives fall into two different groups each with a different type of formation, they all now perform the same function — they are adjectives intensifying the noun or pronoun to which they belong. Near the end of the Middle English period these adjectives, like adjectives in general, were uninflected, hence had no distinctive plural form: 'we *ourself*,' 'you *yourself*,' 'they *themself*.' Of these forms *ourself* and *yourself* were often ambiguous. Before the beginning of the modern period *-s* began to appear in the plural to make the grammatical relations clear: 'we *ourself*' (sing.), 'we *ourselves*' (pl.); 'you *yourself*' (sing.), 'you *yourselves*' (pl.). About 1570 *themself* became *themselves* after the analogy of *ourselves*, *yourselves*. Compare **43** 1.

b. Intensifying Adjectives Used as Pronouns. The pronoun before an intensifying adjective sometimes drops out so that the intensifying adjective must assume the function of the pronoun in addition to its own, thus becoming an emphatic pronoun. This construction is most common in elliptical sentences: 'Did you ever know a woman to pardon another for being handsomer than *hersélf?*' (= *she hersélf was*). It sometimes serves as the predicate of a sentence: 'You are not *yoursélf* today.' A feeling of modesty often suggests its use instead of the pompous *I mysélf*, *me mysélf:* 'General Lee surrendered the Army of Northern Virginia this afternoon on terms proposed by *mysélf*' (U. S. Grant, *Telegram to E. M. Stanton*, Apr. 9, 1865). This old construction is not so common as it was in early Modern English. It is more widely employed in England than in America: 'His stable had caught fire, *himsélf* (in America *he himsélf*) had been all but roasted alive' (Meredith, *The Ordeal of Richard Feverel*). Compare **7** VII *a*.

In early Modern English the intensifying adjective was often used as an ordinary unemphatic personal pronoun: '*Himself* (now simple *he*) and Montmorin offered their resignation' (Thomas Jefferson, *Autobiography*, p. 138). This older usage lingers in the literary language of England: 'There's only *myself* and Louisa here' (Hugh Walpole, *The Duchess of Wrexe*, Ch. XIII) = 'There are only Louisa and *I* here.' It is a feature of American colloquial speech: 'John and *myself* (for *I*) were there.' 'He went with John and *myself*' (for *me*). In older English this form could be used alone in the subject relation unaccompanied by another subject: 'But *himselfe* (now *he*) was not satisfied therwith' (Bradford, *History of Plymouth Plantation*, p. 363, A.D. 1630–1638). This construction is receding in American English in this position, but it is well preserved in Irish English and occurs also in British English: 'MILDRED. Dear me, what's the matter with Jack? — BRIDGET. *Himself* (= *he*) is vexed about something' (Lennox Robinson, *Harvest*, Act II). '*Herself* (= *she*) looked bewitching. She knew that she did' (Hugh Walpole, *Harmer John*, Ch. VII).

For fuller treatment see *Syntax*, **56** D.

3. *Demonstrative Adjectives.* These adjectives point out living beings or lifeless things. The reference often becomes clear with the help of a gesture or the situation or context. These adjectives often point of themselves backward or forward to individuals already mentioned or to be mentioned or described. When they point forward to a following explanatory phrase or clause they are called determinatives. This important group is treated in *e* (p. 53). Some demonstrative adjectives indicate the individual by giving his place in a series or by including each individual in the series.

The adjectives of this important category are: *this, these; that, those;* in popular speech instead of *those* the forms *they* or more commonly *them*, both of which were once employed in the literary language; *the* (see *e*, p. 53), the definite article, the weakened form of an old demonstrative adjective now represented by *that; yonder*, in early Modern English also *yond* and *yon*, the latter of which is still common in American popular speech; *other; the same; one and the same; the identical*, sometimes an equivalent of *the same*, sometimes differentiated in meaning from it; *the very* (see 2 above, last par.), with the force of *identical; such;* in older English *suchlike*, now replaced by *such; a* (see *e*, p. 53), indefinite article; *former, latter; either; neither; both;* often also *each, every, all, half*, which frequently point to definite individuals and hence are not always indefinite, as they are usually classed. A number of these words often experience a change of form when used as pronouns. Their use as pronouns is treated in **7** VII *b* and **42** *b*.

Examples:

You may have *this* book and that one.

You may have *these* books and those.

Did you ever see anything finer than *those* (or in popular speech *them* or *they*) peonies?

I ain't saying nothing agin *they* (= *those*) bars — only that they ain't as fresh as I like 'em (Hugh Walpole, *Harmer John*, Ch. IV).

This railway strike is a serious business.

The warres and weapons are now altered from *them* (now *those*) dayes (Barret, *Theor. Warres*, I, I, 4, A.D. 1598).

What is *that* noise?

I have just read Galsworthy's dramas. I find *these* works as interesting as his novels.

He hasn't returned yet *those* books which I lent him last summer.

These books which I hold in my hand need binding very much.

I want to impress upon you *this* one thing, Don't impose upon your friends.

Among *yonder* hills there are some beautiful little lakes.

See how *yond* justice rails upon *yond* simple thief (Shakespeare, *King Lear*, IV, VI, 155).

Nerissa, cheer *yon* stranger (*id.*, *Merchant of Venice*, III, II, 239).

Yon plank will do (*Dialect Notes*, III, 101).

One of them is my brother. I do not know the *other* boy.

I am using *the same* Latin dictionary that I used as a boy.

Captain Absolute and Ensign Beverley are *one and the same* person (Sheridan, *The Rivals*, I, I).

Even at *one and the same* period different writers did not always use the letters with the same value (Henry Bradley, *English Place Names*, p. 9).

He is wearing *the identical* (or *the same*, or *the very same*) hat that he wore five years ago.

I am *the identical* man you met twenty years ago, but I am not *the same* man any more.

You are *the very* (see 2, 2nd par., p. 48) man I was looking for.

There are few *such* boys as he.

I have been using John's dictionary. I wish I had *such* a dictionary of my own.

There is *such* confusion that I can't collect my thoughts.

The confusion is *such* (predicate adjective) that I can't collect my thoughts.

We need some *such* (adherent adjective; see **8**) rule in every school.

Some *such* (adherent adjective) boys can be found in every neighborhood.

'No *such* (adherent adjective) offer has ever been made before, and *none* [that is] *such* will ever be made again,' or more commonly '*none* [that is] *of the sort* will ever be made again.'

'Cultivated men — professors and *others* [that are] *such*' (Herbert Spencer, *Autobiography*, I, p. 486), or *others of the sort*.

He always gives this excuse or *another* [that is] *such*, or *another of the sort.*

He is a bad boy. I didn't know we had *one* [that is] *such*, or *one of the sort*, in the neighborhood.

These are bad boys. You will find *some* [that are] *such*, or *some of the sort*, in every neighborhood.

'These are bad boys. I didn't know we had *any* [that are] *such*, or *any of the sort*, in the neighborhood,' or 'I hope we haven't *many such*, or *many of the sort*, in the neighborhood.'

In the last examples *such* is a predicate adjective and the form before it is a pronoun. In older English and sometimes still the form before *such* is an adherent (**8**) adjective and *such* is a pronoun: ''Tis plain enough, he was *no such*' (Butler, *Hudibras*, I, I, 44, A.D. 1663), now *none such*. 'Setting aside the hideous vulgarity of the well-to-do stockbrokers and *other such*' (W. Morris, *News from Nowhere*, Ch. XXII), now usually *others such* or *others of the sort*. In early Modern English, after *any, many, other*, we sometimes find *the like* or *suchlike* instead of *such* here: 'as for these objections or any *the like*' (H. Smith, *Works*, II, 97, A.D. 1592); 'and many *the like*' (Bacon, 'Of Seditions and Troubles,' *Essays*, A.D. 1625); 'these scriptures and many *suchlike*' (George Fox, *Journal*, p. 250, A.D. 1656).

a. 'EVERY' AND 'EACH.' Be careful to use *every* and *each* properly: 'There were blackboards *between the* windows,' not 'There was a blackboard *between each* window.' We should say, 'pausing *between the sentences*' or 'pausing *between every sentence and the next*'; not 'pausing *between every sentence*' (George Eliot, *Adam Bede*).

After a possessive adjective or the genitive of a noun *every* and *each* may be employed as an attributive adjective instead of being used as a pronoun before a partitive genitive: 'She indulged *his every whim*,' or *every one of his whims*. 'We indulged *the baby's every whim*,' or *its every whim*, or *every one of its whims*. 'She blocked his *each new effort* at being articulate' (Sinclair Lewis, *Dodsworth*, Ch. XXIV), or *each of his new efforts*. Compare *Syntax*, **10** II 2 H *b* (last par.).

As *every* totalizes (**7** VII *b*, 3rd par.), it forms individual units into a higher unit: 'He comes *every* three days.' Hence its meaning is often very comprehensive with the force of *all possible:* 'There is *every* prospect of success.'

Each and *every* are often used together, *each* individualizing and *every* totalizing, thus strengthening the statement by the two different points of view: 'We will examine carefully *each and every* complaint.'

b. 'BOTH,' 'ALL,' 'HALF,' 'EACH.' With these words there are peculiarities of word-order: '*Both* brothers, or *both* the brothers, are dead,' or 'The brothers are *both* dead.' '*Both* my friends saw it,' or 'My friends *both* saw it.' '*All* the boys saw it,' or 'The boys *all* saw it.' '*All* the boys were there,' or 'The boys were *all* there.' 'I saw them *all* (predicate appositive adjective) there,' or 'I saw *all* (pronoun) of them there.' '*Half* the boys were there.' 'I had only *half* (predicate appositive adjective) a piece,' or 'I had only *half* (pronoun) of a piece.' 'I have only *half* (predicate appositive adjective) what I need,' or 'I have only *half* (pronoun) of what I need.' '*Each* brother has done his full duty,' or 'The brothers *each* have done their full duty.' '*Each* boy received a penny,' or 'The boys received a penny *each*' (or *apiece*, adverb = *severally*). 'I gave *each* boy a penny,' or 'I gave the boys a penny *each*.' For fuller treatment see *Syntax*, **6** C.

c. 'SUCHLIKE' IN OLDER ENGLISH. Older literary use of *suchlike* as an adherent (**8**) adjective survives in popular speech: 'Panoramas and *suchlike* (in the literary language now replaced by *such*) exhibitions have delighted us as well as our fathers.' It even lingers here and there in the literary language: 'Read the records of these and other *suchlike* words in this little treatise' (Edward Gepp, *An Essex Dialect Dictionary,* Introduction, p. 4, A.D. 1920).

d. MEANING OF 'EITHER.' This form has two quite different meanings — the older with the force of *each of the two, both,* now on account of its ambiguity much less used than formerly, the younger meaning with the force of *the one or the other of the two,* now the more common meaning: 'Much may be said on *either side*' (or now more commonly *each side* or *both sides*). 'I received no reply to *either question*' = '*Both questions* remained unanswered.' 'You may take *either side*' (= *one side or the other*).

e. DETERMINATIVES. When demonstrative adjectives and demonstrative pronouns (**7** VII *b*) point forward to a following explanatory phrase or clause, they are called determinatives: '*the* book on the table'; '*the* book I hold in my hand'; '*such* books as instruct'; 'this book and *the one* on the table'; 'these books and *the ones* on the table'; 'this book and *the one* (or *that one*) you hold in your hand'; '*those* (or in popular speech *they* or *them*) books that you lent me'; '*every* book on the table.' Compare **7** VII *b bb*.

Such, a, like that, like those, and, in loose colloquial speech, simple *like* are often used as qualitative determinatives to indicate kind or degree: 'We'll each of us give you *such a thrashing as, a thrashing such as,* or *a thrashing that* you'll remember.' '*Such meat as* is the most dangerously earned is the sweetest.' 'He is not *a man that* can be trifled with,' or 'He is not *a man* to trifle with.' 'Scrooge was not *a man* to be frightened by echoes.' 'John is *a boy that* you can depend upon.' 'John and William are *such boys as*, or *boys that* (with the omission of *a* in the plural), you can depend upon.' 'I am working tonight amid *such confusion* (= *confusion so great*) that I can't keep my thoughts together.' 'The confusion was *such* (predicate adjective) that I couldn't keep my thoughts together,' or 'The confusion was *such* as to render it impossible for me to keep my thoughts together.' 'Nowadays we don't get pies *such as Mother used to make*,' or *like those* (or colloquially simple *like*) *Mother used to make*. Compare **7** VII *b bb* (4th par.). Compare also *Syntax*, **56** A (7th par.).

In older English and sometimes still, *this* or *those* is used instead of *such* as a qualitative determinative or demonstrative to indicate a kind or degree: 'I have not from your eyes *that* (now usually *such*) gentleness as I was wont to have' (Shakespeare, *Julius Caesar*, I, I, 33). 'The town was reduced to *those* (now usually *such* or *so great*) straights that, if not relieved, it must have surrendred in two daies time' (Luttrell, *Brief Rel.*, I, 567, A.D. 1689). 'Katia was a great fight. It's *those* (now usually *such*) fights (the odds against us) that have really daunted the Germans' (Sir Walter Raleigh, *Letter to Lady Wemyss*, Jan. 13, 1917). *Those* is still regularly so used after the indefinite pronoun *one*: 'Mrs. William Morrison was one of *those* people who always speak decisively' (L. W. Montgomery, *Chronicles of Avonlea*, Little Jocelyn).

f. 'SUCH' WITH THE FORCE OF 'THAT,' 'THOSE,' 'THIS,' 'THESE,' 'THE.' In older English, *such* often lost the idea of a particular kind and pointed to definite persons or things, just like *that, those, this, these*, without any difference in meaning: 'That the reader, therefore, may not conceive the least ill opinion of *such a* (= *this*) person, we shall not delay a moment in rescuing his character from the imputation of this guilt' (Fielding, *Tom Jones*, Book VII, Ch. XV). 'But we are sure that the judgment of God is according to truth against them which commit *such* things' (*Romans*, II, 2), here with the force of *this thing*, or simply *this* or *it*, for the reference is to a definite thing, namely, *passing judgment upon others*, mentioned in the preceding verse. 'Thow shalt conceyve a child . . . And his name shalle ȝou Ihesu calle . . . *Suche* (= *these*) wordis were seid to Mary' (*Cursor Mundi*, 10869, about A.D. 1300). *Such*, followed by a relative *as*-clause, is still often used with almost the force of *those*, but it has a meaning a little more indefinite than *those* — which differentiation has preserved it: 'Major Pendennis spent the autumn passing from house to house of *such* country friends as were at home to receive him' (Thackeray,

Pendennis, II, Ch. XXX). Compare **7** VII *b bb* (last par.). Similarly, *such* is often used instead of *this* referring back to a preceding noun where the reference is indefinite: 'A gratuity awarded to any clerk shall be estimated according to the period during which *such* clerk has served' (*Act 41 Vict.* c. 52). We now often prefer *the, this,* or *that* here to *such:* 'That there is a void in a millionaire's life is not disproved by anyone showing that a number of millionaires do not recognize *such* (or *the, this,* or *that*) void.'

g. INTENSIVE 'SUCH.' *Such* or *such a* is often used as an absolute intensive without an expressed comparison, indicating in a general way a high degree of a quality, sometimes standing alone before a noun, sometimes followed by an adjective which expresses the quality more accurately: 'I have never seen *such a storm,*' or more accurately *such a terrible storm,* or with the adverb *so* instead of the adjective *such: so terrible a storm.* The adjective construction is the usual one before a plural noun: 'I have never seen *such children,*' or more accurately *such good children* or *such bad children.*

h. REDUNDANCY. In older English, *same* is used redundantly after a demonstrative — *this, these, that, those, yon:* 'If this *same* palmer will me lead from hence' (Scott, *Marmion,* I, XXV). This usage is still common in popular speech, especially in Negro dialect: 'I'm gwine ter larrup that *same* Mr. Man' (Joel Chandler Harris, *Nights with Uncle Remus,* p. 35). In current popular speech *here* and *there* are similarly used: 'Look at *this here* (or *this 'ere*) book!' 'Do it *thisa* (= *this here*) way!' 'I never saw it done *thata* (= *that there*) way.' Compare *Syntax,* **56** A (2nd par.).

i. EMOTIONAL 'THAT' AND 'THIS.' *That* and *this* are often employed unaccompanied by a gesture and marked by a peculiar tone of voice expressing praise or censure, pleasure or displeasure: 'And then I sit and think of *that* dear wife of mine that I lost a quarter of a century ago' (De Morgan, *Joseph Vance,* Ch. XXXIII). 'Do you think the girls would consider it narrow if I asked them to stop *that* dancing and whooping' (Sidgwick, *Severins,* Ch. III). 'Upon my word, of all the horrid men that I ever heard of *this* publisher of yours is the worst' (R. Haggard, *Meeson's Will*). Compare **27** 4 A *b* (3).

j. 'YE.' The definite article *the* is sometimes still for archaic effect written *ye,* the *y* representing older *þ* and hence pronounced *th:* '*ye* old town.'

4. *Numeral Adjectives.* They indicate number. There are three classes:

a. CARDINAL NUMERAL ADJECTIVES. They are employed in counting: '*two* (or in older English *twain* or *tway*) men,' 'the first *three* years,' '*three* dollars,' '*four* dollars,' '*fifty-five* dollars,' '*one hundred and fifty* dollars'; '*three* years and *a half*,' or '*three and a half* years'; '*one* pound and *a half*,' or '*one and a half* pounds'; '*thirty-one and two-thirds* inches,' '*thirty-one and three-eighths* inches,' etc., but *quarter* is always uninflected as adjective: '*thirty-one and three-quarter* inches.' 'The house cost *a hundred thousand dollars*.' '*Two million* copies of the book have been sold.' 'I have *a hundred and one* (or *a thousand and one*) things to look after.' In early Modern English it was usual to say *one-and-twenty*, *one-and-thirty*, etc.

Other adjective forms often take the place of the regular cardinal adjectives: '*a dozen* eggs,' '*two dozen* eggs,' '*three score* years.' *Odd* (or sometimes *and odd*) is added to a cardinal to indicate an indefinite surplus, cardinal and *odd* (or *and odd*) together forming a compound numeral: 'There were *fifty odd* (or *and odd*) boys there' (i.e. between *fifty and sixty boys*). 'The book has *five hundred odd* (or *and odd*) pages.' The indefinite adjective *some* (**10** 6) is often placed before the cardinal to indicate the idea of approximation: 'The club consists of *some forty* members.' These numerals are called cardinals (from Latin *cardo* 'hinge') because they are the most important words of number on which the others hinge.

The numerals *one*, *only*, *sole*, are used in many idiomatic expressions to indicate oneness: 'Some *óne* man must direct.' 'No *óne* man can do it.' 'I don't know any *óne* house that has so many good points as this.' 'He has the *óne* fault that he is not punctual.' 'There is *óne* napkin too many' (one napkin which is not needed). 'This line has *a* (reduced form of *one*) foot too much' (Note to *Merchant of Venice*, II, VII, 2, in Clarendon Press ed.; more commonly *a foot too many*). 'He is an *ónly* child.' 'This is the *ónly* instance known.' 'This is my *óne* and *ónly* hope.' 'That was his *sóle* reason.'

b. Ordinal Numeral Adjectives. They denote position or order in a series: 'the *first*, *second*, *third*, *last* day of the month.' 'He had now attained his *twenty-fifth* (in older English *five-and-twentieth*) year.' 'After the *twenty-somethingth* attempt to go to sleep I decided to lie where I fell.' From another point of view these adjectives may be classed as demonstratives (**10** 3).

In early Modern English, *fift*, *sixt*, *twelft*, were still in use, but were later replaced by *fifth*, *sixth*, *twelfth*, to bring the form of these ordinals into harmony with that of the other ordinals from *fourth* onwards. In Middle English, French *second* supplanted English *other*. The older English ordinal survives in 'every *other* day.'

c. Multiplicatives. They indicate multiplication, *twofold*, *tenfold*, etc.: 'a *twofold* return for your money,' 'with *twofold* care,' 'a *sixfold* increase,' 'a *double* portion,' 'a *double* row of policemen.' 'The glottis is *twofold*' (predicate adjective). 'I'll return it to you *threefold*' (objective predicate; **8,** 4th par.).

Multiplicatives are most commonly adverbs: 'The fee was *tenfold* what I expected.' 'It repaid me *threefold*.' 'They outnumbered us *a hundredfold*.' 'It is *tenfold, a thousandfold*, worse.' 'He is *double* (or *twice*) my age.' 'He now feels *doubly* guilty.' *Double* is used also as a noun: 'Ten is *the double* of five.'

5. *Relative Adjectives*. There are two groups:

a. Definite 'Which.' This form often points backward to a definite antecedent: 'We traveled together as far as Paris, at *which* place we parted.'

b. Indefinite Relative Adjectives. *Which, what* (more indefinite than *which*), *which(so)ever, what(so)ever*, are widely used as relative adjectives without definite reference. Although these adjectives never refer to a definite antecedent, they are genuine conjunctives in that they link the clause in which they stand to the principal proposition. They introduce a substantive clause, i.e. a noun clause in the relation of a subject or object of the principal verb or an appositive to a noun: 'It is not known *which*, or *what, course he will pursue*' (subject clause). 'I do not know *which*, or *what, course he will pursue*' (object clause). 'The question *which*, or *what, course he will pursue* (appositive clause) has not yet been settled.' 'I will approve *whichever*, or *whatever, course you decide upon*' (object clause). 'I have lost *what little confidence in him I ever had*' (object clause). 'He was not a man given to much talking, but *what little he did say* (subject clause) was generally well said.' 'He has very few books, but *what few he has* (object clause) he reads and rereads.' The object clause may be the object of a preposition, preposition and object clause forming together a unit called a prepositional clause: 'You can rely *upon whatever promises he may make*.' 'Let's hold on *to what certainties we can*.'

The adjectives in *-ever* and simple *which* are used also in adverbial concessive clauses (**15** 2 *i*, **18** B 5): 'I am going to pursue this course, *whatever sacrifices it may demand*.' 'He will find difficulties *whichever* course he may take.' 'Sometimes, turn my head *which way I would* I seemed to see the gold' (George Eliot, *Silas Marner*, Ch. XIX).

In older English, *whether* was often used here with the force of *which of the two*: 'Yet *whether* side was victor note (**57** 4 A *e*) be ghest' (Spenser, *The Faerie Queene*, V, VII, III, A.D. 1590) = 'Yet *which* side [*of the two*] was victor could not be determined.'

6. *Indefinite Adjectives*. They are: *a, an; not a, no* (in older

English *none* before a vowel: 'to *none* effect,' now 'to *no* effect'), *nary* (popular for *ne'er a*, from *never a*); *all; any; ary* (popular for *e'er a*) = *any; this and* (or *or*) *that; this, that, and* (or *or*) *the other; every; a(n) — or so; several; some; some or another* or *some or other; one or another* or *one or other; one or the other; many; many a; the many; a many*, now archaic or poetic though once common, but the modified forms *a good many, a great many*, are still common; *numerous; innumerable; countless; myriad; various; other, another; a certain, certain; divers* (archaic); *sundry* (archaic); *all and sundry* (archaic); *considerable* (of things immaterial; in American colloquial speech also of things material); *much; more* or, in older English where the reference is to number, *mo* or *moe* (Old English *mā*); *little, a little; less; few, a few; enough; sufficient; plenty, plentier, plentiest*, now most common in the predicate relation, but in general obsolete in adjective use in the literary language, though common in all adjective functions in dialect, especially Scotch and Irish; *such* (**10** 3 *f*); *such and such, such or such.*

Examples:

There was *a* (*an* old) man here to see you.

Not a bóy was absent.

Not a múscle of his face moved.

Tibbits is *nót a* (= *nó*, i.e. quite other than a) scholar, *a* genius (Lytton, *Caxtons*, IV, Ch. III).

I am *nó* (= *nót a*, i.e. quite other than a) genius (*ib.*).

I have *no* sécret. I am *nót a* (= *nó*, i.e. quite other than a) quack (Shaw, *The Doctor's Dilemma*, I, 32).

This is *nó* (= *nót a*, i.e. quite other than a) part of my plan.

I am in *nó* hurry = I am *not* in *ány* hurry.

Nó (= *not ány*) occasion could be more appropriate than this.

He did it in *nó* (= *hardly ány*) time.

All boys are not alike.

It took *all* the strength I had to do it.

I haven't *any* money left.

There aren't *any* boys in our neighborhood.

She takes larning easier than *ary* young un ever I seed (Lucy Furman, *The Glass Window*, Ch. III).

Truth must not be measured by the convenience of *this or that* man (Berkeley).

Idle people jot down their idle thoughts, and then post them to *this, that, and the other* newspaper.

She spends *a* week *or so* every summer with her friend.

Several books were damaged.

All of us in our *several* (= *respective*) stations have our work to do.

Each has his *several* (= *individual*) ideal (*Concise Oxford Dictionary*).

The joint and *several* (= *separate*) efforts of all three may be safely left to the contemptuous indifference of the nation (*London Times*).

Some people believe it.
We have *some* good butter today.
We went *some* miles out of our way.
They were *some* little (or considerable) distance ahead of us.
They were *some* fifty yards away from us.
Hardly a day passes in which we do not have *some* visitor *or other.*
Some idiots *or other* have been shooting all night.
Some time *or other* we may be at leisure.
For *some* cause *or other* (or *another*) he was not at home.
Every man has, *one* time *or other* (or *another*), a little Rubicon.
Most applicants are deficient in *one or other* qualification.
You must go *one* way *or the other.*
He has helped *many* men, *many a* man.
Of *the many* men I have met this summer he is the most interesting.
Many (predicate adjective) are the afflictions of the righteous (*Psalms*, XXXIV, 19).
Many's the tale he has told us.
Your gentle, genial letter is as kind and indulgent to me as a favorite relative, and my thanks in return are *many* (predicate adjective) and most fervid (James Whitcomb Riley, *Letter to Frank S. Sherman*, Jan. 8, 1891).
They have not shed *a many* tears, Dear eyes, since first I knew them well (Tennyson, *The Miller's Daughter*, 219).
A great many mistakes have been made.
The plan has *numerous* advantages.
His visit to the old home called up *myriad* (*innumerable* or *countless*) scenes of his childhood.
There were riots in *various* places.
I met him the *other* day on the street.
I am hunting a few *other* examples of this construction.
The little prince's education teaches him that he is *other* (predicate adjective) than you (Meredith, *Egoist*).
I do not want him *other* (objective predicate) than he is.
I will do it *another* time.
That is quite *another* thing.
There was there *a certain* John Smith.
I felt *a certain* reluctance to do it.
There was an incredible frivolity about her sister at *certain* moments.
The old gentleman made *divers* (now more commonly *several*) ineffectual efforts to get up (Smollett, *Peregrine Pickle*, Ch. LXVI, A.D. 1751).
There are *sundry* (more commonly *various*) weighty reasons why I should go.
'He, this school autocrat, gathered *all and sundry* reins into the hollow of his one hand' (Charlotte Brontë, *Villette*, Ch. XV), more commonly *each and every rein.*
He has *considerable* influence.
He has invested *considerable* (colloquial American) money in it.

He has *much* patience, land, property.

Soul, thou hast *much* (now *many*) goods laid up for many years (*Luke*, XII, 19).

They taught *much* (now *many*) people (*Acts*, XI, 26).

Older '*Much* oats is grown here' is now replaced by '*Large quantities of* (or in colloquial speech *lots of*) oats are grown here,' as *much* cannot now stand before a plural mass noun that requires a plural verb.

Send out *moe* (now *more*) horses (Shakespeare, *Macbeth*, V, II, 34).

We need one *more* (= *additional*) teacher.

We need two *more* teachers.

He has *little* patience, land, property.

He needs *a little* patience, *a little* money, *a little* salt.

I can do with *less* money, *less* clothes, *less* troops.

The public wants *more* action and *less* (better than *fewer*, for here the idea of totality is more prominent than that of separate individuals) words (review of a drama).

We can get along with one *less* (after the analogy of *more*) teacher.

Have you *enough* money with you?

There was just *sufficient* water for drinking.

'They (i.e. the factory girls) can earn so much when work is *plenty*' (Mrs. Gaskell, *Mary Barton*, Ch. IX), now usually *plentiful*.

Poets would be *plentier* (J. R. Lowell, *My Study Windows*, 22).

Although there are *plenty* (now usually in the literary language *plenty of*) other ideals that I should prefer (R. L. Stevenson, *Inland Voyage*, 8).

There was *plenty* (in literary English *plenty of*) food of all descriptions (Irish English).

I will meet you at this or *such* other place as shall be deemed proper.

Such and such a cause has *such and such* an effect.

Such and such causes have *such and such* effects.

The question which we contend is of so transcendent moment is, not whether *such or such* knowledge is of worth, but what is its relative worth? (Spencer, *Education*).

a. MEANS OF IMPARTING FEELING. Feeling may be imparted to the statement by placing *ever so* before certain of these adjectives: 'I've taken *ever so much* trouble, but it's no good' (W. E. Collinson). 'I'm afraid I've made *ever so many* mistakes' (*id.*).

b. AMERICAN 'SOME' WITH FORCE OF DESCRIPTIVE ADJECTIVE. In American slang *some* is widely employed as a descriptive adjective expressing a high degree of excellence: 'She is *some* girl.' Often ironically: 'That is *some* car.' This intensive use of *some* has developed out of the literary language, where this force is often to be observed: 'a Person of good Sense and *some* Learning' (Steele, *Spectator*, No. 106, par. 5). In American speech this force has been extended to the adverb *some* described in 42 *c aa* (3rd par.).

c. FORM OF INDEFINITE ARTICLE. The indefinite article *a* or *an*, the reduced form of the numeral *one*, has preserved the *n* of the original word only before a vowel sound: *a* boat; *a* house; *a* union (yūnyən); not *a* one (wun); but *an* apple; *an* heir (with silent *h*).

There is fluctuation of usage before an initial *h* where the syllable is unaccented. In the literary language of England it has long been usual to place *an* here before the *h: an* históorical character; *an* hotél; etc. At the present time, however, this usage is not universal in England. The British scholar H. W. Fowler in his *Modern English Usage* even calls it pedantic. In America it is usual to employ *a* here, although some follow the prevailing British usage. The difference of usage here rests upon an older difference of pronunciation. In America, Ireland, Scotland, and the extreme northern part of England initial *h* has been preserved. In the English dialects it has for the most part been lost, but in standard English under the influence of the written language and Scotch and Irish usage it has been restored. For a long time, however, it was pronounced weakly or not at all in unaccented syllables, which gave rise to the spelling *an* in '*an* históorical character,' '*an* hotél,' etc. Older spelling, such as '*an* hundred crowns' (Shakespeare, *Taming of the Shrew*, V, II, 128), '*an* hill' (*Matthew*, V, 14), shows that in early Modern English initial *h* was not always pronounced in England even in accented syllables.

7. *Interrogative Adjectives.* They are: *what* (indefinite) and *which* (more definite). Like other adjectives, they modify nouns referring to persons or things: '*What* boy (or 'boys') in our neighborhood would do such a thing?' '*What* (*how much*) pudding is there left?' '*What* price are eggs today?' '*What* (pred. adj.) are eggs today?' '*What* (*of what nature*) is the real situation?' '*What* (*how great*) is the extent of the damage?' '*Which* book (or 'boy') did you finally choose?' In indirect questions (**7** VI *b*): 'I asked her *what* girls were going along with her.' 'I asked him *what* the real situation was.' 'I asked him *what* book (or 'books') I should read.' These indirect interrogatives are interrogative conjunctive adjectives (**18** B), i.e. they bind the clause to the principal proposition.

8. *Proper Adjectives.* Proper adjectives, i.e. adjectives derived from a proper noun, often do not denote a kind or a condition, but are limiting adjectives, identifying a being or thing: 'a *Harvard* student,' 'the *United States* flag,' 'the *German* universities,' 'the *English* navy,' 'the *Chicago* post office,' 'the *Presbyterian* church,' 'a *Shakespearean* scholar,' 'the *Smith* residence,' etc. On the other hand, they, of course, often have the force of descriptive adjectives: 'very clever, with a little of the *Tennysonian* leaven in

them' (Longfellow's comment on Matthew Arnold's poems). 'The acting of Kean is *Shakespearean*' (Keats). 'He has *Smith* pluck and energy' (words of Mr. Smith, speaking of his oldest son). Notice that proper adjectives begin with a capital. They, of course, are written with a small letter when they lose their specific application: '*hermetic* seal,' '*quixotic* sentiments,' '*china* dishes,' '*italic* type,' etc.

As can be seen by the examples, proper adjectives are of two kinds — true adjectives and proper nouns used as adjectives. The latter class is quite common: 'the great *Mississippi* flood of 1927,' '*Rocky Mountain* goats,' 'the *Rockefeller* Foundation,' 'the *Field* Museum' (at Chicago). 'He was very *Herries* (family name) in some things: in his passion for England — he had all the *Herries* ignorant contempt for foreigners' (Hugh Walpole, *Rogue Herries*, p. 194). As seen in the last example, proper nouns are used as adjectives not only attributively but also predicatively.

9. *Exclamatory Adjectives.* In exclamations *what* and *what a* are used: '*What* nonsense!' '*What a* shame!' '*What a* beautiful day!' '*What* people!' '*What* (*how great*) babies you are!' '*What* (*how many*) hours I have spent on these useless exercises!' '*What* (predicate adjective = *how great*) was my surprise when I heard that he had resigned!' In these examples *what* with the peculiar tone of voice associated with it indicates that there is something of a surprising or striking nature in the person(s) or thing(s) to which it points.

Such is often used in exclamations with the force of *great:* 'We have had *such* sport!' Often with intensive force: 'We have had *such* a wonderful time!'

CHAPTER IV

THE VERB

11. Definition. The verb is that part of speech that predicates, assists in predications, asks a question, or expresses a command: 'The wind *blows*.' 'He *is* blind.' '*Did* he *do* it?' '*Hurry!*'

12. Classes. There are four classes — transitive, intransitive, linking, and auxiliary.

1. *Transitive Verbs.* A transitive verb is a verb that requires an object (**27** 2 *a*) — noun, pronoun, or clause — to complete its meaning: 'The boy *struck* his *dog*.' 'The girl *loves* her *doll*.' 'The cat *sees* a *bird*, and *is watching it*.' 'They *raise* chiefly *corn* in this section of the country.' 'I *see* by the tracks in the snow *that somebody has been here*.' 'I *believe that he is honest*.' In 'He struck *me*' the object *me* indicates a person toward whom the activity is directed, but in 'He struck a *light*' the object *light* indicates the result of the action. In other sentences the object may have other meanings. The characteristic thing about an object is that it stands in a close relation to the verb, completing its meaning: 'I heard a *groan*.' Compare **27** 2 *a*.

Where the action passes back to the doer we call the transitive verb a reflexive: 'She *is dressing herself*.' 'He *hurt himself*.' 'I usually *shave myself*.' The object here is always a reflexive pronoun (**7** II).

Verbs which are usually intransitive often become transitive by taking a cognate object, i.e. a noun of a meaning cognate or similar to that of the verb, repeating and explaining more fully the idea expressed by the verb. The cognate object is usually modified by one or more adjectives or by an *of*-genitive, which makes it possible to describe the action still more accurately: 'He *died a violent death.*' 'He *is living a sad and lonely life.*' 'He *laughed a little short ugly laugh.*' 'He *sighed a sigh of ineffable satisfaction.*' Of course, a large number of other verbs usually intransitive become transitive when they take an object to complete their meaning: 'Many workless *are walking* the *streets.*' 'He *went* the shortest *way.*' 'He *looked daggers.*' 'She *wept* bitter *tears.*' 'He *ran errands.*' 'They *sat* out the *dance.*' 'He *slept* off his *vexation.*' 'She *cried herself* to sleep.' 'He *smoked himself* into calmness.'

a. CAUSATIVES. There is in our language, as a survival of a once much wider usage, a little group of causatives formed from intransitives and now distinguished from them by a change of vowel or by a change of vowel and a change of consonant: 'The baby *is sitting* (intrans.) on a chair by the windows,' but 'The mother picks up the baby and *sets* (trans. caus.) it on a chair by the window' (i.e. *makes* it *sit* on a chair). 'The baby *is lying* (intrans.) in the cradle,' but 'The mother *lays* (trans. caus.) the baby into the cradle.' 'The tree *falls*' (intrans.), but 'The woodman *fells* (trans. caus.) the tree.' 'He always *rises* (intrans.) to the occasion,' but 'Her family *is rearing* (or *raising;* both trans. caus.) a sumptuous mausoleum over her remains.' 'He *drinks* (intrans.) hard,' but 'The storm *is drenching* (trans. caus.) our clothes' (i.e. *is making* them *drink*).

Today we have little feeling for the construction just described. We often simply use an intransitive as a transitive causative without a change of form, in accordance with the common English principle of using the same form as an intransitive or a transitive: 'The horse *swam* (intrans.) across the river.' 'He *swam* (trans. caus.) his horse across the river.' 'The snow *is melting*' (intrans.). 'The sun *is melting* (trans. caus.) the snow.' 'Here once *stood* (intrans.) a huge oak.' 'I *stood* (trans. caus.) my rifle against the oak.' 'She *flew* (intrans.) across the Atlantic and *flew* (trans. caus.) her own plane.'

In most cases, however, the causative idea is expressed by placing an auxiliary — *cause, make, have, get,* and *let* — before the infinitive or the past participle of the verb to be employed: 'Black spot (disease) *is causing* the rosebush *to drop* its leaves.' 'He didn't want to do it, but I *made* him *do* it.' 'I shall *have* him *cut* the grass soon.' 'I *had* (or *got*) a new suit *made.*' 'I finally *got* him *to do* it.' 'He soon *let* his power *be felt.*' 'He *let* it *be known* to only a few friends.' Compare **49** 2 *e*.

There is another quite different group of causatives, which have come into wide use in the modern period. They are formed by suffixing *-en* to adjectives: 'Travel *broadens* our view of life.' 'Suffering *deepens* our feeling and *widens* our sympathy.' 'A few kind words *lighten* our burdens.' Some of these forms are used either transitively or intransitively: 'Exposure *hardens* (trans.) this stone.' 'This stone *hardens* (intrans.) with exposure.' The suffix *-en* is sometimes added to nouns to form causatives: 'A little encouragement often *heartens* us to further effort.' 'Discouragements from outside only serve to *heighten* his determination.'

2. *Intransitive Verbs.* An intransitive verb denotes a state or simple action without any reference to an object: 'John *is sleeping.*' 'I *dream* every night.' 'He often *acts* rashly.' 'The sun *is melting* (trans.) the snow,' but 'The snow *is melting*' (intrans.).

Transitive verbs are often used intransitively without an object when the thought is directed to the action alone: 'Mary *is dressing* (herself).' 'He *hid* (himself) behind a tree.' 'He *overeats* (himself).' 'He likes *to give.*' 'We *wash* (the linen) every Monday.' Compare *Syntax*, **46.**

A large number of our present-day intransitives were once transitives with a reflexive object: 'Which way will I *turne me?*' (Lyly, *Euphues and His England*, Works, II, p. 142, A.D. 1580). 'At the breach of day we six *made us* for the mountaine' (Lithgow, *Travels*, VI, p. 377, A.D. 1632), i.e. *set* (or *headed*) *ourselves for*. Gradually the reflexive disappeared, as the verb seemed to the English mind sufficient of itself. This development started very early, even in the Old English period. In English it has become perfectly natural to employ a reflexive verb as an intransitive: 'I *dressed* and *shaved* as quickly as I could.' 'She *bowed* to me.' 'I must *wash* before dinner.' In some cases, however, the old reflexive object still lingers: 'Behave!' or 'Behave *yourself!*' In some verbs the reflexive pronoun is still always used: *bestir, betake, pride,* etc.: 'She prides *herself* on her cooking.' Sometimes the simple and the reflexive form are both used, each with a difference of meaning: 'He proved *himself* worthy of the position,' but 'He had made acquaintance with a lady who *proved* to be the countess of Drogheda.' There is the same fluctuation with the use of the reciprocal pronoun. The pronoun may be used or dropped, with a strong tendency for it to disappear: 'The two had never *met each other* before' or more commonly *had never met before*. 'We soon came to a place where two roads *crossed each other*' or more commonly *crossed.* In 'They kissed *each other* tenderly' we still feel the force of the pronoun, but we say 'Kiss and be friends' without the pronoun as we desire to express action pure and simple. Compare *Syntax*, pp. 438, 439.

Many intransitives — both the original stock and those developed from the reflexive form — have developed passive force:

'Snow *is blowing* (= *is being blown*) in at the window.' 'His hat *blew* (= *was blown*) into the river.' 'The grave *had closed* (= *had been closed*) over all he loved.' 'Some letters of a typewriter get more worn than others, and some *wear* (= *get worn*) only on one side.' 'Some builders prefer receiving the graystone lime ground dry as it *mixes* (= *gets mixed*) more readily when it is made up into mortar.' 'These pears don't *cook* (= *can't be cooked*) well.' 'This cloth won't *wash*' (= *can't be washed*). 'This wood doesn't *split* (= *can't be split*) straight.' 'The boat *steers* (= *can be steered*) well under all circumstances.' This usage is most common, as in these examples, where the action seems to take place of itself. We think of the activity pure and simple when we use these verbs and those in the two preceding paragraphs. See also **49** 4. For more examples compare *Syntax*, p. 440.

3. *Linking Verbs.* Although we very commonly make assertions and ask questions by means of verbs, they are not absolutely necessary, and in fact we often do without them: '*A sad experience!*' '*Our sister dead!*' '*John a cheat!*' '*Everything in good order.*' This is an old type of sentence, once more common than now. It is employed when the thing predicated of the subject is an adjective, noun, adverb, or prepositional phrase. It was originally thought sufficient to place the predicate adjective, noun, adverb, or prepositional phrase alongside of the subject, before it or after it. This old type of sentence is called the appositional type as the predicate lies alongside of the subject and predicates of itself without the aid of a finite verb. It is still quite commonly employed when something is predicated of an object: 'I found *him reconciled* to his lot.' 'I have always found *him a true friend.*' 'I found *him in poor health.*' 'She boiled *the egg hard.*' Even in the earliest records of the oldest languages in our family a new style of predication had begun to appear. The predicate adjective, noun, adverb, or prepositional phrase was joined to the subject by means of the copula *be*, as in the following modern English sentences: 'The boy *is* tall.' 'He *is* a carpenter.' 'He *is* up already.' 'Everything *is* in good condition.' The copula *be* performs here merely the function of announcing the predicate. It does not itself predicate; it only links the predicate to the subject. We can still often dispense with it and after a direct object it is still for the most part lacking, although it is now sometimes used here, as illustrated in **8** (4th par.). In the prehistoric period there was a time when there was no such thing as a copula. Later it gradually came into use, but even in the earliest records of the oldest languages it was not freely used as today. Its use spread because there was an absolute need of such a linking word. Its

introduction into our family of languages was one of the greatest events in the history of our family. It has a quality of great value. It has tenses. This copula, like all copulas, was once a full verb with concrete meaning. Later it lost its concrete meaning and developed into a copula, but fortunately it retained its old tenses which it had when it was a full verb. The original appositional type of sentence has no tense forms and hence has only a limited field of usefulness. It can be employed only where the context or the situation makes the thought clear. The introduction of the copula *be* opened up new possibilities of human expression.

We have about sixty copulas in English Their wide and varied use is the most prominent feature of our language. They have been springing up for centuries and within the modern period have been especially active. As these copulas have all with the exception of *be* come into use within the historic period we can study them and see what they are. *Become* in the ninth century meant *come to a place, arrive,* with concrete meaning. In the twelfth century the old concrete meaning began to fade away and go over into the abstract sense of *come to be something, become something* — so abstract that *become* could serve as a copula: 'He *became* blind.' The oldest copula, *be,* was once, like *become,* a concrete verb and later gradually lost its concrete meaning and developed into a copula. In our own time a cow not only *runs into the barn,* but it also *runs* (= *becomes*) *dry.* For centuries *run* has been becoming more abstract, but its old concrete meaning is still common, so that it has not yet become a pure copula. Similarly, *come* is still widely employed as a concrete verb and at the same time is widely used as a copula: 'He *came* (concrete verb) home at ten,' but 'His prediction *came* (copula) true' and 'My shoestring *came* (copula) untied.' With such copulas, especially *feel, smell, taste, sound, ring,* care should be taken that the form following the copula should be an adjective, not an adverb: 'I *feel sad*' (not *sadly*). 'It *smells bad.*' 'It *tastes sour.*' 'His excuse *sounds hollow.*' 'His words *rang true.*' The long list of copulas given in *Syntax,* **6** B contains many words in different stages of development toward the state of copula. No other language shows such a vigorous growth of copulas. As many of them are used also with their old concrete meaning they naturally retain something of it when employed as copulas, so that these words, though copulas, are variously shaded in meaning, thus greatly enriching English expression. Each of these copulas has two forms, the common form and the expanded (**47** 2) form, each with a different shade of meaning: 'He soon *gets* tired.' 'He *is getting* tired.' Thus the use of two forms with differentiated force increases the number of shades in the meaning. The usefulness of these different shades of meaning will become apparent in the next two paragraphs.

Our two participles, present and past, though often true verbs in force, frequently remain adjectives in function, so that they, like any adjective, can serve as predicate after a copula: 'He *is working* in the garden.' 'He got *married* yesterday.' 'This paper on account of its public-spirited editorials and its good news service *has become* widely *read* by both political parties.' Thus the copulas are used to form our active and passive verbal systems. Compare 4 below.

The copulas not only link a predicate adjective, noun, etc., to the subject but also, on account of the different meanings of the different copulas, give various shades of meaning to the predication. They indicate a state, continuance in a state or the continuance of an activity, entrance into a state or the beginning of an activity, a becoming something represented as the outcome of a development or of events or the closing stage of an activity. Simple state: 'He *is* sick.' Continuance in a state: 'He *keeps* still.' Continuing act: 'He *is* working in the garden.' Entrance into a state: 'He *got* sick.' Beginning of an act: 'He *is* just *getting* up.' Outcome of a development: 'He *became* (or *went*) blind.' 'He has lived down a youthful escapade and *has become* respected by everybody.' The ideas now expressed by copulas were in Old English expressed by verbal prefixes: a-deafian *to become deaf*, ge-ealdian *to grow old*, etc. The later wholesale introduction of French and Latin words replacing native verbs with prefixes greatly reduced their number and blunted English feeling for the native prefixes. Moreover, the large Danish population in England had no feeling for the common English prefix *ge-* and dropped it. Conditions were ripe for the development of copulas. In the twelfth century *become* arose followed by *seem, wax, grow, turn,* and *look*. This new development proved so useful that new copulas kept springing up. One of the most handy of the later comers is intransitive *get,* which arose in Shakespeare's day.

We have become so fond of the copula construction that we often use it even when there is a verb which expresses the same thing as copula and predicate noun or adjective: 'There *was* a heavy *snow* last night,' instead of 'It *snowed* heavily last night.' 'I *am fond of* (= *like*) fruit.' The noun *snow* and the adjective *fond* bring pictures before the mind. The English mind is fond of such concrete expression. The predicate adjective, however, is not so common as it once was. Many of the expressions are now only literary: 'You are *forgetful of* (= *forget*) the fact that,' etc. 'I was *ignorant of* (= *didn't know*) these facts.' 'It was a contest *fruitful of* (= *that produced*) animosity and discontent.' 'On every side Oxford *is redolent of* (= *suggests*) age and authority.' Of these predicate adjectives only *fond of* is widely used in colloquial speech. On the other hand, the predicate noun has become very common in colloquial language. A verb is often replaced by a copula and a predicate noun, not only when the noun has a concrete meaning, as *snow* in the example given above, but frequently also when the noun is a verbal noun after the transitive copulas *have, get, do, give,* or *make:* 'After dinner we *had* a quiet *smoke,*' instead of 'After dinner we *smoked* quietly.' 'We *had* several *falls,*' instead of 'We *fell* several times.' 'I *had* a *look* at her just now,' instead of 'I *looked* at her just now.' 'I got *a good shaking* up,' instead of 'I *was shaken* up thoroughly.' 'I *have* not *done* much *walking* since I saw you last,' instead of 'I *haven't walked* much since I saw you last.' 'She *gave,* or *made,* no *answer,*' instead of 'She *didn't answer.*' We feel that *have, get, do, give,* and *make* have a little concrete meaning left. They are not quite like the copula *be. Be* is intransitive, while *have, get, do, give,* and *make* are transitives, but they are all copulas, though in different stages of development. Often their main function is, as copulas, to link the predicate noun to its subject. To English feeling a predicate verbal noun is felt as more concrete and forcible than a pure verb.

4. *Auxiliary Verbs.* An auxiliary verb is one that, although originally independent, now only helps other verbs, transitive, intransitive, or linking, to form some of their parts. Tense auxiliaries: 'He *has* done it.' 'He *has* been sick.' 'He *will* come tomorrow.' Compare **64–68.** Modal auxiliaries: 'He *shall* do it whether he *will* [do it] or not.' Compare **57** 4, **57** 4 A *h.* One of the characteristic forms of English is the auxiliary *do* employed in the so-called *do*-form. The *do*-forms are given in **69** C. The uses of the forms with *do* are described at length in **47** 3. We often use a causative auxiliary with a dependent infinitive or participle instead of a simple causative: 'I *had* him *cut* the grass.' Compare **12** 1 *a* (3rd par.). There are other common auxiliaries of quite a different type — the copulas. These forms link a predicate participle to the subject. The great importance of these auxiliaries for English expression has been shown in 3 above. Their use as auxiliaries of aspect is described in **52** 2 *a, b, c.* Their use as passive auxiliaries is described in **49.**

13. Compound Verbs. A verb often enters into a close relation with an adverb, preposition, prepositional phrase, or object, forming with it a unit, a compound. There are three classes:

a. Adverb and verb often form a firm, inseparable compound in which the stress rests upon the verb, often with figurative meaning: *upróot, uplíft, undernóurish, overchárge,* etc. A preposition often forms such a compound with a verb: 'The river is *overflówing* its banks.' Compare **16** 2 (last par.). Where the preposition or adverb is no longer in use outside of these compounds, as in the case of *be–* (= *over, upon*), it is called a prefix: 'to *bemóan* (= moan over) one's fate,' '*befriénd* (= bestow friendly deeds upon) one,' etc., but with privative force in *behéad.* Such verbs are called derivative verbs.

Such compounds and derivatives are very common in verbs of foreign origin: *pervade, coöperate, proceed, precede,* etc.

b. The verb often enters into a close relation with a more strongly stressed element, usually an adverb, prepositional phrase, or object, forming with it a unit in thought, a real compound, although the parts are often separated and are not written together: 'His father *sèt* him *úp* in business.' 'I *tòok* him *to tásk* for it.' 'He *tòok párt* in the play.'

c. A newer group of compounds is described in **17** (3rd par.).

CHAPTER V

THE ADVERB

14. Definition, Function, Position. An adverb is a word that modifies a verb, an adjective, or another adverb. An adverbial modifier may assume the form of an adverb, a prepositional phrase or clause, or a conjunctional clause: 'He entered *quietly.*' 'Polish it *well.*' 'He entered *in haste*' (prepositional phrase). 'I could see the bird's loaded beak *from where I stood*' (prepositional clause). In the last example a preposition and its dependent clause together form an adverbial element. It is very much more common for a clause to form an adverbial element with the help of a subordinating conjunction: 'He entered *as soon as he had taken off his overcoat.*' The adverbial conjunctional clause is treated in **15 2** *b–k*, **18** B 5, *Syntax*, **25–34.**

An adverb, as indicated by its literal meaning, *joined to a verb,* is an appositive to a verb, i.e. is placed before or after a verb to explain its meaning in the case at hand more clearly, much as an adjective as an appositive is placed before or after a noun to explain it: 'The girl is improving *remarkably*.' The same form is used as an appositive to an adjective or another adverb and here is also called an adverb, although of course it is here not true to its name: 'The girl is *remarkably* beautiful.' 'The girl is improving *remarkably* fast.' An adverb, however, modifies not only thus a single word, but often also a prepositional phrase, a subordinate clause, or an independent statement as a whole: 'He has traveled *entirely* around the world.' 'He is *almost* across the river.' 'He lives *a mile* (adverbial accusative) beyond our house.' 'I arrived *soon* after it happened.' 'I did it *only* because I felt it to be my duty.' For sentence adverb see **15** 1 *b*.

An adverb that modifies an adjective or adjective element or an adverb or adverbial element usually precedes the modified word: 'She is *very* pretty.' 'She sings *very* beautifully.' An adverb that modifies a verb precedes the verb if it itself has a weaker stress but follows the verb if it itself has the stronger stress: 'It's too bad! I *utterly* forgót it.' 'He acted *prómptly*.' After the analogy of 'She would *utterly forgét* her past' many people say, 'She wishes to *utterly forgét* her past.' They feel that the adverb should stand before the more heavily stressed verb. Others think that the second sentence is incorrect, as the adverb stands between the preposition *to* and its object the infinitive *forget*. They call this construction the 'split infinitive' and studiously avoid it, saying here: 'She wishes *utterly to forget* her past.' Those who use the split infinitive feel that *to* is no longer a preposition, but a mere formal introduction to the infinitive clause (**47** 5, 2nd par.) and that consequently the adverb should stand here as elsewhere immediately before the more heavily stressed verb. Almost everybody, however, puts *not* before the *to* of the infinitive, because *not* is felt as modifying not the verb but the infinitive clause as a whole: 'He promised *not to do it again*.' The question of the split infinitive is discussed in detail in *Syntax*, **49** 2 *c*. As copulas and auxiliaries are usually unstressed an adverb follows them. 'I am *always* cáreful.' 'We shall *soon* knów.' 'He doesn'*t* cáre.' 'I have *always* trústed your judgment.' But with change of stress: 'I *always* ám careful.' 'I *always* háve trusted your judgment.' 'I slept beside a spring last night, and I *never* shåll like a bedroom so well' (Meredith, *Amazing Marriage*, Ch. VI). For fuller treatment of the position of adverbs see *Syntax*, **16** 2.

a. *Adverbs in Compounds and Derivatives*. Adverbs often occur as the first component of compounds: *up*root, *over*turn, *under*-

done, *out*lying, *tight*-fitting, *mis*judge, *re*turn, *co*öperate, etc. The adverb *not* is usually replaced here by *un–: un*able, etc. In many foreign words the negative here is *in–* (or *im–*) or *dis–: in*convenient, *im*possible, *dis*obey. Some of these adverbs, *mis–*, *un–*, *re–*, *co–*, etc., which are not used outside of compounds, are called prefixes. Such compounds are termed derivatives.

b. Adverbs Used as Other Parts of Speech. Adverbs are often used as nouns: 'the *ups and downs* of Life'; 'the *ins* (the party in power), the *outs*' (the party out of power). 'He knows *the ins and outs* (details) of every political move.' Nouns made from adverbs are very common in prepositional phrases: until *tomorrow*, after *tomorrow*, since *yesterday*, etc. Compare **16** 2 (2nd par.).

Adverbs are often used as pronouns: 'I saw him a year ago, but since *then* (used as demonstrative pronoun) we haven't met.' 'I saw him a year ago, since *when* (used as relative pronoun) I haven't seen anything of him.' Compare **16** 2 (2nd par.). In older English, adverbs were often used as pronouns in prepositional phrases in which the preposition followed the adverb, adverb and preposition usually being written together as parts of a compound: *therein*, now *in it; therewith*, now *with it; wherein*, now *in what* (interrogative) or *in which* (relative); *wherewith*, now *with what* (interrogative) or *with which* (relative); etc. A few of the old adverbial compounds, however, have survived in common use where they have acquired a special meaning, such as *therefore* (**7** I *b*), *whereupon* (**7** IV *a cc*). In poetical and legal language the old adverbial compounds are still widely used in their original meaning and function. Compare **7** I *b* and **7** IV *a cc*.

Adverbs are often used as adjectives. See **8** *a*, *b*.

On the other hand, adherent (**8**, 3rd par.) and appositive (**8**, 3rd par.) adjectives which modify verbal nouns are in a formal sense adjectives, but they have the force of adverbs: 'his *late* arrival,' 'his last visit *here*.'

15. Classes. Adverbs may be classified from different points of view:

1. *Classification by Function:* There are four groups:

a. SIMPLE ADVERBS. A simple adverb modifies a single word or a group: 'He came *yesterday*.' 'He is *very* industrious.' 'He runs *very* fast.' 'He walked *almost* five miles' (adverbial accusative). The simple adverb often modifies a prepositional phrase employed as an adjective or an adverb: 'He is *almost* across the river.' 'He swam *almost* across the river.' The simple adverb often modifies an adverbial clause: 'I arrived *soon* after it happened.'

b. SENTENCE ADVERBS. A sentence adverb modifies a sentence as a whole: 'You *perhaps* (or *possibly*) underrate my ability.' 'You are *probably* (or '*probably* are') right about it.' 'He must *surely* (or '*surely* must') be there by this time.' 'He has *evidently* (or '*evidently* has') made a mistake.' 'He will *doubtless* (or '*doubtless* will') discover his mistake soon.' '*Unfortunately*, the message failed to arrive in time,' or 'The message, *unfortunately*, failed to arrive in time,' or 'The message failed to arrive in time, *unfortunately*.' Negatives are common sentence adverbs: 'I *never* do such things.' 'He does*n't* do such things.' 'He promises *not* to do it again.' The sentence adverb usually stands before a full verb and after or before a copula or auxiliary. Not infrequently, however, in the case of certain adverbs it may stand also at the beginning or the end of the statement, as in the sixth example. The negative *not* precedes an infinitive. For fuller treatment see *Syntax*, **16** 2 *a*.

There is a peculiar group of sentence adverbs — distinguishing adverbs: *not*, *only*, *solely*, *simply*, *just*, *particularly*, *especially*, *even*, *also*, *at least*, *exactly* (or *precisely*), etc. These adverbs refer to the thought of the sentence as a whole, but at the same time call especial attention to a particular part of it. This particular part — a word or a group of words — is distinguished by placing one of these distinguishing adverbs before it or after it: '*Only* Jóhn (or 'Jóhn *only*') passed in Latin.' 'John *only* (*barely*) pássed in Latin.' 'I have been influenced *solely* by this consideration.' 'I came *just* to see you.' 'Almost all of them arrived on time, *even* Jóhn' (or 'Jóhn *even*'). 'None of them will go; *at least* Jóhn (or 'Jóhn *at least*') will not.' '*Exactly* whát (or 'Whát *exactly*') paganism was we shall never know.' 'Hé did it, *not* Í.' 'He hit mé, *not* hím.' 'He did it for the love of the cause, *not* for personal gain.' In 'Two points in his criticism are *especially* deserving of notice' *especially* is an ordinary adverb modifying the following adjective, but in 'Several of the boys deserve praise, *especially* Jóhn' (or 'Jóhn *especially*') it is a distinguishing adverb.

Nouns are often used as sentence adverbs to express feeling — irritation, surprise, etc.: 'What *the hell* (or *the devil* or *the deuce*) do you want?' 'He is dead.' — '*The devil* he is.' They often express negation: '*Devil* a one!' = '*Not* one!'

c. Conjunctive Adverbs:

aa. Coördinating Conjunctive Adverbs. A conjunctive adverb not only modifies some word in the proposition in which it stands, but also links the proposition in which it stands to the rest of the sentence or to a preceding sentence: 'We are both without money; *there* comes in the difficulty.' 'We played an hour; *then* we went home.' 'There was no one there; *so* I went away.' 'I have had enough.' — '*Then* let us go!' For fuller information see **18** A 1, 3, 5 and *Syntax*, **19** 1 *a*, *b*, *c*, *d*, *e*, **19** 2.

In the strict sense these forms are always simple adverbs, for they always perform the function of a simple adverb in the proposition in which they stand. No formal connective links this independent proposition to the preceding independent proposition. The two propositions lie side by side without a formal binding tie. This is a form of parataxis, described in **18** (5th par.), but yet there is a slight difference. These adverbs, like personal pronouns, not only perform their own function in the proposition in which they stand but also bind it to the preceding proposition. This construction is as old as our language and still has a vigorous life. Alongside of it is coördination with *and:* 'I forgot my pen; *so* I had to use my pencil,' or 'I forgot my pen, *and so* I had to use my pencil.' 'We ate lunch in the park, *then* went rowing,' or 'We ate lunch in the park, *and then* went rowing.'

bb. Subordinating Conjunctive Adverbs. The two adverbial forms *where* and *when* are often used to introduce a subordinate adverbial clause: 'I sat *where I could see them both plainly.*' 'She was very despondent *when I spoke with her last.*' Here *where* and *when* are conjunctive adverbs, i.e. adverbs that have the force of subordinating conjunctions and at the same time perform another important function, namely, they modify as adverbs the verb of the subordinate clause in which they stand.

In reading books from our older literature we often find in such adverbial clauses *there* and *then* where we now employ *where* and *when:* 'The erthe tremelyd *there* (now *where*) Wyllyam stood' *Merch. & Son*, 92, in Hazl. E. P. P. I. 139, sixteenth century). '*Then* (now *when*) hys howndys began to baye, That harde (heard) the jeant *there* (now *where*) he laye' (*Sir Eglam.*, 286, A.D. 1440). As can be seen by the words in parentheses the old demonstrative conjunctives *there* and *then* have been replaced by the indefinite conjunctives *where* and *when*. *There* and *then* were replaced by *where* and *when* also in the adjective clauses described in **7** IV *a cc*. What caused this change in English expression in adverbial and adjective clauses? *There* and *then* were used also as coördinating conjunctions, as described in *aa* above for modern usage. Thus they were not so appropriate for the subordinate clause as *where* and *when*, which were employed in the substantive (noun) clause, a common subordinate clause. *Where* and *when* had for many centuries been widely used in substantive clauses and are still widely employed there, as is illustrated in the second paragraph after this one. Gradually they became established also in the adverbial and the adjective clause.

If the meaning is quite indefinite *ever* is added to *where* and *when* in adverbial clauses: 'She is happy *wherever* she is.' 'He always helps me *whenever* I need him.'

The adverbial forms *where, when, how, why, whither,* etc., are still common, as they have always been, in substantive (noun) clauses, i.e. in subject (**18** B 1), object (**18** B 3), attributive substantive (**18** B 2), and prepositional (**18** B 4) clauses. Here as elsewhere they are conjunctive adverbs, i.e. adverbs that have the force of subordinating conjunctions and at the same time perform another important function, namely, they modify as adverbs the verb of the subordinate clause in which they stand. These conjunctives are either indefinite conjunctives or interrogative conjunctives. Interrogatives are merely a peculiar kind of indefinites, which often assume the special function of calling for an answer in an indefinite situation. As interrogative conjunctives always stand in a subordinate clause they are only indirect interrogatives employed in indirect questions. Examples of indefinite and interrogative conjunctive adverbs: 'It is immaterial to me *where* and *when* (indef.) he goes.' 'It has often been asked *where* and *when* (interrog.) he went.' 'I do not know *where* (indef.) he is.' 'He asked me *where* (interrog.) I had been.' 'I do not know *when* (indef.) he went.' 'She asked me *when* (interrog.) he went.' 'I saw *how* (indef.) he did it.' 'I asked *how* (interrog.) he did it.' 'I asked *why* (interrog.) he did it.'

In older English, alongside of *where,* differentiated in meaning from it, were two other related indefinite forms in common use as indefinite conjunctive adverbs, *whither* and *whence* (or often *from whence*), the former indicating motion toward, the latter motion from. They are still in use in choice language, but in plain prose are replaced by *where* and *where . . . from:* 'I do not know *whither* (in plain prose *where*) he went.' 'I do not know *whence* (or *from whence*) *he came*' (in plain prose *where he came from*). These forms are used also as interrogative conjunctive adverbs: 'Then she asked me *whither* (in plain prose *where*) he went.' 'Then she asked me *whence* (or *from whence*) he came' (in plain prose *where he came from*). In older English, *whether* was often used instead of *whither.*

d. Interrogative Adverbs in Principal Propositions. In indefinite situations where we desire to ask for information, we employ indefinites, not only as interrogative pronouns (**7** VI) and interrogative adjectives (**10** 7), but also as interrogative adverbs, namely, *when, where, whence* (or in plain prose usually *where — from;* see **16** 2, 2nd par.), *whither* (or in plain prose usually *where*), *why, how:* '*When* did he go?' '*Where* does he live?' '*Whence* did he come?' or more commonly '*Where* did he come *from?*' '*Whither* (or more commonly *where*) did he go?' '*Why* did he do it?' '*How* did he do it?' In older English, *whether* was often used instead of *whither*.

In older English, *as* is sometimes placed before the interrogative adverb *how* as a mere formal introduction: 'It is indeed a twofold Grief and a twofold Pleasure.' — '"*As how*, my Dear?" said he' (Richardson, *Pamela*, II, 362, A.D. 1785).

2. *Classification by Meaning.* An adverbial element modifies a verb, adjective, or another adverb by expressing some relation of place, time, manner, attendant circumstance, degree, restriction, extent, cause, inference, result, condition, exception, concession, purpose, or means. Though usually different in meaning from a genitive, dative, accusative, or prepositional object it always performs the same function, i.e. it modifies a verb, adjective, or adverb. The adverbial modifier differs from an object in that its relation to the modified word is less close. For illustrative example see **27** 2 *a*.

A prominent feature of English is the wide use of the predicate appositive construction (**8**, 5th par.) with adverbial force. An adjective, adjective participle, or a noun is placed near the verb, before or after it, to modify it as to some relation of time, manner, attendant circumstance, cause, condition, concession, etc.: '*Tired and hungry* (= *As we were tired and hungry*) we went home.' '*Going down town* (= *As I was going down town*) I met a friend.' '*A younger son in a proud family* (= *As he was a younger son in a proud family*), Hume was really disinherited.' 'She ran into the house *crying*' (manner). 'He came home *tired*' (attendant circumstance). 'He was shunned *as a man of doubtful character*' (cause). As is shown by the many examples given below, the participle is a favorite in this construction.

a. ADVERBS OF PLACE, DIRECTION, ARRANGEMENT. They are: *here; hence* or *from hence* (archaic, poetic, or literary), now usually *from here, away, from now; thence*, or *from thence* (archaic, poetic, or literary), now usually *from there, away; there; yonder; hither* (poetic or literary), now usually *here, to this place; hether*, in older English sometimes used instead of *hither; thither* (poetic or literary), in plain prose now *there, to that place; thether*, in older English sometimes used instead of *thither; in, out, up, down, around; first(ly), secondly*, etc.; *where* (interrog.); *whither* (interrog.; in poetry and choice prose) or now more commonly *where; whence* (interrog.; in poetry and choice prose) or now more commonly *where — from;* etc.: 'He lives *here*.' '*Hence* (now usually *from here*) might they see the full array of either host' (Scott, *Marmion*,

VI, xxiii). '*From hence* (now *from here*) I went to the Card Manufactory' (George Washington, *Diary*, Oct. 28, 1789). 'We must think of what the family needs will be five years *hence*' (literally *from here, from this point of time*). 'I have relatives five miles *hence*' (older English, now *from here* or *away*). 'Barry followed the route taken by the others, along the platform to the corner of the station and *thence* across an area of sun-smitten gravel to the main thoroughfare of Wessex' (R. H. Barbour, *Barry Locke*, Ch. I). 'Two miles *thence* is a fine waterfall.' 'I live in Chicago; I was born *there*. My brother lives in Seattle. I intend to go *there* some day to visit him.' '*Yonder* among the hills are some beautiful little lakes.' 'Harry Esmond, come *hither*' (Thackeray, *Henry Esmond*, IV, Ch. XI), now *here*. 'The old home is a fine place to think of; *thither* in memory I often go.' 'Is your father *in?*' — 'No, sir, he has just gone *out*.' 'He went *in*.' '*Where* does he live?' In popular speech many say '*Where* is he *at?*' to express rest, and 'Where did he go *to?*' to express motion and direction, but in literary language we say here: '*Where* is he?' and '*Where* did he go?' preferring the more simple construction, although it is not so expressive. But even in literary language we must say: '*Where* did he come *from?*' for otherwise the thought would not be clear. Where we use *where* and a preposition (*at*, *to*, or *from*), *where* ceases to be an adverb and becomes a noun (**16** 2).

In colloquial speech *any place, some place, no place, every place*, are often used instead of the literary forms *anywhere, somewhere, nowhere, everywhere* (**7** V *a*).

In older English, *as* was often placed before an adverb or other expression of place as a mere formal introduction: 'Let hym go and marry her, for *as here* he hath no thynge to do' (Berners, *Huon*, CLVI, 602, A.D. 1534).

The adverbial element here often has the form of a prepositional phrase: 'He lives *in that house*.' The object of the preposition may be a substantive clause introduced by the conjunctive (**15** 1 *c bb*) adverb *where:* 'I walked over *to where they were standing*.' Here the preposition *to* forms with its object, the substantive clause, an adverbial prepositional clause. Compare **18** B 4 *b*.

Where often introduces an adverbial clause: 'One likes to live *where one has congenial neighbors*.' Compare **18** B 5.

b. Adverbs of Time. They are: *now, now and then, then, formerly, yesterday, today, tomorrow, immediately, hence, henceforth, henceforward, thence, thenceforth, thenceforward, when* (interrog.), etc.: 'It is not raining *now*.' 'I visited him a few days ago; he seemed as well as usual *then*.' 'Five years *hence*, a fortnight *thence*.' '*When* will he arrive?'

The accusative of a modified noun is often used as an adverb of time: *this morning, last week,* etc. See **71** 1 *a.* Also the genitive is used adverbially: *always,* etc. See **71** 1 *a.*

In older English, *as* was often placed before an adverb or other expression of time as a mere formal introduction: 'a provence untoucht in a manner, and new to us *as till then*' (Bolton, *Florus,* 163, A.D. 1618). This old usage survives in *as yet:* 'He hasn't come *as yet.*' It is much better preserved in British dialect: 'I expect him *as next week.*' A little earlier in the period it was still lingering in the literary language: 'I heard that Mr. Carlyle would be in town *as today*' (Lady Levison in Mrs. Henry Wood's *East Lynne,* III, 223, A.D. 1861).

The adverbial element here often has the form of an adverbial clause introduced by the conjunctive adverbs *when, whenever,* etc. For examples see **15** 1 *c bb,* **18** B 4 *b.*

The form of the adverbial element is often that of a prepositional phrase or a prepositional gerundial clause: 'We are going *after dinner*' or '*after finishing* (or *having finished*) *our dinner.*'

The form is very frequently that of a conjunctional clause: 'We are going *after we have had dinner.*' 'We must finish our work *before we go.*' 'He hasn't written me *since he went away.*' 'I shall come *as soon as I can.*' 'I turned homeward *directly* (British English for *as soon as*) *it began to rain.*' 'John worked *while Henry played.*' '*While* (or *whereas* or *at the same time that,* all with adversative force) *in applied physics we hold our own,* in applied chemistry we have lost much ground.' 'Stay here *until* (or *till*) *I come back.*' '*Until* (preferred to *till* when its clause stands first, as here) *he told me,* I had no idea of it' (*Concise Oxford Dictionary*). 'I met him *as he was coming out of his house.*' For a much larger list of the conjunctions used in this clause see *Syntax,* **27**.

Instead of a conjunctional clause we often employ a participial clause: '*Going down town* I met a friend.' '*Having finished my work* I went to bed.' Compare **47** 4.

Time is sometimes expressed by the absolute nominative construction described in **27** 1: '*The preparations for supper having been completed,* the hungry children were called in.'

c. ADVERBS OF MANNER. They are: *well, slowly, fast, neatly, how, somehow, someway,* etc.: 'He walked *slowly.*' '*How* did you do it?' '*How* does it strike you?' 'I forget how Mrs. Nightingale came into the conversation, but she did *somehow*' (or *someway*).

The adverbial element often has the form of a prepositional phrase or a prepositional gerundial clause: 'She does it *in this way.*' 'It strikes me *in an entirely different way.*' 'She spends her evenings *in practising on the piano.*'

The adverbial element often has the form of a conjunctional clause: 'Do it *how* (indef. conjunctive adv. = *in whatever manner*) *you can.*' 'He differs from his colleagues *in that he spends his spare time in reading.*' 'It struck me *that the whole thing was ridiculous,*' or in the form of a predicate appositive (**8**, 5th par.) adjective introduced by *as:* 'It struck me *as ridiculous.*' 'Do at Rome *as the Romans do.*' 'He looks *as if* (or *as though*) *he were about to speak.*' In colloquial speech *like* is widely used instead of *as:* 'They don't know you *like* (= literary *as*) *I do*' (Hergesheimer, *Balisand*, p. 36). In older English, *like* was used with the force of *as if* (or *as though*), and elliptically with the verb suppressed it is still used with this meaning: 'I ran *like* mad.' 'The dress looks *like* new.' 'Bring in your old faded pictures. They will be made *like* new' (advertisement). *As if* or *as though* is more common here: 'She hurriedly left the room *as if* (or *as though*) angry.' Compare *Syntax*, **28** 1, 2 *a*, *b*.

The form is sometimes that of an infinitival clause: 'Thus ever about her rooms she moved on this mournful occupation until the last thing had been disposed of *as either to be sent back or to be destroyed*' (Allen, *Mistletoe*). 'He raised his hand *as if* (or *as though*) *to command silence.*'

Manner is very frequently expressed by a participle or a participial clause: 'She came in *singing.*' 'He stood *leaning against the gate.*' 'He beat me *jumping.*' 'He was busy *fixing his fence.*' 'It was kind of you to bother yourself *asking her.*' 'Please do not understand me *as having lost hope.*' Compare *Syntax*, **28** 1 *a*.

Manner is sometimes expressed by the nominative absolute construction described in **27** 1: 'He put on his socks *wrong side out.*' 'They walked along *arm in arm.*' 'They sat *side by side.*'

d. Adverbial Elements of Attendant Circumstance. The form here is often that of a prepositional gerundial clause: 'He never passed people *without greeting them.*' 'He never passed people *without their greeting him.*' Compare *Syntax*, **28** 3 *a* (3rd par.).

Attendant circumstance is sometimes expressed by a conjunctional clause: 'The enemy devastated the country *as he retreated.*' 'He never passed anybody on the street *that he didn't greet him*' (or *but* or *but that* or in colloquial speech *but what he greeted him*). 'He was drowned *while he was bathing in the river.*' Compare *Syntax*, **28** 3.

This idea is expressed also by a participial clause: 'He was drowned *bathing in the river.*' Compare *Syntax*, **28** 3 *a*.

Attendant circumstance is often expressed by the absolute nominative construction described in **27** 1: 'He left for the continent, *all his family accompanying him.*' 'He entered upon the new enterprise cautiously, *his eyes wide-open.*' 'We intend to hold a concert, *the proceeds to be devoted to charity.*' 'They decided to start out at random the first day, *each man to use his own best judgment in prospecting.*' The preposition *with* is often placed before the absolute nominative construction, so that the expression in a formal sense becomes a prepositional clause but in spirit remains unchanged: 'He lay on his back, *his knees in the air,*' or *with his knees in the air.*

e. ADVERBIAL ELEMENTS OF DEGREE, RESTRICTION, EXTENT, AMOUNT, NUMBER. The form here is often that of a simple adverb: *very, nearly, almost, about, only, much, little, so, once, twice,* etc. Examples: 'She is *very* kind.' 'We are *nearly* there.' 'He *almost* died.' 'It is *about* empty.' 'I have been there *only* twice.' 'He shot *better* than his father.' 'He shot *best.*' 'He worries *much.*' 'He works *little.*' 'I didn't expect to find him *so* weak.' 'He struck me *twice.*' The accusative of a noun or pronoun is much used to express degree, extent: 'Is he *any* better this morning?' 'He lives *a mile* from here.' 'He lived there *three years.*' Compare **71** 1 *a* (3rd par.).

Certain intensifying adverbs impart feeling to the statement: 'I don't see why people should get up so *déucedly* éarly.' 'It's *dámned* hót today.' Compare **43** 2 B *a*.

The adverbial element of degree is often a prepositional phrase: 'He is taller *by two inches.*' 'He is *by far* more industrious.'

The different categories of degree are frequently expressed by different kinds of adverbial clauses:

A conjunctional clause of simple comparison: 'I am as tall *as she* [*is*].' Compare *Syntax,* **29** 1 A *a*.

A conjunctional clause of proportionate agreement: 'This stone gets the harder *the longer it is exposed to the weather.*' Compare *Syntax,* **29** 1 A *b*.

A conjunctional clause of restriction: '*So far as I could see* they were all satisfied with the arrangement.' Compare *Syntax,* **29** 1 A *c*. The full clause is sometimes replaced by a prepositional phrase: 'He may be dead *for all* I know.' Compare *Syntax,* **29** 1 A *c aa*. The restriction is sometimes expressed by a participial clause: 'The inquiry, *so far as showing that I have favored my own interests,* has failed.' Compare *Syntax,* **29** 1 A *c bb*.

A conjunctional clause of extent: 'I have stood it *as long as I can.*' 'I have walked *as far as I can.*' Compare *Syntax,* **29** 1 A *d*. The full clause can be replaced by an infinitive clause: 'I have gone *as far as to collect statistics for my investigation.*' Compare *Syntax,* **29** 1 A *d aa*. *As far as* in this example is a conjunction. As it is used also as a preposition, it can introduce a prepositional gerundial clause: 'I have gone *as far as collecting statistics for my investigation.*'

A conjunctional comparative clause: 'She is better *than* [*she was*] when I wrote you last.' 'I regard her more highly *than he* [*does*],' but 'I regard her more highly *than* [*I do*] *him.*' Compare *Syntax*, **29** 1 B.

f. Adverbs of Cause. They are: *why* (interrogative), *for what reason* (interrogative), etc.: '*Why* did you do it?'

The adverbial element here often has the form of a prepositional phrase or a prepositional gerundial clause: 'He was punished *for disobedience* or *for disobeying his mother.*'

The commonest form is that of a conjunctional clause: 'He was punished *because he disobeyed his mother.*' '*Now that he is sick* we shall have to do his work.' 'How convince him *when he will not listen?*' '*Once* (or *after*) *you have made a promise* you should keep it.' 'He cannot be tired *since he has walked only half a mile.*' 'The girls could not speak *for fear* or *for fear that* or *lest the tears should come and choke them.*' '*As he refuses* we can do nothing.' 'I saw that I had done something wrong *as they all laughed.*' 'The act was the bolder *that he stood utterly alone.*' 'We were sorry (*that*) *you couldn't come.*' 'I am glad (*that*) *he is going.*' 'I am astonished *that you believe such a thing.*' 'He rejoiced *that he should have received the esteem of his sovereign.*' 'My conscience troubles me *that I have been so remiss.*'

Cause is often expressed by an infinitival or participial clause: 'I was pained *to hear it.*' 'You ought to be ashamed *stealing from a poor widow.*' '*Having run for an hour*, we were almost exhausted.' Compare *Syntax*, **30** *b* (last par.).

Cause is sometimes expressed by the absolute nominative construction described in **27** 1: '*The bridge across the chasm being only a single tree trunk*, we hesitated to attempt the passage.' '*There being no objections*, the minutes were adopted as read.' The absolute nominative may be a clause: 'We bought some more, *what we had not proving sufficient.*' The preposition *with* is often placed before the absolute nominative construction, so that the expression in a formal sense becomes a prepositional clause but in spirit remains unchanged: '*With knowledge increasing by leaps and bounds* we have reached a time when we must be content with specialisms.' 'She is lonesome *with her husband so much away.*'

g. Adverbial Elements of Inference and Result. Simple adverbs: *therefore, consequently, hence, thence, so, thus, then,* etc. Examples: 'No man will take counsel, but every man will take money; *therefore* money is better than counsel' (Swift). 'His means are limited, *hence* he is compelled to economize.' 'There was no one there; *so* I went away.' 'I have had enough.' — '*Then* let us go.' Compare **18** A 5.

The adverbial element here is often a prepositional phrase: 'It has been raining all week; *on that account* (or *for that reason;* both = *consequently*) we have not been able to do our plowing.'

In all these cases the propositions are coördinated. The second proposition is introduced by an adverb or adverbial element with the force of a coördinating conjunctive adverb (**15** 1 *c aa*).

Result is often expressed by a subordinate adverbial clause. Pure result: 'A man ought to have a settled job, with an office in some fixed place, *so that* (in colloquial speech often simple *so*) *you always know where he is.*' 'I must have been blind *that I didn't see that post.*' 'He never played with the children *that he didn't stir up a quarrel*' (or *but, but that,* or colloquially *but what he stirred up a quarrel;* or in the form of a prepositional gerundial clause: *without stirring up a quarrel*). Compare *Syntax,* **28** 5 (6th and 7th parr.). Manner clause of modal result: 'He has always lived such a life *that he can't expect sympathy now.*' Compare *Syntax,* **28** 5 (1st and 2nd parr.). Degree clause of modal result: 'She worried *so that she couldn't go to sleep.*' Compare *Syntax,* **29** 2.

Frequently result is expressed by an infinitival or participial clause. Pure result: 'Put on your gloves *so as to be ready.*' Compare *Syntax,* **28** 5 *d* (3rd par.). Manner modal result: 'He has never lived só *as to inspire respect.*' 'This is not such weather *as to encourage outdoor sports.*' Compare *Syntax,* **28** 5 *d* (1st par.). Degree modal result: 'He was so kind *as to help me.*' 'He was too tactful *to mention it.*' 'He was old enough *to know better.*' Compare *Syntax,* **29** 2 *a*. The infinitive is the usual form where the result is represented, not as the effect of the cause indicated in the principal proposition, but as coming from some independent cause: 'They parted *never to see each other again.*' 'He awoke *to find all this a dream.*' Participial clause of result: 'He mistook me for a friend, *causing me some embarrassment.*' Compare *Syntax,* **28** 5 *d* (3rd par. from end).

After an accusative object, result is often expressed by a prepositional phrase, which, however, is not an adverbial element but an objective predicate (**8,** 4th par.): 'She rocked the baby *to sleep*' (= 'She rocked the baby *so that it went to sleep*'). 'He smoked himself *into calmness.*'

h. Adverbial Elements of Condition or Exception. The form for condition is sometimes that of a simple adverb, a prepositional phrase, or a prepositional gerundial clause: 'Suppose you had never a farthing but of your own getting; where would you be *then?*' (= *in that case*). '*Without him* I should be helpless.' 'He can't walk *without my helping him.*'

The most common form is that of a conjunctional clause: '*If it were not for him* I should be helpless.' 'I would have done it before *if I had had time.*' 'I would come, *only that* (or *were it not that*) *I am engaged.*' 'I shall go *unless it rains.*' 'You may go *on condition that you come home early.*' 'We should have arrived earlier *but that we met with an accident.*' 'I will come *provided* (or *provided that*) *I have time.*' '*In case it rains* I can't go.' 'You may go where you like *so that* (or in colloquial speech *just so* or simple *so*) *you are back by dinner time.*' Compare *Syntax*, **31.**

The conjunctional clause is sometimes replaced by an independent proposition in the form of a question or a command, which is used with the force of a subordinate clause introduced by *if*: '*Is any among you afflicted?* let him pray' (*James*, V, 15). '*Should you find them* (interrogation sign now usually suppressed, as in this example), kindly let me know.' '*Do it at once*, you will never regret it.'

Condition is sometimes expressed by a participial or infinitival clause: '*Left to herself* (= *if she had been left to herself*) she would have been drawn into an answer.' 'This same thing, *happening in wartime* (= *if it should happen in wartime*), would amount to disaster.' 'One would think, *to hear them talk* (= *if one should hear them talk*), that England is full of traitors.' Compare *Syntax*, **31** 2.

Condition is sometimes expressed by the absolute nominative construction described in **27** 1: 'Our ship sails tomorrow, *weather permitting.*' '*Other things being equal* I prefer an August vacation.' Compare *Syntax*, **17** 3 A *c*.

Exception is often expressed by a conjunctional clause: 'I don't believe that God wants anything *but that we should be happy.*' 'Nothing would content him *but I must come.*' 'My boy is as naughty as yours *except that he always begs my pardon.*' The elliptical clause is still more common: 'Who can have done it *but I?*' (Hardy, *The Return of the Native*, V, Ch. I), in colloquial speech often *but me*. 'All *save he and Murray* have pleaded guilty' (*Chicago Tribune*, Nov. 12, 1924). 'Everyone *except me* (or less commonly *I*) seems to dislike him.' Here *I* shows that *except* under the influence of *but* is felt as a subordinating conjunction. The more common *me* here indicates that *except* is more frequently regarded as a preposition or as the imperative of the transitive verb *except*. The usual *me* after *but* in colloquial speech shows that *but* is here felt as a preposition. Compare *Syntax*, **31,** p. 319.

i. Adverbial Elements of Concession. The form is sometimes that of a simple adverb: 'That is how I look at it, *anyway*' (or *anyhow;* both = 'however the case may be'). 'There is something wrong somewhere. *Anyway,* nothing will ever induce me to believe that' (Mackenzie, *Sylvia and Michael,* p. 29).

The form is more commonly that of a prepositional phrase or a conjunctional clause: 'We are going *in spite of the rain.*' '*For all his learning* he is a mean man.' '*For all he laughs and pooh-poohs,* he really suffers.' 'We are going *even if it rains.*' '*Although he seems rough* he is really tender-hearted.' '*Notwithstanding (that) he is being lionized,* he still keeps a level head.' 'It is true *whether you believe it or [whether you do] not [believe it].*' '*Whether he succeed(s) or fail(s),* we shall have to do our part.' An indefinite relative pronoun, adjective, or adverb + *ever* often serves as the conjunction in this clause: 'I am going *whatever he says.*' Compare **7** IV *b* (2nd par.), **10** 5 *b*, and **18** B 5.

The conjunctional clause is often replaced by an expression of will, which, though independent in form, is logically dependent: '*Laugh as much as you like,* I shall stick to my plan.' '*Come what may,* I am bound to see him.' 'Home is home, *be it ever so homely.*' '*Detest him as we may,* we must acknowledge his greatness.' '*Hurry as you will,* you are sure to be late.'

Concession is sometimes expressed by a participial or infinitival clause: 'From dawn to dark in this car, *driving or riding* (= *whether you drive or ride*), you'll never feel that you have put a whole day's miles behind you' (advertisement). See *Syntax,* **32** 2 (4th par.). 'You couldn't do that *to save* your life' (= *even if you would save your life by it*). Compare *Syntax,* **32** 2 (last par.).

Concession is sometimes expressed by the absolute nominative construction described in **27** 1, usually with the predicate of the clause before its subject: '*Granted the very best intentions,* his conduct was productive of great mischief.' The absolute nominative may be a clause: '*Granted that he did so,* what are you going to do?'

j. Adverbial Elements of Purpose. The form is often that of a prepositional phrase, a prepositional gerundial clause, or a conjunctional clause: 'I bought the book *for reference.*' 'John works *for grades.*' 'I came *with the intention of helping you.*' 'They are climbing higher *that* (or *in order that* or *so that* or in colloquial speech simple *so*) *they may get a better view.*' 'He is keeping quiet *that he may not disturb his father*' (or *for fear* or *for fear that* or *lest he should* or *might disturb his father*). Compare *Syntax,* **33.**

Quite frequently the form is that of an infinitival or participial clause: 'I am waiting *to go with John.*' 'I am waiting *for them to go* before I speak of the matter.' 'I am going early *so as* (or *in order) to get a good seat.'* 'Axmen were put to work *getting out timber for bridges.'* Compare *Syntax,* **33** 2.

k. ADVERBIAL ELEMENTS OF INSTRUMENT, MEANS, AGENCY, ASSOCIATION. The form is usually that of a prepositional phrase or clause. Instrument: 'He cut it *with a knife.'* Means: '*By industry and thrift* he has amassed a fortune.' 'He reached the top *by means of a ladder.'* 'All strove to escape *by what means they might.'* '*By using our time and our strength properly* we may become happy and useful.' Agency: 'The trees were trimmed *by a gardener.'* Association: 'He votes *with the Democrats.'* 'Blue does not go *with green.'* 'I walked to town *with him.'* There was once in our family of languages an especial case form of nouns and pronouns — the instrumental case — to express all these relations except that of agency. Compare **27** 5.

CHAPTER VI

THE PREPOSITION

16. Definition, Function, Form. A preposition is a word that indicates a relation between the noun or pronoun it governs and another word, which may be a verb, an adjective, or another noun or pronoun: 'I live *in* this house.' Here *in* shows a relation between the noun *house* and the verb *live*. The preposition *in*, as prepositions in general, has a meaning. It expresses here the idea of place. There are in our language a large number of prepositions, which enable us to express ourselves quite accurately. A rather complete list of these prepositions is given in *Syntax*, **62** 1. Some of the most important ones are treated in the following articles.

In 'I live with *him*' the preposition *with* shows a relation between the pronoun *him* and the verb *live*. The form *him* shows that the preposition today requires its object to stand in the objective case. In Old English different prepositions governed different cases. Now the object of the preposition is always in the objective case, which is an indistinctive form employed for either the dative or the accusative relation. After prepositions we now usually think of the objective case form as an accusative. But this matter of case is of little importance as only a few pronouns have a distinctive form for the object relation. A preposition standing before a noun or pronoun marks the noun or pronoun as an object. Here, as so often elsewhere, position is the distinctive feature.

The preposition does not function singly, but forms a grammatical unit with its object, i.e. the word or words following it: 'I live *in this house*.' This unit is called the prepositional unit. Where the object of the preposition is a single word, as in this example, the prepositional unit is a prepositional phrase. Where the object of the preposition is a clause, as in 'He spoke *of what he had done*,' the prepositional unit is a prepositional clause. An adverb is closely related to a preposition, but differs from it in that it functions singly, i.e. it does not take an object. 'He is *in*' (adverb), but 'He is *in the house*' (prepositional phrase).

The prepositional unit, phrase or clause, has, like a simple word, a function to perform in the sentence. In 'I live *in this house*' the prepositional phrase *in this house* modifies the verb *live*, hence it performs the function of an adverb.

In the following articles the functions and the constituent elements of the prepositional unit, i.e. the functions and the forms of the prepositional unit, will be discussed in detail.

1. *Functions of Prepositional Phrase or Clause.* The prepositional unit performs the functions of (1) an adverb; (2) a noun in the objective relation, object of a verb or an adjective or participle; (3) an adjective in the predicative or the attributive relation.

a. Employed as Adverb. This is a common function: 'He stood *by the window.*' 'He stood *behind me.*' In the first example the preposition *by* connects the intransitive (**12** 2) verb *stood* with the noun *window.* In the second example the preposition *behind* connects the intransitive verb *stood* with the pronoun *me.* In each of the examples the prepositional phrase forms an adverbial element modifying the intransitive verb. The adverbial prepositional phrase is common also in connection with a transitive (**12** 1) verb and its object: 'He is writing a letter *by the window.*' 'We sent a boy *after water.*'

The adverbial prepositional phrase or clause indicates some relation of place, time, manner, result, degree, extent, cause, condition, concession, purpose, means, instrument, agency, association: 'I live *in Chicago*' (place). 'I can see him *from where I stand*' (place). 'I wrote a letter *before breakfast*' (time). 'I read *in bed* (place) *before going to sleep*' (time); but *before* is an adverb in 'I hadn't seen him *before*' and a subordinating conjunction in 'I had not seen him *before* I met him today.' 'I wrote the letter *with care*' (manner). 'He never plays *with the children* (association) *without stirring up a quarrel*' (result). 'I am taller than you *by three inches*' (degree). 'I have gone *as far as collecting statistics for my investigation*' (extent). 'We feel kindly toward him *for his waiting so patiently under such trying circumstances*' (cause). 'He couldn't have done it *without my having helped him*' (condition). 'His wife clings to him *with all his faults*' (concession). '*In spite of his untiring devotion to the community* (concession) he has not received the recognition he deserves.' 'I bought the book *for reference*' (purpose). '*By industry and thrift* he has amassed a fortune' (means). 'He cut it *with a knife*' (instrument). 'The trees were trimmed *by a gardener*' (agency). 'Blue does not go *with green'* (association). 'I walked to town *with him'* (association). The adverbial use of the prepositional phrase or clause is illustrated more in detail in **15** 2 *a–k*.

b. EMPLOYED AS OBJECT. In 'She shot *at him* twice' the prepositional phrase made up of the preposition *at* and its object *him* stands in a little closer relation to the intransitive verb than an adverbial element, forming the necessary complement of the verb, which we call a prepositional object. As the preposition here is often in a closer relation to the intransitive verb than to its own object, it is often felt as a part of the verb, forming with it a compound, a transitive compound verb, as in **17** (last par.). This can be seen in passive form, where the preposition remains with the verb: 'He *has been shot at* twice.' 'He can *be depended upon.*' 'He *is* easily *imposed upon.*' 'He is not a man *to be trifled with.*' The fact that the passive can be used here shows that the intransitive has become a transitive verb. This passive construction is a marked characteristic of English. On the other hand, the preposition is often in closer relation to the noun than to the verb, so that the verb remains intransitive and cannot be put into the passive: 'She went *about her duties* as usual.' 'This obligation devolves *upon you.*' 'This case admits *of no doubt.*' 'This borders *on the commonplace.*' 'This book teems *with blunders.*' 'The bottle smelled *of brandy.*' 'I don't fall *for that kind of conduct'* (American slang = 'I don't believe in, favor,' etc.). This prepositional object is common after an accusative object: 'He wrote a book *on his experiences* in the war.' The noun in this prepositional object is often an infinitive: 'His father forced him *to make* his own living.' 'I persuaded him *to do* it.' 'I can't bring myself *to speak* to him about it.' 'I will leave you *to imagine* my embarrassment.' The *to* of the infinitive in these examples is not a mere sign of the infinitive but a real preposition governing the following infinitive, which is here still a verbal noun although it now takes an accusative object. Compare **47** 5, also *Syntax*, **24** IV *a* and **49** 4 C (1) *d*. The object of the preposition is often a substantive (noun) clause introduced by an indefinite relative pronoun, adjective, or adverb: 'He often spoke *of what he had done and how he had done it.*' 'He told me all *about what had been done, who the leading spirits of the enterprise were, and what valuable experiences they all had had.*' Compare *Syntax*, **24** IV (1st and 5th parr.).

The prepositional phrase is much used also as the object, i.e. as the necessary complement, of an adjective or a participle: 'She is fond *of music, of skating, of reading.*' 'She is dependent *upon her children.*' 'She is devoted *to her children.*' 'He is engaged *in writing* about his experiences in Australia.' After the preposition *to* the noun is often an infinitive: 'I am eager *to go.*' Compare *Syntax,* **24** IV *a* and **49** 4 C (1) *d.* The object of the preposition is often an indefinite relative clause: 'She is proud *of what she has done.*' 'She is fully informed *as to who did it.*' Compare *Syntax,* **24** IV (1st and 5th parr.). The expression is often elliptical: 'I am sure [of it] *that he did it.*' Compare **18** B 4 *a.*

c. Employed as Adjective. The prepositional phrase is employed as an adjective element in the predicative and the attributive relation.

The prepositional phrase is much used in the predicate relation. After a copula (**12** 3): 'The country is *at peace*' (= *peaceful*). Compare **8** *a* and *Syntax,* **7** F (2nd par.). There is no copula when the prepositional phrase is predicated of an object: 'I found *him at home.*' 'I found *him at peace* with himself.' For an explanation of this old construction see **12** 3. Compare **8** (4th par.).

In 'The girl *with dark hair* is my sister' the preposition *with* connects the noun *hair* with the noun *girl.* The prepositional phrase *with dark hair* is an attributive adjective element since it modifies the noun *girl.* It is here equal in force to the descriptive (**8**) adjective *dark-haired:* 'The *dark-haired* girl is my sister.' The prepositional phrase here often has the force of a limiting (**8**) adjective, pointing out one or more individuals: 'the tree *behind the house.*' After verbal nouns (i.e. nouns made from verbs) the prepositional phrase, though in a formal sense an adjective element, often has the force of an object or an adverb: 'a mother's love *for her children*' (with the force of an object); 'a walk *in the evening*' (with the force of an adverb of time).

2. *Constituent Elements of the Prepositional Unit.* The object of the preposition is always a noun or a pronoun, which is uniformly in the accusative: 'He went with *my brother* and *me.*' The preposition usually stands before its object, but it may stand at the end of the sentence or clause: '*Whom* (or in colloquial speech *who* — object of the preposition *with*) do you play *with?*' Though the preposition here is separated from its object, the unity of preposition and object is distinctly felt. The thought holds the parts together. For other examples of this construction see **38** *a* (last par.).

The object of the preposition is often an adverb, a phrase, or a clause which is used as a noun or a pronoun. As a noun: 'for *ever,*' 'until *now,*' 'after *today,*' 'between *now* and *then.*' '*Where* did he come from?' 'Many place-names do not go back to *before the Norman Conquest*' (W. J. Sedgefield, *Introduction to the Survey of the English Place-Names,* Ch. I). 'I have little insight into *what he is doing.*' 'He wrote me about *what he is planning.*' As a demonstrative pronoun: 'I promised him yesterday that I would go with him tomorrow, but since *then* I've had to change my plans.' Relative pronoun: 'I saw him a month ago, since *when* (**7** IV *a cc*) I haven't seen anything of him.'

In the preceding examples the preposition either stands before a noun or pronoun forming with it a phrase, or stands at the end of the sentence or clause. These are the most common uses of the preposition; but with a number of words the preposition is the first component of a compound verb, and its object stands after the verb: 'The enemy *over*ran the whole country.' 'A great principle *under*lies this plan.' 'Water *per*meates the ground.' Compare **13** *a*.

17. Inflectional Prepositions. Prepositions have played a conspicuous rôle in the development of our language. Their numbers are ever increasing. In *Syntax*, **62** 1, a list of those now in use is given. There are now so many of them that we have a wide range of choice in shading our thought. Some do not differ from others in meaning, as *with regard to*, or *with respect to;* they simply serve to vary our expression.

Some prepositions, however, are in certain grammatical relations perfectly rigid, and cannot be replaced by others with the same or a similar meaning. They have often lost a good deal of their original concrete meaning and are no longer felt as prepositions, for they have developed into inflectional particles which indicate definite grammatical relations, often taking the place of older inflectional endings. Thus we now can say 'I gave the book *to my friend*' instead of 'I gave *my friend* the book.' The words *my friend* are in the dative and once had a distinctive ending to indicate the dative relation. Now, as adjectives and nouns have lost their old distinctive dative ending, we often employ the preposition *to* to indicate the dative relation. Similarly, we often use the preposition *of* as an inflectional sign to indicate the genitive relation: 'the father *of the boy*' instead of '*the boy's* father.' Compare *Syntax*, **14** (last par.).

The inflectional preposition is not only placed before words, but often also after them in case of verbs: 'You can depend *upon* him.' The preposition, as *upon* in this example, which once belonged to the word following it, is now often felt as belonging to a preceding intransitive verb, serving as an inflectional particle with the office of converting the intransitive into a transitive. That the preposition and the verb have fused into one word, a real compound, can be seen in passive form, where the preposition remains with the verb: 'He can be *depended upon*.' Compare **16** 1 *b*.

CHAPTER VII

THE CONJUNCTION

18. Definition and Classification. A conjunction is a word that joins together sentences or parts of a sentence: 'Sweep the floor *and* dust the furniture.' 'He waited *until* I came.'

There are two general classes — coördinating and subordinating. A coördinating conjunction, as *and* in the first example, binds together two independent propositions. A subordinating conjunction, as *until* in the second example, joins a subordinate clause to the principal proposition, modifying it in some way. The first example is called a compound sentence, the second example a complex sentence.

The members of a compound sentence, however, are not always complete, each with subject and finite verb, for a natural feeling for the economy of time and effort prompts us, wherever it is possible, to contract by employing a common verb for all members, so that the conjunctions connect only parts of like rank: not 'John is writing *and* Mary is writing,' but 'John *and* Mary are writing,' or 'John *and* Mary are both writing,' or 'Both John *and* Mary are writing.' 'I bought paper, pen, *and* ink.' 'John writes fast *but* neatly.' Care must be taken in contracting when one subject is used with two different verbs each of which stands in a different compound tense: 'All the debts *have been* or *will be* paid,' or 'All the debts *have been* paid or *will be*,' but not 'All the debts *have* or *will be* paid.' Sentences containing these conjunctions, however, are often not an abridgment of two or more sentences, but a simple sentence with elements of equal rank, connected by a conjunction: 'The King *and* Queen are an amiable pair.' 'She mixed wine *and* oil together.'

Coördinating conjunctions also link together subordinate clauses of like rank: 'The judge said that the case was a difficult one *and* that he would reconsider his decision.'

Conjunctions, though often useful in binding sentences and joining clauses to the principal proposition, are not absolutely necessary. In the earliest stage of language development there were no conjunctions at all. This original state of things is still common: 'I came, I saw, I conquered.' Here the close connection of the thoughts holds the different independent propositions together. But such propositions are not always independent. One statement may be subordinate to another in thought, though there is no formal subordination. We place one statement alongside of another, leaving it to the situation to make the relation between them clear: 'Hurry up; it is getting late.' In more formal language we say, 'Hurry up *because* it is getting late.' The construction without a conjunction we call parataxis, i.e. placing alongside of. The construction with a subordinating conjunction, as in the last example with the subordinating conjunction *because,* we call hypotaxis, i.e. subordination of one statement to another. As the intellectual life of the English people unfolded, it developed newer and finer hypotactical forms for fuller expression of its thought and feeling, but it wisely retained a good deal of its older paratactical forms for daily practical use. Parataxis, however, by reason of its elegant simplicity is often employed also in various fields of the literary language. For fuller information about parataxis and hypotaxis see *Syntax*, **19** 3.

When there are three or more coördinated parts of a sentence, usually only the last part is linked by a conjunction: 'He enjoys tennis, golf, *and* baseball.' 'I brought in a basketful of red, pink, white, *and* yellow roses.' The commas between the different words of the series indicate a slight pause and consequently the independence of the parts. The independence is still more marked when the conjunction at the end of the series is lacking: 'She is a wise, sympathetic, hard-working teacher.' On the other hand, this independence disappears in an unlinked series of adherent (**8**, 3rd par.) adjectives that are not separated by pauses. The last adjective is subordinated to the others in that it stands in a closer relation to the governing noun: 'He lives in *the first white* house from here.' 'The saddest of lots is that of *an indigent old* man.'

Nothing in English grammar has changed so much within the Modern English period as our conjunctions. There was in the sixteenth and seventeenth centuries a strong tendency to effect a greater simplicity and accuracy of expression by shortening and differentiating some forms and eliminating others as useless. These developments are described at length in *Syntax*.

In *Syntax* a full list of our English conjunctions is given in connection with a detailed account of their use. The subject is treated here only in outline.

A. COÖRDINATING CONJUNCTIONS

The coördinating conjunctions and conjunctive (**15** 1 *c aa*) adverbs fall into six classes.

1. **Copulative Conjunctions and Conjunctive Adverbs.** They are: *and; both — and; as well as; neither — nor; nor — nor* (in poetry and older English); not — *nor . . . either;* no — *or* (or often *nor* when it is desired to call especial attention to what follows and thus emphasize); *not only — but also* (or *but . . . too*); *too; moreover; besides; again; likewise; further, furthermore; there; then; in the first place; first; secondly; finally; now — now; sometimes — sometimes; partly — partly;* etc.

Examples:

Money is lifeless *and* possessions are vain.

My brother *and* my sister are both married.

He can *both* sing *and* dance.

'He must irrevocably lose her *as well as* the inheritance,' or 'He must irrevocably lose her *and* the inheritance *as well.*'

Neither he *nor* his brother is to blame.

'*Neither* she *nor* I am to blame,' but '*Neither* you *nor* he is to blame.'

It hasn't done me much good, *nor* anyone else *either*.

I can get no rest by day *or* night.

I want no promises *nor notes* (more emphatic than *or notes*); I want money.

'There is *not only* concision in these lines, *but also* elegance' (or '*but* elegance *too*').

We both are without money; *there* comes in the difficulty.

We played an hour; *then* we went home.

Conjunctive adverbs, as *there* and *then* in the last two examples, not only join two independent statements but play the part of an adverb in the proposition in which they stand. Similarly, a demonstrative pronoun or a possessive adjective performs in its own proposition its own part as demonstrative pronoun or possessive adjective and at the same time binds two principal propositions together: 'In this crisis I have often thought of the old home, of Father, of Mother. *That* was a good place to start out in life from. *Their* lives have been an inspiration to me.'

Notice in the case of *neither — nor* where there are subjects of different persons that the verb agrees with the nearer subject, as in the sixth example. On the other hand, if *neither* be construed as a pronoun with two appositives following it the verb is of course in the third person singular: '*Neither*, she nor I, is to blame.'

a. 'And' Employed to Express Number, Repetition, Duration. And is often placed between identical forms of a noun or a verb, not as a conjunction to connect thoughts, but merely as a means to express number, repetition, or duration: 'The entrance to the floor given to executive offices was like the lobby of a pretentious hotel — waiting room in brocade and tapestry; then something like an acre of little tables with typists *and* typists *and* typists, very busy, and clerks *and* clerks *and* clerks with rattling papers' (Lewis, *Dodsworth*). 'We insisted *and* insisted *and* insisted, not once but half a dozen times, at the beginning of the war, on England's adoption of the Declaration of London' (W. H. Page, *Letter*, Aug. 4, 1918). 'I've tried *and* tried, but I've not succeeded.' 'My heart ached *and* ached *and* ached.'

2. **Disjunctive Conjunctions.** They are: *or; either — or; or — or* (in poetry or older English); the disjunctive adverbs *else, otherwise, or, or else:*

Examples:

Is he guilty *or* innocent?
'*Either* John *or* William is to blame,' but '*Either* John *or* I am to blame.'
Seize the chance, *else* (or *otherwise, or*, or *or else*) you will regret it.

Notice in the case of *either — or* where there are subjects of different persons that the verb agrees with the nearer subject, as in the second example, or it may be repeated with its own subject: '*Either* John is to blame *or* I *am*.' On the other hand, if *either* be construed as a pronoun with two appositives after it the verb is of course in the third person singular: '*Either*, John or I, *is* to blame.' Compare **53** *a*.

3. **Adversative Conjunctions and Conjunctive Adverbs.** They are: *but, but then, only* (= *but, but then, it must however be added that*); *still, yet, and yet, however; on the other hand, again, on the contrary, conversely; rather; notwithstanding; all the same; though;*

after all, for all that; at the same time; and withal, yet withal, or *but withal* (= *at the same time, for all that*); *notwithstanding; in the meantime, meanwhile;* etc.

Examples:

He is small *but* strong.

The commander-in-chief has not been quite successful, *but then* he has essayed a difficult task.

He makes good resolutions, *only* he never keeps them.

'I want to go very much; *still* I do not care to go through the rain,' but *still* is an adverb in 'It is raining *still.*'

'I miss him, *yet* I am glad he went,' but *yet* is an adverb in 'It hasn't quit raining *yet.*'

'He has sadly disappointed me. *However*, as a mother I shall not give up hope' or 'As a mother, *however*, I shall not give up hope' or 'As a mother I shall not give up hope, *however.*'

'The sheep which we saw behind the house were small and lean; in the next field *though* (coördinating conjunction), there were some fine cows,' but *though* is a subordinating conjunction in '*Though* it never put a cent of money into my pocket, I believe it did me good.'

The book is stimulating and sound to the core — *yet* difficult reading *withal.*

'Charles is usually cheerful; sometimes, *again*, he is very despondent,' but *again* is a copulative conjunction in '*Again* (often, as here, at the beginning of a paragraph, continuing the discussion), man is greater by leaning on the greatest' (Emerson, *Trust*). *Again* is an adverb of time in 'It is raining *again.*'

'I denied myself everything. *Notwithstanding*, the old skinflint complained without ceasing,' but *notwithstanding* is a preposition in 'I am going *notwithstanding* the rain.'

4. **Causal Conjunction 'For.'** Example: 'This is no party question, *for* it does not touch us as Republicans or Democrats but as citizens.' For the difference between coördinating *for* and subordinating *as* or *since* see *Syntax*, **30** *a* (next to last par.).

5. **Illative Conjunctive Adverbs.** They are: *therefore* (**7** I *b*), *on that account, consequently, accordingly, for that reason, so, then, hence, thence* (= *from that source*, hence also *for that reason*), etc.

Examples:

No man will take counsel, but everybody will take money; *therefore* money is better than counsel (Swift).

The thing had to be done. *Accordingly* we did it.

There was no one there, *so* I went away.

'I am here, you see, young and sound and hearty; *then* don't let us despair' (or 'don't let us despair, *then*'), but *then* is a copulative conjunction in 'First think, *then* act.'

His means are limited, *hence* he is compelled to economize. (Fernald, *Connectives in English Speech*, p. 299).

'Guilt has been variously understood, *thence* (resulting therefrom) have arisen endless disputes about sin, responsibility,' etc. (*ib.*).

6. **Explanatory Conjunctions.** They are: *namely, to wit, viz.* (short for Latin *videlicet*), *that is* (often written *i.e.* for Latin *id est*), *that is to say, or, such as, like, for example* (often written *e.g.* which is for Latin *exempli gratia*), *for instance, say, let us say,* etc.

Examples:

There were only two girls there, *namely,* Mary and Ann.

My wife suggested my going alone, *i.e.* with you and without her.

I passed some time in Poet's Corner, which occupies an end of one of the transepts, *or* cross aisles, of the Abbey.

Take a few of them, *say* a dozen or so.

Any country, *let us say* Sweden, might do the same.

B. SUBORDINATING CONJUNCTIONS

Some of these forms are pure conjunctions; others are real conjunctions, but at the same time play in the clause the part of an adverb, pronoun, or adjective. Such adverbs, pronouns, and adjectives are called conjunctive adverbs, pronouns, and adjectives. Conjunctive adverbs fall into two classes — indefinite conjunctive adverbs and interrogative conjunctive adverbs, as described in **15** 1 *c bb*. Conjunctive pronouns and adjectives fall into three classes — indefinite relative pronouns (**7** IV *b*) and adjectives (**10** 5 *b*), interrogative conjunctive pronouns (**7** VI *b*) and adjectives (**10** 7), and definite relative pronouns (**7** IV *a*) and adjectives (**10** 5 *a*).

The first four of the following groups of conjunctions introduce substantive (noun) clauses. The fifth group introduces adverbial clauses. The sixth group introduces adjective clauses.

1. **Conjunctions Introducing Subject and Predicate Clause.** The most common conjunctions for the subject clause are: *that* (or in popular speech *as*); frequently *because* instead of *that; lest* after nouns expressing fear, sometimes still as in older English used instead of *that;* an illogical *but, but that,* or in colloquial speech *but what,* instead of the more common *that* after *not impossible, not improbable, cannot be doubted; whether* or *if* (especially common in colloquial speech); the indefinite or interrogative conjunctive adverbs *where, when, why, how;* the indefinite or interrogative conjunctive pronouns *who, whoever, what, whatever;* the indefinite or interrogative conjunctive adjectives *which, whichever, what, whatever;* the conjunctions *since, before.*

Examples:

'It is to be hoped *that* nothing has happened,' or 'It is to be hoped [*that*] nothing has happened.'

It is only natural *as* (popular form for *that*) I shuden't git things clear at fust as you've kept me in the dark this two months (Sheila Kaye-Smith, *Green Apple Harvest*, p. 49).

Because (better *that*) they enjoy it is no proof that it is good for them.

My only terror was *lest* my father should follow me (George Eliot, *Daniel Deronda*, I, III, Ch. XX).

It could not be doubted *that* (or now less commonly *but, but that,* or *but what*) his life would be aimed at.

It is doubtful *whether* (or *if*) he is coming.

It is not known *whether* he did it *or* not.

It is not known *how* (indef. conj. adv.) he came by it.

It has often been asked *how* (interrog. conj. adv.) he came by it (indirect question).

What (indef. rel. pron.) you say is quite true.

It is not known *who* (indef. rel. pron.) he is.

The question I want to ask is *who* (interrog. conj. pron.) he is (indirect question).

It is not yet known *which,* or more indefinitely *what* (indef. rel. adj.), road he took.

It is marvelous *what* (indef. rel. adj.) mistakes they continue to make.

It is many months *since* I have seen him.

It will be weeks *before* his disappearance will attract attention.

It was a week ago *that* we first met.

Many other examples are given in *Syntax,* **21** *a, b, c.*

On account of the handiness of the infinitive and the gerund we often prefer an infinitival or gerundial subject clause to a conjunctional clause: 'It is stupid of you *to say it*' (= *that you say it*). '*For* (**47** 5 *a*, last par.) *us to delay* (= *That we should delay*) would be fatal to our enterprise.' 'It is no use *for* (**47** 5 *a*, last par.) *you to say anything,*' or *your saying anything.* '*His saying he is wrong* alters the case.'

The nominative absolute (**27** 1 *a*, 3rd par.) construction is often used as a subject clause. The predicate of the clause is a present participle, the subject of the clause is a nominative absolute, usually a noun, much less commonly a pronoun: 'It is vilely unjust, *men closing two-thirds of the respectable careers to women*' (Sir Harry Johnston, *Mrs. Warren's Daughter*, Ch. III). '*He saying he is wrong* alters the case.' The accusative is sometimes used here: 'It's no use *him wiring back to me*' (J. B. Priestley, *The Good Companions*, p. 594). When the subject is a personal pronoun the usual construction is a gerundial clause. The gerund is the predicate of the clause, its subject is a possessive adjective, which historically is the old genitive of a personal pronoun: 'It's no use *his wiring back to me.*'

The conjunctions for the predicate clause are: *as, before, after, because;* the indefinite relative pronouns *who* (= *man, boy, woman,* etc.) and *what;* the indefinite conjunctive adverbs *where, when, why,* etc. Compare *Syntax,* **22.**

Examples:

Things are not always *as* they seem to be.
It was *before* her mother died that I first met her.
He is not *who* (= *the man*) he seemed to be.
We are not *what* we ought to be.
That is *where* you are mistaken.
Now is *when* I need him most.

2. **Conjunctions Introducing Attributive Substantive (Noun) Clause.** The conjunctions are: *that* (or in popular speech *as*); an illogical *but, but that,* or in colloquial speech *but what* after *no question, no doubt* instead of the more common *that; whether;* the indefinite or interrogative conjunctive adverbs *where, when, why, how;* the indefinite or interrogative conjunctive pronouns *who, whoever, what, whatever;* the indefinite or interrogative conjunctive adjectives *which, whichever, what, whatever.*

After these conjunctions and conjunctive adverbs, pronouns, and adjectives the attributive substantive (noun) clause often stands as an appositive to the noun preceding it. When a conjunctive adverb, pronoun, or adjective is used the attributive element modifying the preceding noun may have also the form of an *of*-genitive or a prepositional clause. As all these clauses are attributive, i.e. modify a noun, they have the force of an adjective.

Examples:

The thought *that* we shall live on after death in another better world consoles many (appositional clause).

I am troubled by another fear, *that* Silvio will send out a search-party (appositional clause).

'I'd a feeling *as* (popular form for *that*) maybe you cud give me,' etc. (Sheila Kaye-Smith, *Green Apple Harvest,* p. 35) (appositional clause).

There is no doubt *that* (or sometimes *but, but that,* or *but what*) he will come (appositional clause).

I have often asked myself the question *whether* I have the right to do it (appositional clause; indirect question).

Now arises the question *when* (interrog. conj. adv.) we should go (appositional clause).

I have no information as to *when* (indef. conj. adv.) he will come (prepositional clause).

I have just read his description of *how* (indef. conj. adv.) he did it (*of*-genitive clause).

We have as yet no information as to *why* (indef. conj. adv.) he did it (prepositional clause).

We have as yet no information as to *who* (indef. rel. pron.) did it (prepositional clause).

'Now arises the question *who* (interrog. conj. pron.) the proper person is to do it' (appositional clause; indirect question), or in the form of a direct question: 'Now the question arises, Who is the proper person to do it?' (appositional clause).

As yet we have no instructions as to *which*, or more indefinitely *what* (indef. rel. adj.), course we are to pursue (prepositional clause).

I haven't the least interest in *what* (indef. rel. pron.) he is doing, in *what* (indef. rel. adj.) views he holds (prepositional clause).

Examples of a little different kind of appositional clause are given in **8** *b* (last par.). For other details see *Syntax*, **23** I.

We sometimes prefer an infinitival or gerundial clause to a conjunctional clause: 'The time *to do something* (= *that we should do something*) has come.' 'I sent him the money in time *for* (**47** 5 *a*, last par.) *it to reach him* (= *that it should reach him*) *by Monday.*' 'That is just our way, *always arriving too late*' or *always to arrive too late*. 'The hope *of John's visiting us soon* (= *that John will visit us soon*) cheers us.' Compare *Syntax*, **23** I *a*.

3. **Conjunctions Introducing Accusative Clause.** This clause is the object of a verb: 'He told me *that he had done it.*' After a passive the clause is retained: 'I was told *that he had done it.*' The conjunctions are: *that* (or in popular speech *as*); *how* = *that; lest,* sometimes still, as in older English, used after verbs of fearing instead of *that; but, but that,* or in colloquial speech *but what,* often used instead of *that not* after a negative or interrogative proposition containing a verb of knowing, thinking, believing, expecting, fearing, or saying; an illogical *but, but that,* or in colloquial speech *but what,* sometimes used instead of the more common *that* after a negative or interrogative proposition containing a verb of doubting, wondering; *whether* or *if* (especially common in colloquial speech); the indefinite or interrogative conjunctive adverbs *where, when, why, how;* the indefinite or interrogative conjunctive pronouns *who, whoever, what, whatever;* the indefinite or interrogative conjunctive adjectives *which, whichever, what, whatever.*

Examples:

'I know *that* he has come' or 'I know [*that*] he has come.'

I don't know *as* (popular form for *that*) I should want you should marry for money (W. D. Howells, *The Minister's Charge*, Ch. XX).

I saw *that* (or *how*) he was falling behind in the race.

He feared *that* (or *lest*) it might anger her.

I don't know *but* (or *but that* or *but what*) it is all true (= *that it isn't all true*).

Who knows *but* (or *but that*, or *but what*) it is all true? (= *that it isn't all true*).

Who doubts *that* (or now less commonly *but*, *but that*, or *but what*) he will win?

I doubt *whether* (or *if*) the catastrophe is over.

I don't know *when* (indef. conj. adv.) he bought it.

He asked me *when* (interrog. conj. adv.) I bought it (indirect question).

I do not know *who* (indef. rel. pron.) did it.

He asked me *who* (interrog. conj. pron.) did it (indirect question).

I couldn't hear *what* (indef. rel. pron.) he said.

He has not told us yet *which*, or more indefinitely *what* (indef. rel. adj.) course he will pursue.

On account of the handiness of the infinitive and the gerund we often prefer an infinitival or gerundial accusative clause to a conjunctional clause: 'I desire him *to go at once*' (= *that he go at once*). 'I don't remember *ever being scolded* (= *that I was ever scolded*) *by her*.' Compare **47** 5 and **47** 6. Notice the peculiar idiom 'We could not help *but laugh*' or more commonly *help laughing*. See *Syntax*, p. 252.

4. **Conjunctions Employed in Prepositional Clause.** This clause is composed of two elements — a preposition and its object, which here is always a substantive (noun) clause. The substantive clause is introduced by a conjunction or an indefinite conjunctive adverb, pronoun, or adjective. These conjunctions are: *that*, *whether;* the indefinite conjunctive adverbs *where*, *when*, *why*, *how;* the indefinite relative pronouns *who*, *whoever*, *what*, *whatever;* the indefinite relative adjectives *which*, *whichever*, *what*, *whatever*. The preposition and its object, the substantive clause, form a grammatical unit — the prepositional clause. This clause serves usually as a prepositional object (**16** 1 *b*) completing as a necessary complement the meaning of a verb or an adjective or participle. Sometimes the relation between the verb and the prepositional clause is less close; then the prepositional clause becomes an adverbial element. Compare **16** 1 *a*.

The relative adverbs, pronouns, and adjectives here are always indefinites, never interrogatives.

a. *Prepositional Clause as Object.* The expression here is often elliptical.

Examples:

I took his word for it *that* he would make an effort.

He boasted [of it] *that* he did it.

I insist upon it *that* you go at once.

You may depend upon it *that* he will do it.
I will see to it *that* he does it.
I am sure [of it] *that* he will do it.
He was afraid [of it] *that* they would discover his dishonesty.
Veblen was right [about it] *that* ideas of this sort are opposed to the chaos of competitive enterprise.
She couldn't make up her mind [to it] *that* the price would have to be lowered.
He was perfectly at a loss [as to] *what* measure he should take.
We are not always conscious of *why* we do things.
I don't care [for] *what* people say.
Be careful (as to) *how* you do it.
She hesitated (as to) *whether* she should break in on his affliction.
I am not informed (as to) *whether* he went.
I am not informed (as to) *when* he will come.
I am curious as to *how* he is going to do it.
He gets furious against *whoever* opposes him.
He never speaks of *what* he has gone through.
I am not informed as to *which* (or more indefinitely *what*) course he will pursue.
He traded with *what* capital he had.

As shown by the above examples, the preposition stands immediately before a clause introduced by an indefinite conjunctive pronoun, adjective, or adverb; but if the clause is introduced by *that* it becomes necessary to place after the preposition the anticipatory object *it*, which points to the following clause, the real object. The *it*, however, is in certain expressions usually dropped.

The conjunctional clause is here often replaced by an infinitival or gerundial clause: 'His father forced him *to make his own living.*' 'I am accustomed *to do* (or *to doing*) *it this way.*' 'He is inclined *to take offense easily.*' 'I am looking forward with pleasure *to seeing you again.*' 'He is dead set *against doing anything for me.*' The infinitive clause here is very interesting. The *to* before the infinitive is still a pure preposition and not a mere sign of the infinitive, as elsewhere. Compare **16** 1 *b*, **47** 5. In a number of cases the infinitival clause is older than the conjunctional clause. In the newer construction the preposition is always suppressed: 'They are anxious *to win*' and 'I am anxious *for* (**47** 5 *a*, close of last par.) *them to win*,' but 'They are anxious *that they should win*' and 'I am anxious *that they should win.*'

b. Prepositional Clause as Adverbial Element.

Examples:

The light came straight towards *where* I was standing (place).
But you do as you like with me — you always did, from *when* first you begun to walk (George Eliot, *Silas Marner*, Ch. XI) (time).

5. **Conjunctions Introducing Adverbial Clause.** The adverbial clause modifies the principal verb by expressing some relation of place, time, manner, degree, cause, condition, exception, concession, purpose, means. The more common conjunctions and conjunctive adverbs are: *where, when, after, before, till, until, while, as, as if, as though, according as, so that, but that, but* (= *but that*), *so far as, as far as, than, that, because, since, if, unless, provided* (*that*), *in case, only that, except that, though, although, in order that,* etc. In concessive clauses an indefinite conjunctive pronoun, adjective, or adverb + *ever* is often used as a conjunction.

Examples:

I live *where* the bridge crosses the river.
When you go home let me know.
Let me know *when* you are ready.
Do at Rome *as* the Romans do.
I went early *so that* I got a good seat.
He was more shy *than* [he was] unsocial.
I am sorry *that* you can't go with us.
The crops failed *because* the season was dry.
They will not go tomorrow *if* it rains.
In case it rains we cannot go.
I would come *only that* I am engaged.
Although he promised not to do so he did it.
They are climbing higher *that* (or *so that* or *in order that*) they may get a better view.
He was resolved to defend himself *whoever* should assail him.
He will find difficulties *whichever* way he may take.
However sick he is, he always goes to work.

Other examples of the adverbial clause are given in **15** 2 *a–j*.

The conjunctional adverbial clause is very frequently replaced by a participial (**47** 4), infinitival, or gerundial clause. Examples are given in **15** 2 *b–j*. Compare **47** 4, **47** 5, **47** 6.

The conjunctional adverbial clause is sometimes replaced by the nominative absolute (**27** 1 *a*, 3rd par.) construction: '*Thou away* (= *When thou art away*) the very birds are mute' (Shakespeare). '*My knife slipping* (= *Because my knife slipped*) I cut myself severely.' Other examples are given in **15** 2 *b, c, d, h, i*. A still fuller treatment will be found in *Syntax*, **17** 3 A.

There is still another adverbial clause — the prepositional clause described in 4 and 4 *b* above.

6. **Relative Pronouns Introducing Adjective Clause.** The relative adjective clause modifies a noun or pronoun: 'The boy *who is leaning on the fence* is my brother.' 'The boy *whom you see leaning on the fence* is my brother.' Here *who*, though an inflected

pronoun, is as much a conjunction as any of the conjunctions in the preceding lists, for it, like a conjunction, links the clause in which it stands to the preceding principal proposition. It is at the same time a conjunction and a pronoun, hence a relative pronoun. The uninflected form *which* is used similarly: 'My brother owns the car *which we rode in yesterday.*' The relative pronouns are treated in **7** IV *a* and **38** *a*.

The relative clause with finite verb is often replaced by a participial clause: 'The circus was all one family — parents and five children — *performing* (= *who performed*) *in the open air.*'

The relative clause with finite verb is often replaced by an infinitive clause: 'He is not a man *to be trifled with*' (= *that can be trifled with*).

The definite relative *which* is sometimes used as a conjunctive adjective introducing an adjective clause: 'We traveled together as far as Paris, at *which* place we parted.' Compare **10** 5 *a*.

CHAPTER VIII

THE INTERJECTION

19. An interjection is an outcry to express pain, surprise, anger, pleasure, or some other emotion, as *Ouch! Oh! Alas! Why!* In general, interjections belong to the oldest forms of speech and represent the most primitive type of sentence. Thus they are not words but sentences. Sentences are older than words (*Syntax* **1** *a*). For fuller treatment see *Syntax,* **17** 1.

ACCIDENCE

20. Accidence is the study of the inflection and order of words, i.e. the change of form and order in words to indicate the part they play in the sentence. In English, the inflection is not so important a factor in the expression of our thought as it once was. The part a word plays in the sentence is now often indicated, not by its form, but by its position in the sentence. The subject of the sentence usually stands before the verb, the object after it: 'The mother (subject) loves her child' (object). Verbs once had many more endings than they now have: Old English *ic lufie, we lufiath*, now *I love, we love*. Today the singular and the plural of the verb have the same form in the first person, while in Old English the endings of the verb indicated singular or plural. We now feel that the subjects *I* and *we* are sufficient to make the thought clear. In the Old English period, as can be seen in **29** and **44** A, nouns and adjectives had endings for case and gender and the case endings varied according to the gender so that English expression at that time was quite complicated. The many endings were, of course, intended to make the grammatical relations clear, but the great complexity of the forms to a certain extent hid these relations, i.e. stood in the way of an easy discernment. The later reduction of the forms and the simplification of the word-order made the grammar visible and the thought easy to understand.

On the other hand, we now often use more words to express ourselves than our ancestors. In Old English the superlative of the adjective always was a single word with a superlative ending, *–est* or *–ost*. We now often put *most* before the simple adjective to form the superlative: 'Mary is the *most beaútiful* and Jane the *most belóved*,' but 'The sisters are all beautiful, but Mary is the *móst beautiful*.' Notice the accents. To emphasize the quality, we stress the adjective, but we stress *most* to emphasize the idea of degree. This shading of the thought is impossible in Old English, since there is only one word there. Alongside of the new superlative, however, we still often employ the old simple form: 'Of the sisters Mary is the *prettiest*.' Thus in English we often find the old and the new side by side. The simple form with an ending we call a synthetic form, the new form with an additional word an analytic form. The old synthetic forms are, in general, best preserved in poetic language, where there is usually a strong tendency to prefer the old, as hallowed by the use of our older masters.

The most remarkable case of an increase in the forms of our language is the introduction of the expanded form of the verb: 'He *is working* in the garden.' It came into the language in the Old English period under the influence of church Latin. At first it was not differentiated in meaning from the common form of the verb, but later in the modern period it gradually acquired distinctive functions of its own, greatly enriching the language. The development and extensive use of the expanded form clearly show that the English people is not averse to the increase of the forms of the language where they add to its power of expression.

In this treatise on accidence, the inflection of words, i.e. their forms or lack of form, is treated in the usual order of the parts of speech, nouns, pronouns, adjectives, verbs, adverbs, prepositions, conjunctions, interjections. In *Syntax*, the manner of using these forms is described more fully. Accidence and syntax are closely related in actual speech, in fact inseparable, but for practical purposes they are separated in this book as much as possible. It is thought helpful to the student to arrange for him in systematic shape all the forms of the language, the bare forms, free from syntactical discussion as much as possible, so that he may always have for ready reference a complete outline of all the formal means of expression in the language. And yet a certain amount of explanation must often be introduced to make the grammatical character of a form clear. At many points a good deal of explanation must be given, for it is important to know all the functions of the form if we are really to know it. In *Syntax* we get to see the form at work in different categories scattered throughout the book and cannot there become acquainted with it as a grammatical form in its entirety. Only in *Parts of Speech* and *Accidence* can we acquire an intimate acquaintance with the forms of the language as means of expression. Hence it often occurs that the important forms of the language are discussed thoroughly here.

CHAPTER IX

INFLECTION OF NOUNS

21. Purposes of Inflection. Nouns are inflected to indicate *number*, *case*, and *gender*

NUMBER

22. Number is that form of a word which indicates whether we are speaking of *one* or *more than one*.

English nouns have two numbers — the singular and the plural: 'The *bird* (singular) is singing.' 'The *birds* (plural) are singing.'

NATIVE ENGLISH WAYS OF FORMING THE PLURAL

23. The plural is formed in different ways.

1. **Plural Formed by Adding –*S*.** In Old English, nouns fell into a number of groups each with a different type of plural. The *s*-plural was only one of these types. Gradually throughout the centuries many nouns from the different groups abandoned their

old form and assumed the *s*-plural. Today this is the only living type. We always employ it with new words. As will be seen below, a few small groups of nouns still preserve their old plural form.

In older English the plural ending was –*es*, but we now shorten it to –*s* wherever it will unite with the singular without forming an extra syllable: 'head, head*s*'; but 'box, box*es*,' as simple *s* will not unite with the simple form. The –*es* is here a survival of older general usage. As we now suppress the *e* of the older ending –*es* whenever we can, it is evident that simple –*s* is now the natural normal plural ending. Only in the written language, however, is –*s* here a single thing. In spoken English it is two things: (1) arm*s*, son*s*, hill*s*, river*s*, bath*s*, boy*s*, flea*s*; (2) hat*s*, back*s*, wrap*s*, cliff*s*, gate*s*, safe*s*, etc. We should note that the –*s* is voiced after a voiced consonant or a vowel, as in the first group of nouns, but it is voiceless after a voiceless consonant, as in the second group. There are many such nouns as the last two in the second group, in which the *e* before the –*s* is a silent letter belonging to the spelling of the singular, hence not a part of the plural.

In one group of words there is a little formal irregularity. Letters, figures, signs used in writing, and parts of speech other than nouns when used as nouns take –'*s* in the plural instead of –*s*: 'Dot your *i*'*s* and cross your *t*'*s*.' 'There are two *9*'*s* in 99.' 'The *I*'*s* and *my*'*s* and *me*'*s* in his speech pass beyond the bounds of modesty and good taste.'

Little irregularities in the pronunciation or the spelling of the plural ending are discussed below.

a. Plural of Nouns Ending in Sibilants. After sibilants (*s, ss, c, sh, tch, ch, g, dg, x, z*) the plural ending is –*es* (pronounced ə*z*), which forms a distinct syllable: gas*es*, mass*es*, vic*es*, dish*es*, ditch*es*, church*es*, ag*es*, edg*es*, box*es*, topaz*es*. Similarly in proper nouns: Perkins, the Perkins*es*, etc. The foreign noun *fracas* is pronounced *frācas* in American English and has the regular plural *fracases*, while in British English it is pronounced *frăcah* and remains unchanged in the plural. In words in which a silent *e* follows a sibilant, as in *rose*, *horse*, we add only –*s* in the plural, but we pronounce ə*z*: *roses*, *horses*.

The –*s* or –*z* should be doubled in the plural after a short vowel in the few words ending in –*s* or –*z*, but this does not always take place: *bus*, *buses* or *busses; quiz*, *quizzes; fez*, *fezzes;* but *gas*, *gases; plus*, *pluses; yes*, *yeses*. The *s* in unaccented –*us*, –*is*, is never doubled: *omnibuses*, *crocuses*, *irises*, etc.

In some dialects, as in Essex and in certain American dialects, –*es* is found not only after sibilants but also after –*sk*, –*sp*, –*st:*

cask, caskes; wasp, waspes; beast, beastes; fist, fistes· nest, nestes; post, postes.

In dialect there is often a double plural –(*e*)*s* + *es: folkses, fisteses, gallowses* (suspenders) or more commonly *galluses.* The double plural in –(*e*)*n* + *s* occurs. See 2 below.

b. Plural of Nouns Ending in –Y. In nouns ending in –*y* preceded by a consonantal sound, *y* is changed to *i* before the addition of –*es* in the plural: lad*y*, pl. lad*ies;* soliloqu*y*, pl. soliloqu*ies;* fl*y*, pl. fl*ies.* But the plural of *dry, fly* (carriage), *stand-by, why,* and proper names in –*y* is regular: *drys, flys* (also *flies*), *stand-bys, whys* (the *whys* and wherefores of it), *Marys, Murphys.* In accordance with a general principle, *y* after a consonantal sound becomes *ie* before the plural ending; but, of course, in the case of proper names the *y* of the singular is retained in the plural before the ending –*s*, since we feel that the identity of the name must be preserved. Certain geographical and historical proper names in –*y*, however, have the plural form in –*ies* where the different individuals form a distinct group: 'the *Alleghenies,*' 'the *Canaries,*' 'the *Rockies,*' 'the Two *Sicilies,*' 'the *Ptolemies,*' etc.

Notice that the plural –*es* here does not mean a distinct syllable, as in *a.* The *e* of the plural ending is silent.

c. Final Consonant of Certain Nouns Ending in –F, –Th, –S, Voiced in the Plural. In native English nouns ending in the spoken language in –*f* preceded by *l* or a long vowel or diphthong, *f* becomes *v* in the plural: *calf, calves; elf, elves; half, halves; self, selves; shelf, shelves; wolf, wolves; knife, knives; leaf, leaves; life, lives; loaf, loaves; sheaf, sheaves; thief, thieves; wife, wives. Beef,* though a French word, follows this model: *beef, beeves.* Notice that the plural –*es* here does not mean a distinct syllable as in *a.* The *e* of the plural ending is silent.

Some native and many borrowed words have a regular plural: *beliefs, chiefs, fifes, gulfs, griefs, hoofs* (also *hooves*), *oafs* (also *oaves*), *loafs* (noun made from the verb *loaf:* 'to obtain surreptitious smokes and *loafs*' — Captain F. Shaw, *Cassell's Magazine of Fiction,* April, 1912, quoted in Kruisinga's *Handbook,* II, p. 7), *proofs, reefs, roofs, safes, spoofs, strifes,* etc. These words do not follow the model of the native words in the preceding paragraph even though the *f* follows an *l* or a long vowel or diphthong. Where the vowel is short or the *f* is doubled, the plural is usually regular: *chefs, cliffs, tiffs, whiffs,* etc.

Scarf forms the plural with –*fs* or –*ves.* The plural of *wharf* is *wharves* or *wharfs.* The plural of *dwarf* is *dwarfs. Staff* has two plurals with different meaning: *staffs, staves.* Compare **25.** *Tipstaff* has the plural *tipstaves.*

In early Modern English, final *f* became *v* before singular genitive *-es* just as before plural *-es,* in both cases the *-ves* appearing in the written language as *ues:* 'his *wiues* brother.' This older genitive singular may survive in 'an old *wives'* tale', where *wives'* is now construed as a genitive plural. In England, the older genitive singular is often preserved in '*calves*-foot jelly.' The American form here is '*calf's*-foot jelly.' The genitive singular *-'s* is now added directly to the singular: *wife's, calf's, wolf's,* etc.

Similar to the change from a voiceless *f* to a voiced *v* in 'cal*f*, pl. cal*v*es' is the change from a voiceless *th* to a voiced *th:* ba*th*, pl. ba*ths*; la*th*, pl. la*ths*; mou*th*, pl. mou*ths*; oa*th*, pl. oa*ths*; pa*th*, pl. pa*ths*; wrea*th*, pl. wrea*ths*. In many words, however, there is no change in the pronunciation of *th* in the plural, the sound remaining voiceless: dea*th*, pl. dea*ths*; heal*th*, pl. heal*ths*; one six*th*, two six*ths*. In a number of words there is fluctuation of usage, the *th* in the plural being pronounced voiced or voiceless: tru*th*, pl. tru*ths*; you*th*, pl. you*ths* (in America more commonly with a voiceless *th* in the plural, while in England the *th* is usually voiced here). Similar to the change from voiceless *th* to voiced *th* in the plural is the change from voiceless *s* to voiced *s* in the plural: hou*s*e, pl. hou*s*es. This is the only word in *-s* that shows this change. In all other words voiceless *s* remains voiceless in the plural: hor*s*e, pl. hor*s*es. The changes discussed in this paragraph, though realities, are not indicated by the spelling.

d. Plural of Nouns Ending in -O. A number of common nouns in *-o* preceded by a consonant take *-es* in the plural, especially *bilbo, buffalo, cargo, dado* (in England pl. *dados*), *dingo, domino* (pieces in a game *dominoes,* in other meanings with the pl. *dominos*), *echo, embargo, go, hero, innuendo, jingo, manifesto, mosquito, motto, mulatto, Negro, no, potato, tomato, tornado, torpedo, veto, volcano. Archipelago, bravado, bravo* (*bravoes* 'daring villains'; *bravos* 'shouts of applause'), *calico, desperado, flamingo, fresco, grotto* (pl. more commonly *grottoes*), *halo, hobo, mango, memento, peccadillo, portico, stucco* (pl. more commonly *stuccoes*), *zero* (pl. more commonly *zeros*) take either *-s* or *-es.* There is a good deal of fluctuation here. All nouns in *-o* preceded by a vowel and a large number preceded by a consonant take *-s,* as *baboo, bagnio, bamboo, boo, cuckoo, cameo, curio, embryo, folio, kangaroo, nuncio, oratorio, pistachio, portfolio, punctilio, ratio, rodeo, seraglio, shampoo, studio, trio, zoo,* etc.; *albino, alto, auto, banjo, basso, bolero, broncho, burro, caballero, canto, capriccio, casino, cello, chromo, commando, contralto, diminuendo, ditto, duodecimo, dynamo, gaucho, gazebo, ghetto, gringo, guanaco, gyro, hidalgo, inamorato, junto, kilo, kimono, ladino, lasso, major-domo, merino, mestizo, octavo, palmetto, photo, piano,* *piccolo, poncho, pro and con* (pl. *pros and cons*), *proviso, quarto, radio, rancho, ridotto, rondo, salvo* (pl. in England *salvoes*), *scenario, scherzo, set-to, silo, sirocco, solo, sombrero, stiletto, stylo, tobacco, torso, tuxedo, violoncello, zemstvo.* Proper names in *-o* and *-oo* take *-s: Lothario, Nero, Eskimo, Filipino, Hindoo,* etc. In general in all the different groups the trend, except in the case of very common words, is toward the plural in *-s.*

Notice that the plural *-es* here does not mean a distinct syllable as in *a* above. The *e* of the plural ending is silent.

2. **Plural Formed by Adding** *-En: Ox,* pl. *oxen.* This plural, common in older English, is now in its simple form restricted to *ox. Children, brethren, kine* (archaic plural of *cow*), are double plurals, resulting from adding the plural ending *-en* to an old plural once in use, *cildru, brothru, cy* (old plural of *cu* cow).

In early Modern English, *eye, shoe, hose,* still had a plural in *-en:* 'Hermia's *eyne*' (Shakespeare, *A Midsummer-Night's Dream,* I, I, 142), 'in clouted *shoon*' (*id., Henry VI,* Second Part, IV, II, 195), 'their *hosen*' (*Daniel,* III, 21). In the British dialects a number of nouns still preserve the old plural ending *-en.* In northern New Jersey the plurals *shoon* and *housen* are still heard in mountain dialect.

In dialect the plural of certain words has a double plural ending *-(e)n + s: sheens* (shoes), *breechens* (breeches), etc.

3. **Plural Formed by Change of Vowel.** This once common plural form is now confined to the following nouns: *foot, feet; goose, geese; louse, lice; man, men; woman, women; mouse, mice; tooth, teeth.*

The plural of *four-foot* is *four-foots:* 'Man on his snowshoes has most wild *four-foots* at his mercy' (E. T. Seton, *Rolf in the Woods,* Ch. XL). The plural of *goose,* a tailor's smoothing iron, is *gooses.*

The plural of *Northman* is *Northmen,* but *Norman* has the regular plural *Normans.* The foreign words *Mussulman, Ottoman, Turkoman, Talisman,* have nothing to do with English *man* and hence have regular plurals: *Mussulmans, Ottomans, Turkomans, Talismans.*

a. The change of vowel in the plural in this little group of nouns is technically called mutation. It was caused by the presence of an *i* that once stood after the final consonant of the stem: Old English *fot* 'foot,' plural *fēt* (from still older *fōti*). For the effects of mutation in verbs see **59** 1 *b.*

4. **Plural with Form of Singular.** This plural goes back to an Old English neuter type of inflection described in **29** I C. There was no distinctive plural sign for the nominative and accusative

plural. There are only two of the original group of neuters that have preserved their old endingless plural form — *deer, sheep:* 'two *deer,*' 'two *sheep.*' Shakespeare still uses *horse* with its old indistinctive plural: 'the galloping of *horse*' (*Macbeth,* IV, I, 140). This old type of plural lingered into the modern period with nouns denoting measurement: 'Some of them weie fiue hundred *pound*' (Pory, *Leo's Africa,* Introduction, p. 39, A.D. 1600). In older English this plural spread in measurements to words originally masculine: 'The indigo Plant grows about two *Foot* high' (*Pomet's History of Drugs,* I, p. 89, A.D. 1712). In certain expressions this plural is still employed: 'ten *hundredweight*'; 'a German liner having 9000 *horse power*'; 'five *brace* of birds'; 'ten *gross* of buttons'; 'a gross = ten *dozen*'; often 'forty *head* of cattle'; 'ten *yoke* of oxen.' 'These lamps must be at least 40 *candle power.*' We often hear 'He is *five foot ten.*' The spread of this plural with measurements shows that a new idea had become associated with it, namely, a collective idea. With measurements this plural has in general passed out of the literary language. It still lingers, however, in colloquial and popular English: 'a couple of *year*' (dialect in the mountains of Kentucky).

In other directions the old plural with the new collective idea has taken a fresh start and is flourishing vigorously. It is especially common in nouns denoting gregarious animals: 'a boatload of *fish,*' 'a string of *fish,*' 'five *bass,*' etc. The old, once common plural *fishes* is now largely confined to reference to different species: 'a large book on our freshwater *fishes,*' 'an illustrated article on our American *basses.*' The old plural with the new collective idea is now widely employed by hunters and is characteristic of their language: 'A farmer raises *ducks,* but a hunter shoots *duck.*' Even in the literary language we usually speak of a jungle abandoned to water *fowl,* but a farmer speaks of the *fowls* going to roost. In books on sport the plurals *lion, elk, antelope, partridge,* etc., are common. Although the American usually thinks of domestic animals as individuals, *hogs, pigs, ducks,* etc., it is quite common to employ *swine* as a collective plural: 'There are millions of *swine* in our country — one-half of a hog for every being in the nation.' In the generic sense *swine* is used also as a singular: *a swine, the swine.* In England the collective plural is used not only in the case of *swine,* but sometimes also in the case of *chicken:* 'Do you keep *chicken?*' (Dean Alford, *The Queen's English*). (This collective plural of *chicken* is given in the *Concise Oxford Dictionary*). There is a tendency to use this plural with names of insects: 'The great thing is to prevent *the moth* from getting into it between seasons' (Galsworthy, *Swan Song,* Part II,

Ch. II). *Vermin* is often used as a collective plural. There is also a tendency to use the old plural with the new collective idea with names of trees, shrubs, flowers: 'woods of *oak* and *beech*.' 'In spring and early summer, daffodils, primroses, *honeysuckle*, cowslips, are seen on every side' (*Calendar of Historic and Important Events*, p. 41, A.D. 1930). This plural is spreading to other categories: 'We traveled on *ski*,' but 'Two broken *skis* were lying on the ground.'

For the differentiation between *folk* and *folks* see **26** 1.

The use of a plural with the same form as the singular, once more common than now, is still common in the second component of compounds: 'a ten-*pound* baby,' 'a ten-*foot* pole,' 'a three-*year*-old,' 'a fort*night*' (i.e. fourteen *nights*), 'a twelve*month*,' etc.

Nouns that are plurals used as singulars, as described in *Syntax*, **59** 2, do not usually change their form in the plural: 'a wheezy old *bellows*' or more commonly 'a pair of wheezy old *bellows*' (pl.), 'two *bellows*' or more commonly 'two pairs of *bellows*' (pl.); 'a high *gallows*,' 'two *gallows*'; *innings*, in British usage singular and plural, as in 'the ninth *innings*' (sing.), 'two *innings*,' but in American English the singular is now *inning*, the plural *innings* except in such figurative expressions as 'The Democrats are now having their *innings*' (sing.) and 'It is your *innings* (= *opportunity*) now'; 'a sure *means*,' 'these *means*'; 'this (in early Modern English usually *these*) *news*,' '*a piece of news*,' never *a news*; *pains* (sing. and pl., usually pl., but sometimes sing., as in 'Much *pains* has been taken'); 'a *scissors*' or more commonly 'a pair of *scissors*,' 'the *scissors*' (usually pl., but sometimes sing.), 'two *scissors*' or more commonly 'two pairs of *scissors*'; 'a *lazy-bones*,' 'all you *lazy-bones*'; 'a *daddy-long-legs*,' 'two *daddy-long-legs*'; *a wood* or *the woods* (pl. referring to one 'wood' or more). We say 'There is *a wood* (not *a woods*) about a mile away.' '*The woods* are about a mile away,' or '*The wood* is about a mile away.' 'You should see the many beautiful *woods* (pl.) of our county.' In colloquial and popular speech it is common to say: 'There is a fine spring in *a woods* (for literary *wood*) near by.' In popular speech the plural ending *-es* is sometimes added to certain of these nouns to indicate the plural idea more clearly: *bellowses*, *gallowses*, etc.

Many nouns made from adjectives and participles have a plural with the same form as the singular: '*the dead* and *the dying*,' '*the poor*,' etc. A rather full treatment of this important group of nouns is given in **43** 3.

In early Modern English, nouns ending in an *s*-sound often had the singular and the plural alike, such as *corpse* (older spelling *corps*), *princess*, *witness*, etc. The plural here is now regular: *princess*, *princesses*.

FOREIGN PLURALS

24. Nouns that have not been thoroughly naturalized retain their original plurals. The tendency to employ the foreign plural is still strong in the technical language of science, but elsewhere in the literary language there is an evident inclination to give to certain words the regular English plural form in *-s* — a tendency that should be encouraged. Foreign words that are the names of favorite flowers and shrubs and common things in general and are thus known to wide circles have become naturalized or are manifesting a tendency to become so in spite of their foreign form: *crocus*, *crocuses*; *nasturtium*, *nasturtiums*; *fuchsia*, *fuchsias*; *libretto*, *librettos* or *libretti* (**24** 8); *soprano*, *sopranos* or *soprani* (**24** 8). The tendency to naturalize names of common things is found even in scientific language, though in much less degree.

There are different groups:

1. Latin words in *-a* with a plural in *-ae* (pronounced as *e* in *react*): *alga*, *algae*; *alumna*, *alumnae*; *ameba*, *amebae* or *amebas*; *antenna*, *antennae*; *camera*, *cameras* (photographic apparatus), *camerae* ('chambers,' term used in anatomy); *cesura*, *cesuras* or *cesurae*; *cicada*, *cicadas* or *cicadae*; *corona*, *coronae* or *coronas*; *curia*, *curiae*; *differentia*, *differentiae*; *drachma*, *drachmas* or *drachmae*; *fauna*, *faunas* or *faunae*; *fibula*, *fibulae* or *fibulas*; *flora*, *floras* or *florae*; *formula*, *formulas* or *formulae*; *gemma*, *gemmae*; *lacuna*, *lacunae*; *lamella*, *lamellae*; *lamia*, *lamiae* or *lamias*; *lamina*, *laminae*; *larva*, *larvae*; *ligula*, *ligulae* or *ligulas*; *macula*, *maculae*; *mammilla*, *mammillae*; *mamma*, *mammae*; *maxilla*, *maxillae*; *minutia*, *minutiae*; *nebula*, *nebulae*; *papilla*, *papillae*; *papula*, *papulae*; *pelta*, *peltae*; *pinna*, *pinnae*; *pleura*, *pleurae*; *plica*, *plicae*; *pupa*, *pupae*; *quadriga*, *quadrigae*; *retina*, *retinas* or *retinae*; *scintilla*, *scintillae*; *scoria*, *scoriae*; *stria*, *striae*; *struma*, *strumae*; *taenia*, *taeniae*; *tessera*, *tesserae*; *tibia*, *tibiae*; *trachea*, *tracheae*; *ulna*, *ulnae*; *umbra*, *umbrae*; *ungula*, *ungulae*; *vagina*, *vaginae*; *verruca*, *verrucae*; *vertebra*, *vertebrae*; *vesica*, *vesicae*; *vitta*, *vittae*; etc.

Many nouns in *-a* from the Latin have become naturalized and now have the regular plural in *-s*, and of course there are from other languages many nouns in *-a* that have become naturalized, so that there are a large number of nouns in *-a* that have the regular plural in *-s*: *acacia*, *area*, *arena*, *camellia*, *cedilla*, *chimera*, *cinema*, *cornucopia*, *corolla*, *cupola*, *dahlia*, *encyclopedia*, *era*, *fistula*, *fuchsia, hyena, idea, lama, llama, panacea, peninsula, propaganda, quota, replica, sofa, sonata, subpoena, ultima, umbrella, uvula, veronica* (shrub), *villa, vista, wisteria,* etc.

2. Latin words in *-us* with a plural in *-i* (pronounced as *i* in *mine*): *abacus, abacuses* or *abacī; acanthus, acanthuses* or *acanthī; alumnus, alumnī; alveolus, alveolī; bacillus, bacillī; bronchus, bronchī; cactus, cactī* (in science) or *cactuses* (in general use); *calculus, calculī; cirrus, cirrī; colossus, colossī* or *colossuses; cothurnus, cothurnī; cumulus, cumulī; discobolus, discobolī; esophagus, esophagī* or *esophaguses; eucalyptus, eucalyptī* (in science), *eucalyptus* or *eucalyptuses* (in general use); *famulus, famulī; focus, focuses* or *focī; fucus, fucī; fungus, fungī* or *funguses; gladiolus* (*gladiŏlus, gladíolus*, or, in England, often *glădiolus*), *gladiŏluses, gladiŏlus, gladíolī,* or *glădioluses; hippocampus, hippocampī; hippopotamus, hippopotamuses* or *hippopotamī; humerus, humerī; iambus, iambuses* or *iambī; ichthyosaurus, ichthyosaurī; literatus* (now little used), *literatī* (more common than the singular); *loculus, loculī; locus, locī; magus, magī; modulus, modulī; narcissus, narcissus(es)* or *narcissī; nautilus, nautiluses* or *nautilī; nidus, niduses* or *nidī; nimbus, nimbuses* or *nimbī; nodus, nodī; nucleus, nucleī* or *nucleuses; obelus, obelī; ocellus, ocellī; papyrus, papyrī; plesiosaurus, plesiosaurī; polypus, polypī* or *polypuses; radius, radiī; ranunculus, ranunculuses* or *ranunculī; scyphus, scyphī; senarius, senariī; stimulus, stimulī; stratus, stratī; syllabus, syllabī* or *syllabuses; talus* (anklebone), *talī,* but *talus* (slope), *taluses; tarsus, tarsī; terminus, terminī; thalamus, thalamī; thesaurus, thesaurī; torus, torī; tumulus, tumulī; umbilicus, umbilicī; uterus, uterī; villus, villī; vitellus, vitellī;* etc.

But some nouns from the Latin have a plural in *-us, -ora,* or *-era,* as in Latin: *apparatus, apparatus* or, especially in England, *apparatuses; corpus, corpora; genus, genera; hiatus, hiatuses* or *hiatus; ictus, ictuses* or *ictus; lusus, lusus; meatus, meatus* or *meatuses; nexus, nexus* or *nexuses; opus, opera; plexus, plexus* or *plexuses; rictus, rictuses* or *rictus; saltus, saltus; sinus, sinuses* or *sinus; viscus, viscera;* etc.

Some nouns in *-us* from Latin and other languages have become naturalized and now take the regular *-es* in the plural: *bolus, bonus, callus, campus, caucus, census, chorus, circus, Columbus, conspectus, convolvulus, crocus, fetus, excursus, hibiscus, ignoramus, impetus, incubus, isthmus, lotus, mandamus, minus, mittimus, octopus, omnibus, platypus, plus, prospectus, rebus, rhombus, vidimus, virus,* etc. *Ignoramus* (i.e. *we do not know*), *mandamus* (i.e. *we command*), *mittimus* (i.e. *we send*), *vidimus* (i.e. *we have seen*), are Latin verbs used as nouns. *Omnibus* is a Latin dative plural = *for all. Rebus* is the Latin ablative plural of *res* 'thing.' These six words never take *-i* in the plural. *Rumpus* is an English word and, of course, takes *-es* in the plural.

3. Latin words in *-um* with a plural in *-a: addendum, addenda; agendum, agenda; animalculum, animalcula,* sometimes *animalcula* (plural construed as singular), *animalculae* (new plural), but now in the singular usually *animalcule,* which has a regular plural; *antrum, antra* or *antrums; aquarium, aquariums* or *aquaria; arboretum, arboreta* or *arboretums; arcanum, arcana; auditorium, auditoriums* or *auditoria; bacterium, bacteria; candelabrum, candelabra* or *candelabrums; cerebellum, cerebella* or *cerebellums; cerebrum, cerebra* or *cerebrums; cilium, cilia; compendium, compendiums* or *compendia; corrigendum, corrigenda; cranium, crania* or *craniums* (jocular use for *heads*); *curriculum, curricula* or *curriculums; datum, data; desideratum, desiderata; dictum, dicta; effluvium, effluvia; emporium, emporiums* or *emporia; epithalamium, epithalamiums* or *epithalamia; erratum, errata; exordium, exordiums* or *exordia; frenum, frena* or *frenums; frustum, frustums* or *frusta; fulcrum, fulcrums* or *fulcra; gymnasium, gymnasiums* or *gymnasia; gymnasium* (German classical school), *gymnasia* or in German form *gymnasien; honorarium, honoraria* or *honorariums; interregnum, interregna* or *interregnums; labium, labia; lustrum, lustrums* or *lustra; mausoleum, mausoleums* or *mausolea; maximum, maxima* or *maximums; medium, mediums* (of things and persons, always so of persons) or *media* (of things); *memorandum, memoranda* or *memorandums; menstruum, menstrua* or *menstruums; millennium, millenniums* or *millennia; minimum, minima* or *minimums; momentum, momenta; moratorium, moratoria* or *moratoriums; operculum, opercula; opusculum, opuscula; ovum, ova; palladium, palladia; phylum, phyla; planetarium, planetaria* or *planetariums; plectrum, plectra; podium, podia; propylaeum, propylaea; proscenium, proscenia; pudendum, pudenda* (usually employed in the plural, but the singular is sometimes used with the same meaning); *residuum, residua; rostrum, rostra* (ships' beaks) or *rostrums* (pulpits, platforms, in these meanings sometimes also *rostra*); *sacrarium, sacraria; sanatorium, sanatoriums* or *sanatoria; scholium, scholia; scrinium, scrinia; scriptorium, scriptoria; scutum, scuta; septum, septa; simulacrum, simulacra; solarium, solaria; solatium, solatia; spectrum, spectra* or *spectrums; speculum, specula; sputum, sputa; stadium, stadia; sternum, sterna* or *sternums; stratum, strata; substratum, substrata; sudatorium, sudatoria; symposium, symposia; tintinnabulum, tintinnabula; trapezium, trapeziums* or *trapezia; triclinium, triclinia; triforium, triforia; tripudium, tripudia; triquetrum, triquetra; tympanum,*

tympana; ultimatum, ultimata or *ultimatums; vacuum, vacuums* or *vacua; vasculum, vascula; velamentum, velamenta; velum, vela; vexillum, vexilla; vibraculum, vibracula; vinculum, vincula; vivarium, vivariums* or *vivaria;* etc. A number of scientific terms occur only in the plural: *carnivora, herbivora, infusoria, mammalia,* etc.

Some nouns in *-um,* whether of Latin or other origin, usually take *-s* in the plural: *album, antirrhinum, asylum, chrysanthemum, decorum, delphinium, Elysium, encomium, factotum, forum, geranium, hoodlum, lyceum, museum, nasturtium, nostrum, pandemonium, pendulum, petroleum, premium, quorum, referendum, serum, Targum, vellum, viburnum,* etc. *Quorum* (i.e. *of whom*) is a Latin genitive plural and hence cannot take *-a* in the plural.

The Latin neuter *stamen* had the plural *stamina.* In English, *stamen* has a regular plural, *stamens.* The old Latin plural *stamina* has become in English a singular, an abstract noun without a plural.

4. Words in *-ex, -ix, -yx, -trix, -is, -sis,* with a plural in *-ēs.* The plural *-ēs* is not added to the singular, but to an altered or shortened form of it, or, on the other hand, *-ĕs* is often after English fashion added to the regular singular form: *apex, apexes* or *apicēs; codex, codicēs; cortex, corticēs; index, indexes* (**25**) or *indicēs* (**25**); *murex, muricēs* or *murexes; vertex, verticēs* or *vertexes; vortex, vorticēs* or *vortexes; appendix, appendixes* or *appendicēs; helix, helicēs* or *helixes; radix, radicēs* or *radixes; calyx, calyxes* or *calycēs; administratrix, administratricēs; cicatrix, cicatricēs; executrix, executricēs* or *executrixes; heritrix, heritricēs* or *heritrixes; inheritrix, inheritricēs* or *inheritrixes; matrix, matricēs* or *matrixes; mediatrix, mediatricēs* or *mediatrixes; prosecutrix, prosecutricēs* or *prosecutrixes; testatrix, testatricēs* or *testatrixes; amanuensis, amanuensēs; analysis, analysēs; apodosis, apodosēs; arsis, arsēs; axis, axēs; basis, basēs; chrysalis, chrysalises* or *chrysálidēs; crisis, crisēs; diagnosis, diagnosēs; dieresis, dieresēs; ellipsis, ellipsēs; emphasis, emphasēs; hypothesis, hypothesēs; metamorphosis, metamorphosēs; matathesis, matathesēs; metempsychosis, metempsychosēs; narcosis, narcosēs; neurosis, neurosēs; oasis, oasēs; parabasis, parabasēs; parenthesis, parenthesēs; periphrasis, periphrasēs; proboscis, proboscises* or *proboscidēs,* but not *proboscēs; prognosis, prognosēs; protasis, protasēs; psychosis, psychosēs; sclerosis, sclerosēs; syllepsis, syllepsēs; synopsis synopsēs; synthesis, synthesēs; thesis, thesēs,* etc. There are other words with the plural in *-ēs*: *pāriēs, parĭetēs; vibrio, vibriōnēs.*

Iris, metropolis, usually have English plurals, *irises, metropolises,* but the former sometimes has the foreign plural *īridēs. Calliopsis, coreopsis, clematis,* and often *iris* remain unchanged in the plural. See **23** 4 (2nd par.).

5. Greek words in *–on* with a plural in *–a*: *anacoluthon, anacoluthons* or *anacolutha; asyndeton, asyndeta* or *asyndetons; automaton, automatons* or *automata; criterion, criteria; ganglion, ganglia* or *ganglions; hyperbaton, hyperbata* or *hyperbatons; noumenon, noumena; organon, organa* or *organons; oxymoron, oxymorons* or *oxymora; perispomenon, perispomena; phenomenon, phenomena; prolegomenon, prolegomena* (usually in plural); etc. Instead of *ephemeron* (pl. *ephemera* or *ephemerons*) we may use *ephemera* (pl. *ephemeras*).

There are a number of naturalized nouns in *–on* — from this Greek declension and from others, also from other languages — so that there are now many nouns in *–on* that have the regular plural in *–s*: *anion, archon, canon, cation, colon, semicolon, cotyledon, demon, electron, lexicon, mastodon, pylon, rhododendron, siphon, skeleton, tenon,* etc.

6. Greek words in *–ma* with a plural in *–mata: anathema, anathemas* or *anathemata; diploma, diplomas* or sometimes in the rarer meanings *diplomata; dogma, dogmas* or now rarely *dogmata; fibroma, fibromata; gumma, gummata* or *gummas; miasma, miasmata* or *miasmas; neuroma, neuromata; sarcoma, sarcomata* or *sarcomas; scleroma, scleromata; stemma, stemmata; stigma, stigmas* or, in ecclesiastical and scientific senses, *stigmata; stroma, stromata; zeugma, zeugmas* or *zeugmata;* etc.

Dilemma and *panorama* have the regular plural in *–s*: *dilemmas, panoramas.*

7. *Species, series, superficies, abatis,* have the same form for singular and plural. *Chamois, corps, patois, rendezvous,* and *Dumas* (name) have the same spelling for singular and plural, but in the spoken language the final *s* is silent in the singular and spoken in the plural. *Forceps* is either a singular or a plural: 'this or these *forceps*,' 'a pair of *forceps*.'

Cȳclŏps has a variant form *Cȳclŏp. Cȳclŏps* has the plural *Cȳclŏpses* or *Cȳclōpēs. Cȳclŏp* has the plural *Cȳclŏps.*

Sioux has the same form for singular and plural, the final *x* silent in the singular and in the plural either silent or pronounced *z*. Thus it is treated either as a noun made from an adjective or as a pure noun. *Iroquois* has the same form for singular and plural, always with silent final *s*, both in the singular and the plural. Thus it is treated as a noun made from an adjective. Compare **23** 4 and **43** 3 (4th par.).

Larynx and *mēninx* have the plurals *larýngēs* and *meníngēs.* The plural of *phálanx* is *phalángēs* in anatomy and botany, elsewhere *phálanxes.* The singular of *phalángēs* is also *phálange.*

8. Italian words with the plural in *–i* (pronounced as *e* in *react*):

bandit, bandits or *banditti; carbonaro, carbonari; cicerone, ciceroni* or *cicerones; conversazione, conversaziones* or *conversazioni; dilettante, dilettanti* or *dilettantes; Facista, Facisti* or in English form *Fascist*, pl. *Fascists*, as adjective always *Fascist*, as in '*Fascist* doctrine'; *graffito, graffiti; intermezzo, intermezzos* or *intermezzi; lazzarone, lazzaroni; libretto, librettos* or *libretti; niello, nielli* or *niellos; sbirro, sbirri; soprano, sopranos* or *soprani; virtuoso, virtuosi* or *virtuosos*. The plural of the compound *prima donna* is *prima donnas* or *prime donne*.

9. French. *Madáme, monsiéur* have the plurals *mesdámes, messiéurs*. The following nouns — accented in the case of words of more than one syllable upon the last syllable except in *búreau, flámbeau, tableau* (*tábleau* or *tabléau*), *portmánteau*, and *rondeau* (*róndeau* or *rondéau*) — take in the plural *-s* or *-x*, which is pronounced as *s* in *rose: adieu, adieus* or *adieux; beau, beaus* or *beaux; bureau, bureaus* or *bureaux; chateau, chateaux* or *chateaus; flambeau, flambeaux* or *flambeaus; plateau, plateaus* or *plateaux; portmanteau, portmanteaus* or *portmanteaux; rondeau, rondeaus* or *rondeaux; rouleau, rouleaux* or *rouleaus; tableau, tableaux* or *tableaus; trousseau, trousseaux* or *trousseaus*. *Purlieu* always has the plural *purlieus*.

The contracted form *Messrs.* (*mĕsrz*) is used as the plural of *Mr.* In direct address the plural of *Madam* is *Ladies*.

Chassis has the same spelling for singular and plural, but it is usually pronounced *shăsē* in the singular and *shăsēz* in the plural. It is sometimes pronounced *chasis* in both singular and plural. In England the usual pronunciation is *shăsē* for singular and plural.

10. Hebrew: *cherub, cherubim* or *cherubs* (in the sense of 'darlings' always *cherubs;* in older English with the singular *cherubin* or *cherubim* and the plural *cherubins* or *cherubims*); *seraph, seraphim* or *seraphs; sephardi, sephardim*. *Teraphim* is used as a collective plural = 'the household gods.' This form is sometimes used as a singular with the plural *teraphims*. The singular is sometimes *teraph* with the plural *teraphs*. The plural of *rabbī* is *rabbīs*.

11. Latin: *triumvir, triumvirs* or *triumviri; naiad* (*nīăd* or *nāyăd*), *naiads* or *naiadēs*.

12. Japanese. The Japanese coin *yen* has the same form for the singular and the plural.

13. Arabic: *fellah, fellaheen* or *fellahs*. The usual plural of *Moslem* is *Moslems*, but the Arabic form *Moslemin* is sometimes employed. Some use *Moslem* also as a plural in a collective sense: 'All *Moslem* (more commonly *Moslems*) are bound to study it' (i.e. the Koran) (Carlyle, *Heroes and Hero-Worship*, II, 104).

TWO PLURAL FORMS WITH DIFFERENTIATED MEANING

25. When different plural forms arise, there is a tendency to differentiate them in meaning. Notice the following differentiations: *brother*, pl. *brothers* (by blood), *brethren* (of a religious or secular order or community); *cherub*, pl. *cherubs* (darlings), *cherubim* (angels); *cloth*, pl. *cloths* (different pieces or kinds of cloth), *clothes* (collective pl., one's garments); *die*, pl. *dies* (stamps), *dice* (cubes used in games); *genius* (person of high mental power; in this meaning pronounced *jēnyŭs*), pl. *geniuses; genius* (pronounced *jēnĭ-ŭs*) or *genie* (pronounced *jēnĭ*), both in the sense of a good or evil spirit with the plural form *geniī*, or instead of *genie* the Arabic form *jinnee* is sometimes used with the plural *jinn; penny*, pl. *pennies* (individual coins), *pence* (collectively, as in 'Can you give me six pennies for this sixpence?'), the latter of which can be used as a singular noun with a regular plural, as in *a sixpence, two sixpences; index*, pl. *indexes* (tables of contents), *indices* (algebraical signs); *seraph*, pl. *seraphs* (sweet singers), *seraphim* (angels); *staff*, pl. *staves* (musical term), *staffs* (military or newspaper staffs, flagstaffs, etc.).

In older English, *pease* is a singular as well as a plural. The old singular form is still sometimes used in *pease-pudding* (now usually *pea pudding*, *pea soup*, etc.). From the plural *pease* was formed the new singular *pea*, a so-called back-formation. To this new singular there were for a long time two plurals, *peas* (individual *peas*), and *pease* (for a mass of *peas*), now usually *peas*.

For further discussion see *Syntax*, **59** 1.

PLURAL OF COMPOUND NOUNS

26. There are three groups:

1. **Old Compounds.** Our oldest compounds and most of our newer ones are forms representing a unit of thought, hence are treated as simple nouns, the final element, if a noun, assuming the plural form that it would have as a simple word: *toothpick, toothpicks; horseman, horsemen; housetrap, housetraps; womanhater, womanhaters; washerwoman, washerwomen; bird's-nest, bird's-nests* or *birds' nests; crow's-foot*, the *crow's-feet* about his eyes; *Peter's penny, Peter's pence;* etc. If the final element is not a noun, the plural usually ends in *-s: bucketfuls, handfuls, spoonfuls, breakdowns, drawbacks, setbacks, hold-ups, stop-overs, stowaways, godsends, merry-go-rounds, go-betweens, forget-me-nots, cure-alls, four per cents* (last element a phrase), *four o'clocks*, etc.

Inflection usually takes place only in the final element, but in certain compounds containing two nouns as components both nouns have plural form: *maid servants, girl cashiers, woman* (more commonly *women*) *clerks, chief justices, lieutenant colonels, lieutenant governors,* etc., but *men servants, men friends, gentlemen boarders, women students, women singers,* etc. It would be more in accordance with our modern feeling, as described in *Syntax,* **10** I 2, to construe the first element in many such expressions as an adjective, and the following word as the governing noun. Some of these expressions, however, such as *chief justice, lieutenant governor,* etc., are real compounds.

In a few words a difference of accent is associated with a difference of meaning: *mankínd* (the human species), *mánkind* (the males of a household, the male sex) or sometimes still in accordance with older usage *ménkind.* In America the colloquial expression is *men folks. Womankínd* has the force of *all women,* while *wóman-kind* or *wómenkind* means *women folks* ('our, his, etc., *women folks*'). In England the forms *menfolk* and *womenfolk* are used instead of *men folks* and *women folks.* Americans often employ *menfolk, womenfolk* in literary style: 'As the wife of a celebrated senator, mother of his successor in the Senate and of the Governor of Wisconsin, her (i.e. Belle Case LaFollette's) personality along with her work was merged in the fame of her *menfolk*' (*The New York Times,* Editorial, Aug. 20, 1931). Similarly in formal language we say 'my (his, etc.) *kinsfolk,*' but colloquially we use more commonly 'my (his, etc.) *relatives,*' 'my (his, etc.) *people,*' or 'my (his, etc.) *folks.*' 'My (his, etc.) *folks,*' however, refers most commonly to the members of a single household. Compare *Syntax,* **59** 1.

2. **Syntactical Compounds.** Although in the old compounds in 1 the components stand in a syntactical relation, the relation is often not indicated by their form; hence we can easily add the plural sign at the end of the group. But in many compounds where the syntactical relation is indicated by the form, especially where the first component is a noun which is modified by a genitive, prepositional phrase, adverb, or adjective, we plainly feel the force of the noun and give it plural form if there is a reference to more than one: *men-of-war, mothers-in-law, brothers-in-law, sons-in-law, daughters-in-law, heirs-at-law, commanders-in-chief, editors-in-chief, aides-de-camp, autos-da-fé, lookers-on, goings-on* or sometimes *on-goings* (both usually in the plural), *passers-by, coats-of-mail, justices-of-the-peace, postmasters-general, governors-general, attorneys-general, courts-martial, notaries public, poets laureate, knights-errant, billets-doux.* In a number of such compounds,

however, the concrete force of the noun is felt so little and the oneness of the compound is felt so strongly that the regular plural ending *-s* is added at the end: *will-o'-the-wisps, good-for-nothings, jack-in-the-pulpits* (American plant), *brigadier generals, major generals, lieutenant generals, attorney-generals* (perhaps more common than *attorneys-general*), etc.; often *court-martials* instead of *courts-martial;* in popular speech often *mother-in-laws*, etc. While we say in the literary language 'my *brothers*-in-law' we must, on the other hand, say 'my brother-in-*law's* house.'

When in compounds the second component is a noun in apposition with the preceding component, both components usually have plural form: *Knights Templars, Knights Hospitalers, Lords Justices, Lords Lieutenants, Lords Chancellors*, etc. But there is considerable fluctuation in usage with some of these words: *Lord Lieutenants* (both components felt as a unit), *Lords Lieutenant* (second component felt as an adjective), etc.

3. **Plural of Titles**: 'Messrs. (mĕsərz) Smith' or 'the Messrs. Smith'; 'Messrs. Smith and Brown'; 'the two Mr. Smiths'; 'Mr. Paul [Smith] and Mr. John Smith' or 'Messrs. Paul and John Smith'; 'Master Smith'; 'the two young Master Smiths' or 'the two young Masters Smith'; 'Drs. William Smith and Henry Brown'; 'Professors Smith and Brown'; 'the two Miss Smiths' or 'the two Misses Smith,' but only 'the two Mrs. Smiths'; 'the Miss Smiths' or in more formal language, as in addressing a letter, 'the Misses Smith'; 'the Misses Mary and Ann Brown'; 'the Misses Smith, Brown, and Reed.'

CASE

27. Case is that form of a noun or pronoun which marks it as the subject of a verb, or as the object of a verb, adjective, or preposition, or as playing the part of an adjective or an adverb. Once the Germanic (German, English, etc.) languages, in large measure, indicated these grammatical relations by inflectional endings, i.e. endings which the nouns, pronouns, and adjectives assumed to show the part they were playing in the sentence. Of the many case endings once used English has, in nouns, preserved only one, namely the *-s* of the genitive. Apart from the genitive relation, these grammatical relations are now indicated by the position of the noun with regard to the verb or preposition, or by means of inflectional prepositions (**17**), which have taken the place of the old inflectional endings, or often by the context alone; that is, the context without the aid of word-order or inflectional preposition suggests the grammatical relation, as illustrated in 3 *a* below.

In the genitive relation we still frequently employ the genitive ending *–s*, but employ also frequently the inflectional preposition *of*, as described in 4 A *b* (2) (p.134).

There are now four cases, nominative, accusative, dative, genitive, and in Old English as a fifth case the instrumental. The cases other than the nominative are called the oblique cases.

Nominative

1. **Functions.** The nominative performs three functions. It plays the rôle of subject, predicate, and direct address.

a. Subject. The subject relation is shown by a clear nominative form only in the case of a few pronouns: *I, he, she, we, they, who.* Nouns and most pronouns can no longer show by their form that they are performing the part of subject, but they become clear subject nominatives through their position, i.e. by being placed before the verb, and even the pronouns that have a distinctive nominative form have this position: 'The *wind* blows.' 'The *winds* blow.' '*He* is industrious.' '*They* are industrious.'

In transferring a sentence with active verb to a form of statement with passive verb the accusative object of the active becomes nominative: 'He beat *me* in tennis today' (active). '*I* was beaten by him in tennis today' (passive). If there are a dative and an accusative object in the active there will be a double form in the passive. Active form: 'He gave *them ample warning.*' In the passive the accusative of the active becomes nominative and the dative is retained, or the dative of the active becomes nominative and the accusative is retained: '*Ample warning* was given *them*' or '*They* were given *ample warning.*' Notice that in questions the retained accusative may introduce the sentence: '*What* was he paid?' Compare *Syntax*, **15** I 2 *a*.

The subject nominative usually, as in the preceding examples, stands before a finite verb, i.e. a verb that agrees with its subject in number and person. In subordinate clauses, however, the subject nominative sometimes stands before a predicate participle, adjective, noun, adverb, or prepositional phrase: 'Off we started, *he* remaining behind' (= *while he remained behind*). 'It is doubtful if he had quite listened — *he having* (= *because he had*) so much to not listen to at the Home Office that the practice was growing on him' (Galsworthy, *Freelands*, Ch. XVI). 'We sail on Tuesday, *weather* permitting' (= *if the weather permits*). 'He lay on his back, his *knees* in the air, his *hands* crossed behind his back.' '*Thou* away, the very birds are mute' (Shakespeare). In colloquial speech the accusative is often used instead of the nominative: 'You wouldn't expect anything else, would you, *me* (instead of choicer *I*) being here like this, so suddenly, and talking face to face with you' (Arnold Bennett, *Sacred and Profane Love*, Act I, p. 25). This style of predication without the aid of a finite verb is the old appositional type of predication explained in **12** 3. The literary nominative employed in these clauses is called the nominative absolute. The construction is described in detail in **18 B 1**, **15** 2 *b*, *c*, *d*, *f*, *h*, *i*, also in *Syntax*, **17** 3 A, B, C.

On the other hand, in infinitive clauses the subject of the infinitive, as explained in **47** 5 *a*, is often a dative, an accusative, or *for* + an accusative: 'I told *him* (dative) to do it.' 'I begged *him* (accusative) to do it.' '*For me* to back out now would be to acknowledge that I am afraid.' The subject in gerundial clauses is a genitive or an accusative: 'I do not approve of my *son's* (or *son*) doing such a thing.' The form of the subject of the gerund is discussed in **47** 6 *a*. Thus it is evident that the subject of a verb is not always a nominative. In the course of the development of English other cases have come into use here in certain constructions.

b. *Predicate*. The predicate nominative is recognized by its position after a linking (**12** 3) verb: 'It is *he*.' 'She is my *sister*.' Here the subject of the sentence is a nominative. Where something is predicated of an accusative object the predicate is an accusative. See 2 *c* below.

Only a few personal pronouns have a distinct nominative form for the predicate relation: *I*, *he*, *she*, *we*, *they*. In choice English these forms are the usual ones for the predicate nominative relation, but in colloquial speech they are replaced here by the corresponding accusatives: 'It was *me*, *him*, *her*, *us*, *them*,' instead of the literary forms *I*, *he*, *she*, *we*, *they*. Compare *Syntax*, **7** C *a*.

The predicate nominative is found not only after a linking verb, i.e. a copula, as in the preceding examples, but also after the passive forms of certain transitive (**12** 1) verbs: 'He was made *a general*.' 'He was proclaimed *king*.' 'He is considered *the best man* for the place.' The predicate nominative is often introduced by the particle *as*: 'She is regarded *as the best teacher* in the school.' The predicate nominative in the passive form of statement corresponds to the predicate accusative in the active form of statement: 'The President made him *a general*.' Compare **27** 2 *c* (2nd par.).

c. *Direct Address*. The nominative of address is known by its peculiar intonation and its independent position in the sentence, having a close relation to the thought, but without any relation to the grammatical structure: 'O *Mary*, go and call the cattle home!' In older languages the noun in direct address often had a special case form called the *vocative*.

Accusative

2. **Functions.** The accusative has three functions. It plays the rôle of object, adverb, or objective predicate (i.e. the noun that predicates something of an object).

a. Accusative Object. The accusative of a noun or pronoun is widely used to modify the verb closely — here called accusative (or direct) object. Its relation to the verb is a little closer than that of an adverbial element. The pause between verb and adverb is greater than that between verb and object, but, of course, in both cases the pause is slight. We might say that there is no pause between verb and object and a slight one between verb and adverb. Jespersen in *The Philosophy of Grammar* (p. 103) tells the story of a boy who in reading a passage understood 'Job cursed *the day* (object) that he was born' as meaning 'Job cursed (slight pause) *the day that he was born.*' If *cursed* and *the day* are closely connected in thought, *the day* is an object. If there is a slight pause between *cursed* and *the day*, what follows the pause is an adverbial element. The boy, pausing in thought where he ought to have read straight on, got a wrong idea of the sentence.

An interesting variety of this object — the cognate object — has come into wide use in English: 'He lives *a sad and lonely life.*' For a fuller description see **12** 1 (3rd par.).

But a noun or a pronoun may be the object of another part of speech than a verb. It may serve also as the object of a preposition or an adjective. The object function is indicated by placing the noun or the pronoun after the verb, preposition, or adjective: 'The dog bit my *brother* and *me.*' 'He is sitting by *me* on the *sofa.*' 'This book is worth (adjective) *reading.*'

A full discussion of the use of the accusative as the object of verbs is given in *Syntax*, **11** 1, 2. The various uses of the accusative as the object of prepositions have already been given in **16** 1 *b*. *Worth* is the only adjective that takes an accusative object: 'He isn't worth *a dollar.*' 'It is worth *while, doing, having, troubling* oneself about.' '*What* is the house worth?' Adjectives usually have as object a prepositional phrase, a so-called prepositional object consisting of a preposition and its object: 'She is fond *of music.*' 'He is eager *for gain.*' Compare **16** 1 *b* (2nd par.). Also an intransitive (**12** 2) verb may have a prepositional object: 'He is shooting *at a mark.*' Compare **16** 1 *b*.

b. Adverbial Accusative. The accusative of a noun or pronoun is often used adverbially as a modifier of a verb, an adjective, or an adverb: 'He stayed *an hour.*' 'This pole is *a foot* longer.' 'He stayed *a day* longer than I did.' 'He died *the next day.*' 'He died *that year.*' The adverbial accusative of time is common with the relative pronoun *that*: 'The day *that* he died was a momentous one for America.' *That* is sometimes an adverbial accusative of manner: 'This is not the way *that* you are expected to act.' Certain of these accusatives impart feeling to the statement: 'I don't care *a damn*' (or '*a* tinker's *cuss*'). This force is often conveyed, not by the accusative but by the adjective that stands before it: 'He doesn't care a *blessed* thing for us.' 'She is a *deuced* deal cleverer than lots of men.' Compare **7** VII *c cc*. For fuller treatment see **71** 1 *a*.

c. Predicate Accusative. A noun or pronoun which is predicated of an accusative object is in the accusative and is called an objective predicate or a predicate accusative: 'They supposed us to be *them.*' 'A boy whom I believed to be *him* just passed.' Compare **47** 5 *a* (8th par.).

A clear accusative form, of course, is found only in the case of pronouns that have a distinctive accusative, as in the preceding examples. Usually only the function shows that we have to do with a predicate accusative: 'The president made him *a general.*' 'The king dubbed his son *a knight.*' 'They elected him *temporary chairman.*' 'We thought the fellow *a coward.*' 'We consider him *a very fine teacher.*' 'They named him *John.*' 'He called me *a liar.*' The predicate accusative is often introduced by the particle *as:* 'They represent him *as a reliable man.*' The objective predicate may be also a clause: 'His rigid discipline has made me *what I am.*'

The predicate accusatives in the first paragraph are linked to their accusative subjects by the copula (**12** 3) *be*. The predicate accusatives in the second paragraph are a much older type of predicate, a predicate without the aid of a copula, as explained in **12** 3.

Dative

3. Function and Forms. The dative modifies the verb closely and is thus an object. To distinguish it from the accusative (or direct) object (**27** 2 *a*), with which it is often connected, we call it the dative (or indirect) object. The dative object indicates that an action or feeling is directed toward a person or thing to his or its advantage or disadvantage. This function is indicated in two ways — by a simple noun or pronoun, or by a preposition + the noun or pronoun. The preposition here is a mere formal sign to mark the following noun or pronoun as a dative.

We usually call this case the dative of advantage or disadvantage, as in 'He offered (or 'refused') *me* his support,' but we often call it the dative of reference where the related idea of personal reference is prominent: 'He offered (or 'refused') *me* his support, but he didn't offer (or 'refuse') it *to my brother.*' 'It doesn't seem fair *to me.*' 'His hat is too large *for me.*' 'He bowed *to me.*' As in the last three examples, the dative of reference is often used with intransitives (**12** 2). Compare *Syntax*, **12** 1.

a. Simple Dative. We still often employ the simple form of the noun or pronoun: 'This woman is making *her little son* a new coat.' The dative is recognized by its position before the accusative, the direct object of the verb. It has held its position before the accusative for thousands of years, and its position is so much a characteristic feature of it that we can often recognize it by its position although it often does not have a distinctive form. Sometimes, however, the context alone indicates that the noun or pronoun is performing the dative function: 'The woman who makes *a man* (dative = *to the advantage of a man*) a good wife also makes *him* (accusative, direct object of the verb) a good husband.' 'They chose *him* (dative) a wife,' but 'They chose *him* (accusative) king.' English is here at its simplest. Form disappears entirely. The context alone distinguishes dative and accusative. Compare *Syntax*, **11** 1.

b. Prepositional Dative. This dative has the same force as the older simple dative. As the older dative has lost the distinctive endings that it had in older English the newer form is often preferred as a clearer dative form. It is made by placing the inflectional preposition (**17**) *to* or *for* before the simple noun or pronoun: 'The mother is making a new coat *for her boy John.* She will give his old one *to his little brother.*' 'The mother is sewing *for her boy;* she is making a new coat *for him.* She will give it *to him* when he comes home from school.' The prepositional dative forms with *for* and *to* both express advantage here, but the same forms may express also discomfort, disadvantage: 'I set a trap *for the mouse.*' 'She gave the scolding this time *to the girls,* where it properly belonged.' Thus for many centuries the same forms have been used for both advantage and disadvantage. There is a tendency at present to differentiate English expression here — to employ *to* and *for* for advantage and *on* for disadvantage. *On* cannot be freely used for disadvantage, but in the colloquial language of our time it is playing an important part: 'He played his *father* (old simple dative) a mean trick,' or 'He played a mean trick *on his father*' (new prepositional dative of disadvantage). 'She hung up [the receiver] *on him.*' 'He turned the light out *on them.*' 'They raised the rent *on us.*' The *on*-dative is common in Irish English, which at this point may be influencing American English.

But for many hundreds of years there has been a similar *on* in the literary language. It is used for advantage or disadvantage: 'She smiled *on* me.' 'He turned his back *on* me.' But the idea of disadvantage is ever becoming more prominent in *on*; so that *on* + noun (or pronoun) is developing into a dative of disadvantage worthy of use in choice language: 'His pursuers are gaining *on him.*' 'This strain is beginning to tell *on her.*' This distinctive form for disadvantage enables us to express our thought more accurately than in older English. For fuller discussion see *Syntax*, **11** 1, **12** 1 B *a*, *b*, *c*.

Genitive

4. **Functions, Forms, Meanings.** The genitive has three functions, four forms, and a number of distinct but related meanings. These things will be discussed in the following articles.

A. *Attributive Genitive.* This genitive is treated at considerable length in *Syntax*, **10** II. Attention is directed here chiefly to matters of form and an outline of its functions.

a. Function and Meaning. The attributive genitive modifies a noun or pronoun and thus plays the part of an adjective. It expresses many related ideas, *origin, possession, subject, object, material, composition, characteristic, measure, apposition, a whole from which a part is taken:* '*Shakespeare's* (origin) dramas'; '*John's* (possession) hat'; '*mother's* (subject) love for us'; '*Caesar's* (object) murderers'; 'an idol *of gold*' (material); 'a flock *of birds*' (composition); 'a *child's* (characteristic) language'; 'an *hour's* (measure) delay'; 'the gift *of song*' (apposition); 'a piece *of bread*' (whole from which a part is taken). These meanings are described at length in *Syntax*, **10** II 2.

b. Form. There are four forms of the genitive.

(1). *S*-Genitive. An *'s* is added to a noun not ending in an *s*-sound: 'the *girl's* hat,' etc. Of course we write *Descartes's, Dumas's*, for the *s* and *es* before the genitive ending are silent. An *'s* is added also to plurals not ending in *-s:* '*men's* clothing.' The *'s* in all these examples is pronounced as a simple *s*.

An *'s* is usually added to nouns ending in an *s*-sound: '*James's* hat.' The *'s* here is never pronounced as a simple *s* but always as *ĕs*. This is the survival of older usage when all nouns could take *ĕs* in the genitive singular. This older usage was still lingering in Shakespeare's day: 'as white as whalĕs bone' (*Love's Labor's Lost*, V, ii, 332). The *e* of the old genitive ending began to disappear about 1380 and finally in the early part of the Modern English period disappeared entirely except in the case of nouns ending in an *s*-sound, where it in general survives although it is not written. In the Middle English and early Modern English periods the *s* of the genitive ending was often suppressed in nouns ending in an *s*-sound. This older usage lingers: '*Cards*' pride' (Hugh Walpole, *Fortitude*, p. 80), 'greatly to *Charles*' surprise' (Hergesheimer, *The Bright Shawl*, p. 20). This older usage survives especially in a few set expressions and a few foreign names difficult to pronounce with the genitive *s*-ending: for old *acquaintance*' sake, for *goodness*' sake, for *conscience*' sake, Jesus', Xerxes', Socrates', etc. In general, however, the *'s* of the genitive ending is more common in nouns ending in an *s*-sound than it was in early Modern English, and is gradually becoming established. On the other hand, *s* is never added in the genitive plural to nouns ending in *–s* in the plural: 'the *ladies*' club,' 'the *girls*' hats,' 'the *Joneses*' garage.'

In compounds the genitive *'s* is added to the last component: 'Hop-o'-my-*thumb's* mother,' 'my brother-in-*law's* new house.' In such compounds as the latter of these examples the plural ending *–s*, in contrast to the genitive ending *–'s*, is added to the first component: 'my two *brothers*-in-law.'

In older English, when there were two *s*-genitives connected by a coördinating conjunction, the genitive ending was often added only to the second genitive, while present usage requires each genitive to take the ending: 'My *wife* (now *wife's*) *and children's* ghosts will haunt me still' (Shakespeare, *Macbeth*, V, vii, 16).

The apostrophe is not found with the *s*-genitive in older English: 'in *Gods* care' (Chettle, *Kind-Hartes Dreame*, p. 22, A.D. 1592), '*Gods* grace' (Bradford, *History of Plymouth Plantation*, p. 32, A.D. 1630–1648). The apostrophe began to appear about 1680, gaining ground at first only slowly. Its use cannot possibly rest upon a careful observation of the spoken language. In '*James's* hat' the vowel before the second *s* in *James's* is not suppressed. The apostrophe before the second *s* here probably arose from the misconception that *James's* is a contraction of *James his*, the old *his*-genitive (see (4) p. 136), which was still employed at the time when the apostrophe came into use. This theory does not explain the use of *'s* after a feminine or a plural noun. The *'s* spread by analogy from masculine nouns to feminines and plurals. The old *s*-genitive without an apostrophe survives in *his, hers, ours, yours, theirs.*

(2). *Of*-Genitive. This form is composed of the inflectional preposition *of* (**17**) and a noun. This prepositional phrase indicates exactly the same grammatical relation as the simple *s*-genitive, and historically has taken the place of the old simple *s*-genitive and the other old inflectional genitives that in Old English stood after the governing noun. As originally, the *of*-genitive still always follows the governing noun. The simple *s*-genitive originally stood either before the governing noun or after it but is now restricted to the position before it, so that now the simple *s*-genitive stands before the governing noun and the *of*-genitive stands after it: '*the man's* son' or 'the son *of the man*'; 'the *fox's* tail' or 'the tail *of the fox*.'

The simple *s*-genitive and the *of*-genitive always have the same grammatical function but do not always have exactly the same meaning. When there are two forms for the same thing there is a tendency for them to become differentiated. Today the *s*-genitive has become associated with life and cannot usually be used with nouns that denote lifeless things. Thus today we say '*a boy's* leg' but not 'a *table's* leg.' For things we usually employ the *of*-genitive: 'the leg *of the table*.' The *s*-genitive is used with names of things only when in lively language they are thought of as having life: 'the *ocean's* roar,' '*Duty's* call,' 'for the sake of the *mind's* peace.' 'A *book's* chances depend more on its selling qualities than its worth.' On the other hand, with reference to persons and other living beings both genitive forms are used without a difference of meaning: '*the man's* son' or 'the son *of the man*.'

It is interesting to see how we lost the old *s*-genitive that in the Old English period stood after the governing noun. In Old English it became ever more common for the *s*-genitive to stand after the governing noun, and in this position it was at that time a perfectly clear form: 'þa leaf *þæs treowes*' = 'the leaves *of the tree*.' In Old English the article þæs before the *s*-genitive was inflected, had an *s*-genitive form itself, so that the thought was clear. When the article later lost its inflection the old *s*-genitive in this position disappeared, since its reduced form — 'the leaves *the trees*' — conveyed no meaning. It was replaced by the *of*-genitive: 'the leaves *of the tree*.' In (3) below we shall see that the *s*-genitive in somewhat changed form later came back into use in the position after the governing noun. It cannot, however, be so freely used in this position as the *of*-genitive. See (3) below.

(3). Double Genitive. The *s*-genitive that in the Old English period stood after the governing noun disappeared in Middle English, as described in the last paragraph of (2) above. It had scarcely disappeared when its loss was keenly felt. About 1300, attempts were made to restore it. To avoid the lack of clearness that had come into the *s*-genitive in the position after the governing noun the new genitive sign *of* was placed before the old *s*-genitive so that there arose a clear new somewhat changed *s*-genitive, a double genitive, a form having the same force as the simple *s*-genitive and, like it, referring to persons: 'a friend *of my father's,*' 'this only son *of our mayor's,*' 'this remark *of Carlyle's,*' 'after quoting a word or two *of Shakespeare's,*' 'an admirer *of Mary's.*' This form is common also with possessive pronouns, which are old genitive forms: 'He is no friend *of mine.*' 'That is no business *of yours.*' 'What business is that *of yours?*' We say 'a beautiful picture *of hers*' (i.e. belonging to her) in contrast to 'a beautiful picture (i.e. likeness) *of her.*' The double genitive is often associated with emotional *this* and *that* (**10** 3 *i*), so that it is a common feature of lively language expressing praise and censure, joy and displeasure: '*that* dear little girl *of yours,*' '*that* old dog *of yours,*' '*this* broad land *of ours,*' '*that* ugly remark *of her father's,*' '*that* kind wife *of yours,*' '*that* ugly nose *of his.*'

(4). *His*-Genitive. In older English instead of an *s*-genitive a genitive formed with *his, her, their,* was often used: '*John his* book,' '*Mary her* book,' '*the boys their* books.' This genitive was occasionally used in Old English. It became common between 1500 and 1700, and later gradually disappeared from the literary language. It survives in popular speech. Compare *Syntax,* **10** II 1 (5th par.).

B. *Predicate Genitive.* After the verbs *be, become, seem, feel,* a predicate genitive is used to express several ideas found also in the attributive genitive, namely, characteristic, origin, possession, material, and the partitive idea: 'I am quite *of your opinion.*' 'We are *of the same age.*' 'He was not *of the poor class.*' 'Render therefore unto Caesar the things which are *Caesar's,* and unto God the things which are *God's*' (*Matthew,* XXII, 21). 'The floors are *of tiles.*' 'But ye believe not because ye are not *of my sheep*' (*John,* X, 26).

The genitive is used also as objective predicate: 'He showed himself *of noble spirit,*' or 'He showed himself *to be of noble spirit.*'

The predicate genitive is treated more fully in *Syntax,* **7** A *e.*

C. *Adverbial Genitive.* In Old English the *s*-genitive of nouns was often used adverbially: 'He com to him *anes nihtes*' = 'He came to him *one night.*' As can be seen by the translation we now employ the accusative here. But the old genitive survives here and there: *always, nowadays,* must *needs,* etc. The old *s*-genitive survives in many adverbs: *once* (from *ones*), *twice* (from *twies*), *thrice, unawares, afterwards,* etc. The old *s*-genitive has been replaced in certain expressions by the newer *of*-genitive: '*of late years,*' '*of a Sunday afternoon,*' etc.: 'He often comes in *of an evening.*' Compare **71** 1 *a.*

Notice that there is now, as originally, no apostrophe with the *s*-genitive in adverbial use.

Instrumental

5. **Function, Form, Meaning.** The central idea of the old instrumental case was that of association. In Old English, it indicated that something was associated with an act in the way of an instrument or a cause: '*Sweorde* swebban' 'to kill *with* a sword'; 'lustfullien þaes biscopes *wordum*' 'to rejoice *on account of the words* of the bishop.' It was used also with adjectives to indicate in what respect a quality could be associated with a person or thing: '*feðrum* strong' 'strong *with respect to its wings*.' The old instrumental survives in adverbial *the* (**71** 1 *c*), the old instrumental case of demonstrative *that:* 'We are *the* better for mastering difficulties,' literally, 'We are better *on that account* — for our mastering difficulties.' The instrumental has ceased to be felt as a case, although it in fact is used as much as ever. As can be seen by the translations of the Old English instrumentals just given, we express the ideas contained in the old instrumental by prepositional phrases, the different prepositions now used conveying the thought more accurately than the old instrumental. In Old English, the instrumental case no longer had a special case form for nouns, the dative here performing the functions of dative and instrumental. Thus the dative was overburdened by functions, so that later, in order to make the thought clearer, it was felt as expedient to relieve the dative of its instrumental functions and at the same time express these ideas more accurately by employing prepositions. Compare **15** 2 *k*. The modern instrumental phrase, like the old instrumental case, has adverbial force. Compare **15** 2 *k*.

GENDER

28. Gender is the distinction of words into masculine, feminine, and neuter. Our nouns follow natural gender. Names of male beings are masculine: *man, father, uncle, boy,* etc. Names of female beings are feminine: *woman, mother, aunt, girl,* etc. The names of inanimate things are neuter: *house, tree, street, stone, whiteness,* etc. Some feminine nouns, as *duck, goose,* and many masculine, as *dog, horse, teacher, editor,* are often used to denote either sex where there is no desire to be accurate. Such nouns are said to be of common gender.

In modern English sex is usually indicated by the meaning of the noun itself, much less commonly by a formal sign: man, woman; boy, girl; uncle, aunt; king, queen. By a formal sign: Joseph, Joseph*ine*; Franc*is*, Franc*es*; deacon, deacon*ess*; hero, hero*ine*; aviator, aviatr*ix*; sultan, sultan*a*. The list of such words is given in full in *Syntax*, **60** 1 *c*. Some of the formal signs are of foreign origin and still felt as such. The commonest of the formal signs that have been in use a long time is *-ess*. The list of words in *-ess* (*Syntax*, **60** 1 *c*), though still long, has been steadily decreasing for centuries. *Teacheress*, *singeress*, etc., sound strange to us today. Formal signs are losing their hold on English feeling. The present tendency is to employ a noun or a personal pronoun used as an adjective: *girl* cashier, *woman* clerk, *man* friend, *men* friends, *girl* friend, *girl* friends, *women* voters, *she* bear, *he* bear, *billy* goat, *nanny* goat, *tom* cat, *tabby* cat, *buck* rabbit, *doe* rabbit, *hen* pigeon, etc. Fuller list in *Syntax*, **60** 1 *b*. Also adjectives are employed here: *male* cat, *female* cat, *fair* readers. The necessities of life require us still in a large number of cases to indicate sex, but in the literary language and in our daily life there is a marked and growing disinclination to do this with reference to man or beast. With such nouns as *editor*, *lecturer*, *leader*, *teacher*, *doctor*, etc., we avoid the use of a feminine sign for fear it might suggest the idea of inferiority. On the other hand, when we desire to speak disparagingly there is always a handy word for each sex: *frump*, *dowd*, *slattern*, *termagant*, *virago*, *minx*, *hussy*, *prude*, etc.; *dude*, *fop*, *masher*, *bruiser*, *ruffian*, etc. We can hit hardest with the pronouns *that* and *it* for reference to males: 'Would you like to marry Malcolm? Fancy being owned by *that!* Fancy seeing *it* every day!' (Elinor Glyn, *Vicissitudes of Evangeline*, p. 127). Compare **33** *b*.

In plain normal English every gender form indicates sex or sexlessness. Thus modern English gender is of a character radically different from that of the other languages that belong to our family and radically different also from that of the oldest stage of English itself. In Old English there was grammatical gender, i.e. for grammatical purposes the names of lifeless things were often masculine or feminine. *Stone* was masculine, *book* feminine, *sun* feminine, *moon* masculine, etc. A similar order of things is found in all the related languages ancient and modern. In the early periods of the oldest languages of our family the imagination may have played an important rôle in assigning gender to nouns. Even much later in the Old English period the imagination was still active, but for the most part the gender forms in both nouns and adjectives had become mere grammatical devices to link adjectives to the nouns that they modified. In Old English, adjectives had more distinctive forms for gender and case than nouns had. As they stood before the nouns that they modified they indicated not only their relation to the noun but indicated also the part that the noun played in the sentence, i.e. they showed whether the noun was subject or object.

In the course of the Middle English period the English people utterly destroyed the old system of distinctive endings for gender and case in noun and adjective and replaced it by a system of distinctive position for noun and adjective. In the subject relation the noun was placed before the verb, in the objective relation it was placed after the verb, and the adjective was left in its old position before the noun. As position now indicated the function of noun and adjective, the old endings for gender and case — except the *-s* of the genitive of nouns — disappeared as useless forms.

With the gender forms disappeared also in serious prose the conception of life which had been associated with many nouns that denoted lifeless things. Thus serious English prose changed its character somewhat. It became more composed. Elsewhere, however, the old association of life with lifeless things survived, and became a characteristic feature of animated English. The older conceptions of gender could not be preserved intact because the gender forms had disappeared and there was nothing left to recall the older order of things. The old gender of certain very familiar things lingered a long while, for instance the conception of the *sun* as feminine, but the older gender could not be maintained. Foreign ideas of gender as found in French and Latin suggested themselves and came into wide use in animated language. *Ship* was treated as feminine under the influence of the corresponding Old French word. *Sun* finally became established as masculine under the influence of the corresponding Latin noun. In the choice animated language of poetry and higher diction the following usage is widely observed. *Sun, time, ocean, love, anger, discord, murder, rivers, mountains, winds, seasons,* are treated as masculine. *Earth, moon, church, nature, religion, soul, night, charity, liberty, victory, mercy, cities, countries, ships,* etc., are treated as feminine. But the gender of animation has its widest boundaries in colloquial and popular speech. Here usage differs in the different sections of a country and in different countries, but there is a general trend toward the feminine gender. In America the feminine gender has long been such a favorite that the masculine has almost disappeared: It is used for everything without regard to literary usage: '*Sun she* rise up en shine hot' (Joel Chandler Harris, *Nights with Uncle Remus,* p. 34). 'That helps the blood to draw the *wart,* and pretty soon off *she* comes' (Mark Twain, *Tom Sawyer*). 'My fiddle? — Well, I kind o' keep *her* handy' (James Whitcomb Riley, *Neighborly Poems,* p. 36). In literary English, Americans usually follow literary usage: 'The *sun* moves steadily northward, and with *him* come hepatica and wake-robin' (*The Chicago Daily News,* Editorial, Feb. 29, 1932).

But even in the literary language in general the fondness for the feminine gender may assert itself in animated style. In *The National Geographic Magazine*, August, 1933, Lieut. Col. L. V. S. Blacker, O.B.E., writes in an article on flying over Mt. Everest: 'A moment later came Everest *herself*, flanked by the snowy pyramid of Makalu.'

OLDER INFLECTION OF NOUNS

29. Old English Inflection of Nouns. The Old English inflections of nouns are presented here in only general outlines, for our present inflections are not in a large measure developed out of them, but represent almost an entire break with the older systems. But as certain of the older types of inflection have been in part preserved, a study of the older systems is helpful in understanding our inheritance. Some of the irregularities and peculiarities in current usage become intelligible to us only in the light of these older conditions. This brief study of the older inflections of nouns will serve another useful purpose. It will enhance the appreciation of our present improved means of expression, whose simplicity and clearness should become evident in contrast to the complexity and not infrequent ambiguity of the older inflections.

I. Strong Inflection

A. Masculine Nouns

	stone	*son*	*foot*	*man*	*brother*
			Singular		
Nom.	stān	sun*u*, *-o*	fōt	man(n), manna	brōþor
Acc.	stān	sun*u*, *-o*	fōt	man(n), mannan	brōþor
Dat.	stāne	suna	fēt	men(n)	brēþer
Gen.	stānes	suna	fōtes	mannes	brōþor
			Plural		
Nom.	stānas	suna	fēt	men(n)	brōþor, broþru
Acc.	stānas	suna	fēt	men(n)	brōþor, brōþru
Dat.	stānum	sunum	fōtum	mannum	brōþrum
Gen.	stāna	suna	fōta	manna	brōþra

B. Feminine Nouns

	tale	*herd*	*hand*	*book*	*mother*
			Singular		
Nom.	tal*u*, *-o*	heord	hand	bōc	mōdor
Acc.	tale	heorde	hand	bōc	mōdor
Dat.	tale	heorde	handa	bēc	mēder
Gen.	tale	heorde	handa	bēc, bōce	mōdor

Plural

Nom.	tal*a*, *–e*	heord*a*, *–e*	handa	bēc	mōdor, mōdru
Acc.	tal*a*, *–e*	heord*a*, *–e*	handa	bēc	mōdor, mōdru
Dat.	talum	heordum	handum	bōcum	mōdrum
Gen.	tal*a*, *–ena*	heord*a*, *–na*	handa	bōca	mōdra

C. Neuter Nouns

Singular

	word	*hole*	*wonder*	*knee*	*child*
Nom.	word	hol	wundor	cneo(w)	cild
Acc.	word	hol	wundor	cneo(w)	cild
Dat.	worde	hole	wundre	cneowe	cilde
Gen.	wordes	holes	wundres	cneowes	cildes

Plural

Nom.	word	hol*u*, *–o*	wundor	cneo(w)	cild, cildru
Acc.	word	hol*u*, *–o*	wundor	cneo(w)	cild, cildru
Dat.	wordum	holum	wundrum	cneowum	cildrum
Gen.	worda	hola	wundra	cneowa	cildra

Notice that in this old period the apostrophe was not used with the genitive ending *–s*.

II. Weak Inflection

	Masculine	Feminine	Neuter
		Singular	
	name	*tongue*	*eye*
Nom.	nama	tunge	eage
Acc.	naman	tungan	eage
Dat.	naman	tungan	eagan
Gen.	naman	tungan	eagan
		Plural	
Nom.	naman	tungan	eagan
Acc.	naman	tungan	eagan
Dat.	namun	tungum	eagum
Gen.	namena	tungena	eagena

30. Middle English Inflection of Nouns

I. Strong Inflection

A. Masculine Nouns

Singular

	stone	*son*	*foot*	*man*	*brother*
Nom.	stōn	sone	fōt	man	brōther
Acc.	stōn	sone	fōt	man	brōther
Dat.	stōn(e)	sone	fōt(e)	man(ne)	brōther
Gen.	stōnes	sones	fōtes	mannes	brōther(es)

Plural

Nom.	stōnes	sones	fēt	men	brēther brētheren brōtheres
Acc.	stōnes	sones	fēt	men	brēther brētheren brōtheres
Dat.	stōnes	sones	fēt	men	brēther brētheren brōtheres
Gen.	stōnes	sones	fētes	mennes	brēther brētheren brētheres

B. Feminine Nouns

Singular

	tale	*herd*	*hand*	*book*	*mother*
Nom.	tale	herde	hand	bōk	mōder
Acc.	tale	herde	hand	bōk	mōder
Dat.	tale	herde	hand(e)	bōk(e)	mōder
Gen.	tal*e*, *–es*	herd*e*, *–es*	hand*e*, *–es*	bōkes	mōder, mōdres

Plural

Nom.	tales	herdes	handes	bōkes	mōder mōdres, mōdren
Acc.	tales	herdes	handes	bōkes	mōder mōdres, mōdren
Dat.	tales	herdes	handes	bōkes	mōder mōdres, mōdren
Gen.	tales	herdes	handes	bōkes	mōder mōdres, mōdren

C. Neuter Nouns

Singular

	word	*hole*	*wonder*	*knee*	*child*
Nom.	word	hole	wonder	knē	child
Acc.	word	hole	wonder	knē	child
Dat.	word(e)	hole	wonder	knē(e)	child(e)
Gen.	wordes	holes	wondres	knēes	childes

Plural

Nom.	wordes	holes	wondres	knēes	children, childer
Acc.	wordes	holes	wondres	knēes	children, childer
Dat.	wordes	holes	wondres	knēes	children, childer
Gen.	wordes	holes	wondres	knēes	children, childer

II. Weak Inflection

	Masculine	Feminine	Neuter
		Singular	
	name	*tongue*	*eye*
Nom.	name	tonge	eye
Acc.	name	tonge	eye
Dat.	name	tonge	eye
Gen.	name, *–es*	tonge, *–es*	eye, *–es*
		Plural	
Nom.	nam*en*, *–es*	tong*en*, *–es*	ey*en*, *–es*
Acc.	nam*en*, *–es*	tong*en*, *–es*	ey*en*, *–es*
Dat.	nam*en*, *–es*	tong*en*, *–es*	ey*en*, *–es*
Gen.	nam*en*(*e*), *–es*	tong*en*(*e*), *–es*	ey*en*(*e*), *–es*

a. In all the above Middle English groups only the synthetic genitive — the genitive formed by an ending — is given, but alongside of it was in wide use the newer *of*-genitive, which arose in Old English, at first employed in only a few categories, but gradually spreading to others. Notice that in this older period the apostrophe was not used with the genitive ending *–s*.

b. The Old English gender of the above Middle English words has been given merely for the purpose of comparison with the Old English. In fact Middle English nouns no longer had grammatical gender (**28** 3rd par.). The breaking up of the older inflections of nouns and adjectives and the consequent loss of distinctive endings had contributed a good deal to its final elimination from the language. Compare **31** and *Syntax*, **60** 2. This disintegration of the older inflections began in the North at the close of the Old English period and gradually spread southward. There was little left of the old grammatical gender in the Midland at the beginning of the thirteenth century; it had disappeared from the Southern dialects by the close of the fourteenth.

31. General Principles at Work in the Development of the Inflection of English Nouns. As can be seen by a glance at the Old English inflections there was in this early period of our language an intricate system of indicating number, case, and gender. But Old English expression of number, case, and gender, in spite of the multiplicity of their forms, often lacked clearness, and, by reason of this multiplicity, always lacked simplicity. The peculiar circumstances of the Middle English period facilitated a marked development in the direction of greater simplicity. In the early formative part of the period English was not a widely used literary language with firmly fixed usage. It had been abandoned by people of culture in their literary expression and was used by them only in their practical everyday life. Thus the development of English was largely left to the plain and practical common people, who stood close to the present with its pressing needs and had little to do with the literary language of the past and hence were little influenced by its fixed usage. The weakening of the older full vowels to *e* in the unstressed Middle English case endings rendered unclear the grammatical relations in the genitive singular and throughout the plural. The common people, untrammeled by literary tradition, chose from among the different endings used to mark the genitive singular and the four cases of the plural the common ending *-s* as the clearest of the available forms to mark the genitive in the singular and all the cases of the plural. In Middle English in the South of England, the *en*-plural manifested for a time a tendency to spread, but it too was finally for the most part supplanted by the *s*-plural. The *en*-plural survives in only a few words, *oxen*, *children*, *brethren*, etc. Compare **23** 2.

Other Old English types of expression have become fixed in certain words: *man*, *men; foot*, *feet; sheep*, *sheep;* one *fish*, a boatload of *fish;* etc. In the first two examples the retention of the old form is explained by the great frequency of the words. In the last two examples the old form has been retained as we have put into it a new meaning and thus made it useful. The identity of form in the singular and the plural here suggests the employment of this plural form when we desire to indicate that the idea of mass is more prominent in our feeling than that of separate individuals. For fuller discussion see **23** 4.

One of the outstanding features in the Middle English period was the persistent struggle to secure a clear uniform plural for nouns. In Old English, the nominative and accusative plural was often the same as case forms of the singular. The plural idea was frequently expressed by the plural form of the adjective that stood before the noun, so that the adjective was not only a word that modified the meaning of the noun but also a grammatical form that indicated the number and the case of the noun: '*þa þing* þe ge hyrdon' '*the things* that you have heard.' Here the article *þa* has distinctive plural form, while the noun *þing*, though in the plural, has the same form as the singular. As can be seen by the translation, the noun now has plural form, while the preceding adjective is uninflected. Since the noun now has a clear plural form, there is no need of inflecting the adjective, so that the adjective, once characterized by its rich inflection, has become invariable. This development began in Middle English and by the close of the period was an accomplished fact. Of the many Old English inflected adjectives only two now have forms to indicate the plural: *that, those; this, these.* A number of adjectives, such as *many, five, six, few,* etc., indicate a plural idea by virtue of their meaning. But in general we now feel that the plural idea should be expressed by the noun alone, for it has nothing to do with the meaning and the function of most adjectives. This development has greatly simplified the structure of our language.

Another important step was taken in the direction of simplicity when grammatical gender was entirely discarded. By a glance at the Old English inflections in **29** it will be seen that many nouns designating inanimate objects, such as *stone, tale, book,* etc., were once masculine or feminine. The beautiful and useful simplicity that has resulted from the disappearance of grammatical gender in Middle English is the result of a long development. A feeling for natural gender in contrast to grammatical gender began to manifest itself in Old English. Even in this early period the selection of a masculine or feminine personal pronoun in harmony with sex was quite common when the reference was to a neuter noun denoting a living being. This strong sense of sex helped develop the idea of sexlessness, so that a neuter personal pronoun was sometimes used when the reference was to a masculine or feminine noun denoting a lifeless thing. The development of the feeling for sex and sexlessness was greatly facilitated by the loss in Middle English of distinctive adjective endings to mark the gender. Compare **28** (4th par.).

One of the most marked developments in the Middle English period was the suppression of the adjective and noun endings that were employed to indicate the case relations of nouns. Except in the case of the *-s* of the genitive of nouns all the case endings of nouns and attributive adjectives disappeared. The new word-order, subject before the verb and object after it, made the grammatical relation here so clear that endings in nouns and attributive adjectives were felt as unnecessary.

CHAPTER X

INFLECTION OF PRONOUNS

32. Purposes of Inflection. Pronouns, like nouns, are inflected to indicate number, case, and gender. There are now only two numbers — the singular and the plural. In Old English, personal pronouns (**33** I) had a third number — the dual, for reference to two persons. Compare **34.** Later, the plural number was employed to express reference to two persons or things as well as reference to more than two.

The means employed in English to express number in nouns are in general simple, but the means employed to express number in pronouns lack this simplicity and vary from class to class. The variety of expression here comes from the fact that the different classes are of different origin. A number of the indefinites (**7** V) — *numbers, lots, worlds,* etc. — have an *s*-plural, as they were originally nouns. The plurals of the personal pronouns (**33** I) are peculiar old forms that stand all alone. In older English many pronouns that were formed from adjectives ended in the plural in the unstressed vowel *e*, the adjective plural ending. Today many of these pronouns are without an ending in the plural, as this old plural ending has disappeared: *many, both, some,* etc. In the case of *many, both,* etc., the meaning shows that the forms are plurals. In other cases the context indicates the number: '*some* (sing.) of the sugar,' '*some* (pl.) of the men.' '*Which* (sing.) of the books *is* the most interesting?' '*Which* (pl.) of the books *are* the most interesting?' Where the context does not indicate the number we now often employ a *one*-form to make the thought clear: 'I saw him looking over the books, but I don't know *which one* (sing.), or *which ones* (pl.), he selected.' For the development of the *one*-form see **43** 1 (2nd par.).

The cases of pronouns have the same force as those of nouns, as described in **27** 1, 2, 3, 4. The inflectional forms, however, are in part different. Personal pronouns (**33** I) and relative, interrogative, and indefinite *who* (**38** *a*) have more distinctive case forms than nouns, preserving certain older features of their inflection. The means employed to indicate the case relations vary from class to class, as described in detail below.

In general pronouns cannot indicate sex, but personal pronouns (**33** I) have special forms for this purpose. The pronoun *who* has a still older feature. It cannot distinguish sex, but it distinguishes life from lifeless. It now indicates a person or persons.

The seven classes are presented here in the same order as in 7.

I. PERSONAL PRONOUNS

33. These pronouns have three persons: the first person representing the speaker; the second the person spoken to; the third the person or thing spoken of. The forms for the third person have in the singular three genders (**28**), masculine, feminine, neuter.

Their inflection is as follows:

	FIRST PERSON	SECOND PERSON		THIRD PERSON		
	Singular	*Singular*		*Singular*		
		Old Form	Common Form	Masculine	Feminine	Neuter
Nom.	I	thou	you	he	she	it
Acc.	me	thee	you	him	her	it
	me	thee	you	him	her	it
Dat.	to me	to thee	to you	to him	to her	to it
	for me	for thee	for you	for him	for her	for it
	mine	thine	yours	his	hers	its
Gen.	my	thy	your		her	
	of me	of thee	of you	of him	of her	of it
	Plural	*Plural*		*Plural for All Genders*		
Nom.	we	ye	you		they	
Acc.	us	you	you		them	
	us	you	you		them	
Dat.	to us	to you	to you		to them	
	for us	for you	for you		for them	
	ours	yours	yours		theirs	
Gen.	our	your	your		their	
	of us	of you	of you		of them	

The use of the dative forms is described in **27** 3 *a*, *b*. Compare *Syntax*, **12** 1, **12** 1 B *a*, *b*, *c*.

Of the above forms the simple genitives were formerly used as personal pronouns, but they are now employed as possessive adjectives (**10** 1) and possessive pronouns (**7** VII *e*, **7** VII *e aa*, **42** *e*). Compare *Syntax*, **10** II 2 D (last par.).

Notice that, in accordance with older usage, there is still no apostrophe before the genitive *-s* in these pronouns. Compare **42** *c cc*. Differing from the other personal pronouns, *its*, earlier in the present period, often took the apostrophe: *it's* or *its*, now only *its*.

a. Use of the Third Person for the Second. Sometimes, as an especial mark of respect, a noun in the third person is employed instead of a personal pronoun in the second person: 'How is *the*

Captain this morning?' or more commonly 'How are *you* this morning, Captain?' The pronoun *it* is often, in playful humor, used instead of *you:* '"What's the matter, sweet one?" coming up and caressing Molly. "Is *it* worrying *itself* over that letter?"' (Mrs. Gaskell, *Wives and Daughters*, III, p. 69). *This* is often used instead of *you* or *I*. Compare **7** VII *b*, p. 24.

b. Use of 'It' for Reference to Things, Persons, Animals, Ideas. *It* is the usual form for reference to things. It is often used also for reference to a baby or a little child: 'As I came up to her little baby *it* stretched out *its* little arms to me.' This *it*, thus closely associated with the idea of the lack of personality, is often used disparagingly of persons, similarly also *that* and *what:* 'Would you like to marry Malcolm? Fancy being owned by *that!* Fancy seeing *it* every day!' (Elinor Glyn, *Vicissitudes of Evangeline*, p. 127). 'Well — [she is] the sort that takes up with impossible people — you really never know *What* you may meet in Agnes Hyde's rooms' (Mrs. Cecily Sidgwick, *The Severins*, Ch. XVI).

It often has the abstract idea of estate, rank, dignity: 'She is a queen and looks *it*.'

It can be used for reference to animals, although *he* and *she* are also employed. See *Syntax*, **60** 1 *d*.

It is often used as subject referring to some person or thing that is disclosed to us not by words but by the situation — situation *it:* '*It*'s John, or Anna, or the boys' (uttered by someone upon hearing approaching steps). 'Somebody sat behind him. A little later I saw that *it* was his brother.' 'Somebody sat behind him, but I couldn't see who *it* was.' Compare *Syntax*, **4** II A.

Situation *it* is often used as predicate: 'In the dance *it* (= *the important thing*) is grace. In a cigarette *it* is taste' (advertisement). 'In mathematics he is *it*' (superior). 'He thinks he is *it*.' Compare *Syntax*, **7** C (last par.).

Situation *it* is often used as object, as a convenient complement of transitive or intransitive verbs without definite reference, leaving it to the situation to make the thought clear: 'You will catch *it*.' 'They had to fight *it* out.' 'That's going *it* rather strong.' 'We footed *it*.' 'She (the typist) dons her freshest blouse and shadiest hat, and with her girl friend tubes *it* to Hampstead or trams *it* to Kew, there to forget for a time the carking cares of business' (*Everyman*, Feb. 28, 1913). Compare *Syntax*, **11** 2 *b*.

It is widely used as anticipatory subject: '*It* is necessary *that you exert yourself*' (logical subject) or *to exert yourself*. '*It* was my two brothers *who did it*' (logical subject). '*It* is immaterial *what names are assigned to them*' (logical subject). '*It* is vilely unjust, *men closing two-thirds of the respectable careers to women*' (logical subject). '*It* is marvelous *what mistakes they continue to make*' (logical subject). The main verb is in the singular because the logical subject is a clause, a grammatical and logical unit. Compare **18** B 1 and *Syntax*, **4** II C.

It is widely used as anticipatory object: 'I found *it* difficult *to refuse him his request*' (logical object). Compare **18** B 4 *a*, also *Syntax*, **11** 2 *b*.

It is often employed as an impersonal subject: '*It* snows, rains, hails.' Compare *Syntax*, **4** II B.

It often refers to the thought contained in a word or a group of words. See **7** I *c*.

c. *Editorial 'We.'* The first person plural is often used by authors and speakers instead of the first person singular, and the possessive *our* instead of *my*, the author or speaker thus modestly turning the attention away from himself by representing his readers or hearers as accompanying him in thought: 'Thus far *we* have been considering only the outward condition of things at Luther's birth, now *we* are to turn (or 'let *us* turn') our attention to his early home influences.' A speaker or writer often modestly employs *we* since he speaks also for those associated with him: '*We* (the editor speaking for the editorial staff) owe an apology to the public for not noticing this work on its first appearance.' In these examples *we* still has the original associative force, but it now often refers to only one: '*We* (the reviewer of the book) do not say that everything in these essays is as good as what *we* have quoted.' 'It will be easier to explain this later on, when *we* have said something about what is called the history of language' (Wyld, *The Growth of English*, Ch. I, 8). The Plural of Modesty in its earliest forms is very old, for we find a quite similar usage in classical Latin.

Instead of *we* some authors employ here a noun with the third person of the verb: 'The *author* would remark,' etc.

d. *Plural of Majesty*. Of later origin than editorial *we* is the associative *we* first used in the third century in imperial decrees, in that period of Roman history when two or three rulers reigned together and hence were associated in the official proclamations. Later, whenever the political power was centered in one emperor the old *we* was retained, so that although the associative force was present, since the ruler included his advisers, the associative *we* developed into royal *we*, the Plural of Majesty, since the ruler spoke of himself in his official announcements in the plural instead of the singular, as 'We decree' instead of 'I decree.' This usage spread to the different European courts and was common in the Old English period.

e. '*We*' = '*You.*' *We* is often used with the force of *you:* 'Are *we* downhearted today?' Often sarcastically: 'How touchy *we* are!' 'Oh, ain't *we* select since *we* went to that hen college!' (Sinclair Lewis, *Babbitt*, Ch. II, II) (retort of a boy to his sister, who has graduated from Bryn Mawr, and on the occasion in question has spoken to him sarcastically).

f. '*Thou,*' '*Thee,*' '*Ye,*' '*You.*' In Middle English, it was still possible to express the idea of number in the personal pronouns of the second person. In the singular, *thou* was used as subject and *thee* as dative and accusative object, while in the plural *ye* served as subject and *you* as dative and accusative object. These grammatical functions for *ye* and *you* were widely observed until the middle of the sixteenth century, and survive in the biblical and higher poetical language of our time. In the fourteenth century, however, the form *you* — with reference to one or more — sometimes replaced *ye* in the subject relation in the usual intercourse of life, and later in the course of the sixteenth century became more common here than *ye*. Occasionally we find the opposite development in older English — *ye* was used instead of *you* in the object relation: 'I do beseech *ye*' (*Julius Caesar*, III, I, 157). In older English, *ye* is thus not infrequently used in both the subject and the object relation, often in the form of *ee:* '*D'ee* (*do ee*) know this crucifix?' (Middleton and Rowley, *The Spanish Gipsie*, III, III, 40, A.D. 1661). 'I commend me *t'ee,* sir' (Chapman, *The Gentleman Usher*, III, II, 208, A.D. 1606). This usage survives in British dialect. The outcome of this development for the literary language is *you* for nominative, dative, and accusative. In biblical language *ye* is now uniformly employed as nominative and *you* as dative and accusative, as can be seen in the present text of the King James Version of the Bible. In the original text of this version this usage was not so uniform, as there were in it a number of *you's* where we now find *ye*. Both *ye* and *you* are here still always plural forms as originally.

The use of the plural forms *ye* and *you* for reference to one person is closely related to the use of the Plural of Majesty *we* described in *d* above. As a ruler often spoke of himself in the plural, others in addressing him felt that they should employ the plural form. After this model it became general in continental Europe to address by a plural form every person of high rank in church and state. At last, plural form became a mark of politeness in general and was used in speaking to an equal as well as to a superior. The use of the plural form for reference to a single person began to appear in the written language in the second half of the thirteenth century. This usage arose under the influence of

French, which here followed continental Latin usage. The new polite form of addressing one person by the plurals *ye* and *you* did not at once displace the older usage of employing *thou* and *thee* here. For a long while the old and the new forms often alternated with each other, but gradually the new form was distinctly felt as more polite. Thus, in older English, the forms were often differentiated. *Thou* was used in familiar intercourse, and *you* employed as a polite form in formal relations. In Pecock's *Donet* (about A.D. 1449) the father, throughout the book, addresses his son by *thou* and *thee*, while the son out of deference uses *ye* and *you* to his father. The British dialects of the South and South Midland still distinguish between *thou* or *thee* used in intimate relation and *you* or *ye* (often written *ee*) employed in polite language in more formal intercourse. In the eighteenth century, Richardson in his *Pamela* lets Lady Davers use *thou* to her brother in moments of strong emotion and employ *thou* to Pamela in moments of anger and tenderness. This usage survives in British dialects.

In the standard prose English of the eighteenth century, *thou* and *thee* were entirely replaced by *you*, so that the form of polite address became general in the common intercourse of life, the one form *you* serving without distinction of rank or feeling for one or more persons and for the nominative, dative, and accusative relations. The lack of clearness here has called forth in the popular speech of America, Australia, and Ireland a plural ending for this form to indicate more than one, *yous* (or *youse* and in Ireland also *ye, yees, yez, yiz*): 'He'll settle *yous* (= *you kids*), *yous guys*.' It is not unknown in British English. Horace Walpole in a letter to Miss Mary Berry, March 27, 1791, in speaking of her and her sister Agnes writes playfully: 'I have been at White Pussy's (i.e. Lady Amherst's) this evening. She asked much after *yous*.' This advantage, however, is sometimes lost through the popular tendency to simplify, i.e. to employ *yous* also as a singular: 'So! At last I found *youse*' (cartoon in *Chicago Tribune*, Sept. 16, 1923).

In the southern states, *yóu all* is used as the plural of *you*: 'He'll settle *yóu all*.' The genitive *yóu all's* is also in use: '*yóu all's* business.' *Yóu all* may be addressed to a single person provided the form is felt as a plural comprising a definite group of individuals: 'Do *yóu all* (addressed to a clerk representing the different members of the firm) keep fresh eggs here?' (Alphonso Smith, *The Kit-Kat*, IX, p. 27). The *all* in *you all* is often reduced to *'ll*, as it is only weakly stressed: 'Boys, I want *you'll* to stop that noise' (*ib.*). In the literary language *you áll* is used, but the stressed *all* indicates that the thought is different from the normal southern use of *yóu all,* which is simply a plural of *you:* '*You áll* are wrong,' or 'You are *áll* wrong.' In popular speech *you uns* is often used as the plural of *you.* The genitive is *you uns'.* In certain British dialects *you together* is used as plural of *you.* In the literary language and in ordinary colloquial speech we bring out the plural idea here by placing some plural noun after *you:* 'you gentlemen,' 'you boys,' 'you kids,' etc.

The older universal use of *thou* and *thee* in the singular and *ye* and *you* in the plural for all persons has survived in the higher forms of poetry and elevated diction, where the thoughts soar, but in the realistic forms of poetry the actual language of everyday city and country life holds almost complete sway, even where the thoughts rise somewhat from earth, the poet forgetting that the language of earth keeps us on earth: 'Oh, when I was in love with *you,* Then I was clean and brave, And miles around the wonder grew, How well did I behave' (Housman, *A Shropshire Lad,* XVIII). Thus the old poetic forms, long used to elevate thought and feeling, are in our own time breaking down; it may be because the poetic elevation of thought and feeling that once gave them meaning is no longer present.

In older English, *thee* is sometimes seemingly used as a nominative subject, where in fact it may be an ethical dative (*Syntax,* **12** 1 B *c*): 'Hear *thee* (possibly an ethical dative, but now felt as a nominative), Gratiano!' (*Merchant of Venice,* II, II, 189). This same form is also sometimes found in older English as a real nominative, perhaps after the analogy of *you,* which has one form for all the cases: 'How agrees the devil and *thee* about thy soul?' (Shakespeare, *I Henry the Fourth,* I, II, 127). 'What hast *thee* done?' (Marlowe, *Jew,* 1085, about A.D. 1590, ed. 1636). 'If *thee* wilt walk with me, I'll show thee a better' (words of a young Quaker to Benjamin Franklin, as quoted in Franklin's *Autobiography, Writings,* I, p. 255). This usage lingered much later in popular speech: 'I know *thee* dost things as nobody 'ud do' (George Eliot, *Adam Bede,* Ch. IV).

Thou and *thee* are still used by Quakers, often with the nominative form *thee* in connection with a verb with the personal ending *-s,* as explained in **54** (close of 2nd par.): '*Thou knowest* (or now more commonly *Thee knows*) better.' The Quaker address originally had a deep meaning in that it was used toward all men irrespective of rank, and hence emphasized their equality, but it has become a mere symbol of sect since society in general recognized this democratic principle by the employment of *you* without respect to social station.

g. Personal Pronouns for Indefinite Reference. The personal pronouns usually refer to definite persons, but now and then the reference is indefinite. On the other hand, the indefinite pronoun *one* (**7** VII *c ee*) is occasionally used for *I*. *One, we, you,* are sometimes employed with the same general or indefinite force: 'As long as *one* is young, *one* easily acquires new friends.' '*We* don't like to be flatly contradicted.' '*You* don't like to be snubbed.'

We often use *they* here, but with a somewhat narrower meaning, since it usually refers to a smaller circle or one remote, always excluding the speaker and the person addressed, hence often used by the speaker to assert something modestly, representing it as coming from others: 'In fashionable society *they* talk of the impending nuptials of the Duke of Clarence.' 'In that crowd *they* mostly play cards.' 'In Japan *they* generally marry without love.' '*They* say best men are moulded out of faults' (Shakespeare).

When a writer or speaker desires to refer to himself modestly, there is a tendency at present to employ the indefinite *one* instead of the sharply precise *I* or *me: 'One* (or *a person, a fellow*) *doesn't* (instead of *I don't*) like to be treated that way.' 'Under such circumstances you might offer to help *one*' (or *a fellow* instead of *me*). Compare **7** VII *c ee.*

OLDER INFLECTION OF PERSONAL PRONOUNS

34. Old English Forms of the Personal Pronouns:

FIRST PERSON

	Singular	*Dual*	*Plural*
Nom.	ic	wit	wē̆
Acc.	mec, mē̆	unc, uncit	ūsic, ūs
Dat.	mē̆	unc	ūs
Gen.	mīn	uncer	ūser, ūre

SECOND PERSON

	Singular	*Dual*	*Plural*
Nom.	þū̆	git	gē̆
Acc.	þec, þē̆	inc, incit	ēowic, ēow, īow
Dat.	þē̆	inc	ēow, īow
Gen.	þīn	incer	ēower, īower

THIRD PERSON

	Masculine	Feminine	Neuter
		Singular	
Nom.	hē̆	hīo, hēo	hit
Acc.	hine, hiene	hīe	hit
Dat.	him	hiere, hire	him
Gen.	his	hiere, hire	his

Plural for All Genders

Nom.	hīe, hī̆
Acc.	hīe, hī̆
Dat.	him
Gen.	hiera, hira, hiora, heora

35. Middle English Forms of the Personal Pronouns:

FIRST PERSON

	Singular	*Plural*
Nom.	ic, ich, i	wē̆
Acc.	mē̆	ū̆s
Dat.	mē̆	ū̆s
Gen.	mīn, mȳn, mīne, mȳne, mī, mȳ	ūre, oure, our(e)s

SECOND PERSON

	Singular	*Plural*
Nom.	thu, thou, thow	ȝē̆, ye(e)
Acc.	thē̆, thee	ȝou, you, yow
Dat.	thē̆, thee	ȝou, you, yow
Gen.	thīn, thȳn, thīne, thȳne, thī, thȳ	ȝūre, youre, your(e)s

THIRD PERSON

	Masculine	Feminine	Neuter
		Singular	
Nom.	hē̆, ha, a	hē, hō, ȝhē, ȝhō (East Midland) schē (shee, she, sse) (Northern) schō (sco, sso)	hit, it
Acc.	him	hire, hir, here, her	hit, it
Dat.	him	hire, hir, here, her	him
Gen.	his	hire, hir, her, hir(e)s, her(e)s	his, hit, it

Plural for All Genders

Nom.	hī̆, he, thei, they
Acc.	hem, theim
Dat.	hem, theim
Gen.	her(e), hir(e), theire, their(e)s

a. The feminine form *she* probably comes from Middle English *schē*, which, though used as a personal pronoun, was in fact not a personal pronoun at all but a Middle English form corresponding to Old English *sīo* (**44** C 1), the feminine form of the demonstrative pronoun. The Middle English feminine personal pronoun was *hē*. Some recent scholars, however, are not satisfied with this explanation of the origin of *she*. They regard our modern personal pronoun *she* as naturally developed from the Old English feminine personal pronoun *hīo* (**34**), which suffered a change of pronunciation when it followed a verbal form in *–s*, the *–s* of the verb being carried over to the following personal pronoun: *was hio* becoming *was sio,* finally developing into *was she.* Whatever the origin of this *she* may be, its establishment as the regular feminine personal pronoun was facilitated by the fact that the masculine and the feminine of the original personal pronoun had fallen together in the form *hē.* The old order of things — *he* for reference to male or female — has survived in the British dialects of the East and South, where, however, *he* is now pronounced *ee.* Also preserved in America in the Gullah Negro dialect: 'Doll (name of a woman) is de luckiest 'oman I ever seen. *E* (= *she*) got de finest man ever was for a husband' (Julia Peterkin, *Scarlet Sister Mary,* Ch. XXI). 'Unex (name of a boy) is gone. *E* (= *he*) went off and left me' (*ib.,* Ch. XXVI). In this Negro dialect *e* may refer also to lifeless things, as also in British dialect: 'De bes time to kill grass is wen *e* (= *it*) young' (John G. Williams, *Brudder Coteny's Sermons,* Sermon III). '*E* (= she) said smokin would help me to stop bein so nervish.' — 'Sho *e* (= *it*) will, if you learn to smoke right' (Julia Peterkin, *Scarlet Sister Mary,* Ch. XIV). It is employed also as subject of an impersonal verb: '*E* (= *it*) is gettin dark' (*ib.,* Ch. XXIX). The accusative of *e* is *em* with reference to male, female, or lifeless thing: 'I'd like to kill Cinder (woman) — kill *em* dead' (*ib.,* Ch. XII). 'You better smoke you pipe. Le me fill *em* fo you' (*ib.,* Ch. XXI).

b. The accusatives *him* and *her* are old datives. At the close of the Old English period the datives *him* and *her* began to be used as accusatives, so that the datives served for both the dative and the accusative relation.

On the other hand, the old masculine accusative *hine,* reduced to *un, en,* or *'n,* continued to be used for centuries in the South of England as a colloquial form for the accusative and the dative relation: 'I expect *un* (acc.) every minute' (Fielding, *Tom Jones,* Book VI, Ch. VII, A.D. 1749). 'Why, gi' *un* (dat.) thy hand this minute' (*ib.,* Book XVIII, Ch. XII). This usage survives in the South of England in popular speech.

Similarly, the Old English neuter accusative *hit* survived in Middle English, and later in the Modern English period in its reduced form *it* supplanted the old dative *him,* so that it now serves both for the accusative and the dative relation: 'See how nice the old house looks since I have painted *it* (acc.). I have given *it* (dat.) two coats of paint.' The initial *h* disappeared between the twelfth and fifteenth centuries. In certain dialects the *h* is still often heard, as in Scotland and the mountains of Kentucky, often also in Negro dialect.

The Old English neuter genitive *his* began to be replaced in Middle English by *hit, it;* and later, in the seventeenth century, *it* was replaced by *it's,* later *its:* 'Ye are the salt of the earth, but if the salt have lost *his* (at this time also *it* and *it's,* later replaced by *its*) savor,' etc. (*Matthew,* V, 13). The old genitive *it* survives in British dialect: 'Put th' orse mobs (blinkers) on *it* yed' (head) (Huddersfield dialect).

c. About 1300 there began to appear, in the South, genitives in *-n* corresponding to the northern *s*-forms, after the analogy of the genitives *min, thin,* namely, *hisn, hern, ourn, yourn, theirn.* These *n*-genitives survive in the southern British dialects and here and there in American popular speech. Compare **7** VII *e aa.*

d. About 1200 the Middle English plural *hi* began to be replaced by the Danish (Scandinavian) demonstrative plural *thei,* at first in the nominative and later also in the other cases. The fact that such a common form of speech as a personal pronoun could be borrowed from the invaders indicates very clearly that the Danes must have settled in England and lived long in close, intimate relations with the English.

e. In dialect and colloquial speech, the old third person plural *hem* survives in the form of *'em* in unaccented positions: 'Call *'em.*'

II. REFLEXIVE PRONOUNS

36. These pronouns (**7** II), *myself, yourself,* etc., have no change of form in the accusative, and in the dative take *to* or *for* before them except before an accusative, where they still have their old simple form: 'She is dressing *herself.*' 'He is true *to himself.*' 'He bought a new hat *for himself,*' or 'He bought *himself* a new hat.' The form itself indicates the number and person and in part also the gender.

In older English, the personal pronouns were used as reflexive pronouns. This older usage lingers on in Shakespeare, although the newer forms are more common: 'A (= he) bears *him* like a portly gentleman' (*Romeo and Juliet,* I, v, 68). 'Let every soldier hew *him* down a bough' (*Macbeth,* V, IV, 4). The long forms have become established in the third person on account of the ambiguity of the short forms: 'She bought *herself* a new hat.' The old short forms, however, linger in popular speech: 'Rutheney she never even stops to ax Link may she ride in to town — she jest ketches *her* a nag and lights out' (Lucy Furman, *The Quare Women,* Ch. II). In the first and second persons the short forms are often heard also in colloquial speech: 'I bought *me* (or *myself*) a new hat.' 'Did you buy *you* (or *yourself*) a new hat?'

The older short forms, however, are still the usual ones in adverbial prepositional phrases which express local relations in a literal sense: 'He looked about *him,* around *him,* ahead of *him,* above *him,* beneath *him.*' 'He had no money with *him.*' 'He shut the door behind *him.*' 'She sat looking before *her.*' 'The horse sprang over the precipice bearing its rider with *it.*' But in a figurative sense, the fuller forms are the usual ones here: 'Look into *yourself.*' 'You can't do that by *yourself.*' 'They will succeed in the special aim they have put before *themselves.*' Compare *Syntax,* **12** 2 *c.*

a. Origin of Reflexive Pronouns. As described in **36** (2nd and 3rd parr.), we sometimes still use the accusative form of the personal pronouns *me, him,* etc., as reflexive pronouns. This was normal usage in Old English and long remained so. To distinguish reflexive from personal pronouns and thus emphasize the reflexive idea, intensifying *self* was in Old English often added to the personal pronoun. These old intensive forms have become the modern normal reflexive pronouns *himself, herself, itself, themselves* (until about A.D. 1550 *themself*). This usage, once found with all the reflexives, is now confined to these four words. As early as the thirteenth century *herself,* which originally consisted of *her,* the accusative form of the personal pronoun *she,* and intensifying *self,* was sometimes construed as being the possessive adjective *her* and the noun *self.* This conception affected other reflexive pronouns, so that we now employ several reflexives of this type: *myself, thyself, ourself* (after the Plural of Majesty and editorial *we* = *myself*), *ourselves* (in older English *ourself*), *yourselves* (in older English *yourself*), instead of *meself, theeself, usselves, youselves.* In the seventeenth and eighteenth centuries *its self* was in limited use, but is now replaced by *itself.* In popular speech *hisself, theirselves,* are common forms. In England the indefinite reflexive is *oneself.* In America the older form *one's self* is still used, but is yielding to the newer form *oneself.*

The simple form *self* survives as a noun made from the old adjective *self:* 'a truth which purifies from *self*'; 'love of *self.*' 'The next morning all the guests at the hotel except *us* (or *ourselves,* or *our two selves*) went back.' 'Have you hurt your little *self?*' 'Baby fell and hurt its dear little *self.*' 'I hope you are your old *self* again.' 'You must not blame anybody but your own *self.*' 'A man's better *self* should lead him.' 'Sometimes one must think of one's own *self.*' The compound forms are sometimes needlessly used here instead of the simple form: '*Himself* is the only consideration with himself' (Meredith, *The Egoist,* 231), instead of '*Self* is the only consideration with him.'

III. RECIPROCAL PRONOUNS

37. These pronouns (**7** III), *each other, one another,* have the old *s*-genitive, but in the dative have only the newer form with *to* or *for:* 'The two never weary of *each other's* (or *one another's*) company,' or 'the company of *each other*' (or *one another*). 'All true friends bear *one another's* (or *each other's*) burdens.' 'The two are kind *to each other*' (or *one another*). In the object relation these pronouns follow a verb or a preposition: 'The two love *each other* (or *one another*) dearly.' 'The three gentlemen looked at *one another* (or *each other*) with blank faces when these words were uttered.' There is a tendency to employ *each other* for reference to two persons and *one another* for reference to more than two, but this has not yet become fixed usage. Sometimes *one another* is employed for reference to two persons and *each other* for reference to more than two.

In older English, the long reflexive pronouns were sometimes used for reciprocal pronouns: 'Get thee gone; tomorrow We'll hear *ourselves* (instead of *each other*) again' (Shakespeare, *Macbeth*, III, IV, 31). Although this old usage has in general passed away, it is still often found after the prepositions *among* and *between*, perhaps prevails here: 'They quarreled *among themselves*' (but *with one another*). 'We are still quarreling *among ourselves*.' 'They resolved *between themselves* to start immediately.'

a. Older Use of 'Each Other' and 'One Another.' *Each other* and *one another* are now felt as compound plural pronouns, but each element in the present compounds was originally a separate word with its own grammatical function, *each* and *one* being in the nominative singular and *other* and *another* being in the accusative, dative, or genitive according to the structure of the sentence. *Other* could be singular or plural. Either the newer form *others* or the older form *other* could serve as plural. *Another* could serve as singular or plural. A peculiarity of this older usage was the absence of the definite article before *other* for definite reference, as still observed in the case of proper names and such abstract nouns as *justice, honesty, youth,* etc. In this old time, as illustrated also in **7** VII *b*, the *an* in *another* could have the definite force of *the*, referring to a definite single individual. On the other hand, *another* often pointed to a number of individuals taken two by two. *Other* or *another* referring to a single definite individual: '*Eche* of them fersly regarded *other*' (Lord Berners, *Huon*, I, p. 41, A.D. 1534), now *the other*. 'So aprochyd *eche* to *other* (now *the other*) and so fought *eche* with *another*' (*ib.*, p. 42), now *the other*. 'They wer so nere togyder that *eche* of them understode *others* (now *the other's*) langage' (*id.*, *Froyssart*, I, LXI, 83, A.D. 1523). 'When we are married and have more occasion to know *one another*' (Shakespeare, *The Merry Wives of Windsor*, I, I, 255), originally = *one the other*, but now felt as a compound reciprocal pronoun. *Others* referring to a number of more or less definite individuals: 'Pages blush'd at him, and men of heart look'd wond'ring *each at others*' (Shakespeare, *Coriolanus*, V, VI, 100, First Folio, A.D. 1623). Later editions often have here *other*, the older plural. *Another* referring to a number of individuals taken two by two: 'A plague upon it when thieves cannot be true *one* to *another*' (Shakespeare, I *Henry the Fourth*, II, II, 28).

Where the reference is more or less definite, the old usage described above still lingers, now, however, with the definite article before *other* or *others:* '*Each* blamed *the other,*' or negatively '*Neither* blamed *the other.*' '*Each* blamed *the others,*' or negatively '*No one* blamed *the others.*' 'There were two old cats there, *each* ready to tear out *the other's* eyes,' but 'There were three old cats there, *each* ready to tear out *the others'* eyes.' Notice here the position of the apostrophe before or after the final *s* in *the other's, the others'* according as the reference is to one or more. In the compound *each other,* however, the apostrophe is always before the genitive –*s* since *each other* is always a plural form and consequently the genitive –*s* takes the apostrophe before it as after other plural forms, as in *men's, children's,* etc.: 'The two, or three, old cats were tearing out *each other's* (not *others'*) eyes.' Notice also that we can say, 'We *each* know what the *other* wants,' but we should not say, 'We know what *each other* wants,' for the compound *each other* cannot be used in the subject relation, a reciprocal pronoun always standing in an oblique (**27**) case. Only in poetry does the old form with simple *other* survive: 'For many a petty king, ere Arthur came, Ruled in this isle, and ever waging war, *Each* upon *other,* wasted all the land' (Tennyson, *The Coming of Arthur,* 7).

b. 'Either Other' instead of 'Each Other.' In early Modern English, the compound reciprocal pronoun *either other* was sometimes still used instead of *each other:* 'Thus both were bent to deceive each other, and to take the advantage of *either others* (now *each other's*) disadvantage' (Sir Philip Sidney, *Arcadia,* Book III, p. 47, A.D. 1593).

Originally each member of the compound was a separate word with its own grammatical function, as in the case of *each other,* described in *a* above: 'Membres helpen *eyther other*' (Trevisa, *Bartholomaeus,* V, I, 99, A.D. 1398). There was no definite article here before *other,* as in the case of *each other,* as explained in *a* above. Where the old original construction still lingers, there is now a definite article before *other:* 'the rights of *either* to disturb *the other*' (Morley, *Compromise,* 103, A.D. 1874). '*Either* was ready to help *the other.*'

c. Less Common Substitutes for '*Each Other.*' In older English or in poetry there are still other words that may be used instead of *each other:*

In older English, *either* sometimes has the force of *each other:* 'Treason and murder ever kept together, As two yoke-devils sworn to *either's* purpose' (Shakespeare, *Henry the Fifth,* II, II, 105).

In poetic language *each — either* is sometimes used instead of *each other:* 'And *each* at *either* dash from either end' (Tennyson, *Gareth and Lynette,* 535).

In poetic language *each — each* is sometimes used instead of *each other:* 'Then *each,* dishorsed and drawing, lash'd at *each'* (Tennyson, *The Marriage of Geraint,* 563).

In poetic language *either — either* is sometimes used instead of *each other:* '"We two were born together, and we die Together by one doom," while he spoke Closed his death-drowsing eyes, and slept the sleep With Balin, *either* lock'd in *either's* arms' (Tennyson, *Balin and Balan,* last stanza).

IV. RELATIVE PRONOUNS

38. There are two groups:

a. **Relative Pronouns with Antecedent.** These pronouns (**7** IV *a* and **8** *b*, last par.), *who, which, that, what* (**8** *b*, last par.), etc., have all except *who* and the *who*-forms, as *whoever,* etc., lost their old inflectional forms, even the genitive ending *-s,* which is still common in nouns. Hence the case relations here are indicated by modern means. The subject stands before the verb, and the dative and the genitive have inflectional prepositions (**17**) before them as case signs, *to* or *for* before the dative and *of* before the genitive: 'He is the boy *that* (nom.) gave it to me.' 'He is the boy *to whom* I gave it,' or '*that* (dat.) I gave it *to,*' or with the suppression of the relative pronoun: 'He is the boy I gave it *to.*' 'He is the boy *for whom* I bought the new coat.' 'He is the boy *that* (dat.) I bought the new coat *for.*' In the case of the relative pronoun *that,* the case sign *to* or *for* stands at the end of the clause, as explained in *Syntax,* **62** 4 (3rd par.).

The *of*-genitive here often follows the governing noun, indeed always when the governing noun stands in a prepositional phrase: 'This is the tree in the shade *of which* we often rest.' *That,* however, has no genitive form.

The relative pronouns proper all have the same form for singular and plural.

Relative pronouns which are the object of a verb have a position in the sentence different from that of all other objects. As they have conjunctive force, i.e. as they link the clause in which they stand to the rest of the sentence, they must stand at or near the beginning of the clause, hence cannot follow the verb. They indicate the grammatical relations here by a peculiar word-order. If the verb follows the relative immediately or soon, the relative is a nominative: 'He is the boy *that* (nom.) did it.' 'That is the man *who* (nom. sing.) did it.' 'The things *that* (nom. pl.) have often been censured as Shakespeare's conceits are completely justifiable.' 'The things *that* (nom. pl.) chiefly count at national elections are the shibboleths of party.' If a noun or pronoun follows the relative, the relative is in the object relation: 'He is the boy *that* (acc.) I saw do it.' 'That is the book *that* (acc.) he wants.' 'He is the boy *that* (acc.) the dog bit.'

If the relative pronoun is the object of a preposition, it stands at the beginning of the clause after the preposition, or it stands in the first place in the clause and the preposition in the last place: 'This is the pen *with which* I write,' or 'This is the pen *which* I write *with*,' or 'This is the pen I write *with*' (*Syntax*, **23** II, **62** 4).

aa. 'Who'-Form. This relative originally had indefinite force, like the *who* in *b* below, from which it has developed. It gradually acquired definite force, and can now refer to a definite antecedent. It has inherited from indefinite *who* a valuable property which is making it a favorite among the definite relatives. It indicates clearly that the reference is to a person or persons. But it does not indicate the sex.

It inflects as follows, each form serving as singular and plural:

Nom.	who
Acc.	whom
Dat.	whose to whom for whom
Gen.	whom of whom

bb. Case of Relative and Its Agreement with Its Antecedent. The relative pronoun performs a double function: It is a pronoun in the clause in which it stands and is also a connective joining the clause in which it stands to the governing noun. As a pronoun it has the case required by its function in the relative clause, i.e. is subject, direct or indirect object, or a genitive limiting some noun in the clause: 'The man *who* (subject) was sick is now well.' 'The boy *whom* (object of the verb of the clause) I trusted has proved worthy of my confidence.' 'The boy of *whom* (object of the preposition *of*) I spoke yesterday will soon be here.' 'The boy *to whom* (indirect object) I gave a knife has lost it.' 'The boy *whose* (genitive limiting *knife*) knife was lost has bought another.' In loose colloquial speech we sometimes hear *who* as accusative instead of the correct *whom.*

As a connective or conjunctive pronoun the relative has relations to its antecedent, with which it agrees as far as possible in gender, number, and person. Gender: 'The boy *who* is standing by the gate is my brother,' but 'The book *which* lies upon the table is a history.' *That* is the appropriate form where the reference is to two or more antecedents representing both persons and things: 'The cabmen and cabs *that* are found in London.' However, we use also *which* here and this form must be used where a preposition stands before the relative: 'The Company had indeed to procure in the main for themselves the money and the men by *which* India was conquered.'

As relative pronouns have the same form for both numbers and all three persons, their number and person can be gathered only from the number and the person of the antecedent. This becomes important wherever the relative is the subject of its clause, for it then controls the number and person of the verb: '*I, who am* your friend, tell you so,' where *am* is in the first person singular agreeing with its subject *who*, which agrees with its antecedent *I*. 'For help I look to *thee who art* all-powerful and able to help.' 'The *road that leads* to the shore is sandy.' 'The *roads that lead* to the shore are sandy.' An antecedent which is in the vocative, i.e. in the case of direct address, is felt as being in the second person: 'Dark *anthracite, that reddenest* on my hearth!'

The relative often in loose colloquial speech, sometimes even in the literary language, agrees incorrectly with some word closely connected with the antecedent instead of agreeing with the antecedent itself, since this word lies nearer the thought of the speaker or writer than the grammatical antecedent, with especial frequency in the case of a plural partitive genitive that is dependent upon the numeral *one*, which is erroneously felt as the antecedent: 'That is *one* of the most valuable books (true antecedent but here not felt as such) that *has* (instead of the correct *have*) appeared in recent years.' 'Tyranny is *one* of those evils which *tends* (instead of *tend*) to perpetuate *itself*' (instead of *themselves*) (Bryce, *American Commonwealth*, Second Edition, II, p. 344). The singular form of the verb here is quite old: 'Thauriso, þat is a full fair cytee and a gret and on (one) of the beste þat *is* in the world for marchandise' (Mandeville, *Travels*, Ch. XVII, fourteenth century, MS. Cotton, A.D. 1410–1420).

cc. Personality and Form. Current English stresses the idea of personality much more than older English. Even a little earlier in the period *who* was used of animals, while we today usually employ *that* or *which* here since we feel the absence of personality: 'Though the weather is raw and wintry and the ground covered with snow, I noticed a solitary robin, *who* (now *that*) looked as if *he* needed to have *his* services to the Babes in the Woods speedily requited' (Thoreau, *Journal*, I, p. 21). The relative is always near the antecedent, hence the incongruity of placing a personifying form alongside of a noun designating a being without personality is more keenly felt than in the case of personal pronouns, which stand farther away: 'We have one cow *that* (or *which*) we highly prize. *She* is a Jersey.' With children the idea of individuality increases with their age. We say 'the last child *which* was born.' but 'our only child *who* is now at college.'

The idea of personality varies considerably in collective nouns denoting persons. We employ *which* here wherever the idea of oneness or a mass or masses is more prominent than that of a number of independent individuals: 'The Garth *family*, *which* was a large one,' etc. (George Eliot, *Middlemarch*, p. 217). 'His mother had ten children, of *which* he was the oldest' (*Scribner's Magazine*, XXXV, 114), but 'Every faction is attended by a crowd of camp-followers, an useless and heartless *rabble who prowl* round its line of march' (Macaulay). 'He instructed the *crowds which* surrounded him,' but '*People who* have enjoyed good educational opportunities ought to show it in their conduct and language.'

In older English, after the names of cities, countries, and other organizations implying persons, *who* was often used as relative, but it has been entirely replaced here by *which*, since the idea of organization is now uppermost in the mind: 'France, *which* is in alliance with England'; 'that party in England *which*,' etc.

Similarly, we often employ *which* after a noun denoting a person where we desire to express the idea of estate, rank, dignity rather than to speak of a person: 'He is exactly the man *which* such an education was likely to form' (Trollope, *The Warden*, Ch. II). 'He was surprised to find that he had come out upon quite a different Clark from the one to *which* he had been accustomed' (Barry Pain, *The Culminating Point*). 'He did not understand, and could not without giving up his own idea of her, the May Gaston *which*, as she said, he had made for himself' (A. Hope). 'Most of the critics have been kind. I only saw one *which* was not' (Sir Henry Jones, *Letter*, May 29, 1919). *Which* is especially common here in the predicate relation: 'Like the clever girl *which* she undoubtedly was' (Benson, *Relentless City*, 84). 'He is not the man *which* his father wants him to be.' *That* might be used instead of *which* in all of these examples. Although *which* and *that* are both used here, *which* is the more distinctive form and is, in general, winning out, but in the predicate relation *that* and also *as* are still quite common: 'But Hilda, like the angel of mercy *that* she was, whispered,' etc. (Grant Allen, *Hilda Wade*, Ch. I, p. 19). 'I will do my best to stop you, madman *as* you are'

(Thackeray, *The Newcomes*, I, Ch. XXIX). We often omit the relative here where it would not impair the thought: 'It is a part of Torrence's business to counsel widows, which he does like the honorable man [that] he is' (Meredith Nicholson, *Lady Larkspur*, Ch. II, p. 69).

When the relative refers to both persons and things we cannot, of course, in one word indicate both personality and lack of it, hence we here choose the colorless *that*, which can refer both to living beings and lifeless things: 'He spoke largely of the men and the things *that* he had seen.' Of course we cannot use *that* after prepositions, where we must use *which*. See *bb* (2nd par.) above.

When the reference is to a person we always employ after the indefinite pronoun *one* the form *who* as relative to make it clear that we have to do with a person: 'one *who* (not *that*) has gone through such an experience will never forget it.'

In sharp contrast to the principle of indicating personality or the lack of it, which now prevails in the use of the nominative and objective cases of the relative, as described above, is the employment of the genitive *whose* for reference to persons, animals, and living and lifeless things: 'the man *whose* watch was stolen,' 'a dog *whose* name is Carlo,' 'the tree *whose* top was trimmed,' 'the house *in whose shade* (or *in the shade of which*) we sit.' Where the reference is to lifeless things, colloquial language prefers the new prepositional genitive *of which*, although the convenient old form *whose* is still not infrequent. In poetry and choice prose the old form is still the favorite: 'a little white building *whose* small windows were overgrown with creepers' (Galsworthy, *The Patrician*, p. 40). The use of *whose* for persons and things is the survival of older usage, which knew nothing of the differentiation described above. In the genitive the convenient agreeable simple form has thus far proved stronger in our feeling than the logical distinctions which sway us in the nominative and objective relations. Even in choice language, however, the simple genitive is only in limited use, for it cannot be used at all in the relation of an objective genitive: 'In its sensuous purity this woman's face reminded him of Titian's "Heavenly Love," *a reproduction of which* (not *whose reproduction*) hung over the sideboard' (Galsworthy, *The Man of Property*, p. 301).

dd. Descriptive and Restrictive Relative Clauses. There is a tendency in English at present to distinguish between descriptive relatives, introducing a descriptive, independent fact, and restrictive relatives, introducing a clause confining or limiting the application of the antecedent. Descriptive clauses stand in a loose relation to the antecedent and hence are separated by a pause, indicated in print by a comma, while restrictive clauses are quite closely linked to the antecedent in thought, so that they follow immediately without pause, and hence are not usually cut off by a comma: 'I like to chat with John, *who* (not *that*) is a clever fellow,' but 'What is the name of the boy *that* (or *who*) brought us the letter?' 'Next winter, *which* (more common than *that*) you will spend in town, you know, will give you a good opportunity to work in the library,' but 'The next winter *that* (or *which*) you spend in town will give you a good opportunity to work in the library.' There is often a double restriction, the second relative clause restricting the antecedent as restricted by the first relative clause: 'How seldom do we find a man *that has stirred up some vast commotion who does not himself perish, swept away in it*' (Carlyle, *Heroes and Hero-worship*, 127). The descriptive relative clause is in a formal sense a dependent clause; but it does not in any way limit the application of the antecedent, so that it is logically an independent proposition. Compare *Syntax*, **20** 1 (3rd par.). In a descriptive relative clause the relative pronoun must be expressed, for its suppression might change the thought or obscure the expression: 'This fact, *which* you admit, condemns you,' not 'This fact, you admit, condemns you,' which is another thought. Compare *Syntax*, **23** II 6.

b. **Indefinite and General Relative Pronouns.** Of the indefinites in **7** IV *b* *who* and *what* have each a marked peculiarity. *Who* refers indefinitely to a person or persons. *What* points indefinitely to something that is without life. Today *what* is an uninflected form. *Who* and the *who*-forms inflect as follows, the same form in each case serving as a singular and a plural:

Nom.	who	whoever	whosoever
Acc.	whom	whomever	whomsoever
Dat.	whom to whom for whom	to whomever for whomever	to whomsoever for whomsoever
Gen.	whose of whom	whose-ever whoever's (colloquial)	whosesoever whosoever's (colloquial)

As we have abandoned the use of the old case forms in relative pronouns — except the *who*-forms given above — and now indicate the grammatical relations by means of the word-order, there is a strong tendency in colloquial speech to abandon also these special *who*-forms and employ non-inflection also here: 'I don't know *who* (instead of *whom*) he plays with.' 'I will go with *whoever I like*,' instead of *whomever I like* [*to go with*]. But of course: 'I will go with *whoever is* or *are going my way*.' 'I do not know *who was* or *were there.*' The relative pronoun always has the case form required by the construction of the clause in which it stands. Thus in the last two examples it is nominative since it is subject. In the preceding example it is the object of the preposition *with* understood. We should withstand the strong drift here toward the modern forms and use the more expressive older ones. One old *who*-form, the genitive *whose*, is well preserved: 'I don't know *whose* child it is.' 'I will not hurt a hair of her head, *whose-ever* (or, colloquially, *whoever's*) daughter she may be' (Goldsmith, *Good-nat. Man*, V, 155). 'It's mine now, *whose-ever* (the usual form when, as here, there is no noun following) it was a while back' (Hergesheimer, *Mountain Blood*, 294).

The *who*-forms are often followed by the appositive adverb *else:* 'I don't know *who else* (i.e. distinct from him) could have done it.' Relative pronouns often enter into a close relation to *else*, forming with it a compound. 'I don't know *whose else* (older usage), or now usually *who else's*, child it could be.' 'If it isn't his child, I don't know *whose else* (still in use when there is, as here, no noun following), or *who else's*, it could be.' 'His love will never fail, *whoever else's* (or *whosoever else's*) may.' Notice that in accordance with older usage there is still no apostrophe before the genitive *-s* in *whose*, while in *whoever's, whosoever's, who else's, whoever else's, whosoever else's*, the apostrophe is employed in harmony with modern usage. Compare **42** *c cc*.

There are four indefinite relative pronouns that have been formed from indefinite relative adjectives — *what* and *whatever* with quite indefinite force, especially the second form, and with less indefinite force *which* and *whichever*. Differing from all other relative pronouns these words are limiting (**8**) adjectives used as pronouns, hence they may have the *one*-form, like other limiting adjectives in substantive (**43** 1, 2nd par.) function: 'I haven't much butter, but *what* (singular) I have is good.' 'My father is a man of few affections, but *what* (plural) he has are very strong' (Mrs. Gaskell, *Wives*, I, Ch. XVIII). 'Every day he questions us on some particular grammatical point, but we never know in advance *what one* he will bring up.' 'I desire to profit from these experiences and *what ones*, or *whatever ones*, I shall encounter in the future.' 'Here are two hats, but I don't know *which one* is mine.' 'Here are some new books. I don't know *which ones* to select.' 'I want to give you one of these books. You may have *whichever one* you may select.' 'I want to give you several of these books. You may have *whichever ones* you may select.' *Which* and *whichever* refer not only to things but also to persons: 'We have two fine speakers in our class. We do not yet know *which* of them will represent us.' 'There are several very able men in our community. We shall be well represented *whichever one* of them we may select.' Other examples are given in **7** IV *b*.

The *one*-form cannot be used when, as in the first example of the preceding paragraph, the reference is to an indefinite mass that has no fixed individuality. Compare **43** 1 (3rd par.). In the second example of the preceding paragraph either *what* or *what ones* might be used. The reference is indefinite but points to fixed individualities. Simple *what* is still often used here when the reference is to more than one individual thing.

The *one*-forms have a genitive singular in *-s*, which has the force of a possessive pronoun, for it can be used, like a possessive pronoun, as subject or object: 'All three boys have a good record at school, but I do not know *which one's* (subject) is the best.' Compare **7** VII *e* (2nd par.).

39. Older Inflection of Relative Pronouns. In Old English, where there was a reference to a definite antecedent, the demonstrative forms, *se, sio, þæt* were used also as relative pronouns, with the same inflection as in demonstrative function, as described in **44** C 1: 'Me wæs lareow Albinus, *se* wæs wide gefaren and gelæred' (Bede) = 'My teacher was Albinus, who had traveled much and was learned,' originally 'My teacher was Albinus, that one, [he] had traveled much and was learned,' the demonstrative, or rather determinative (**7** VII *b bb*), *se* pointing to the following explanatory clause. After the determinative (*se, sio,* or *þæt*) there often stood the determinative adverb *þe* (= *there*): 'Albinus, *se þe* wæs wide gefaren' = 'Albinus, *who had traveled much,*' originally 'Albinus, *that one there:* [*he*] *had traveled much.*'

In Middle English, the demonstrative *se* lost its inflection here, so that the old neuter form *that* now serves for all cases, genders, and numbers: 'the boy *that* I play with'; 'the girl *that* I play with'; 'the pencil *that* I write with'; 'the boys *that* I play with.' Compare *Syntax* **23** II.

In Old English, the determinative adverb *þe* often served alone as a relative pronoun: 'ealle þa þing *þe* þanon cumaþ' = 'all the things which come from there.' Compare **7** IV *a cc* (last par.).

In Old English, the indefinite relative pronouns *who* and *what* inflected as follows:

	Masculine	Neuter
Nom.	hwă	hwæt
Acc.	hwone	hwæt
Dat.	hwǣ̆m, hwām	hwǣ̆m, hwām
Gen.	hwæs	hwæs
Instr.		hwȳ, hwī

In Middle English, *what* became an uninflected form. *Who* inflected: *whō* (nom.), *whōm* (dat. and acc.), *whōs* (gen.).

The old simple indefinite relative pronoun is still widely used in substantive (i.e. noun) clauses (**18** B): '*Who* goes light travels fast.' 'It is not known *who* did it.' 'I do not know *who* did it.' The old instrumental form, indicating association, instrument, cause, survives in *why* in causal function: 'I do not know *why* (= *on account of what*) he did it.' It is also used in questions, direct and indirect, as indefinite *what* is in general used also interrogatively: '*Why* (= *on account of what*) did you do it?' 'He asked me *why* I did it.' Compare **7** VI *b*, *c*.

In Old English, the adverb *so* (Old English *swa*) was often placed before and after *who* and *what*, thus forming a compound indefinite to emphasize the idea of indefiniteness: *swa hwa swa*, now *whosoever*, *whoever; swa hwæt swa*, now *whatsoever*, *whatever*.

Out of the old simple and compound indefinites *hwa* and *swa hwa swa* has developed the common relative pronoun *who* with a definite antecedent. This development took place in the Middle English period. Compare *Syntax*, **23** II 1.

Out of the old simple indefinite pronoun *who* has developed also the interrogative pronoun *who*. But this development is very old, having taken place before the time of historical records. In Old English, the indefinite and the interrogative pronoun had the same inflection. Compare *Syntax*, **23** II 1 (last par.).

In the Middle English period, the accusative of the relative and the interrogative *who* disappeared, the dative early assuming the accusative function in addition to its own.

In Old English, *which* (Old English *hwilc*) was often, as today, an indefinite relative, but it could not be used for reference to a definite antecedent to point to a definite person or thing, as later in Middle English. Today we may use it to point to a definite thing, but not to a definite person, as in Middle English and early Modern English. The development of *which* into a relative pronoun referring to a definite person or thing is described in *Syntax*, **23** II 3.

In Old English, *which* was inflected like a strong adjective, as described in **44** A 1. In the Middle English period it became uninflected except that it often took an *e* in the plural: *which* (sing.), *whiche* (pl.). Later the plural *-e* disappeared.

V. INDEFINITE PRONOUNS

40. Of these pronouns (**7** V) the forms in *-body*, i.e. *somebody*, *anybody*, *everybody*, *nobody*, have preserved the old genitive in *-s*, which they retain alongside of the newer *of*-form: 'I don't want *anybody's* help,' or 'the help *of anybody*.' The other compound forms have preserved the old *s*-genitive only when used as the subject of the gerund: 'I haven't heard of *anything's* (or *anything*, an accusative; see **47** 6 *a*) being wrong.' Elsewhere we employ the modern means of expressing the grammatical relations: subject before verb and object after it; *to*-dative or *for*-dative; *of*-genitive. Most of these indefinite pronouns have no plural. On the other hand, a few — *men, people, folks, we, you, they* — as indefinite pronouns are used only in the plural. See **7** V. A number of these indefinite pronouns — *numbers, lots, heaps,* etc. — have an *s*-plural, as they were originally nouns. In the case of *a lot* and *lots, a heap* and *heaps, a world* and *worlds,* there is often no essential difference of meaning between singular and plural, both numbers indicating a large quantity or number. The plural is perhaps more emphatic.

The compound *somebody or other* has the old genitive in *-s* or the newer *of*-genitive: 'It is odds that you touch *somebody or other's* sore place,' or 'the sore place *of somebody or other.*'

The compound pronouns are often followed by the appositive adverb *else,* which has the force of a predicate adjective: 'Did he want anything *else?*' (additional). 'It couldn't mean anything *else*' (different). 'It wasn't he; it was somebody *else*' (i.e. distinct from him). These compound pronouns often enter into a close relation with *else* here, forming with it a compound indefinite pronoun: 'It can't be *anybody else's* hat,' instead of older '*anybody's else* hat.' 'That is my business and *nobody else's,*' or sometimes as in older English *nobody's else.* Older usage usually survives here only when there is no noun following *else,* as in the last example.

For the use of the apostrophe before the genitive *-s* of these compounds see **42** *c cc.*

The accusative of a number of these pronouns is used adverbially. See **7** V *c.*

VI. INTERROGATIVE PRONOUNS

41. There are five interrogative pronouns: *who, what;* with quite indefinite force *what one*(*s*); with less indefinite force *which, which one*(*s*). The last three of these are limiting (**8**) adjectives used as pronouns; hence, like other limiting adjectives in substantive (**43** 1, 2nd par.) function, they have a *one*-form: 'Of the innumerable effects or impressions, of which the heart, the intellect, or (more generally) the soul is susceptible, *what one* shall I on the present occasion select?' (Poe, *Philosophy of Composition,* p. 2). 'All the words belong to some attitude or other — all but one.' — '*What one* is that?' (Bernard Shaw, *Plays Unpleasant and Pleasant,* II, p. 133). 'Good idea, if we had a play . . . but we — No, by Jinks, we have got one.' — '*What one?*' asked Lillie de Lisle (Alice M. Williamson, *Lord Loveland Discovers America,* Ch. XXXIV). 'We must add some new juvenile books to our collection. *What ones* would you suggest as appropriate?' '*Which* of the two brothers is the stronger?' 'Here are two hats. *Which one* is yours?' 'You have read Tarkington's novels. *Which*, or *which ones*, are the best?' These pronouns formed from limiting adjectives have a genitive singular in *-s*, which has the force of a possessive pronoun, for it can be used, like a possessive pronoun, as subject or object: 'All three brothers have a good record at school.'—'*Which one's* (subject) is the best?' Compare **7** VII *e* (2nd par.).

The pure interrogative *what* is not inflected. The grammatical relations are shown by the word-order: subject before the verb; the object before a verb which is followed by the subject: '*What* (subject) is worrying you?' '*What* (subject) are their names?' '*What* (object) does he want?' *What* and *who* are often predicates when they stand before a linking (**12** 3) verb which is followed by the subject: '*What* is he?' '*Who* is he?' Often also in exclamations: '*What* was my astonishment when I saw her there!' Predicative exclamatory *what*, as found in this example, is now felt as an adjective. See **10** 9.

When *what* is the object of a preposition it stands at the beginning of the sentence after the preposition, or much more commonly it stands in the first place, and the preposition in the last place: '*About what* are they talking?' or '*What* are they talking *about?*'

The pure interrogative pronoun *who* inflects as follows, the same form in each case serving as a singular and a plural:

Nom.	who
Acc.	whom
Dat.	to whom *or* for whom
Gen.	whose

The older inflection of *who* is given in **39**.

As we have in general abandoned the use of the old inflectional endings in favor of modern means of expression, there is also here in colloquial speech a strong tendency to employ modern forms—except in the genitive relation, where the old form is well preserved: '*Who* (instead of *whom*) did you meet?' '*Who* did you give it *to?*' instead of '*Whom* did you give it *to?*' or '*To whom* did you give it?' '*Who* did you get it *from?*' instead of '*Whom* did you get it *from?*' or '*From whom* did you get it?' In choice language the tendency is to withstand the very strong drift here toward the modern forms and use the more expressive older ones. In the genitive relation we always use the older form: '*Whose* car is it?' This old genitive form is often used as a possessive pronoun, for it can be used, like a possessive pronoun, as subject or object: 'His achievements have never measured up to his aims, but then *whose* have?' (Barrett H. Clark, *Eugene O'Neill*, p. 197). Compare **7** VII *e* (2nd par.).

The *who*-forms are often followed by the appositive adverb *else*, which has the force of a predicate adjective: '*Who else* (i.e. distinct from those mentioned) were there?' The interrogative often enters into a close relation to *else*, forming with it a compound: '*Whose else* (older usage), or now usually *who else's*, son should he be?' 'It is my book; *whose else* (still widely used when there is, as here, no noun following), or now also *who else's*, should it be?' We sometimes say here: '*Whose* should it be *else?*' Also *what* is followed by *else:* '*What else* (further, more) do you want?' '*What else* (with the force of *different*) could it mean?'

Notice that in accordance with older usage there is still no apostrophe before the genitive *-s* in *whose*, while in *who else's* the apostrophe is employed in harmony with modern usage. Compare **42** *c cc*.

VII. LIMITING ADJECTIVES USED AS PRONOUNS

42. The five groups given in **7** VII *a*, *b*, *c*, *d*, *e* are inflected as follows:

a. **Intensifying Adjectives Used as Personal or Indefinite Pronouns.** The intensifying adjectives (**7** VII *a*), *myself*, *ourselves yourself*, *yourselves*, *themselves*, etc., have all lost their old case endings and even when used as pronouns must indicate the case relations by modern means: e.g. *yourself*, a subject when standing before the verb, but an object when following a preposition or any verb except a linking (**12** 3) verb, where it is a predicate; *to*, and *for*, *yourself*, dative. For examples see **7** VII *a*.

The form of these pronouns always indicates the number and the person.

b. **Demonstrative Pronouns.** Of the words in this group (**7** VII *b*) *this one*, *that one*, *the one*, *such a one*, *the same one*, *the former*, *the latter*, *the first one*, *the second one*, etc., *the last one*, *either*, *either one*, *neither*, *neither one*, *each one*, and *every one* still have in the singular the old *s*-genitive alongside of the newer *of*-genitive: 'John and Sam and *the latter's* sister,' or 'the sister *of the latter*.' 'I should be welcome at *either's* house,' or 'at the house *of either* of them.' 'Two men applied for the place, but *neither's* looks pleased me,' or 'the looks *of neither* of them pleased me.'

Most of the other forms in this group indicate the case relations by modern means, also the forms given above when used in the plural: 'I know most of the students present, but I don't know the names *of these*,' or 'the names *of the last ones* in the row.'

The genitive of *other* is *other's* in the singular and *others'* in the plural: '*the other's* record,' or 'the record *of the other*'; '*the others'* records,' or more clearly 'the records *of the others*.'

For the use of the apostrophe before the genitive *-s* of these pronouns see *c cc*, p. 176.

Some words indicate the singular and the plural by their forms: *this, these; that, those; the one, the ones; the other, the others* or *the other ones; such a one, such ones; the same* (*one*), *the same* (*ones*); *the first* (*one*), *the first* (*ones*); *the last* (*one*), *the last* (*ones*). The meaning of *both* indicates the plural: '*Both* of the men, *both* of the speeches, are good.' *All, half, the former, the latter,* are either singular or plural: '*All* of the speech was good.' '*All* of the speeches were good.' '*Half* of the speech was good, *half* of it was very bad.' '*Half* of the speeches were good.' 'The cake was cut in *half* (or *two,* both forms limiting adjectives used as plural pronouns) or into *halves*' (plural noun). 'He has a whole apple, but I haven't even *half a one*.' 'John and William both spoke well, only *the former* spoke a little too long and *the latter* didn't speak quite long enough.' 'I am going either today or tomorrow; *the latter* is more likely.' 'I prefer milk to coffee; *the latter* is more pleasant to the taste, but *the former* is more wholesome.' 'The struggle between Alfred and the Danes resulted in the overthrow of *the latter*.' *Either* and *neither* are usually employed only in the singular, but *neither* is not infrequently used also as a plural: '*Neither* of us *are* dukes' (H. G. Wells, *The New Machiavelli*, p. 316). Compare *Syntax*, **8** I 1 *e*. Many examples containing demonstratives are given in **7** VII *b*.

The plural form *the other ones* has more individualizing force than *the others:* 'These houses are newer than *the other ones* we were looking at' (the speaker thinking of each house), but 'I like these houses better than all *the others*' (the speaker thinking of the others as a mass or group).

The accusatives of the pronouns *this, that, all, half,* like the accusatives of the indefinite pronouns in **42** *c aa* are used as adverbs: '*This* (or *that* or *thus* or *so*) much I hold to be true.' 'She is dressed *all* in white.' 'The work is only *half* done.' For fuller treatment see **71** 1 *a, b*.

c. **Indefinite Limiting Adjectives Used as Indefinite Pronouns.** Of the words in this group (**7** VII *c*) *anyone, everyone, someone, someone or other, such and such a one, many a one, one, no one, another, another one, a certain one, this* (*one*) *and that one,* and *this, that, and the other one,* still have in the singular the old *s*-genitive alongside of the newer *of*-genitive: '*someone's* boy,' or 'the boy *of someone*'; '*no one's* boy,' or 'the boy of *no one*.' '*One* must often make up *one's* mind quickly.' 'It is likely that you will touch *someone or other's* sore place.' In older English, the *s*-genitive of *any* and *none* was in use: 'I haue taken as great delight in thy company as ever I did in *anyes*' (John Lyly, *Euphues and His England*, Works, II, p. 76, A.D. 1580), now *anyone's*. 'Wisedome will that we should refrayne From foolishe deming (deeming) and *none's* (now *no one's*) death discuss' (Barclay, *Shyp of Folys*, 58, A.D. 1509).

Others is the only word that has the simple genitive in the plural: 'She thinks only of *others'* good,' or 'the good *of others.*' In older English, also, other words had the simple plural genitive: 'In *many's* looks the false heart's history Is writ in moods and frowns and wrinkles strange' (Shakespeare, *Sonnet* 93). 'Howso'er it shocks *some's* self-love, there's safety in a crowd of coxcombs' (Byron, *Juan*, XIII, xxx). With the exception of *other* these words now have in the plural only the *of*-genitive. *Other* has here either the simple genitive or the *of*-form.

All the other pronouns of this group regularly indicate the case relations by modern means, also usually the pronouns given above when used in the plural.

Five indicate the plural by their form: *others, other ones; this, that, and the other ones; such and such ones; certain ones.* Earlier in the period *other* was without an ending in the plural, as the old Middle English plural ending *-e* had been lost and the new plural ending *-s* had not yet appeared: 'This ignorauncie in men whyche (now *who*) know not for what tyme and to what thynge they be fit causeth some to desire to be maysters and rule *other* (now *others*), whiche (now *who*) neuer yet began to rule themselfe' (Roger Ascham, *Toxophilus*, p. 153, A.D. 1545). The old plural *other* is now and then still found lingering on, especially before a modifying *of*-genitive: 'The wide influence of this and *other* (or more commonly *others*) of his books is shown by the fact that most of them have reached a sixpenny edition' (*Athenaeum*, Aug. 28, 1915). Other examples are given in **7** VII *c*.

Eleven indicate the plural by their meaning: *several, various, sundry, numerous, many, a many* (once common, now archaic or poetic), *a good many, a great many, certain, few, a few.*

All, any, enough, more, none, some, such (**7** VII *b, c*), *such and such* (**7** VII *c*), are either singular or plural. *None*, which was originally a singular and is sometimes still so used, is now more commonly a plural. Compare **7** VII *c*. In the singular it is usual to employ *nó one:* '*Nó one* (more common than *none*) knows it so well as I.' *Not óne* (numeral), or colloquially *not a óne*, is more emphatic than *none* or *nó one:* 'There is *none*, no, *not óne* in whom

I trust' (M. H. Hewlett). 'Nó one came to the meeting, no, *not a óne.*' Compare *Syntax*, **57** 5 *b*.

Less is now usually a singular: 'It is worth that much. I will not take *less.*' Though it often points to a number of persons or things, it does not refer to them as individuals, but, like a singular collective noun, represents them as a single unit, an aggregate, while *fewer* represents them as separate individuals: 'No doubt the receipts in December 1909 were *less* than normal' (*Westminster Gazette*, No. 5507, 1). 'There are about 228,000 colored workers on the mines now. In 1903 there were many *less.*' (*London Daily News*, No. 21003, 10). 'There are *fewer* in our colleges now who can read and appreciate the Greek classics than in the last century.' *Less than* and *more than* are often adverbs: 'There were *less than* (adverb) sixty (= sixty people) there,' or '*fewer* (= fewer people) than sixty there.' '*More than* (adverb) one has found it so.' 'There are *more* (plural indefinite pronoun) than one' (G. Washington Moon, *The Dean's English*, 7th ed., p. 70). 'There are more (adjective) reasons than one,' but 'There is *more than* (adverb) one reason.' Compare *Syntax*, **8** I 5.

aa. Neuter Indefinite Pronouns Used Adverbially. All, other, any, none, some (= *a fair amount*), *much, more, little, a little, less, enough*, etc., are often used as neuter pronouns: 'He felt that he already possessed in this world *all* that his heart really craved.' 'Nor could his private friends do *other* than mournfully acquiesce.' 'I don't want *any* of your nonsense.' 'It is *none* of my business.' '*None* of this concerns me.' 'I should like to have *some* of your patience.' The accusative of a number of these neuter pronouns is much used adverbially, especially with a comparative: 'It is *all* gone.' 'It is *all* the same to me.' 'He is *all* the better for it.' 'He cares *little* about it.' 'He was *a little* (*not a little*) vexed.' 'It is *much* too large.' 'Is he resting *any* better today?' 'He is *none* the worse for his fall.' 'He is *some* (colloquial accusative for the literary adverb *somewhat*) better this morning.' 'He had learned *some* more about the world' (Jack London, *White Fang*, p. 87). The adverbial use of *some* with verbs is especially characteristic of Scotch English. It is common also in American English: 'I think *some* of attending the great antislavery convention' (J. G. Whittier, quoted from the year 1843 in Pickard's *Life*). 'She was very sick during the night, but she rested *some* toward morning.' The adverbial accusative of *other* (= *otherwise*) was once used and still lingers: 'Who dares receive it *other?*' (Shakespeare, *Macbeth*, I, VII, 77). 'It could not have been carried out *other* than by the mammoth vessels' (quoted by Fowler in his *Modern English Usage*, p. 411). Compare **7** VII *c cc*. For fuller discussion see **71** 1 *a*.

Sometimes the nominative can be used adverbially: 'It is *all* but impossible to get anything done under these circumstances,' literally 'It is *everything* short of impossible,' etc. 'He was *all* but drowned.' '"It's a pity he (the horse) can't talk," she said. — "Oh but he can — *all* but"' (D. H. Lawrence, *Sons and Lovers*, p. 297). Originally *all* was here a predicative nominative, and after a moment's reflection this older function is often still easily discernible, but *all* is now more commonly felt as forming with *but* a compound adverb with the force of *almost*, modifying an adjective or a verb. Similarly in 'She is *anything but* strong' we may construe *anything* as a predicative nominative or now more commonly may regard *anything but* as an adverb with the force of *far from*. These are apt illustrations of the changes that take place in the functions of words.

In American slang adverbial *some* is much used to express a high degree: 'We drove *some*, I'll say.' 'I tell you, I'm *some* tired tonight.' Compare **10** 6 *b*.

bb. 'Else' after Indefinite Pronouns. These pronouns are often followed by the appositive adverb *else:* 'It wasn't he; it was *someone else*' (i.e. distinct from him). These pronouns often enter into a close relation with *else* here, forming with it a compound indefinite pronoun: 'It must be *someone else's* hat,' or in older English '*someone's else* hat.' 'That is his business and *no one else's*,' or sometimes still as in older English *no one's else*. Older usage usually survives here only when there is no noun following *else*, as in the last example.

cc. Use of Apostrophe in the Genitive. The apostrophe began to be used with the genitive of nouns about 1680, but it was used very little at first, the old genitive without the apostrophe prevailing with both nouns and pronouns: 'Yet could she tell the touch of that woman from *any ones else*' (Increase Mather, *Remarkable Providences*, Ch. V, Jan., 1684). Later, the apostrophe gradually became established with nouns and pronouns, but the personal, relative, and interrogative pronouns still follow older usage. For the history of the apostrophe with the genitive see **27** 4 A *b* (1), last par.

d. **Numeral Adjectives Used as Pronouns:**

aa. Cardinal Numeral Adjectives Used as Pronouns. These adjectives (**10** 4 *a*) when used as pronouns never have an ending, except *only* and *sole*, which take the *one*-form: 'There were *seventy-five* there.' 'There are *four* of us.' 'These trees are planted too closely together. *Three* will be taken out.' '*Fifty odd* of the eggs were broken.' 'Some *fifty* of them were broken.' 'You may select any *óne*, any *twó*, any *thrée*, of the books.' 'He is the *óne* in the family you can depend upon.' 'They are the *twó* in the family you can depend upon.' But: 'He is the *ónly one* that can do it.' 'Here is the dictionary, the *ónly one* we have in the house.' 'They are the *ónly ones* who can do it.' 'These two passages are the *ónly ones* in which Plato makes mention of himself.' 'They made him their agent, the *sóle one* for this community.' 'He is the *sóle one* in this mystery' (Keats, *Otho the Great*, III, II, 254). Milton used simple *sole* as a pronoun: 'O *sole* in whom my thoughts find all repose' (*Paradise Lost*, V, 28), now 'O *sóle one* in whom,' etc.

In the written language there is a peculiar ambiguity in the use of *one*. 'I can't find *one* of my books' means that either all or one of the books is missing. In the spoken language we stress *one* to convey the former meaning, and speak it lightly to convey the latter meaning. In fact unstressed *one* is not now felt as a numeral but has developed into an indefinite pronoun (**7** VII *c*).

bb. Ordinal Numeral Adjectives Used as Pronouns. These adjectives (**10** 4 *b*) when used as pronouns may take the *one*-forms, and thus can indicate the singular and the plural idea: 'Of the speakers *the first* (or *the first one*) was interesting.' 'Of the speakers *the first ones* were interesting. *The last ones* were very tiresome.' 'The first volume is more interesting than *the second*,' or *the second one*.

e. **Possessive Adjectives Used as Pronouns.** The substantive, i.e. pronominal, forms of the possessive adjectives *my, thy, his, her, its, our, your, their,* are *mine, thine, his, hers, its, ours, yours, theirs,* two adding *-n* in the substantive relation, four adding *-s*, two, *his* and *its*, remaining unchanged. This list may be greatly increased, for many nouns and pronouns may become possessive pronouns by the addition of *-s:* 'Mý son is tall, but *my síster's* (subject nominative) is still taller.' 'All three boys have a good record at school, but I do not know *which one's* (subject nominative) is the best.' 'Both John and William have a good record. I regard *the latter's* (accusative object) as a little better.' This new type is described more fully in **7** VII *e*. The old possessives once rich in inflectional endings haven't a single ending left. They now indicate the grammatical relations by modern means. The subject stands before the verb, the object after the verb. The preposition *of* indicates the genitive relation, the prepositions *to* and *for* indicate the dative relation. The possessive pronouns of the newer type are treated in the same way. Examples illustrating the use of both types are given in **7** VII *e*. A mere glance at these examples will show how simple and yet clear English now is at this point. The simplicity almost amounts to elegance. The pronouns of the old type that refer to the third person indicate the gender, a rich inheritance from the personal pronouns from which they were formed.

In the nineteenth century arose the usage of suffixing *one* to the possessive adjectives to form possessive pronouns. This development has never been strong, and is for the most part confined to British English: 'When a woman is old . . . But *my one!* She's not old' (Trollope, *The Duke's Children*, III, 163). '*Hers*, the absolute form of the possessive pronoun *her*, used when no noun follows = *her one, her ones*' (*Oxford Dictionary*). 'I ought to give you my name. It's Rattray, of one of the many Kirby Halls in this country. *My one's* down in Lancashire' (Hornung, *Dead Men Tell No Tales*, p. 40). When a genitive follows the possessive pronoun, the suffix *one* cannot be dispensed with if the possessive construction is retained: 'Leaning back in *his one* of the two Chippendale armchairs in which they sat' (Juliana Ewing, *Jackanapes*, p. 26). Professor Jespersen, who in his *English Grammar*, II, p. 261, furnishes the first and the last of these quotations, gives also another containing a noun used as a possessive pronoun: 'Her parasol is fine, but her *sister's one* is finer.' Professor Jespersen quotes here from the spoken words of an English gentleman. The second example is the words of the editor of the *Oxford Dictionary*, which gives some dignity to the construction. To the author of this Grammar, who is an American, all these examples seem strange. The quotation from Juliana Ewing, however, indicates that this new form might become useful. Compare **7** VII *e* (last par.).

For the origin of the old possessive pronouns see **7** VII *e aa*.

CHAPTER XI

INFLECTION OF ADJECTIVES

PRESENT INFLECTION OF ADJECTIVES

43. In Old English, adjectives indicated by their inflection case, gender, number, and the degrees of comparison, the comparative and the superlative. A mere glance at the Old English inflection of adjectives in **44** A will give a general idea of the intricate means of expression employed in our oldest historic period. A wealth of forms does not at all mean a wealth of expression. The later increase of power in English expression was for a long time accompanied by a simplification of English form. In the course of the Middle English period, as explained in part in **31**, the inflectional endings for case, gender, and number in adjectives entirely disappeared. The following paragraphs describe our present simple means of inflecting adjectives.

1. Inflection of the Positive

In the course of the Middle English period the adjectives for the most part ceased to be inflected. In the position before the governing noun *this* and *that* alone show traces of their former rich inflection. They can still indicate the plural: *these, those.* In the position after the governing noun or pronoun the identifying (**10 2**, **10 2** *a*) adjectives take *-s* in the plural: 'we *ourselves*,' 'you *yourselves*,' 'they *themselves*.' Near the end of the Middle English period the forms of these words were: *ourself, yourself, themself*, i.e. they were uninflected, like most adjectives. The first two forms were often ambiguous. Before the beginning of the modern period *-s* began to appear in the plural to make the grammatical relations clear: 'we *ourself*' (sing.), 'we *ourselves*' (pl.); 'you *yourself*' (sing.), 'you *yourselves*' (pl.). About 1570 *themself* became *themselves* after the analogy of *ourselves* and *yourselves*.

The reduction of adjective inflection in the Middle English period was too radical. It had hardly disappeared when it became apparent that something valuable had been lost. The inflectional endings for case, gender, number, had served the useful purpose of linking the adjective to its governing noun. The lack of an ending was not felt when the adjective stood immediately before the noun, as in 'a *black* hat,' and the suppression of the endings here for case, gender, and number was a great improvement, for it brought into the language a remarkable simplicity, which made English expression easier and more forcible. But in substantive function, i.e. when the adjective stood alone separated some distance from its governing noun, the lack of the ending was sorely felt: 'My brother bought a white hat, and I bought a *black*.' The need of something after *black* to link it to its governing noun *hat* was felt as early as the thirteenth century, and people began to put the numeral *one* after it: 'My brother bought a white hat, and I bought a *black one*.' The linking force of *one* was felt much more strongly than its original meaning *one*, so that the plural *ones* was employed to link the adjective to a plural noun: 'My brother bought two white hats, and I bought two *black ones*.'

Thus *ones* in this example has entirely ceased to have a relation to the numeral *one*, for it means *two*. It has the same force as the old inflectional ending that once stood in the same place. In spite of the fact that it has always been written as an independent word, it has become an inflectional ending of the adjective with the function of linking it to its governing noun. Of course, *one* is employed with a noun or a group of nouns used as an adjective, sometimes also with a genitive that has the force of a descriptive adjective: 'I like this pipe better than a *clay one*.' 'On a side line was a little train that reminded Peter of *the Treliss* (town) *to Truro* (town) *one*' (Hugh Walpole). 'The higher course is a *two years' one*' (*London Times*, Aug. 8, 1918). In harmony with its origin *one* can refer only to individuals, persons and things that can be counted; hence it never points to mass words (*sand*, *milk*, etc.): 'this hat and *that one*'; not 'this butter and *that one*,' but 'this butter and *that*.' As a suffix, *one* is usually without stress, while numeral *one* often has a strong accent: 'Here are some fine apples. You may select *ány one* (substantive form of *any*) of them you choose,' but 'You may select any *óne* (numeral), or any *twó*, of them you choose.' '*Nó one* (substantive form of *no* used as an indefinite pronoun) can do that,' but 'No *óne* (numeral) of you can do that.' 'Helen hated boys, and she would have liked to whip *thís one* long and often,' but 'Except this *óne* nearest friend he was alone in the world.' In emphatic language, however, the *one* of the substantive form of the adjective may have a stress: 'I want *évery óne* of you to come.' 'Not a *bléssĕd égg* was fresh,' but with *blessed* in the substantive relation: 'Not a *bléssĕd óne* of the eggs was fresh.' For an explanation of the double stress here see *Syntax*, **57** 1 (6th par.).

The use of *one* to indicate substantive, i.e. pronominal, function, as in the above examples, is quite general with descriptive (**8**) adjectives, since the thought requires it here. But with limiting (**8**, **10**) adjectives it has not become so well established, in some of the groups in **10** not being used at all, in other groups being used with some adjectives and never found with others. The meaning in limiting adjectives is often so concrete that *one* or *ones* is not needed in the substantive relation to make the thought clear. The cardinal numeral adjectives and many other limiting adjectives, as *many*, *several*, *few*, etc., though they have no plural ending, indicate the plural relation clearly by their meaning: 'these books and *the six* on the table.' *These*, *those*, indicate the plural by their form: 'that book and *these* in my hand'; 'these books and *those* on the table.' 'Associate with *those* that you can look up to.' '*Those* who have themselves suffered are apt to sympathize with others.'

A number of limiting adjectives, however, need *one* or *ones* in the substantive, i.e. pronominal, relation to make the thought clear: 'Here are several books. I don't know *which one*, or *which ones*, would please you most.' We say either '*each*, or *each one*, of the books.'

In Old English the adjective had the same inflectional ending for adjective and pronominal function, while today it is uninflected in adjective function and has the *one*-form in pronominal function, so that there is a distinctive form for each of the two functions. Thus, although Modern English is less rich in form than Old English it has a clearer expression for these two functions.

There are other ways of indicating the substantive, i.e. the pronominal, relation. The pronominal forms of the possessive adjectives *my, thy, his, her, its, our, your, their*, are *mine, thine, his, hers, its, ours, yours, theirs*, two adding in the pronominal relation an *–n*, four adding an *–s*, and two, *his* and *its*, remaining unchanged: 'my hat and *yours*'; 'your hat and *mine*'; 'his house and *ours*'; 'our house and *his*.' Other examples are given in **7** VII *e*. These pronouns have for the most part a distinctive ending, *–n* or *–s*. Originally they were the genitive forms of the personal pronouns. Gradually they developed into possessive adjectives and pronouns. The present difference of form for the two functions is the result of a long development described in *Syntax*, **57** 5 *a*. The pronominal forms here are peculiar. Elsewhere the common way to make a pronominal form is to add *one* to the adjective form. In England *one* is actually coming into use also here: 'Leaning back in *his one* of the two Chippendale armchairs in which they sat' (Juliana Ewing, *Jackanapes*, p. 26). Compare **7** VII *e* (3rd par.) and **42** *e* (2nd par.).

The limiting adjective *other* takes an *–s* in the substantive, i.e. the pronominal, relation in the plural: 'this book, and *the others* on the table.'

As in the above examples, the substantive forms of limiting adjectives point to a preceding noun or a following *of*-genitive, a prepositional phrase, or a relative clause. They are here always employed as convenient substitutes for a noun or a noun and its modifying adjective, so that in fact they are pronouns: 'these books and *those* (= *those books*) on the table.' As these pronouns are among the commonest in the language, the question of their proper form is of considerable importance. Their form is treated in detail under the head of pronouns in **7** IV *b*, **7** VI, **7** VII *b, c, d, e*, **38** *b*, **41**, **42** *b, c, d, e*. This subject is treated at considerable length in *Syntax*, **57** 1, 2, 3, 5 *a, b, c*.

Also the substantive forms of descriptive adjectives are pronouns, for they are only convenient substitutes for nouns and their modifying adjective: 'the black sheep and the *white one*' (= white sheep).

The substantive forms of both limiting and descriptive adjectives, though pronouns by function, differ from pure pronouns such as *I*, *you*, *he*, *she*, etc., in one important point. They not only perform the pronominal function, but they describe or point out, i.e. they have meaning, while the pure pronouns, meaningless and colorless, are mere conventional symbols standing for persons and things. These substantive forms differ from pure pronouns also in that they are freely modified by adherent (**8**) adjectives, betraying thus their substantive origin, their relation to some noun understood: 'quaint old houses and *beautiful new ones*'; 'these books and *all those*'; 'these books and *many more, some more, a few more*'; '*some fifty* of them'; 'John, Fred, and *some others*'; '*some few* of us'; etc.

2. Comparison of Adjectives

There are three degrees — the positive, the comparative, the superlative. The positive is the simple form of the adjective: 'a *strong* man.' The comparative indicates that the quality is found in the person or thing described in a higher degree than in some other person or thing: 'the *stronger* of the two men.' 'This tree is *taller* than that.' The superlative is relatively the highest degree and often indicates that the quality is found in the highest degree in the person or thing described: 'Mt. Everest is the *highest* mountain in the world.' Often, however, the superlative is used in a relative sense, indicating that of the persons or things compared a certain person or thing possesses the quality in the highest degree, which need not be a very high or the highest degree in general: 'John is the *strongest* of these boys, but there are others in the school stronger than he.'

In general, comparison is characteristic of descriptive adjectives, the comparative and the superlative indicating different degrees of a quality. But a number of limiting adjectives are compared. Here the comparative and the superlative do not indicate different degrees, but point out different individuals: the *former;* the *latter;* the *first;* the *last;* the *topmost* round; the *southernmost* island of the group. In the following discussion of comparison, descriptive and limiting adjectives are, for convenience, treated together.

A. **Relative Comparison.** In contrast to the older uniform use of endings to construct the comparative and the superlative, we today with some adjectives employ the old terminational, or synthetic, form in *-er* and *-est;* with others, influenced by our fondness for analytic form, as described in *b*, p. 188, we prefer comparison with *more* and *most;* with others we fluctuate between the old terminational, or synthetic, form and the new analytic form. The wide use of the analytic form with *more* and *most* in modern English is explained not only by its expressiveness, as described in *b*, p. 188, but also by its agreeableness of sound and its ease of pronunciation in the case of long adjectives.

Monosyllabics and a large number of dissyllabics are compared by means of the comparative ending *–er* and the superlative ending *–est: quick, quicker, quickest; sturdy, sturdier, sturdiest.* Before adding the comparative or superlative ending: (1). Drop *e:* larg*e*, larg*er*, larg*est*. (2). Change *y* to *i* if a consonant precedes, but retain the *y* if a vowel precedes: laz*y*, laz*ier*, laz*iest;* dr*y*, dr*ier*, dr*iest*; but gra*y*, gra*yer*, gra*yest*. In British English, however, *sly* and usually *shy* retain the *y* although a consonant precedes: sl*y*, sl*yer*, sl*yest;* sh*y*, sh*yer*, shy*est*. In America the forms *–ier, –iest,* are the usual ones: sl*y*, sl*ier*, sl*iest;* sh*y*, sh*ier*, sh*iest*. (3). In monosyllabic words double the final consonant after a short vowel: hot, hot*ter*, hot*test*. The British scholar Alfred West on page 114 of his English Grammar remarks, 'A few other adjectives, not monosyllabic, exhibit the same orthographical change: crue*ller*, hopefu*ller*.' In American usage the *l* here is not doubled, as it stands in an unaccented syllable: cruel*er*, hopeful*er*. Americans prefer here, however, the analytic forms with *more* and *most: more cruel, most cruel,* etc.

While we may thus compare with *–er* and *–est* a number of dissyllabics, especially those in *–er, –le, –y, –ly, –ow, –some,* such as *tender, bitter, clever, sober, able, noble, idle, holy, goodly, narrow, handsome, wholesome, winsome,* and some words accented upon the last syllable, such as *profound, remote,* etc., and also others that cannot be easily described, such as *pleasant, cruel, quiet,* etc., or in these same words and many others may use both the old form in *–er* and *–est* and the newer analytic form with *more* and *most,* as in *pleasanter* or *more pleasant, crueler* or *more cruel, serener* or *more serene,* in many others we usually prefer comparison by means of *more* and *most,* as in the case of *earnest, eager, proper, famous, comic, docile, fertile, hostile, certain, active, content, abject, adverse,* and participles in *–ed* and *–ing* and adjectives in *–ful* and *–ish,* as *learned, strained, charming, useful, childish,* etc.

A few monosyllabics, *like, real, right, wrong,* and *wan,* which do not naturally incline to comparison, are usually compared by *more* and *most* when they are compared, although the terminational form occasionally occurs; in the case of *like,* however, only in older English, and sometimes still in poetry and dialect, never in colloquial or literary prose: 'I'm *liker* (now usually *more like*) what I was than you to him' (Dryden, *All for Love,* I, 247, A.D. 1678).

'Father is *more like* himself today.' 'The figures of Spartacus, Montrose, Garibaldi, Hampden, and John Nicholson were *more real* to him than the people among whom he lived' (Galsworthy, *Freelands*, Ch. X). 'It is wrong to even think it; it is *more wrong* to do it.'

Monosyllabic adjectives, however, are often compared by *more* when the adjective is placed after the noun to give it more emphasis and at the same time impart descriptive (**8**, 3rd par.) force. With classifying force 'There never was a *kínder* and *júster* man,' but with descriptive force 'There never was a man *more kínd* and *júst*.'

In ordinary literary language, words of more than two syllables are seldom compared otherwise than by *more* and *most: beautiful, more beautiful, most beautiful.*

a. Irregular Comparison:

Positive	*Comparative*	*Superlative*
bad, ill, evil	worse, badder (in older English)	worst, baddest (in older English)
far	farther, further	farthest, furthest
fore	former	foremost, first
good, well	better	best
late	later, latter	latest, last, lattermost
little	less, lesser	least
much, many	more, or in older English, mo or moe	most
nigh	nigher	nighest, next
old	older, elder	oldest, eldest
	after	aftermost
east, eastern	more eastern	easternmost
end		endmost
hind	hinder	hindmost, hindermost
	inner	inmost, innermost
low	lower	lowest, lowermost
north, northern	more northern	northmost, northernmost
	nether	nethermost
	outer, utter	outmost, outermost, utmost, uttermost
rear		rearmost
south, southern	more southern	southmost, southernmost
top		topmost
under		undermost
up	upper	uppermost, upmost
west, western	more western	westernmost

In older English, *mo* or *moe* (Old English *mā*) was used instead of *more* when the reference was to number: 'Send out *moe* horses' (Shakespeare, *Macbeth,* V, III, 34).

In a few cases the variant forms indicate a differentiation of meaning or function. The usual comparative and superlative of *old* are *older, oldest,* always so in the predicate relation; but we may use *elder, eldest,* in the attributive and the substantive (**43** 1) relation and *elder* as a noun, especially of relationship and rank: the *elder* brother; the *elder* Pitt; I am the *elder;* He is my *elder* in service; the *eldest* brother, etc. 'He is an *elder* in the church.'

We use *farther* and *further* with the same local and temporal meaning, but *further* has also the meanings *additional, more extended, more:* 'The cabin stands on the *farther* (or *further*) side of the brook.' 'I shall be back in three days *at the farthest,*' or *at the furthest.* But: *further* details; without *further* delay. 'After a *further* search I found her.' 'Have you anything *further* (= *more*) to say?' In adverbial function *farther* and *further* are used indiscriminately: 'You may go *farther* (or *further*) and fare worse.' There is, however, a decided tendency to employ *further* to express the idea of additional, more extended action: 'I shall be glad to discuss the matter *further* with you.'

Later and *latter* are now clearly differentiated in meaning.

The terminations in some of these forms, as *lesser, innermost,* etc., express the degree two or three times instead of once. Compare *aa* below.

aa. OLDER COMPARISON, PLEONASM, EXCESS OF EXPRESSION. In older English, *old* was not the only adjective that might have a change of vowel in the comparative and superlative. Once this change, called mutation, was with certain words the rule. Later, the tendency toward uniformity brought the vowel of the positive into the comparative and superlative. In the early part of the sixteenth century there are still two adjectives which have mutation, but alongside of the old mutated form is the new unmutated, both forms with exactly the same meaning: *long, lenger* or *longer, lengest* or *longest; old, elder* or *older, eldest* or *oldest.* Toward the close of the century the old mutated form of *long* disappeared, while *old* kept both forms but now with differentiated meaning, as described in the second paragraph on this page.

In older English, the comparative and superlative were formed by means of suffixes, not only in the case of monosyllabics but also in the case of longer adjectives, often where it is not now usual: 'Nothing *certainer*' (Shakespeare, *Much Ado about Nothing,* V, IV, 62); 'one of the *beautifullest* men in the world' (Thomas Fuller, *The Holy State and the Profane State,* V, II, 362, A.D. 1642). Long terminational comparatives and superlatives can still be heard in popular speech, which here preserves older usage: *beautifuler, beautifulest,* etc. This older usage still occurs also in emphatic and excited colloquial speech, especially in the attributive relation: 'The machine was perfect as a watch when we took her apart the other day; but when she goes together again the 15th of January, we expect her to be *pérfecter* than a watch' (Mark Twain, *Letter to Joseph T. Goodman*, Nov. 29, 1889). 'There was no *cráftier* or *cróokeder* dírector in the habitable world' (Sinclair Lewis, *Arrowsmith*, Ch. XXX, IV). 'Joe Twichel was the *delíghtedest* old bóy I ever saw when he read the words you had written in that book' (Mark Twain, *Letter to W. D. Howells*, Dec. 18, 1874). 'Our baby is the *bléssedest* little bundle of súnshine Heaven ever sent into this world.' 'It is the *stúpidest* nónsense!' The analytic forms with *more* and *most* began to appear in the thirteenth century in connection with participles, where they are still the most thoroughly established. This tendency to place the comparative and superlative of an adverb before a participle had already begun in Old English, where the forms *swiþor* and *swiþost* were used, which were replaced by *more* and *most* in the thirteenth century. The participles as verbal forms could take adverbs before them just as finite verbs do. The adverbs *more* and *most* were often retained when the participles were used as adjectives, since *more* and *most* as common adverbs had more concrete force than the endings *-er* and *-est*. This new usage spread to adjectives. It was and still is absolutely necessary in the case of nouns, adverbs, and prepositional phrases used as adjectives, as in 'He was *more knave* than fool' and 'I was *more in doubt* about it than any of them.' The general development in the direction of *more* and *most* was facilitated by the strong English trend toward analytic forms and was also furthered by French influence.

The new analytic forms at first gained ground only slowly, not becoming common until the sixteenth century, then gradually establishing themselves in the literary language alongside of the terminational forms, as we find them today.

The new analytic forms occur also in popular speech, but for the most part only pleonastically alongside of the usual terminational forms: a *more abler* man; the *most carelessest* man. Such double forms were once in use in the literary language: 'we will grace his heels With the *most boldest* and best hearts of Rome' (Shakespeare, *Julius Caesar*, III, I, 120). In older literary English, we often find double comparison in *worser*, which still survives in popular speech. Double comparison still survives in the literary language in *lesser*, which replaces *less* in attributive and substantive function in certain expressions, especially with reference to concrete things: in *lesser* things; the *lesser* grammarians; the *lesser* of two evils; but *less* with more abstract reference, as in *less* degree; at a *less* depth; also to express amount and quantity, and in adverbial use, as in 'He has *less* money than I' and 'He works *less* than I.'

We no longer feel the double comparison in *near* (comparative of *nigh*, but now felt as a positive with regular comparison, *near*, *nearer*, *nearest*) and adjectives in *-most* (now confounded with *most*, but in older English with the form *mest*, which consists of the two superlative suffixes, *-m* and *-est*), as in *foremost*, *hindmost*, *inmost*, *utmost*. From the superlative *foremost* the comparative *former* has been formed. In *aftermost, hindermost, innermost, nethermost, outermost, uppermost, uttermost,* we have a comparative + the two superlative suffixes *-m* and *-est.*

While we today in general avoid pleonastic comparison, we do not feel such forms as *more perfect, most perfect, deader, deadest, more unique,* etc., as pleonastic, since we have in mind degrees of approach to something perfect, dead, or unique.

Somewhat similar to the pleonasm of older English was its excess of expression in using the superlative with reference to two, which still survives in popular and colloquial speech, as in 'the *smallest* of the two.' Sometimes in the literary language: 'They (i.e. the two squirrels) seemed to vie with one another who should be *most bold'* (Thoreau, *Journal,* XIII, p. 189).

bb. Blending of Superlative and Comparative. In comparisons where there is present the idea of a group or class, the superlative represents the group as complete, while the comparative represents the separation of one or more from all the others in the group. Hence we should say: 'His versification is by far *the most perfect of all English poets,'* or *more perfect than that of any other English poet,* but we should not blend the two forms, as in *the most perfect of any English poet* or *the most perfect of all other English poets.*

b. Advantages of the Analytic Forms. It should be noticed that in the old terminational form the sign of the degree is intimately associated with the stem, so that it is a mere suffix and can never be stressed. On the other hand, in the analytic form the sign of degree, *more* or *most,* is still an independent word and is often stressed. There are here two parts, one indicating the degree, the other the meaning. We here, as in **47** 3 (1), (2), are fond of using the analytic form, since by means of it we can better shade our thought. We stress the adjective when we desire to emphasize the meaning, but stress the *more* or *most* when we desire to emphasize the idea of degree: 'She is more béautiful than her sister,' but 'She is indeed béautiful, but her sister is still móre beautiful.' 'Of the sisters Mary is the most béautiful and Jane the most belóved,' but 'The sisters are all béautiful, but Mary is by far the móst beautiful.'

c. Use of the 'One'-Form in Different Degrees and Different Functions. The different degrees have different forms when used substantively (**43** 1), the form with *one* being for the most part required in the positive but often felt as unnecessary in the comparative and superlative. The comparative and the superlative of descriptive adjectives frequently do not need *one,* since in connection with the definite article, the degree ending, and the context they become in large measure limiting adjectives; i.e. they do not describe persons and things but point them out and thus mark them so clearly as definite individuals that *one* is not necessary to indicate the grammatical relation: 'Which of the two brothers did it?' — '*The younger*' or '*The younger one.*' But in '*the younger* of the two brothers,' '*the youngest* of the brothers,' *one* is not usually felt as necessary. *One*, however, is now, in contrast to older usage, felt by most people as indispensable after the indefinite article, since the reference is not clear and definite: 'This cord will not do; I need *a stronger one.*' 'I am not looking for a room today. I have just found *a most cómfortable one.*'

There is also a difference of usage in different functions: 'This cord is *strong*' (predicate adjective) or *a strong one* (used substantively). 'This cord is *stronger*' (predicate adjective), or in substantive use *the stronger* or *the stronger one*, but always *a stronger one*. 'This cord is *strongest* (predicate adjective) at this point,' but in substantive use 'This cord is *the strongest*,' or *the strongest one*. 'The lake is *deepest* (predicate adjective) at this point,' but in substantive use 'Of these lakes this one is *the deepest*,' or 'This lake is *the deepest one*,' or simply *the deepest*. The pure predicate superlative represents the highest degree attained by a person or a thing as compared with himself or itself at different times, places, or under different circumstances: 'The storm was *móst violent* towards morning.' 'The lake is *deepest* here.' 'He is *happiest* when left alone.' There is usually no *the* here before the superlative, but it is now creeping in, as explained in *d* below.

d. Predicate Superlative in Form of Adverbial Accusative or Prepositional Phrase. Instead of the pure predicate adjective superlative described in *c* (2nd par.) we sometimes employ in the predicate relation the adverbial accusative (**71** 1 *a*) of a noun made from the adjective superlative by placing the definite article *the* before it: 'I doubt whether the actions of which we are *the very proudest* will not surprise us, when we trace them, as we shall one day, to their source' (Thackeray, *Pendennis*, Ch. XXXI), instead of *indeed proudest*. 'The rooks settle where the trees are *the finest*' (Lytton, *My Novel*, I, Ch. V), instead of *finest*. 'Of these specimens my friend is naturally *the móst proud*' (J. Conrad, *A Set of Six*), instead of *móst proud*. 'It was, perhaps, at this time that Mrs. Henry and I were *the móst uneasy*' (R. L. Stevenson), instead of *móst uneasy*. This superlative is always used when it is modified by a restrictive relative clause: 'On that day she looked *the happiest* that I had ever seen her,' or often with suppressed relative pronoun: 'Louise was sitting in a deep chair, looking *the happiest* [that] I had ever seen her' (Mary Roberts Rinehart, *The Circular Staircase*, Ch. XXXIV). 'On that day she looked *the most beauti-*

ful that I had ever seen her.' As described in **71** 2 *a bb,* this adverbial accusative is sometimes used with verbs as the superlative of the adverb, hence it is used also here in the predicate, just as adverbs in general are often used in the predicate with adjective force (**8** *a*).

In the predicate instead of the simple superlative without *the* or the adverbial accusative of the superlative with *the,* we may use also a prepositional phrase (**16** 1 *c*) composed of *at* and the superlative modified by a possessive adjective: 'The steps are *at their steepest* (or *steepest,* or *the steepest*) just here' (F. M. Peard, *Madame's Granddaughter,* p. 74). 'She knew that she looked *at her best* in this attire' (C. Garvice, *Staunch as a Woman,* p. 83). Similarly, as objective predicate: 'She first saw the hill *at its gayest* when that brief, brilliant hour before autumn bedecked Cosdon' (Phillpotts, *The Beacon,* I, Ch. VI). 'In "Doctor Dick" we have the author *at his most useful'* (*Literary World,* Apr. 19, 1895, p. 362). Sometimes *the* takes the place of a possessive here: 'It was now sunset — the throng *at the fullest'* (Lytton, *What Will He Do with It?* I, Ch. I).

e. Two Qualities of One Person or Thing Compared. In comparing two qualities of one person or thing we usually employ *more:* 'She is *more proud* than *vain.*' 'He is *more shy* than *unsocial.*' However, in the case of a few monosyllabics, *long, wide, thick, high,* we still regularly employ the old simple comparative, usually with full clause form in the subordinate clause: 'The wall was in some places *thicker than it was high.*'

f. Comparative of Gradation. To indicate that the quality increases or decreases at a fairly even rate we place *ever* before the comparative, or we repeat it: 'The road got *ever worse* (or *worse and worse*) until there was none at all.'

g. Comparison of Other Parts of Speech Used as Adjectives. Here we usually employ *more* and *most:* 'John is *more in debt* than I am.' 'She is *more mother* than wife.' 'Though the youngest among them, she was *more woman* than they.' Where we feel a comparative more as a pronoun than as an adjective we say: 'Charles was *more of a gentleman* than a king, and *more of a wit* than a gentleman.' 'Smith is *more of a teacher* than his brother.'

h. Comparative of Limiting Adjectives Not Used in Predicate. The comparative of limiting adjectives, *inner, outer, former, latter,* etc., cannot be used as a predicate followed by *than,* since, according to **43** 2 (2nd par.), limiting adjectives do not indicate degrees, but merely point out individuals. The comparative *older* can, as a descriptive adjective, be used as a predicate; but *elder* cannot be so used, for it is a limiting adjective: 'He is *older* (not *elder*) than I,' but 'This is the *elder* brother.'

i. Comparison of Compounds. We compare the first element of a compound where this is possible, usually employing the terminational form, but if the first element is a word that does not admit of this form we use *more* or *most*: 'the *biggest-chested* and *longest-armed* man I ever saw,' but 'This is the most *up-to-date* book I know.' Even if the first element admits of the terminational form, we employ *more* or *most* if the first element has fused with the other component so closely that it is not felt as a separate element with a separate function: *well*-known; *better*-known; but 'the *more well-to-do* tradesmen.'

Of course, we compare the last component if it contains the element capable of comparison, usually employing the form we should use if it were an independent word: *bloodthirstier, bloodthirstiest; praiseworthiest,* or *most praiseworthy;* etc.

B. Absolute Comparison:

a. Absolute Superlative. In all the preceding examples the degrees express superiority in a relative sense, some person or thing excelling all the members of a definite group in the possession of a certain quality, while in fact the higher or highest degree here may be a comparatively low degree: 'John is *the taller* of the two, *the tallest* of them all, but he is notwithstanding quite small.' We may in the case of the superlative, quite commonly, express superiority in an absolute sense, indicating a very high degree in and of itself, not necessarily, however, the very highest.

In lively style, we here often place unstressed *most* before the stressed positive of the adjective or participle: (relative superlative) 'It is *the móst lovely* flower in the garden,' but in an absolute sense: 'He has *the most béautiful* of gardens.' 'Everything about the place tells of *the most dáinty* order, *the most éxquisite* cleanliness' (Mrs. Gaskell, *Life of Charlotte Brontë*, Ch. I). 'It was *a most magníficent* exhibition of courage.' 'We shall soon see George and *his most béautiful* wife.' '*Most lóvely* flowers everywhere greet the eye and *most frágrant* perfumes fill the air.' We can distinguish only by the stress '*Most réputable* (absolute superlative) writers have now abandoned this claim' from '*Móst* (= the great majority of) *reputable* writers have abandoned this claim.'

Instead of the usual absolute superlative with *most*, we sometimes in the case of adjectives which admit of the terminational form employ the simple superlative, often drawling it out and stressing it: 'Oh, he made *the rú-dest* remark!' 'The letter did not meet with *the wármest* reception.' 'Thus he was perfectly rational, though when others beheld him he appeared *the insánest* of mortals' (Meredith, *Amazing Marriage*, Ch. VI). 'I'm in *the bést* of health.' 'She is in *the bést* of company.' 'At all times her dress was of *the póorest.*' 'Humphrey's ideas of time were always of *the váguest* order' (Florence Montgomery, *Misunderstood*, Ch. III). 'The letter was written in *the kíndest* terms.' Besides such expressions we find this form sometimes, especially in our own time, when the superlative is modified by a limiting adjective, *my, any, every, each, no, some, certain*, etc., or, on the other hand, sometimes when it is entirely unmodified, especially in the case of abstract and plural nouns: '*my déarest* darling'; '*any pláinest* man who reads this' (Trollope, *Framley Parsonage*, Ch. XIV); 'so completely did it fulfil *every fáintest* hope'; 'there is *no smállest* doubt.' 'It was perhaps on *some dárkest, múddiest* afternoon of a London February' (*Times Literary Supplement*, June 9, 1918). 'A stronger lens reveals to you *certain tíniest* hairlets, which make vortices for these victims' (George Eliot, *Middlemarch*, I, Ch. VI). 'Michael and Guy left Oxford in the mellow time of an afternoon in *éarliest* August' (Compton Mackenzie, *Sinister Street*, p. 760). 'I owed her *déepest* gratitude' (Elinor Glyn, *Reflections of Ambrosine*, III, Ch. V). 'Our friendship ripened into *clósest* intimacy.' 'From *éarliest* times.'

The most common way to express the absolute superlative is to place before the positive of the adjective a simple adverb, such as *very, exceedingly, highly, absolutely*, etc., or in colloquial speech *awfully, dreadfully, terribly, beastly*, etc., sometimes without the suffix *-ly*, as in the case of *awful*, even regularly so in the case of *real* (**71** 1; widely used in America), *mighty, jolly* (British colloquial for *very*), *devilish, damned, bloody* (British), *bally* (British), etc.: *very cold* weather; an *exceedingly intricate* problem; a *highly polished* society. 'I am *awfully* (sometimes *awful*) *glad.*' 'It's *real cold.*' 'I'm *jolly glad* anyhow.' 'It's *damned hot.*' Also *only too, simply too, just too*, and *just* are so used: 'I shall be *ónly tóo glád* if you accept my invitation.' 'It's *símply tóo bád* of him!' 'It's *júst tóo áwful!*' 'It's *júst spléndid!*' In older English, *pure* was used with the meaning of *absolutely:* 'It is *pure* easy to follow god and serue hym in tyme of tranquylite' (Caxton, *Chast. Goddes Chyld*, 89, A.D. 1491). This usage is preserved in certain American dialects: 'Dey hides is *pure tough*' (Julia Peterkin, *Scarlet Sister Mary*). Compare *Syntax*, **16** 2 *a*.

b. Absolute Comparative. The absolute comparative is not as common as the absolute superlative: the *lower* classes; the *higher* classes; *higher* education; a *better*-class café; the *more complex* problems of life; 'the mist, like a fleecy coverlet, hiding every *harsher* outline' (H. Sutcliffe, *Pam the Fiddler*, Ch. I).

We usually place here before the positive of the adjective a simple adverb, such as *tolerably*, *fairly*, *rather*, etc.: a *tolerably* (or *fairly*, or *rather*) long walk; *somewhat* talkative; etc.

C. **Comparison to Denote Degrees of Inferiority.** Here we uniformly employ *less* and *least*: *wise*, *less wise*, *least wise*.

3. Adjectives and Participles Used as Nouns

In English more easily than in most languages a word can be converted, i.e. made into another part of speech. This usually takes place without any modification whatever, except, of course, the necessary change of inflection. Thus the noun *eye* is converted into a verb by merely giving it verbal inflection: 'They *eyed* the prisoners with curiosity.' As adjectives are now always uninflected, the conversion of nouns, adverbs, phrases, and sentences into adjectives is very easy. Compare **8** *a*. On the other hand, the conversion of adjectives into nouns is more difficult and irregular. In old English, adjectives, converted into nouns, often retained their old adjective form. In many cases this old usage survived even after the adjective endings had disappeared; in other cases the loss of the adjective endings brought about new forms of expression. The breakdown of the adjective inflection at the close of the Middle English period forced the English people, who are fond of short-cuts in language, to do something contrary to their nature — to go a roundabout way to express themselves. If we now say *the good* it can only mean *that which is good*, but in older English, according to the form of article, it could mean *the good man*, *the good woman*, *the good thing*. We now regularly use *man*, *woman*, and *thing* here, but there are numerous individual survivals of the older use of the simple adjective where the situation of itself without the help of the form of article or adjective makes the thought clear. Of persons: the *deceased;* the dear *departed;* my *intended;* the *accused;* the *condemned;* a lover clasping his *fairest;* my *dearest* (in direct address); etc. In a few cases a modern genitive form has been created: the *Almighty's* strong arm; her *betrothed's* sudden death; etc. A large number have a genitive singular in *–'s* and a plural in *–s*, since they have become established as regular nouns: a *savage*, genitive a *savage's*, plural *savages*. Similarly, *native*, *equal*, *superior*, *private*, *male*, *three-year-old*, *grown-up*, *Christian*, *criminal*, *red* (anarchist), etc. 'She is such *a silly*.' 'They are *such sillies*.' 'Our *wets*' (opponents of prohibition) in Congress.' (Arthur Brisbane, Jan. 1, 1932).

Alongside of modern plurals here in *–s* are a number of older plurals without an ending, which are the reduced forms of still older inflected forms: my *own* (i.e. my kindred); the *rich;* the *poor;* the really (adverb) *poor;* the seriously (adverb) *wounded;* the worst (adverb) *wounded;* the *living* and the *dead;* the *blind;* our *wounded;* 2000 homeless *poor;* a new host of *workless* walking the streets; four other *accused;* 2000 *killed* and *wounded; rich* and *poor; old* and *young; big* and *little.* These nouns usually have no case ending throughout the plural, taking the modern forms of inflection: *the wounded;* gave food and drink *to the wounded;* the friends *of the wounded.* The *s*-genitive is rare: 'Always just the pausing of folks for the bit of offhand chat and then the hurrying away to their own dinner bells and their *own's* voices, calling' (Fannie Hurst, 'White Apes,' in *Forum,* Mar. 1924, p. 290).

These nouns without an ending in the plural have been preserved because in the competition between the old and the new plural in older English they became differentiated in meaning. They acquired collective force: 'the *poor* of our city,' but 'the two *poor men* entering the gate'; 'the state of *the heathen* and their hope of salvation,' but 'Smith and Jones are regular *heathens.*' On account of the lack of a plural ending the old uninflected plural, however, is usually ambiguous, so that we often cannot use it at all. We may say 'the *poor* of the South,' but we must say 'the *blacks* (or the *black people*) of the South,' for *the black* now suggests a singular idea since it is sometimes used in the singular, thus now being felt as a noun: '"Fetch a light," she said to *the black* who opened for us' (S. Weir Mitchell, *Hugh Wynne,* Ch. XXVII). We say also '*the whites* of the South.' The old form is thus in quite limited use. A pastor might say to his congregation 'I urge *old and young,*' but he could not say 'I desire to meet after our service *the young.*' He would say *the young people.* But we say 'a picture of a willow-wren feeding its *young*' (or *young ones*). In a broad sense *the young* is used also of human beings: 'Men rode up every minute and joined us, while from each village *the adventurous young* ran afoot to enter our ranks' (T. E. Lawrence, *Revolt in the Desert,* p. 303).

Since the names of some peoples have been made from adjectives, as *the English, the French,* the old uninflected adjective plural has become productive here, and is now used with many names of peoples: the *Swiss* (in older English *Swisses*), *Portuguese* (in older English *Portugueses*), *Japanese, Chinese,* etc. We sometimes use the same form for the singular just as we use 'the *deceased*' for the singular, but we avoid these singulars since we feel these forms as plurals and prefer to say 'a *Portuguese gentleman, lady,*' etc. In *Chinaman,* plural *Chinamen* or *Chinese,* we have, for singular and plural, forms which may become established. The singular

Chinee, a back-formation from the plural *Chinese,* is common in a derogatory sense. We usually say 'three, four *Chinamen,*' but '10,000 *Chinese, the Chinese*' (not *the Chinamen,* although in a narrow sense we may say '*the Chinamen* sitting on the bench yonder'). The uninflected plural is especially common with the names of uncivilized or less civilized peoples: the *Iroquois, Navaho, Hupa, Ojibwa, Omaha, Blackfoot, Duala, Bantu, Swahili,* etc. Here the same form is freely used also as a singular: a *Blackfoot,* etc. We say *the English, the French,* or *Englishmen, Frenchmen,* but in the singular only *Englishman, Frenchman.* Many other words, however, may assume the new, more serviceable, type with the genitive singular and the plural in *-s*: a *German,* a *German's,* the *Germans;* an *American,* an *American's,* the *Americans;* a *Zulu,* a *Zulu's,* the *Zulus;* and even many of those given above with uninflected plural: an *Omaha,* an *Omaha's,* the *Omahas.* The plural of *Blackfoot* is often *Blackfeet.*

In some cases we make nouns out of the substantive form (**43** 1), i.e. the *one*-form: the *Crucified One;* the *Evil One.* 'He is a *queer one.*' My *dear ones;* our *little ones;* my *loved ones;* the *great ones* of earth, etc.

In a few cases nouns made from adjectives may drop the article as in older English: 'My good lady made me proud as *proud* can be' (Richardson, *Pamela,* III, 241). 'Eleven years *old* does this sort of thing very easily' (De Morgan, *Joseph Vance,* Ch. XV). 'Sweet *Seventeen* is given to daydreams.' '*Slow* and *steady* wins the race.' 'For 'tis the eternal law That *first* in beauty should be *first* in might' (Keats, *Hyperion,* II, 228). '*First* come, *first* served.' '*First* come, *first* in.' In plain prose an article is usually placed before the noun: 'He is strong for *an eleven-year-old.*' 'I was *the first one* served.' 'We were *the first ones* served.'

Nouns made from adjectives often denote lifeless things, usually with a meaning more or less general or indefinite. They are usually preceded by the definite article or some other limiting adjective: *the present* (= *the present time*); *the beautiful; the sublime.* 'You ask *the impossible.*' 'He did *his best.*' As such forms, though now employed as nouns, were originally adjectives, they still are often, like adjectives, modified by adverbs: the genuinely *lovable;* the relatively *unknown;* etc. There are still many neuter nouns made from adjectives, but in older English the tendency to use them was stronger than today. A number of these nouns have since been replaced by other words: 'Let me enjoy my *private*' (Shakespeare, *Twelfth Night,* III, II, 99), now *privacy.* 'Whereat a sudden *pale* (now *paleness*) . . . Usurps her cheeks' (*id., Venus and Adonis,* 589).

While the neuter nouns made from adjectives now usually have the definite article or some other limiting adjective before them, we still not infrequently find the older articleless form, especially in the case of two adjectives connected by *and:* 'I can spy already a strain of *hard* and *headstrong* in him' (Tennyson). 'That is *good*, but there is *better* to follow.' 'There is *worse* ahead.'

The modified or unmodified form has become fixed in many set expressions: in *the dark;* after *dark;* through *thick* and *thin;* from *grave* to *gay;* to keep to *the right;* to go to *the bad;* to go from *bad* to *worse;* to make *short* of *long;* *the long* and *the short* of it; before *long*. 'After frequent interchange of *foul* and *fair*' (Tennyson, *Enoch Arden*, 529). 'The police came up to see *fair* between both sides' (*London Daily News*, Mar. 11, 1891). 'That's no *fair*' (common in the language of children).

A large number of neuters have become concrete nouns: *German;* Luther's *German;* the *German* of the present time; my *German;* a *daily* (paper), pl. *dailies;* a *weekly*, pl. *weeklies;* the *white* of an egg, the *whites* of eggs. 'They sent him a *wireless*.' 'He at last got in one with his *left*' (left hand). 'The combats between the moderates and the extreme *left*' (more democratic section of European legislative chamber). 'What is the *good* of lying?' 'It is no *good* trying to conceal it,' but the plural *goods* has a much more concrete meaning. A large number are employed only in the plural: *greens, woolens, tights, necessaries, movables, valuables, the Rockies*, etc.

Most of the adjectives used as nouns in the examples given above are descriptive adjectives, but also some limiting adjectives are used as nouns: 'He has lost his *all*.' 'He and *his* (**7** VII *e bb*) are all well.' 'I wrote you the details in my *last*' (= *last letter*). 'He was successful from *the first*' (= *the beginning*). Proper adjectives are often (**10** 8) limiting adjectives. They can, of course, be used also as nouns: *a German; a German's; the Germans;* etc. The use of these adjectives as nouns is treated on page 195.

OLDER INFLECTIONS OF ADJECTIVES

44. An outline of older inflection is given below to indicate clearly what a great gain has come to English at this point in the direction of simplicity of expression.

A. **Old English Inflection of Descriptive Adjectives.** In Old English, there were two different types of descriptive adjective inflection — the strong and the weak. The strong type was the usual one for adjectives that were not modified by a limiting adjective: 'þes mann is *eald*' = 'This man is *old*.' 'þas menn sindon *ealde*' = 'These men are *old*.' The strong form was used also after one limiting adjective — the indefinite article.

The original meaning of the weak adjective was to point out a definite individual or definite individuals. It was used after limiting adjectives except the indefinite article: 'þes *ealda* mann' = 'this old man'; 'þas *ealdan* menn' = 'these *old* men.' The weak form was always used in the comparative, while the superlative could be inflected strong or weak, as in the case of the positive, but was usually weak. The comparative was formed by adding *-r* and the superlative by adding *-ost* or *-est*. To the comparative stem the regular weak endings were added, to the superlative stem the regular strong or weak endings. The following examples illustrate the inflectional changes for the nominative masculine singular in the different degrees of comparison: leof or leof*a* 'dear,' leof*ra* 'dearer,' leof*ost* or leof*esta* 'dearest'; eald or eald*a* 'old,' ield*ra* 'older,' ield*est* or ield*esta* 'oldest.' In Old English there were special endings for the different genders, cases, and numbers, as can be seen in the examples of inflection given below. Some adjectives, as in the case of *eald*, had a change of vowel in the comparative and the superlative. *Elder*, *eldest*, as in 'the *elder*, or *eldest*, brother,' are survivals of this older usage. Compare **43** 2 A *a aa*.

The forms of the two Old English types of adjective inflection are illustrated below by the inflection of *eald* 'old':

1. STRONG ADJECTIVE

	Masculine	Feminine	Neuter
		Singular	
Nom.	eald	eald	eald
Acc.	ealdne	ealde	eald
Dat.	ealdum	ealdre	ealdum
Gen.	ealdes	ealdre	ealdes
Instr.	ealde		ealde
		Plural	
Nom.	ealde	eald*a*, *-e*	eald, ealde
Acc.	ealde	eald*a*, *-e*	eald, ealde
Dat.	ealdum	ealdum	ealdum
Gen.	ealdra	ealdra	ealdra

The nominative of the feminine singular and the nominative and the accusative of the neuter plural in adjectives with a short stem end in *-u* or *-o*, as in the case of the corresponding nouns in **29** I B and C: *blacu* or *blaco*, nom. fem. sing. and nom. and acc. neut. pl. of *blæc* 'black.'

2. WEAK ADJECTIVE

	Masculine	Feminine	Neuter
		Singular	
Nom.	ealda	ealde	ealde
Acc.	ealdan	ealdan	ealde
Dat.	ealdan	ealdan	ealdan
Gen.	ealdan	ealdan	ealdan

Plural

Nom.	ealdan	ealdan	ealdan
Acc.	ealdan	ealdan	ealdan
Dat.	ealdum	ealdum	ealdum
Gen.	eald*ra*, *–ena*	eald*ra*, *–ena*	eald*ra*, *–ena*

B. **Middle English Inflection of Descriptive Adjectives.** In this period all adjectives became uninflected except monosyllabics ending in a consonant, and they preserved but little of the old wealth of adjective form, as shown by the following inflection of *ōld* 'old':

1. Strong Adjective

For All Genders

Singular

Nom., Acc., Dat., Gen.	ōld

Plural

Nom., Acc., Dat., Gen.	ōlde

2. Weak Adjective

For All Genders

Singular

Nom., Acc., Dat., Gen.	ōlde

Plural

Nom., Acc., Dat., Gen.	ōlde

C. **Older Inflection of Limiting Adjectives.** In older English *that* and *this* had forms not only for number, but also for gender and case:

1. Old English Inflection of 'That'

Singular

	Masculine	Feminine	Neuter
Nom.	sē̆	sīo, sēo	þæt
Acc.	þone	þā	þæt
Dat.	þǣm, þām	þǣre	þǣm, þām
Gen.	þæs	þǣre	þæs
Instr.	þȳ, þon		þȳ, þon

Plural

For All Genders

Nom.	þā
Acc.	þā
Dat.	þǣm, þām
Gen.	þāra, þǣra

In Middle English, under the influence of the forms in the oblique cases, *sē* was replaced by *þe*, which by 1300 had everywhere developed into the uninflected definite article *the* and was replaced as a demonstrative by *that*. In the early part of the period, however, *that* was used not only as a demonstrative but also as a definite article for all genders, so that there were two definite articles, *the* and *that*. *That*, as definite article, was gradually replaced by *the*, but it survived for centuries before adjectives or pronouns beginning with a vowel, especially in the expressions *that one, that other* = *the one, the other*. *That other* in the contracted form *t'other* was still in wide literary use in the eighteenth century and survives in dialect. From 1300 on, the usual function of *that* was that of a singular demonstrative adjective and pronoun for all genders and cases.

The Old English plural *þā* became *þō* in Middle English. Alongside of it there was in common use another plural form — *thōs*, the Middle English form of Old English *þās*, plural of 'this.' As described in 2 below, *þōs* was brought into relation to *þō* by the sameness of vowel. The two forms were long used side by side with the same meaning until the gradual disappearance of *þō* in early Modern English and the final victory of *thōs* in the form of *those*. The Middle English plurals *þō* and *þōs* were used for all genders and cases.

The Old English neuter instrumental survives in adverbial *the*: '*The* more money he has, *the* more he wants.' Compare **71** 1 *c*.

2. Old English Inflection of 'This'

Singular

	Masculine	Feminine	Neuter
Nom.	þēs	þīos, þēos	þis
Acc.	þisne	þās	þis
Dat.	þis(s)um	þisse	þis(s)um
Gen.	þis(s)es	þisse	þis(s)es
Instr.	þӯs, þīs		þӯs, þīs

Plural

	For All Genders
Nom.	þās, þǣs
Acc.	þās, þǣs
Dat.	þis(s)um, þiosum
Gen.	þissa, þisra

In Middle English, the neuter form *this* was early used as a singular for all genders and cases. The Old English plural *þās* became in Middle English *thōs*. The Old English plural *þǣs* developed in Middle English several variants, *thēs, theos, thüs*. The singular *this* was for a time employed also as a plural. Alongside of the plurals *thēs, thüs, this*, sprang up the new plurals *thēse, thüse, thise*, which had been formed by adding the adjective plural ending *-e* to the plurals *thēs, thüs*, and *this*. All these plurals were used for all genders and cases. The plural *these* alone survives in this meaning. The plural *thōs* gradually ceased to be felt as the plural of *this*, and was employed, as described in 1 above, as the plural of *that* alongside of the regular plural *tho*. *Thōs*, though originally the plural of *this*, was brought into relation to *thō*, the plural of *that*, by the sameness of vowel, being felt as a form of *thō*, a form with a distinct plural ending *-s* and for this reason finally replacing *thō* entirely. This could be brought about since *thōs* was not vividly felt as the plural of *this* and was not needed, for *this* had at that time other plurals besides *thōs*, as described above. Of the later spellings of *thōs* — *those*, *thoose*, *thoos*, and *thoes* — only *those* survives. In early Modern English the spellings *thees* and *theese* were used alongside of *these*.

CHAPTER XII

INFLECTION OF VERBS

FORMS OF THE VERB

45. The English verb has forms called voices, moods, tenses, aspects, numbers, and persons, which represent the action suggested by the verb as limited in various ways, such as in person, number, time, manner of conception, etc. A verb that can be limited in all these ways is called a finite verb: I *go*, he *goes*, they *go*, he *went*, he *may* go, he *might* go, etc. The infinite forms of the verb — the participle (**47** 4), the infinitive (**47** 5), and the gerund (**47** 6) — are limited in fewer ways.

One of the marked features of the growth of English in the modern period is the amazing activity in the field of the verb. Not only entirely new structures have been reared but also new life has been injected into older creations that were living before only feebly.

VOICE

46. There are two voices, the active and the passive.

Active Voice

47. The Six Forms and Their Uses. The active voice indicates that the subject does something, is, or is becoming, something. There are six forms, which fall into two groups. The forms of the first group — the common form, the expanded form, the *do*-form — are finite (**45**); the forms of the second group — the participle, the infinitive, the gerund — are infinite (**45**). The forms of the first group must agree with the subject in person and number (**53** *a*): 'Our bird *sings* very little.' 'Birds *sing*.' 'The boat *is sinking*.' 'The boats *are sinking*.' 'I *am sinking*.' '*Does* he *do* his work well?' '*Do* they *do* their work well?' Finite verbs in present-day English are not so rich in endings as in the older periods, but they must agree with the subject whenever they can. The forms of the second group do not have inflectional endings, hence they can never indicate their agreement with the subject: '*Going* (= *As I was going*) down the street I met a friend.' '*Going* (= *As we were going*) down the street we met some friends.' 'I believe *him to be* (= *that he is*) honest.' 'I believe *them to be* (= *that they are*) honest.' '*After finishing* (= *After he finishes*) his work he goes to bed.' '*After finishing* (= *After they finish*) their work they go to bed.' The infinite forms have fewer tenses than finite verbs, but they express the time relations fairly well. Participle and gerund lack forms for mood and aspect (**52**). They cannot express mood at all and can express progressive action only in the perfect tense. See **69** B. The infinitive lacks forms for mood but has forms for the two aspects: 'I expect him *to work* tomorrow.' 'I expect the engine *to be working* by this time tomorrow.' 'He is reported *to have done* it.' 'He is reported *to have been playing* there at that time.' Compare the full inflection of verbs, **69** A, B. The finite forms can express finer shades of thought than the infinite forms as they are richer in means of expression, hence they must often be used; but the infinite forms are great favorites in practical life by reason of their handiness and are highly prized in choice language by reason of their elegant simplicity. The improvements that in the last five centuries have been gradually introduced into the infinite forms by making them clearer means of expression and by making it possible to use them more extensively show that the English people has appreciated their good qualities and intends to give them a wider place in its everyday speech. The infinite forms, however, are restricted to subordinate clauses. Here they compete with finite verbs, as shown in some of the examples given above. They do not differ from the finite forms in meaning. They are usually only convenient substitutes for them. On account of the great usefulness of the infinite forms they are treated with considerable care in this book.

A description of the six forms follows.

1. *Common Form:* 'Mary *makes* good bread.' 'Mr. Smith *is* a banker.' 'I *have* just *received* good news.' For full inflection see **69** A.

The common form has two distinct uses. (1) It expresses a general truth, a fact, a habitual act: 'Water *runs* down hill.' 'Honesty *pays*.' 'He *smokes*.' (2) It expresses a particular act: 'I *hear* him coming up the stairs.' 'I *see* him coming up the street.' Although the common form often expresses something general, as in (1), it often expresses something particular, as here. It always expresses an accomplished fact, but the fact is sometimes of a general nature, sometimes refers to a particular occurrence. The idea of a single particular occurrence is indicated not by some peculiarity of form but by the situation, as in these two examples. But sometimes the situation does not show that the act is a particular one. To make it perfectly clear that the act is a particular one, not general, we employ the expanded form, as illustrated in 2 *b* below.

As seen in the preceding paragraph, the common form has two quite different meanings. They are united, however, in a higher unity. Both meanings represent the act as a whole, as an accomplished fact. Thus the common form always has terminate force. Compare **52 1**.

a. Pro-Verb 'Do.' To avoid the repetition of the common form of a verb that has just been mentioned we employ the pro-verb *do* in its stead: 'He behaves better than yóu *do*,' instead of *behave*. 'We shall have a hard time of it if competition advances as it *hás done* for several years.' 'He has never acted as he *shóuld have done*.'

In colloquial speech *has* or *have* is often used elliptically for *has done* or *have done*: 'It is very unkind of you to inconvenience us as you *háve*.'

2. *Expanded Form.* It is made up of a form of the copula *be* and the present participle of the verb to be conjugated: 'He *is writing* a letter.' For full inflection see **69** B. The expanded form from its frequent use with progressive force, as described in *a* below, is often called 'the progressive form.' It has, however, sometimes still the meaning of the common form, as described in *b* below. In the Old English period, when it first, under the influence of church Latin, came into use, it was not differentiated in meaning from the common form. The present differentiation of the two forms is the result of hundreds of years of development. In Shakespeare's day the expanded form was used as today but not so often and so regularly: 'What *do you read* (now *are you reading*), my lord?' (*Hamlet*, II, ii).

The expanded form, though now widely used, is not employed at all with the copula *be* if it is desired to impart progressive force. Thus we still say, as in older English, 'I *am* sick,' 'I *have been* here a month,' not 'I *am being* sick,' 'I *have been being* here a month.' The expanded form of the copula *be* always has terminate force. See *b* below.

The expanded form as used today has two quite different meanings.

a. With Progressive Force. The expanded form usually represents an act as going on: 'He *is working* in the garden.' There is thus usually an idea of progression or continuance associated with this form. Hence with such a verb as *know* we cannot use it at all, for *know* denotes a fact, something complete within itself, not something uncompleted that is still going on: 'I *have known* (not *have been knowing*) him for ten years.' Similarly we say, 'I *hear* (not *am hearing*, for the act of perception is completed) him coming up the stairs.' On the other hand, the expanded form cannot be employed with verbs denoting a condition, state, even though the idea of continuance is prominent, for it is generally restricted in its use to verbs denoting action: 'I *have been* (not *have been being*) sick all week.' We use the common form here. Such verbs as *sit, lie, stand, remain,* however, are thought of as acts, not conditions, for we can prolong the acts at will: 'He *has been sitting* on the porch for an hour.' Of course, there are acts beyond the power of our will, such as *rain, snow, thunder, perspire,* etc. It is here self-evident that these are acts of nature. With all verbs denoting acts the particular phase of the progression is indicated by the meaning of the verb or verbal phrase. With duratives (**52** 2 *a*) the expanded form represents the subject as in the midst of the action: 'He *is working* in the garden.' With iteratives (**52** 2 *b*) this form represents the subject as in the midst of action that is often repeated: 'The clock *is ticking.*' 'The girls *are giggling.*' With ingressives (**52** 2 *c*) it represents progression towards the beginning of an act or state, i.e. a preparing to, a tending to, the initial stage to: 'It *is going* to rain.' 'Look out! I *am going* to shoot.' 'I *am getting* tired.' 'The baby *was waking up* as I entered.' With effectives (**52** 2 *c*) the expanded form indicates that the action is progressing toward, is approaching an end: 'The lake *is drying up.*' 'His strength *is giving out.*' Compare **52** 2 *c*.

The progressive idea was once expressed by the common form, which, however, was used also with its present meaning. The introduction of the expanded form to express progressive force was a great improvement of English expression. Compare **52** 1.

b. WITH TERMINATE FORCE. The expanded form often represents the act as a whole, hence it has terminate (**52** 1) force: 'I am sorry you doubt my statement. I *am telling* you the truth.' The common form, 'I *tell* the truth,' could not be used here, for its meaning, as in (1) in 1 (2nd par.) above, is so general that it is not felt as suitable for reference to this particular case. The action here is not represented as going on. The reference is to an act as a whole. We must thus often employ the expanded form to indicate that the statement is not general but refers to a particular case. It must not be inferred, however, that the common form cannot be used for reference to a particular case. It often indicates a particular act, as illustrated in (2) in 1 (2nd par.) above. Usually in such cases the situation makes it clear that the reference is to a particular act: 'I *hear* him coming up the stairs.' 'I *demand* that you go at once.' But when the situation does not make it perfectly clear that the reference is to a particular act we employ the expanded form: 'I know that I *am demanding* a good deal of you when I ask this of you, but I hope that you will do it.' Thus though the expanded form is often not employed to indicate a particular act it always stands ready for service when the common form is not a clear means of expression. We have been so often told that we should associate the expanded form with progressive force that we have overlooked the fact that it often has terminate force, i.e. indicates an act or state as a whole, as a fact. The expanded form of the copula *be* is always terminate: 'Perhaps I *am being* a fool, dearest one. I will go up to my music-room and play myself into reason and leave you to your own work' (Charles Morgan, *The Fountain*, p. 289). The expanded form refers to the particular moment in question.

The expanded form with terminate force is often associated with our inner convictions and feelings so that statements having this form contain a strong personal element expressing emphasis or feeling: 'When Elizabeth put Ballard and Babington to death she *was* not *persecuting*' (Macaulay, *Essays*). 'Somebody *has been tampering* with my alarm clock!' The references here are to particular cases, but the expanded form with terminate force often refers also to a general fact imparting likewise emphasis and feeling: 'A rich man who spends his money thoughtfully *is serving* (much more emphatic than *serves*) his country as nobly as anybody' (Milne, *Mr. Pym Passes By*, p. 10). 'You *are helping* me, darling. You *are being* an angel' (Noel Coward, *The Vortex*). 'John *is doing* fine work at school' (spoken in tone of praise). 'John *has been neglecting* his work recently!' (vexation). 'You children *are* always *getting* in my way when I am at work' (scolding). 'Our vacation is almost over. We shall soon *be having* to go down to the old shop every morning' (unpleasant thought). The lively tone associated with the terminate expanded form makes this form peculiarly suitable for use in descriptive style: 'We *are tramping* over the hills and *reading* and *writing* and *having* a restful time' (Jean Webster, *Daddy-Long-Legs*, p. 225).

The terminate force of the expanded form is very old. It was in use in the Old English period. It is probably the oldest meaning of the form. Throughout the centuries progressive force has been becoming more and more associated with this form, but the old terminate force is still often found with it, as seen in the above examples.

3. *'Do'-Form.* In the present and the past tense of verbs of complete predication the simple verb is often replaced by a periphrastic form made up of *do* and a dependent infinitive: 'Thus conscience *does make* (= *makes*) cowards of us all' (Shakespeare), originally '*causes a making* of cowards out of us all.' At first, *do* was a full verb with an infinitive as object. Later, it lost its concrete force and became a mere periphrastic auxiliary. In older English, as in the example from Shakespeare, there was usually no clear difference of meaning between the simple and the periphrastic form. This periphrastic form with *do* was rare in Old English, but

it began to become common in the fourteenth century and was at its height between 1500 and 1700. After the periphrastic and the simple form had long been used interchangeably, a desire for more accurate expression led to a differentiation of their meaning, as described in detail below. Present usage became fixed about 1750, but with certain verbs the old simple forms lingered on even in plain prose long after they had elsewhere passed away, indeed here and there linger still, especially in set expressions, as *if I mistake not, I care not, I doubt not, I know not, what say you? what think you?* etc. Of course, the poet makes still more liberal use of the old forms when it suits his purpose. In popular speech there is a tendency to employ the *do*-form with the copula *be* in declarative sentences, which is contrary to literary usage: 'Some days she *do be* awful about her food' (Dorothy Gerard, *The Eternal Woman*, Ch. XV).

In plain prose we now employ *do* in the following categories:

(1) In the present and the past tense of a verb of complete predication accented *do* stands in a question, a declarative statement, or an entreaty where there is a desire to emphasize the idea of actuality, the truthfulness of a claim, realization or a desire of realization: '*Dídn't* he work?' '*Díd* he work?' '*Dóes* he cheat?' 'I still maintain that you didn't *dó* it.'—'But I *díd* do it.' 'Why don't you *wórk?*'—'I *dó* work.' 'I am so happy to learn that you *dó* intend to come.' '"My dear, you *díd* (painful realization) tread on my toe."—"I didn't *méan* to," muttered Soames' (Galsworthy, *Swan Song*, Part II, Ch. II). '*Dó* finish your work' (desire of realization).

(2) Unaccented *do* is used in the present and the past tense in declarative sentences with inverted word-order and in entreaties and questions in which there is no desire present to emphasize the idea of actuality: 'Never *did I sée* such a sight.' 'Bitterly *did we repént* our decision.' '*Do fínish* your work.' '*Does* he *belíeve* it?' 'How'*s* (= how does) it *stríke* you?' (Jack London, *The Sea-Wolf*, Ch. VII). 'What'*s* he *sáy?*' 'What *did* he *ánswer?*'

The old simple forms are now used in questions only when the subject is an interrogative pronoun: '*Who met* you?' In older English, the simple forms could be used also when some other word was subject: '*Discern'st thou* aught in that?' (Shakespeare, *Othello*, III, iii, 101). The old simple forms are still used for archaic effect in historical novels: '*Saw* you ever the like?' (Wallace, *Ben Hur*, Ch. X). Also in certain dialects, as in Scotch English, the old simple forms are still used: 'What *paid* ye for't?' (George Macdonald, *Robert Falconer*, Ch. XXI). The older simple form survives widely in the literary language in the case of ***have,*** especially in England: '*Have* you swordfish?' alongside of the more common *do*-form, '*Do* you *have* swordfish?' The old simple form is still often, especially in England, employed with *used:* '*Used you*, or *did you use*, to do such things?' In indirect questions the old simple form is preserved with all verbs: 'When *did* you *come* back?' but 'I asked him when he *came* back.'

(3) *Do* is employed also in the negative form of questions, declarative statements, and commands when simple *not* is the negative, but only in the present and past tense of verbs of complete predication. It is therefore not employed in the case of the copula *be*, the tense auxiliaries, the modal auxiliaries *can, must*, etc., the auxiliary-like verb *ought*, often also the auxiliary-like verbs *need, dare, used*, which, however, may take *do;* usually also not in the case of *have* in unemphatic statements: '*Doesn't* he *líve* here?' but '*Isn't* he here?' 'I *do not* often *forgét* it,' but 'I *must not forget* it.' 'I *do not go* home till eight,' but either 'I *need not go* home till eight' or 'I *do not need to go* home till eight.' 'She *dared not tell* (or *to tell*) him,' or 'She *did not dare tell* (or *to tell*) him.' 'He *did not use*, or *used not*, to smoke,' or colloquially 'He *didn't use*, or *usedn't* (*usen't*), to smoke,' where Americans prefer the *do*-forms, Britishers the simple form. In America and England both constructions are often blended in colloquial and popular speech: 'I *didn't used* to mind your embarrassing me' (Sinclair Lewis, *Dodsworth*, last Ch.). 'I *didn't used*' (Gepp, *Essex Dialect*, p. 120). Usage fluctuates with *have*, often even in the same sentence: 'I *haven't* or *don't have*, it with me,' but in emphatic statement 'I *do nót have* it with me,' where, however, in colloquial speech we may employ also the form without *do:* 'You have it with you.' — 'I *hável't*.' In commands and entreaties: '*Don't tóuch* me!' '*Dón't* you *touch* me!' '*Don't have* a thíng to dó with him!' '*Dón't go* yet!' In negative commands and in positive and negative entreaties *do* is used also with the copula *be*, as *do* has become associated with negative commands and both positive and negative entreaties: '*Don't be* láte!' '*Dón't* you *be* late!' '*Dó be* reasonable!' '*Dón't be* unreasonable!' In popular speech *do* is used also elsewhere with *be:* 'Now boy, why *don't* you *be* perlite and get up and give one of these young ladies a seat?' (*Punch*).

Although in negative statements the old simple forms have disappeared from simple prose, the charm of the beautiful older simplicity often asserts itself in the language of our better moments: 'We cannot do wrong to others with impunity. Our conscience *résts not* until the wrong be righted.'

(4) In our popular southern American English the *do*-form is used also in the present perfect tense, as in older Scotch English

(*Syntax*, **6** A *d*): 'I [*have*] *done tell* you 'bout Brer Rabbit makin' 'im a steeple' (Joel Chandler Harris, *Nights with Uncle Remus*, p. 97). The dependent infinitive following the past participle *done* is often attracted into the form of the past participle: 'I 'speck I [*have*] *done tole* (instead of *tell*) you 'bout dat.' (*ib.*, p. 97).

4. *Participial Form.* The forms of the participle are given in **69** and **70**. The time relations expressed by them are described in **56** 1 *d*, **65** *a*, and **70** A *a*. The participle often has full verbal force and at the same time performs the function and has the position of an adjective. It is used in subordinate clauses as predicate or as predicate appositive. Predicate in adjective relative clauses: 'The boy *playing* (= *who is playing*) in the yard is my brother.' 'His last novel, *written* (= *which was written*) in 1925, is his best.' 'He is a man *broken* (= *who has been broken*) by misfortune.' It is very common as objective predicate (**8**, 4th par.): 'I see him *working* in his garden.' It has here progressive (**52** 2) force. To express terminate (**52** 1) force, i.e. the idea of an action as a whole, as a fact, we must employ the infinitive as objective predicate: 'He said he didn't do it, but I saw him *do* it.' In adverbial clauses the participle often stands as a predicate appositive (**8**, 5th par.) alongside of the predicate or near it, modifying it as to some relation of time, manner, attendant circumstance, cause, condition, concession, purpose. Time: '*Going* (= *As I was going*) down town I met an old friend.' '*Having finished* (= *After I had finished*) my work I went to bed.' Manner (an unusually common category in English): 'I beat him *jumping*' (indicating manner, respect in which he excelled). 'He *was* (= *was busy*) two years *writing* the book.' 'Are you through *asking* questions?' Attendant circumstance: 'He was drowned *bathing* in the river.' Cause: 'I feel it as a rare occasion *occurring* (= *since it occurs*) as it does only once in many years.' '*Feeling* (= *Since I feel*) tired I'll stay at home.' 'I was proud of him *acting* (= *since he acted*) so unselfishly.' Condition: 'The same thing, *happening* (= *if it should happen*) in wartime, would amount to disaster.' Concession: 'Even *assuming* (= *Though we assume*) a great willingness on the part of our members to work, we are not properly prepared for the task.' Purpose: 'He went *fishing*' (= *that he might fish*). Other examples are given in **15** 2 *b*, *c*, *d*, *e*, *f*, *g*, *h*, *i*, *j*.

The subject of the participle is usually not expressed within the participial clause. It is implied in some noun or pronoun near by to which the participle as a predicate or predicate appositive adjective belongs. The subject of the participle is expressed only in the nominative absolute (**27** 1 *a*, 3rd par.) construction: 'Off we started, *he remaining* (= *while he remained*) behind.' The use of the different forms of the participle in the nominative absolute construction is illustrated in **15** 2 *b, c, d, f, h, i*, **18** B 1. On the other hand, the participle often has no subject expressed or implied — the dangling (or unrelated) participle. This construction is usually censured by grammarians, but on account of its easy formation it is in wide use and is even approved natural English expression wherever the reference is quite general and indefinite: 'Generally *speaking* (= If *one* may speak in a general sense), boys are a nuisance.' 'So how could I have stolen him from her, even *supposing* (= if *one* should suppose) I had the slightest desire to' (Sinclair Lewis, *Dodsworth*, Ch. XIX).

The participial form was little used in Old English with the full force of a verb. Later in Middle English, under the influence of church Latin, it came into wider use with this force. Little by little it has become a powerful construction, a general favorite by reason of its convenience and forcible terseness.

5. *Infinitival Form*. The forms of the infinitive are given in **69** and **70**. The time relations expressed by them are described in **56** 1 *d*, **65** *a*, and **47** 5 *b*. The infinitive was originally a verbal noun. It was often used as the object of the preposition *to*, and this older usage survives in many expressions. Preposition and infinitive together form a prepositional object, which is used to complete the meaning of a verb, adjective, or participle: 'Hunger drove him *to steal*' or *to stealing*. 'I finally induced him *to do* it.' 'He is eager *to do* it.' 'He is inclined *to take* offense easily.' Compare **16** 1 *b*.

The *to* before the infinitive, however, is now usually a conjunction rather than a preposition. It is now for the most part a mere formal introduction to the infinitive clause just as *that* is often a mere formal introduction to the full clause with a finite verb. The infinitive itself is the verbal predicate in the subordinate clause in which it stands. It is now widely used in subordinate clauses. Adjective relative clause (**8** *b*, **18** B 6): 'John is the boy *to do it*' (= *who should do it*). 'That is the thing *for you to do*' (= *that you should do*). Attributive substantive clause (**18** B 2): 'His desire *to succeed* (= *that he should succeed*) spurred him on.' 'It is time *for you to begin your work*' (= *that you should begin your work*). Subject clause (**18** B 1): 'It is stupid of you *to say it*' (= *that you say it*). Object clause (**18** B 3): 'I hope *to see him today*' (= *that I may see him today*). Adverbial clause: 'I am going early *so as* (or *in order*) *to get a good seat*' (clause of purpose = *so that I may get a good seat*). Adverbial infinitive clauses of different kinds are given in **15** 2 *c, d, f, g, h, i, j*.

As shown in the examples just given the infinitive clause is an equivalent of the full clause with a finite verb. As it is usually felt as an easier way of talking, it is a favorite in colloquial speech; but by reason of its elegant simplicity it is much used also in more formal language.

The expression here is often elliptical: 'I shall go to the celebration tomorrow, or at least I am planning *to* [*go*].'

For the split infinitive see **14** (3rd par.).

a. SUBJECT OF THE INFINITIVE. The subject of the infinitive is often not expressed in the clause, but is some noun or pronoun performing some function in the principal proposition and at the same time serving as the subject of the infinitive: '*He* desires *to go* at once' (= He desires *that he may go* at once). Here *he*, the subject of the principal verb, serves also as the subject of the infinitive.

The infinitive construction often has the force of a relative clause. The subject of the infinitive is the noun or pronoun that precedes it: 'This road car is the latest *to be offered* to the public' (= *which has been offered*). 'He has an ax *to grind*' (= *which he wants to grind*). 'The king has no children *to succeed* him on the throne' (= *who can succeed him*).

In 'She gave *him* (dative) *to understand* that he should not come back again' *him*, the dative object of the principal verb, is also subject of the infinitive. Likewise in the two following examples: 'I told *him* (dative) where *to find* it' (= *where he could find it*). 'I taught *him* (dative) how *to do* it.' In the passive the infinitive is retained: 'He was told how *to do* it.'

In 'I am depending upon *him to do* it' *him* is the object of the preposition *upon* and serves at the same time as the subject of the infinitive.

The subject of the infinitive is most commonly an accusative, which serves as the object of the principal verb and as the subject of the infinitive: 'He begged *me* (accusative) *to go* at once.'

After verbs of permitting, allowing, commanding, and ordering the dative object serves also as the subject of the infinitive: 'I permitted *her* to take the books out of the library.' 'I ordered *him* to bring in the prisoners.' When the infinitive is put into passive form its former accusative object becomes its new accusative subject: 'I permitted *them* (i.e. the books) to be taken out of the library.' 'I ordered *them* (i.e. the prisoners) to be brought in.'

The infinitive with an accusative subject has its simple form after *let, bid, make, have* (cause, experience), *see, notice, look at, observe, perceive, watch, feel, hear, overhear, listen to*: 'Bid *him come* in.' 'I had *him do* it yesterday.' 'I had *the gypsies steal* my hens.' 'I saw *him do* it.' 'Look at *him run!*' 'I heard (or 'overheard') *him say* it.' Compare *Syntax*, **15** III 2 B. In the passive statement the infinitive is retained, but it takes *to:* 'He was heard *to say* it.' 'He was seen *to do it.*'

The accusative is used as the subject of the infinitive after another, quite different group of verbs, namely, *want, wish, desire, like, know, think, believe, suspect, suppose, take* (= *suppose*), *imagine, expect, declare, report, represent, reveal, find, prove,* etc. The infinitive here arose in the objective predicate (**8,** 4th par.) construction: 'She wishes *him happy.*' 'She wished *him here.*' 'I imagined *him a respectable man.*' 'I can't imagine *anyone in better health.*' 'They represented *me as having forsaken* my former principles.' Here an adjective, adverb, noun, prepositional phrase, or a participle is predicated of the preceding object without the aid of the linking verb *be,* as is usual in this construction, but there is a natural modern tendency to employ the linking verb here as elsewhere: 'She wished *him to be* here.' 'I know *him as an honest man* or *him to be an honest man.*' 'I thought, supposed *him to be the owner* of the house.' 'He thought, supposed *Richard to be me*' (**27** 2 *c*). 'I took *him to be nearer* sixty than fifty.' 'They report *him to be very sick.*' Likewise in the passive: 'She wished *the rubbish removed* or *the rubbish to be removed.*' The old objective predicate construction without the linking verb *be,* as in the last example, is still common in the passive.

In the objective predicate construction the predicate is not only an adjective, adverb, noun, prepositional phrase, or participle, but now also an infinitive: 'She wishes *him here with her*' or *him to stay with her.* 'His father wants *him to give* more time to his studies.' 'She reports *him as improving* or *him to be improving.*'

When the subject of the infinitive is general or indefinite, it is often not expressed: 'It is wise *to be cautious*' (= *that one should be cautious*).

In Old English the subject of the infinitive was never in native expression formally expressed, but was merely implied in some word in the principal proposition, as in all the examples in the first six paragraphs. The construction was widely felt as very handy, but it could not be used where there was no word in the principal proposition which might serve as its subject. In the fourteenth century arose the desire to extend the use of the construction. The infinitive began to be used with a subject of its own if there was no word in the principal proposition that could serve as its subject. This subject is always preceded by the preposition *for.* The history and explanation of this *for* is given in *Syntax,* **21** *e.* Though most people know nothing of the origin of this *for* everybody feels clearly that it must stand before the subject of the infinitive. This new construction occurs most commonly in the subject clause and in adverbial clauses, much less commonly in object clauses: '*For me to back out now* (subject clause) would be to acknowledge that I am afraid.' 'All that I want is *for somebody to be thinking about me*' (Arnold Bennett, *The Glimpse*) ≐ *that somebody should be thinking about me* (subject clause). 'He was too near *for me to avoid him*' (adverbial clause of result). 'I know how deeply she must have offended you *for you to speak like that*' (adverbial clause of cause). 'I should be glad *for Mary to go*' (adverbial clause of condition). 'I see no way out of the difficulty *except for them to offer an apology*' (adverbial clause of exception). 'There was nothing now *but for him and the footman to get into the carriage*' (adverbial clause of exception). 'I am waiting *for them to go*' (adverbial clause of purpose). 'I hope *for the book to make its mark*' (Meredith, *Letters*, p. 550) (object clause). It is common as object of an adjective: 'I am eager *for her to see it.*'

b. Use of the Tenses of Infinitive after Full Verb. The tenses of the infinitive express time relative to that of the principal verb. The present tense indicates time contemporaneous or future with reference to that of the principal verb: 'I wish *to do* it.' 'He was foolish *to do* it,' not usually now as in older English 'He was foolish *to have done* it.' 'I managed *to do* it without his help' (I did it without his help). Of course, the present infinitive refers to the past after the annalistic present (**51**), for the annalistic present itself refers to the past: 'This is the fourth case of lockjaw *to occur* (i.e. *that has occurred*) within a week.'

The perfect tense of the infinitive indicates time prior to that of the principal verb: 'I am proud *to have been* able to help.' 'It gives recreation a better relish *to have* first *accomplished* something.' To indicate non-realization many still say 'I intended *to have written* a line to you,' a survival of older usage. As the perfect infinitive, according to present usage, points to time prior to that of the principal verb, it does not now express here the idea intended. Hence it is now more common in the literary language to say: 'I had intended *to write* a line to you.' 'He would have liked *to have hugged* his father' (Hughes, *Tom Brown's School-Days*, I, Ch. IV) is now usually replaced by 'He would have liked *to hug* his father.'

The use of the tenses of the infinitive after modal auxiliaries is treated in **50** 2 *d* (next to last par.).

6. *Gerundial Form.* The forms of the gerund are given in **69** and **70.** The time relations expressed by them are described in **56** 1 *d*, **65** *a*, and **47** 6 *b*. The present participle now has the same form as the gerund. This unfortunate development is described in **56** 4 *e*. Although the gerund is not differentiated from the

present participle in form, it is distinguished by its function. While the participle has the function and the position of an adjective, the gerund has the function and the position of a noun: '*Rearing* a large family is no easy task.' Here *rearing* has the full force of a verb, but at the same time it has the function of a noun, for it is the subject of the sentence. A sentence with a subject clause often begins with anticipatory *it* and closes with a gerundial clause as logical subject: '*It* is no use (predicate) *your saying anything about it.*' Compare **18** B 1 (3rd par.). In 'I like *working* out my own problems' *working* has the full force of a verb, but at the same time it has the function of a noun, for it is the object of the principal verb. Thus the gerund is widely used in subject and object clauses. See **18** B 1 (3rd par.) and **18** B 3 (last par.).

One of the most common functions of the gerund is to serve as the object of a preposition. Preposition and gerund together form a prepositional clause, which modifies a verb, adjective, participle, or noun. Such a prepositional clause is of course an adjective element if it modifies a noun: 'his disappointment *over attaining so little.*' If the prepositional clause modifies a verb, adjective, or participle it is an object if its relation to the governing word is very close, but it is an adverbial element if its relation to its governing word is less close. Prepositional clause as object: 'Hunger drove him *to stealing*' or *to steal.* 'He insisted *upon his wife's joining him in the deceit.*' 'I am afraid *of their seeing it.*' 'I am accustomed *to doing* (or *to do*) *it this way.*' Adverbial prepositional clause: '*After finishing my work* (clause of time) I went to bed.' 'He differed from his colleagues *in spending his spare time in reading*' (clause of manner). 'He never passed people *without greeting them*' or *without their greeting him* (clauses of attendant circumstance). 'I have gone *as far as collecting statistics for my investigation*' (clause of extent). 'I can't do anything *for thinking of her*' (clause of cause). 'He can't walk yet *without my helping him*' (clause of condition). 'I didn't come *with the object of destroying the good feeling prevailing among you*' (clause of purpose).

The gerund, as a noun, often follows a noun in the capacity of a modifying genitive: 'In the language of scholars the art *of speaking simply* is almost a lost art.'

The gerund, as a noun, can stand in apposition to a preceding noun: 'I now have very pleasant work, *preparing boys for college.*'

As a noun the gerund often forms the first component of a compound: *báking*-pòwder, *íroning*-bòard, *díning*-càr, *drínking*-wàter, *sléeping*-quàrters. A present participle in the same position is distinguished from the gerund by its adjective force and its weaker stress: *slèeping* chíldren.

a. SUBJECT OF GERUND. In Old English the subject of the gerund was always in the genitive, the subjective (**27** 4 A *a*) genitive, for the subject of a verbal noun was regularly in the genitive. In general this rule still holds for verbal nouns: '*man's* love of fairness.' We often still employ as the subject of the gerund a genitive or a possessive adjective, which historically is an old genitive: 'I am provoked at *John's* (or *his, her, your, their*) treating him so rudely.' In contrast to usage with other verbal nouns the genitive subject of our modern gerund with the force of a full verb is always an *s*-genitive, never an *of*-genitive. For centuries the English people has been growing ever fonder of the handy, forcible gerund. As soon as it became a favorite means of expression widely used, there arose a serious formal difficulty, which had to be overcome. To the ear the singular and the plural of the *s*-genitive sound alike. The natural impulse to speak so as to be understood led to an improvement of English expression here. A simple means of removing the difficulty suggested itself. It soon became common to employ an accusative as subject instead of the genitive, for the accusative always distinguishes singular and plural by the form: 'I don't approve of *my son* (sing.), or *my sons* (pl.), doing that.' There is a natural inclination to avoid the *s*-genitive of a noun denoting a lifeless thing. Rather than use the queer obsolete *s*-genitive here most people prefer to employ an accusative subject: 'You better not depend on *this address reaching* me but address c/o Guaranty' (Sinclair Lewis, *Dodsworth*, Ch. XIX). There are a large number of uninflected pronouns that have no *s*-genitive. Of course we have here no choice. We must employ an accusative: 'Some families may have moved away on account of the repeated failure of crops, but I do not know of *any having done* so.' If there is after the subject of the gerund a modifier of any kind the accusative is now always used as subject: 'Did you ever hear of *a man* (never *man's*) of good sense *refusing* such an offer?' Enough has been said to explain the wide use of the accusative today as subject of the gerund. The question is discussed more in detail in *Syntax*, **50** 3. In one group of pronouns, however, the genitive is still preferred — the old genitives *my, thy, his, her, its, our, your, their:* 'The fact of *his* (or *her, their*) *being convicted* so promptly is gratifying.' On the other hand, the gerund often has no subject of its own, as there is elsewhere in the sentence a noun or pronoun which is felt not only as performing its own function but as serving also as the subject of the gerund: 'I am afraid *of hurting* his feelings.'

b. ORIGIN OF GERUND. The gerund was originally a verbal noun. Its object was in the genitive, like that of any other verbal noun, as in 'the persecution *of the early Christians.*' This old construction is still common: '*The shooting of birds* (genitive object) is forbidden.' 'I don't like *his trusting of the secret* to his friends.' The gerund, like every other verbal noun, can take an article or a possessive adjective before it, as in these examples. The article or possessive adjective, however, disappears when the verbal force of the gerund becomes strong, and the genitive object is replaced by an accusative object, as required by verbs: '*Shooting birds* is useless.' This is the verbal construction that has been treated above. This verbal force has become so strong that, since 1500, forms for tense and voice have been gradually coming into ever wider use: 'After *having finished* my work I went to bed.' 'The fact of his *being* (or *having been*) *convicted* so promptly is gratifying.' Though the gerund now often has the full force of a verb and can, like a verb, take an accusative object, it does not, like a verb, take a nominative subject. Just as every verbal noun has a genitive subject, as in '*a man's* love of fairness,' so may the gerund often still take a genitive subject, as in the early period when it was a mere verbal noun. Examples are given in *a*. Moreover, the gerund always has its original construction, i.e. it is still always a noun — the subject or object of a verb or the object of a preposition.

Passive Voice

48. Meaning and Use. The passive voice represents the subject as acted upon: 'John *was punished* for disobeying his mother.' 'Our house *is being painted.*' Only transitives (**12** 1) can form a passive. Some transitives, however, on account of their meaning do not readily take passive form, especially certain verbs in **12** 1 (2nd and 3rd parr.).

The passive is a favorite form of expression in English. See **7** VII *c bb* for a peculiar feature of our language that has contributed to the spread of the passive.

49. Formation of the Passive. The active verb is often a simple form, but the passive is always a compound. It is made in the following ways, of which the forms in 1, 2, 3, 4 are finite, those in 5 infinite (**45**).

1. *Common Actional Passive Form.* The common literary form is made by combining some form of the copula *be* with the past participle: 'The house *is painted* every year.' 'The house *was painted* last year.' 'The house *has* just *been painted.*' In early Modern English, *is* is often used instead of *has been:* 'Besides I met Lord Bigot and Lord Salisbury, With eyes as red as new-enkindled fire, And others more, going to seek the grave Of Arthur

whom they say *is* (now *has been*) *kill'd* tonight On your suggestion' (Shakespeare, *King John*, IV, II, 162). In this older English the participle had not only the force of a predicate adjective expressing a state, as in 'The house is *painted*,' but also the force of a passive verb pointing to the past, as in the example from Shakespeare. The common actional passive form represents the act as a whole, as a fact, hence it has terminate (**52** 1) force. Although it always represents the act as a whole, as a fact, it has two quite different meanings. It indicates a single occurrence or a customary, habitual occurrence, the context alone deciding which of the two meanings is present. Single occurrence: 'The attitude of the community *is* well *described* in today's issue of our local paper.' 'Our house *was painted* last month.' Customary occurrence: 'Our house *is painted* every two years.' 'The end of the struggle is nearly always that the public *is conceded* everything.' For full inflection see **70** A.

To represent the beginning or the end of the occurrence as a fact we place the simple form of *begin* or *cease* before the passive infinitive: 'Our house *has begun to be painted*.' 'This oil well *has ceased to be worked*.' If we desire to represent a progressive action as just starting or as approaching an end we must employ the expanded form, as explained below in 3 *a* (last par.).

2. *New Passive Actional Forms*. Within the modern period have sprung up several valuable new passive forms.

a. 'GET'-PASSIVE. The common actional form is employed also as a statal passive, i.e. to express a state: 'The door *was shut* (state) at six, but I don't know when it *was shut*' (act). This is explained by the simple fact that in our copula *be* are merged two quite different verbs — *is* and *be*. *Be* had effective (**52** 2 *c*) force with the meaning of our modern effectives *get* and *become*. The modern forms of *be* still often have their old effective force: 'The door *was* (= *got* or *became*) *shut* at six.' Effective *be* indicates an act, but unfortunately *be* does not always have this meaning. It more commonly indicates a state, retaining the old meaning of *is*. Compare **52** 3. We still have a certain feeling for both meanings of the forms of *be*, but the matter is not vividly clear to us, and there has arisen a widely felt desire to express ourselves more clearly. There is a strong drift in England and America to employ *be* to denote a state and use effective *get* to denote an act: 'He *is married* (state) now, but I can't tell you when he *got married*' (act). 'Your nature is an overbearing one, Sophia, and for once you *got punished* for it' (A. Marshall, *Many Junes*, Ch. I). 'The men say: "Good stunt, Mont! But not practical politics, of course." And I've only one answer: Things as big *got done* in the war'

(Galsworthy, *The Silver Spoon*, Ch. VII). 'I suppose it *will get whispered* about, and they'll hear it' (Tarkington, *Gentle Julia*, Ch. XVIII).

b. 'BECOME'-PASSIVE. This form is made by combining some form of *become* with the past participle: 'Beatrice *became* more and more *influenced* by Randal's arguments' (Lytton, *My Novel*, II, II, Ch. III). *Get* and *become* as effectives (**52** 2 *c*) have in general the same meaning, but in passive constructions they are becoming differentiated. The *get*-passive denotes a simple act, as illustrated in *a*, while the *become*-passive represents the occurrence as the final outcome of a development: 'Good and readable as these addresses are, we should like to see those which deal with these larger topics gathered into a single smaller volume, which at a modern price might *become* widely *read* by the people of both countries' (*London Times*, Educational Supplement, A.D. 1914). 'He *became seized* with a profound melancholy' (McCarthy, *History of Our Own Times*, I, p. 228). 'For the first time the immensity of what she was doing *became borne* in upon her' (Dorothea Gerard, *Exotic Martha*, Ch. V). This is the youngest of the passive constructions, but has already on account of its fine distinctive meaning become common. It is strange that it has been overlooked by grammarians. It is not mentioned even in the great *Oxford Dictionary*. The first example and the last two are taken from Poutsma's large English Grammar, II, Section II, p. 100. This Dutch scholar quotes these interesting sentences as examples of English passive formations, but he does not describe their peculiar character.

As *become* is used here in the common form it represents the development as a fact. If we desire to represent the development as approaching its culmination we employ the expanded form, as explained below in 3 *b*.

c. 'COME-TO'-PASSIVE, 'GET-TO'-PASSIVE. This passive is made by combining some form of *come* or *get* with a passive infinitive: 'He *came* (or *got*) *to be highly respected* by everybody in the community.' The *get-to* passive is not so choice English as the *come-to* passive, and moreover it becomes impossible in the present perfect tense on account of the ambiguity of the form: 'He has *come* (not *got*) to be treated more kindly by his associates.' *Has got* here would indicate that the speaker is determined to bring about a better treatment of the person in question. After *come* we sometimes employ the past participle instead of the present passive infinitive: 'I can now tie my shoes so that they *won't come untied*,' instead of *won't come to be untied*. This construction is after the analogy of 'It *comes true*' (**52** 2 *c*).

The *come-to*-passive is sharply differentiated from the *become*-passive: 'He used to be so hard-headed, but he *has* gradually *come to be influenced* by his wife. Evidently, he *has become softened* by gentleness and kindness.' Both constructions indicate the end of a development or the outcome of events. *Become* directs our attention only to the final outcome, while *come to* points also to the preceding course of events. In 'O'Connell *became seized* with a profound melancholy' *became* cannot be replaced by *came to be,* for the reference is to a sudden development.

As *come* and *get* are used here in the common form they represent the development as a fact. If we desire to represent the development as approaching its culmination we employ the expanded form as explained below in 3 *b*.

d. Passive of Experience. There is another passive, which, though it did not absolutely arise in the present period, first became common in modern times. It is now widely employed in colloquial speech and is found also in the literary language. It represents the subject of the sentence as experiencing something. In this peculiar construction there is always a past participle with passive force. This participle serves as an objective predicate, predicating something of the object of the principal verb, which is regularly *have* or *get:* 'Last week I *had* (or *got*) *my right leg húrt* in an accident.' 'I have just *had* (or *got*) *gíven* me (or 'to me') *a fine new knife.*' In more careful language the usual auxiliary is *have:* 'In life I *have had this truth* repeatedly *dríven* in on me.' 'In this grammar the spoken language *has had its proper importance assígned* to it.'

e. Passive after Causatives. The construction is the same as in *d*, but *have* and *get* are here stressed: 'I *hád* (or *gót*) a new suit made.' 'We *háve* our work *done*' (We employ others to do it), but with quite different meaning 'We *have* our work *dóne*' (It is done, completed). Thus accent can play a rôle in English grammar.

3. *Expanded Form.* The expanded form has different meanings with different kinds of verbs.

a. With Duratives and Iteratives. With duratives (**52** 2 *a*) and iteratives (**52** 2 *b*), we employ the expanded form of the copula *be* in connection with the past participle to indicate that the subject is receiving the action continuously and that the attention is directed to the midst of the action: 'The bread *is being baked* in the new oven.' 'He *is being beaten* by some ruffians.' Here the common form of the copula *be* represents the action as going on, but the common form of another copula, even though it have strong durative force, represents the action, not as going on, but as a whole, as a fact: 'For a long while she *kept being disturbed* by her conscience.' 'She *kept being startled* by the stump of his missing finger' (Robert Raynolds, *The Brothers in the West*, p. 15). Compare **52** 2 *a*. The passive expanded form with the copula *be* is used only in the present and the past tense. In other tenses, on account of the clumsiness of the form, it is replaced by the shorter form described in the next paragraph. For full inflection of the two forms as now used in the literary language see **70** B.

There is another expanded passive form than the one described above. It was widely employed between 1700 and 1825, and in the literary language is still in limited use in the present and the past tense and is the usual literary construction for the present perfect, past perfect, and future. It is made by combining a form of the copula *be* with the present participle, which here contains the passive idea, although elsewhere it usually has active force: 'There *is* a new bridge *building*.' This construction first appeared about the middle of the sixteenth century. It gradually replaced in the literary language the much older gerundial construction, 'There is a new bridge *a-building*,' from older *on building*, *in building*. The contracted form *a-building* survives in popular speech, like many other older literary means of expression.

It does not seem probable that the passive construction 'There *is* a new bridge *building*' developed entirely of itself. There was alongside of it, from the start, an older passive with the same construction, i.e. active in form but passive in meaning. It represented something as going on of itself as a natural process or development: 'The heel of my right shoe *is wearing* badly on the outer side.' 'There *is* a storm *brewing*.' 'There *is* mischief *brewing*.' See 4 on page 222 for other examples of this passive. It is a marked peculiarity of our language that intransitives develop passive force. Compare **12** 2 (last par.). The presence of this passive must have facilitated the establishment of the passive 'There *is* a new bridge *building*.'

The passive 'There *is* a new bridge *building*' was after 1825 to have a serious competing construction in another passive form, which first appeared about 1447 and was thus a century older but had not yet made much headway: 'There *is* a new bridge *being built*.' The present and past tenses, *is being built*, *was being built*, though heavier than *is building*, *was building*, were felt as clearer passive forms and gradually came into favor and for the most part supplanted the shorter forms. But on account of the impossibility of such clumsy forms as *has been being built*, *had been being built*, *will be being built*, the longer passive construction has not become established in the present perfect, past perfect, and future. On account of the clumsy combination of *be being* the longer construction cannot be used also in the present infinitive. On account of these formal difficulties in the way of the long construction the shorter present perfect, past perfect, and future forms — *has been building, had been building, will be building* — have been retained. In our colloquial speech is a still younger form, which is both handy and accurate. It is made by combining *get* and the past participle. It can form all the tenses: 'A new bridge *is getting built, was getting built, has been getting built*,' etc. As the literary language has no form in the present infinitive the *get*-passive is now used here: 'It is, however, an excellent thing that bicycles should *be getting called* simply wheels' (Abercrombie, *Poetry and Contemporary Speech*). The expanded *get*-passive may later become more useful in the literary language.

To express the idea of the beginning or end of progressive action with duratives we place the expanded form of *begin* or *cease* before the passive infinitive: 'This paper *is beginning to be* widely *read*.' 'The village was greatly excited over the murder, but the subject *is* now *ceasing to be discussed*.'

b. WITH POINT-ACTION VERBS. With point-action verbs (**52** 2*c*) we employ the expanded form to indicate a beginning or an approaching end: 'The work *is* just *being* (or *getting*) *started*.' 'The last bit of our patience *is being* (or *getting*) *exhausted*.' The passive constructions described in 2 *b*, *c* above become progressive effectives (**52** 2 *c*) when they have the expanded form: 'Our patience *is becoming exhausted* by these constant annoyances.' 'This paper *is becoming* widely *read* by the people of this community.' 'He is *coming* (or *getting*) *to be* highly *respected* by everybody.' The development is here represented as culminating.

4. *Passive Force with Active Form.* Many intransitives which represent something as going on of itself as a natural process or development acquire passive force: 'The hat *blew* (= *was blown*) into the river.' 'Muscles, nerves, mind, reason, all *develop* (= *are developed*) under play.' 'My coat *caught* (= *got caught*) on a nail.' 'The plans *worked out* (= *were worked out*) successfully.' 'The books *sold out* (= *were sold out*) in a week.' 'The vessel *steers* (= *can be steered*) with ease.' Compare **12** 2 (last par.).

The expanded form is used with many of these verbs to express the progressive idea: 'The plans *are working out* successfully.' 'The books *are selling* rapidly.' 'Snow *is blowing* in at the window.' This passive has not shared the fate of the passive construction of the same form described in 3 *a* above: 'The bridge *is building*,' now supplanted by the more expressive 'The bridge *is being built*.' We say *is being built* when we think of something being constructed by visible human hands, but we say 'The lecture hall *is* rapidly *filling up* with students and townspeople' and 'Snow *is blowing* in at the window' because we think of something proceeding of itself, i.e. spontaneously, naturally, without the aid of the conscious effort of hand or brain. The two shades of passive thought were not differentiated in form in early modern English but are now clearly distinguished by the form of expression.

There is another common construction in which the verb usually has passive force with active form. In older English a predicate infinitive after the copula *be* had passive force with active form. Only a few expressions survive in the principal proposition: 'This house *is to let*' (= *is to be let*). 'He *is to blame*' (= *is to be blamed*). In abridged relative clauses this old usage is still common: 'He is not a man *to trifle with*' (= *that can be trifled with*). 'It is not a place *to visit* (= *that should be visited*) at night.' For fuller treatment see *Syntax*, **7** D 2, p. 47.

5. *Infinite Passive Forms.* The passive participial, infinitival, and gerundial forms are given in **70**. These forms are widely used in subordinate clauses: 'His last novel, *written* (= *which was written*) in 1925, is his best.' '*Frightened* (= *As he was frightened*) by the strange sound he halted.' '*Being oppressed* (= *As I am oppressed*) by financial troubles I am not enjoying life much.' 'We are expecting *him to get punished* (= *that he will get punished*) for it.' '*After becoming discouraged* (= *After he had become discouraged*) by so much misfortune, he gave up entirely.' '*Having come to be treated* (= *As he had come to be treated*) more kindly by his associates, he found life easier.' '*Having had* (= *After I had had*) my chickens *stolen* twice, I took greater precautions to save them.' Compare **47** 4, 5, 6.

MOOD

50. Moods are the changes in the form of the verb to show the various ways in which the action or state is thought of by the speaker.

There are three moods:

1. **Indicative Mood.** This form represents something as a fact, or as in close relation with reality, or in interrogative form inquires after a fact. A fact: 'The sun *rises* every morning.' In a close relation to reality: 'I shall not go if it *rains*.' The indicative *rains* here does not state that it *is* raining, but indicates that the idea of rain is not a mere conception, but something close to a reality, for the speaker feels it as an actual problem in his day's program with which he has to reckon and is reckoning.

The complete inflection of the indicative is given in **69** and **70.**

2. **Subjunctive Mood.** There are two entirely different kinds of subjunctive form — the old simple subjunctive and the newer forms consisting of a modal auxiliary and a dependent infinitive of the verb to be used. The complete inflection of the simple subjunctive is given in **69** and **70.** The forms of the modal auxiliaries are found in **57** 4. A brief treatment of the meaning of the subjunctive forms and the use of the subjunctive tenses follows. They are discussed in detail in *Syntax*, **41–44.**

The function of the subjunctive is to represent something, not as an actual reality, but as formed in the mind of the speaker as a desire, wish, volition, plan, conception, thought; sometimes with more or less hope of realization, or, in the case of a statement, with more or less belief; sometimes with little or no hope or faith. The present subjunctive is associated with the idea of hopefulness, likelihood, while the past and the past perfect subjunctive indicate doubt, unlikelihood, unreality, modesty, politeness: 'I desire that he *go* at once.' '*May* he *return* soon.' 'O that he *were* alive and *could see* the fruits of his labor.' 'I *would buy* it if I *had* the money.' 'I fear he *may* come too late.' 'I am becoming worried; he *might come* too late.' 'I *would have* bought it if I *had had* the money.' 'I *should think* it rather unfair.' 'You *should go* at once.'

The various meanings may be classified under two general heads — the optative subjunctive and the potential subjunctive. The optative subjunctive represents something as desired, demanded, or required (by a person or by circumstances). The potential subjunctive marks something as a mere conception of the mind, but at the same time represents it as something that may probably or possibly be or become a reality or on the other hand as something that is contrary to fact. The optative subjunctive is often closely related in meaning to the imperative.

In the four following articles sentences will be given to illustrate the two principal meanings of the subjunctive and the use of the subjunctive tenses.

a. Optative Subjunctive. Examples: '*Part* we in friendship from your land!' (Scott, *Marmion*, 6, 13) now with the auxiliary *let:* '*Let* us *part* in friendship!' 'Everybody *stand* up!' or with the auxiliary *let:* '*Let* everybody *stand* up!' For stronger expression of will we use *must:* 'We *múst* go!' Also *have to* and in colloquial speech *have got to:* 'I insist on it. You *have* (or *have got*) *to* do it,' or 'You *must* do it.' 'We *have to* (or *must*) sell our house' (constraint of circumstances). To indicate the will of the speaker we often use *will* in the first person and in questions also in the second person, but in declarative statements employ *shall* in the second and third persons: 'I *will* do all I can' (promise). 'I *won't have* you children playing in my study.' '*Won't* you *sit* down?' (kind in tone). 'You *shall have* some cake' (promise). 'You *shall smart* for it' (threat). 'You *shall do* as I say.' 'You *should go* at once' is polite, while 'You *shall go* at once!' is stern. 'We *should hurry!*' (admonition). 'You *should mind* your own business!' (polite in form, but stern in tone).

Moral constraint: 'We *ought to* (or *should*) do something to help him.' Ideal constraint, i.e. fitness and expediency: 'She *ought to* (or *should*) *be praised* for that.' 'A liar *ought to* (or *should*) *have* a good memory.' We often employ *is to, are to,* here: 'Such women *are to be admired.*' *Is to, are to,* here and elsewhere are as clearly modal forms as are the so-called modal auxiliaries *shall, should,* etc. In expressions of will we often employ *is to, are to:* 'You *are* always *to shut* the door when you come in.' This form also represents something as planned: 'He *is to go* soon.' 'He *is to be promoted* soon.'

In permissions *may* is the usual auxiliary: 'You *may play* until noon.' 'Rooms *may* not be *subrented.*' In colloquial speech *can* is widely used in negative form: 'Children, you *cannot* (or *must not*) play in the street.' Also in figurative use: 'Society *cannot* disown its debts.' (J. Arthur Thompson, *What Is Man?* p. 218.)

In wishing we use the simple subjunctive in a few expressions, but we now for the most part employ auxiliaries: 'The Lord *have* mercy on us!' 'God *bless* you!' '*May* you *see* many happy returns of this occasion!' 'Too late! O *might* I *see* her just once more!'

The past subjunctive is much used in modest expressions of desire: 'I *would* rather *stay* than *go.*' 'He *would like* to go,' but 'I *should like* to go,' for in the first person *would* expresses desire and its use here would be tautological, as this idea is contained in *like.* '*Would* you *tell* me the time, please?' 'You *might call* at the baker's and *get* some bread.' Instead of the past subjunctive *would* with the infinitive we sometimes use the past subjunctive *had* with the infinitive: 'I *had* rather *stay* than *go.*'

Shall, is to, are to, represent something as the inevitable outcome of events: 'Better days *are* soon *to* (or *shall* soon) follow.'

The optative subjunctive can of course be used also in subordinate clauses: 'I beg that I *may go,* too.' 'I require that you *be* back by ten.' 'She insisted that he *accept* and, indeed, *take* her with him.' 'Though he *may make* (concession) every effort he cannot succeed.' 'Even though he *might make* (concession) every effort he could not succeed.' 'I am now going down to Garden City and New York till the President *send* for me; or if he do not send for me, I'm going to his house and sit on his front steps till he *come* out!' (Walter H. Page, *Letter to Irwin Laughlin*, August, 1916). 'Is she going to keep a lonely vigil till that time *shall* come?' 'You should be kept at work until you *finished* it.' 'I locked myself into my study that I *might* (purpose) not *be disturbed*.' 'What this country needs now more than it ever did before, what it *shall* (or *is to*) need the years following is knowledge and enlightenment.' (Woodrow Wilson, Dec. 9, 1902).

b. Potential Subjunctive. Examples: 'It *may rain* today.' 'It *might rain* today.' 'We *can* (stronger than *may*) expect opposition from vested interests.' '*Could* he *have meant* it?' 'I *should think* it rather unfair' (modest statement). 'That *would have been* rather difficult' (modest statement). 'He *could* easily *do* it.' 'Eclipse (horse) *ought to* (or *should*) *win*.' 'You *must* (or *should*) *be* aware of this' (inferred or presumed certainty). 'You *must* (or *should*) *have been* aware of this.' The past subjunctive *had* with a dependent infinitive is often used to express a statement modestly: 'He *had* better *go*' (= He *should regard* going as better).

The potential subjunctive is common also in subordinate clauses: 'It is not impossible that he *may change* his plans.' 'I have heard that he *may return* soon.'

The potential subjunctive often occurs in conditional sentences. It is least common when the reference is to the immediate future: 'We shall all be sorry if it *rains* tomorrow.' As in this sentence, the indicative is the usual form here. The simple subjunctive was once common here and is still sometimes found in choice literary expression: 'If he *confess* (more commonly *confesses*) I shall overlook the offence.' Similarly when the reference is to the immediate past: 'Such an impression is bound to be dissipated if one stay (more commonly *stays*) long enough to love the land, and if one *have* (more commonly *has*) *come* in the first place remembering that the Master lived a human life amid commonplace surroundings' (Harry Emerson Fosdick, *A Pilgrimage to Palestine*, Ch. VIII). If the reference is to the future outcome of events the *shall*-subjunctive is still sometimes used, as in older English: 'If you *shall fail* to understand What England is . . . On you will come the curse of all the land' (Tennyson).

When future events present themselves to our mind in only a vague, indefinite way we employ a past subjunctive in the condition: 'If we *missed* (or *should miss* or *were to miss*, indicating decreasing grades of probability) the train we *should* (**67** 1, 3rd par.) have to wait an hour at the station.' 'If he *missed* (or *should miss* or *were to miss*) the train he *would* (**67** 1, 3rd par.) have to wait an hour at the station.' 'If I *missed* (or *should miss*, or *were to miss*) the train I *would* (**67** 1, 3rd par.) come back and try it again to-morrow.'

When the condition is contrary to fact we employ the past or past perfect subjunctive in the condition: 'If he *were* here I *would speak* to him.' 'If he *had been* here I *would have spoken* to him.' 'If Father *were* here and *saw* this we *should have* to suffer.' 'If they *had have* (or *a* or *of*) *said* (instead of the correct *had said;* see *Syntax*, **49** 3 *b*, 3rd par.) so, you'*d a sat* and *listened* to them.'

The potential subjunctive is common in conditional sentences, as in all the above examples, but the optative subjunctive is also used here, especially after *provided* and *on condition* (*that*): 'She was granted a year's probation on condition she *send* (or *should send*) her son to school.'

The potential subjunctive is often used of actual facts, as the abstract conception, the principle involved, is more prominent in the mind than the concrete fact: 'That many men *should enjoy* it does not make it better' (Matthew Arnold, *Essay on Keats*). 'It seemed incredible that one so young *should have done* so much' (William B. Maxwell, *Gabrielle*).

c. Old Simple Subjunctive. In looking over the examples of the optative and the potential subjunctive in *a* and *b* above, it will become apparent that the old simple form does not occur so often as the newer form with a modal auxiliary. The latter by virtue of its finer shades of meaning has gained the ascendancy in both literary and colloquial language. The old simple form, however, as older forms in general, is still highly prized in elevated diction for its peculiar effect. Although its use is not now for the most part common in colloquial speech, the simple past tense is still widely used there in the subordinate clause where the idea of unreality is prominent, i.e. where the idea of a future act presents itself to the mind in only a vague indefinite manner or where a condition is contrary to fact or a wish is impossible of fulfillment: 'Even if he *said* (optative subj.) it himself (concessive clause), I shouldn't believe it.' 'If he *struck* (potential subj.) me (conditional clause), I would strike him.' 'If I *had* (potential subj.) the money (condition contrary to fact), I would buy it.' 'O that he *were* alive and *could* see the fruits of his labor!' The present tense of the old simple optative subjunctive is still common only in a principal proposition with an indefinite subject and in a subordinate clause after a strong expression of will or in a subordinate concessive clause that has the form of a principal proposition: 'Everybody *stand* up!' 'I demand, insist that he *do* it at once!' '*Sink* [I] or *swim* [I], I shall undertake it.' '*Detest* [we] him as we may, we must acknowledge his greatness.' Elsewhere the old simple optative subjunctive survives in normal English only in set expressions: 'Long *live* the King!' 'God *bless* you!'

Except in the case of the verb *be* the simple past subjunctive and the past indicative are identical in form; but they are not confounded, for the past indicative points to the past and, according to *d*, the past subjunctive points to the future: 'He *struck* (past indic.) me yesterday.' 'If he *struck* (past subj., pointing to the future) me, I'd strike him.'

d. Use of the Tenses of the Subjunctive. The two groups of tenses employed in the subjunctive — the present tense forms (present, present perfect, or *will*, *may*, or *shall* with a dependent infinitive) and the past tense forms (past, past perfect, or *would*, *might*, or *should* with a dependent infinitive) — stand out in general quite distinctly from each other. The different tenses within each group mark different distinctions of time, while the tenses of one group as compared with those of the other group do not mark different distinctions of *time*, but differ only in the *manner* in which they represent the statement. Thus the present and the past subjunctive both denote present or future time, but they usually differ in the manner of the statement, the past tense indicating a greater improbability, or even unreality: 'If there *be* a misunderstanding between them, I don't know of it,' but 'If there *were* a misunderstanding between them, I should know of it.' 'If it *rain*, I'll not go,' but 'If it *were to rain*, I wouldn't go.' Likewise the present perfect and the past perfect subjunctive both denote past time, but differ in the manner of the statement: 'I ask that every man of any standing in Rome be brought to trial even if he *have remained* (a quite probable case) neutral' (Masefield, *Pompey the Great*, Act II). 'Even if he *had been* (contrary to fact) here, I should have said the same thing.' We feel the distinctions of manner today most vividly in the auxiliaries. *Will*, *may*, *shall*, on the one hand, and *would*, *might*, *should*, on the other hand, all represent present or future time, but the two groups differ markedly in the manner in which they represent the thought: 'I am hoping that he *may* come this evening,' but 'I think he *might* come this evening but I am not expecting him.'

In oldest English, when there were only two tenses, the present and the past, the past subjunctive, like the past indicative, pointed to the past, differing from it only in that it represented the act as a mere conception or as contrary to reality. It is sometimes still employed for reference to the past where it is desired to represent something not as a concrete reality but as conceivable, as probably occurring: 'If it *were* so, it was a grievous fault' (Shakespeare, *Julius Caesar*, III, II, 84). 'If ever poet *were* a master of phrasing, he (Tennyson) was so' (A. C. Bradley, *Commentary on Tennyson's 'In Memoriam,'* Ch. VI). 'No Thanksgiving dinner was quite complete unless there *were* a baby on hand belonging to some branch of the family' (George F. Hoar, *Autobiography,* I, 57). In Old English the past subjunctive was still used for reference to the past to express unreality. This old usage still lingers in a limited way: 'I would have denied it if I *could*' (Hope, *Dolly Dialogues,* 25). The context here makes the thought clear. Now when it is desired to express unreality the past perfect is the usual subjunctive form for reference to the past: 'I would have denied it if I *had been* able to do so.' As the modal auxiliaries, however, are defective verbs that have never had a past perfect subjunctive, we have to employ here another means to express unreality when the reference is to the past, namely, the past subjunctive of the auxiliary in connection with a dependent perfect infinitive: 'He *might have succeeded* if he had tried' (past perfect subjunctive). Similarly, the present tense subjunctive forms of these auxiliaries with their implication of greater probability may be used for reference to the past if they are associated with a perfect infinitive: 'The train *may have arrived* by this time.'

As shown in the first paragraph of this article the tense of the subjunctive employed is a point of vital importance. Unfortunately, however, this feeling for the meaning of the subjunctive tenses is only active after a present tense form (present, present perfect, future). After a past tense it is destroyed by our law of the sequence of tenses, which requires a past tense to be followed by a past tense: 'I *am* hoping that he *may* come this evening,' but 'I *was* hoping that he *might* come that evening.' Here *might* does not have the usual force of a past subjunctive, for it is a present subjunctive that has been attracted into the form of a past tense after a past tense.

3. **Imperative Mood.** This form is the mood of command, request, admonition, supplication, entreaty, warning, prohibition. It now has many forms. One of them, the simple imperative, is one of the oldest forms of our language: *Go! Run!*

The old simple forms of the imperative are given in **69** and **70.**

With the simple imperative the subject was expressed in older English: '*Enter ye* in at the strait gate . . . because strait is the gate and narrow is the way' (*Matthew,* VII, 13). We do not usually express the subject today, but it must stand when we desire to indicate a contrast — now with the subject before the imperative: 'I don't know what to say. Norah, *yóu* go!' The subject is expressed also in lively language to indicate that the person addressed should take an interest in something, or that it is intended for his good or for his discomfiture, or that it should concern or not concern him especially: '*Yóu mark* my words. He won't do it.' 'He's not an unpleasant fellow at all.'—'Just *yóu get* better acquáinted with him and *sée!*' '*Yóu follow* my advice and dón't go!' '*Yóu leave* that alone!'

Negative commands are expressed by the form with unstressed *do:* '*Don't tálk* so loud!' In older English the simple form was used here. This older usage survives with the adverb *never:* 'Never *méntion* it again!' In poetry it occurs also elsewhere: '*Tell* me not in mournful numbers . . .'

The form with *do* is often employed in entreaties and as an emphatic prohibition or a negative entreaty, here usually with stressed *do:* '*Dó go,* please!' '*Dón't go!*' '*Dón't you do* that!' '*Dón't you forget!*'

The simple optative subjunctive is used in a number of expressions as a mild imperative: 'Everybody *stand* up!' 'What do you say *wé black* our faces and *give* a little party, now the guests will be asleep?' (Anderson and Stallings, *Three American Plays,* p. 69). '*Say* [*we*] what we will, he doesn't mind us.' '*Cost* [*it*] what it may, I shall buy it.' More commonly with the auxiliary *let:* '*Let* him *come* in!' In pleading tone: '*Dó let's come* to an understanding!' Negative form of *let*-form: '*Let's* not *dó* that!' In pleading tone: '*Dón't let* us *do* that!' In colloquial speech the negative is often *don't* instead of *not:* '*Let's dón't* be serious, George. Let's tálk of something pleasant' (Tarkington, *The Magnificent Ambersons,* Ch. XVII). '*Let's dón't do* anything of the kind!' (P. G. Wodehouse, *The Coming of Bill,* Ch. VII).

We often employ the imperative of the expanded form (**47** 2): 'Up, *be doing* everywhere, the hour of crisis has verily come!' (Carlyle, *Latter-Day Pamphlets,* 28). In colloquial speech *get* takes the place of *be:* '*Get* going!' The indicative of the expanded form is common in commands: 'You sit down! You'*re* not *going* yet!'

We often employ modal auxiliaries, which are subjunctive forms: 'You *cán't do* that! You *shán't do* it. By God you *shán't!*' (Clemence Dane, *Legend,* p. 173). 'Positively, you *shall* not *do* that again!' or in kinder tone 'You *should* not *do* that again.' 'You *múst behave!*'

We employ the future indicative when we desire to speak courteously and at the same time indicate that we are confidently expecting that our wish will be fulfilled: 'Heads of departments *will submit* their estimates before January first.'

In lively language, expression is often terse, since the situation makes the thought clear, so that nouns, adverbs, prepositional phrases, etc., serve as imperatives: 'The *salt,* please!' 'All *aboard!*' '*Down* in front!' 'Hats *off!*' '*Forward*, brave companions!' A noun or a noun and an adjective often serve as a warning: 'Danger!' 'Fresh paint!'

The gerund preceded by *no* has the force of a negative command: '*No parking* here' = 'Do not park here.'

Commands such as have been treated in the foregoing articles usually have reference to the present moment or the future. We sometimes use also the present perfect tense of the imperative to represent the action as already performed: *Have done!* or in popular speech '*A*' *done!* '*Have done* with such nonsense!'

The uses of the imperative are treated in considerable detail in *Syntax*, **45.**

TENSE

51. Tenses are the different forms which a verb assumes to indicate the time of the action or state. There are six tenses, present, past, present perfect, past perfect, future, future perfect: I *return* (present), *returned* (past), *have returned* (present perfect), *had returned* (past perfect), *shall return* (future), *shall have returned* (future perfect). For formation see **55–70.**

There were in oldest English only two tenses in general use — the present and the past. These two forms performed the functions of the six tenses we have today. With the rising culture of the Old English period new forms arose to relieve the present and the past of some of their functions.

The present functions of our six tenses are fairly well defined by their names — present, past, present perfect, past perfect, future, future perfect.

Only the present tense is loaded with functions. It represents the act as going on: 'He *is writing*.' 'He *is playing*.' It represents an act as habitual, customary, repeated, characteristic: 'I *live* in Chicago.' 'I *call* on him whenever I *go* to town.' 'He *sings* beautifully.' It expresses a general truth: 'Twice two *is* four.' It is used as a historical present bringing historical events vividly before us: 'Lincoln *stands* with bowed head. He *looks* up and *begins* to speak. It *is* evident that he *is* under the sway of a strong emotion.' Similar to the historical present is the annalistic present, which registers historical facts as matters of present interest: 'It *is* not till the close of the Old English period that Scandinavian words *appear*. Even late Northumbrian (of about 970) *is* entirely free from Scandinavian influence' (Sweet, *New English Grammar*, p. 216). The present tense is still, as in Old English, widely used to point to the future: 'The ship *sails* tomorrow.' 'We are waiting till he *comes*.'

In **65** *b* are some remarks upon characteristic differences in meaning between the present perfect and the past.

The meaning and use of our tenses are described in detail in *Syntax*, **37**.

ASPECT

52. It is a marked characteristic of our language that we usually — almost always — must indicate the aspect of an act, i.e. we must almost always indicate whether the act is thought of as a whole, a fact, or, on the other hand, as going on, as continuing. Hence there are two aspects. Each aspect has six tenses. Thus in our language tense is subordinated to aspect. The six tenses of each aspect indicate the time relations of the aspect.

In the following articles the form of the two aspects and their use are treated, also the meanings of the component elements of the forms.

1. **Terminate Aspect.** This aspect represents the act as a whole, as a fact. It is usually expressed by the common form of the verb: 'He *shot* a duck.' 'He *wrote* a letter.' 'I *see* him coming up the road.' 'I *write* a letter every day.' 'Our clock *ticks* too loudly.' 'He *wakes up* early every morning.' 'We *have* no scraps in our house. We *eat up* everything every meal.' 'He *will go* tomorrow.' In this aspect the action is always thought of as completed, now or in the past or in the future, for it is represented as a whole, as a fact. Thus it stands in contrast to the second of our aspects, the progressive (2 below), which represents the act as going on.

The terminate aspect has become closely associated in English with the common form of the verb. In oldest English the common form was used also to express progression. In the Old English period under the influence of church Latin the expanded form came into use. At first it had the same meaning as the common form. Later it gradually acquired progressive force and relieved the common form of this function. Gradually the common form was restricted to terminate use — one of the most important developments in the history of our language. Thus it has become possible in English to indicate an action as a whole — something impossible in many languages.

Although the common form always has terminate force, it has two quite different meanings. It expresses a general or a particular fact: 'Lead *sinks*' (general fact). 'I *see* him coming' (particular act). The situation makes it clear in the second example that the act is a particular one and not general. Sometimes the situation does not make it clear that the act is a particular one. In this case we must employ the expanded form to bring out this idea: 'In honoring him you *are honoring* yourself.' 'You *are exaggerating!*' (directed to the person addressed after he had made a rash statement). If the speaker had said in the second example 'You *exaggerate*' it might have been interpreted as a general statement, not a reference to a particular occasion as it really was. The expanded form shows that the reference is to a particular case. The situation or context alone marks this expanded form as terminate. Otherwise it cannot be distinguished from the expanded form with progressive force. Compare **47** 2 *a*. This expanded form with terminate force is often associated with emphasis and feeling. Examples are given in **47** 2 *b* (2nd par.).

2. **Progressive Aspect.** This aspect represents the action as progressing, proceeding, hence as not ended. It is expressed by the expanded form (**47** 2). This form is used also with verbs like *sit, lie, stand, remain,* etc., to express the similar idea of continuation. Compare **47** 2 *a*. The progressive action naturally falls into three classes on the basis of the meaning of the verb or verbal phrase.

a. With Durative Verbs. Such verbs express duration. To express progression we employ the expanded form (**47** 2). The scene is laid in the midst of the activity, which is still progressing, proceeding: 'He *is working* in the garden.' 'He *is plowing* corn.' 'Several books *are lying* on the table.' The idea of duration may be contained in a verb and yet some other idea may overshadow it: 'He *kept working* until he was tired.' The verb *work* has strong durative force, but the common form *kept* indicates clearly that the sentence is a statement of fact, the report of an occurrence in its entirety. It is not represented as going on, as unfinished. Even in 'He is very tired, but he *keeps on working*' our attention is not directed to an action going on, but to the persistency of the person at work. The common form of the verb always expresses an act as a whole, as a fact. Here it calls attention to the fact of persistency on the part of the person at work. To indicate that the action is actually going on we employ the expanded (**47** 2) form: 'He *is working* in the garden.' The different tenses of the expanded form are used to indicate the different time relations: 'He *was working* in his garden when I drove by.' 'He *has been working* in his garden all day.' 'You find me at work, and I *shall* probably *be* still *working* when you return.' Notice that with the present perfect tense, as in the next to the last example, the action is represented as still going on.

It should, however, be noted that the expanded form does not always express duration. It expresses duration only with verbs whose meaning is durative. Compare **47** 2 *a*.

The common form of a durative has terminate force, i.e. denotes an action as a whole, as a fact: 'He *works* in his garden every day.'

b. With Iterative Verbs. Such verbs express repetition, iteration. To express progression we employ the expanded form: 'He *is haw-hawing* again.' 'The fire *is crackling* on the hearth.' 'Leaves *are dropping* from the trees.' The idea of duration is closely related to that of iteration. In 'He *has been working* on this book for several years' the first impression is that of duration, but in the exact sense the expression is iterative, for the work was often interrupted.

The common form of such verbs of course has terminate force: 'The clock *is ticking*' (progressive iterative), but 'A clock *ticks* (terminate iterative) louder than a watch.' 'I *have been trying and trying* (progressive iterative), but have not succeeded yet,' but 'I *have tried and tried* (terminate iterative), but have not succeeded.' Only the terminate common form is employed with *used* and *would:* 'They *used* (as tense found only in the past) to nod to each other when they met, and now and then they *would* exchange a word or two.' But both terminate and progressive forms are employed with the participle *accustomed:* 'I *am accustomed* (terminate) to do promptly what I have to do.' 'I *become* easily *accustomed* (terminate) to do promptly what I have to do.' 'I *am becoming accustomed* (progressive) to do promptly what I have to do.' Instead of *accustomed* we may employ *used* or *wont* (**60** B): 'I *am used* (or *wont*) to do promptly,' etc.

If we desire to give ingressive (i.e. beginning) or effective (i.e. approaching an end) force to an iterative we place *is beginning* or *is ceasing* before the iterative: 'The clock *is beginning,* or *is ceasing, to tick.*'

The expanded form with iterative force does not always have progressive iterative force: 'He *is* always *getting* angry.' 'He *is* always *smoking.*' The *always* in these sentences gives general force to the statement. The reference is to the act as a whole, hence the aspect is terminate. The expanded form is the terminate expanded form described in **47** 2 *b.*

c. With Point-Action Verbs. Such verbs call attention, not to an act as a whole, but to only one point, either the beginning or the end. A verb that calls attention to the beginning of something is an ingressive: 'I *am getting* tired.' If the verb calls attention to the end it is an effective: 'I *am getting* deaf.' In the first example the reference is to the beginning of a temporary state. In the second example the reference is to the end, the outcome of a long development. The verb *get* is used with ingressive or effective force. The context alone shows whether the force is ingressive or effective. In English we have a very useful group of copulas, which, like *get*, can be used with ingressive or effective force. See **12** 3 (next to last par.).

Certain verbs other than copulas express these ideas. A number of these verbs, such as *begin, commence, start*, etc., have only ingressive force, while others, such as *cease, stop, quit, finish, leave off*, etc., have only effective force.

Ingressive or effective force often lies, not in a copula or other verb with ingressive or effective meaning, but in an adverb or a prefix. Ingressive force: 'Baby is waking *up*,' or 'Baby is *a*waking.' 'Baby is dozing *off*' (beginning to sleep). 'The children quieted *down*.' Effective force: 'He ate *up* the apple.' 'He paid *off* the men and discharged them.' 'He put the rebellion *down*.'

The expanded form (**47** 2) of an ingressive indicates progression toward the beginning of an act or state, i.e. a preparing to, a tending to, the initial stage to: 'It *is going* to rain.' 'Look out! I *am going* to shoot.' 'I *am getting* tired.' 'Baby *was awaking* as I entered.' The *a-* in *awake* is an old ingressive prefix. We now more commonly employ an ingressive adverb here. The adverbs *up* and *off* are common: 'Baby *was* just *waking up* as I entered.' 'He *is dozing off*.' 'He *is* just *taking off* for a nonstop flight to Paris.' The ingressive adverb *out* is widely used: 'The lilacs *are coming out*' (beginning to bloom). The idea of ingression often lies in the verb: 'He *is* just *starting* for town.' 'He *was* just *starting* for town as I arrived.' 'Within a week we *shall be starting* for Europe.' 'The baby *was* just *going* to sleep as I entered.' 'I *am getting* tired.' 'We *were getting* quite tired when John unexpectedly came up with the auto.' It should be noted that the expanded form has pure ingressive force only with ingressives. If it is desired to call attention to the beginning of progressive action expressed by a durative we must employ the expanded form of an ingressive and place it before the durative: 'The baby *is starting to cry*.' 'It *is beginning to rain*.'

In the imperative, to express ingression, we place the imperative of *be* before the present participle: 'Up, *be doing* everywhere, the hour of crisis has verily come' (Carlyle, *Latter-Day Pamphlets*, 28). In colloquial language we employ *get* instead of *be*: '*Get* going!' 'Let's *get* going!'

The common form of such verbs has terminate ingressive force: 'The boat *slowed up* (began to go slower) as it came in.' 'The spot where the horse *took off* to where he landed is above eighteen feet' (*Sporting Magazine*, XLIII, 287, A.D. 1814). 'On May 20, 1927, the brave airman Charles Lindbergh *took off* alone from New York for a successful nonstop flight across the Atlantic to Paris.' 'That *set* me *thinking.*'

The expanded form of an effective indicates that the action or state is progressing toward, is approaching an end or a culmination or realization: 'The lake *is drying up.*' 'He *is becoming* (or *going*) blind.' 'All that he said *is coming* true.' 'The cost of this enterprise *is coming* high.' 'He *is coming to see* the error of his ways.' 'I *am* just *getting* through with my work.' 'I came up just as they *were getting to blows,*' i.e. the final outcome of the dispute was blows. 'His strength *is giving out.*' 'He *is* finally *getting* the machine *running.*' 'We *are* at last *getting to understand* each other better.' 'Of late we *have been getting to understand* each other better.' 'This bright little boy *is going to be* a great man some day' represents the speaker as standing in the present looking forward to the probable outcome of a development. It should be noted that the expanded form has pure effective force only with effectives. If it is desired to call attention to the approaching end of progressive action expressed by a durative we must employ the expanded form of an effective verb and place it before the durative: 'It *is ceasing to rain.*' With terminate force we say 'It *has stopped raining,*' but on account of the unpleasant repetition of *-ing* we do not employ the expanded form to express progressive effective force: 'It *is stopping raining.*' But where the situation makes the reference clear we may say 'It *is stopping*' or in American colloquial speech 'It *is letting up.*' With terminate force we say 'I *have finished reading* the novel,' but to express progressive effective force we say 'I *am* just *finishing* it.' The connection makes it clear whether the reference is to the reading or the writing of the novel. We do not hesitate to say 'Many people *are* now *leaving* off *sleeping* with the windows shut,' as *off* separates the two forms in *-ing*.

The common form of such verbs has terminate effective force: 'It *stopped raining.*' 'The baby *stopped crying.*' 'He *quit smoking.*' 'They *ate up* everything that was on the table.' 'I *hunted up* (indicating attainment) my old friend Collins.' The beginning of something new is often itself the end, the result, the outcome of preceding circumstances, preceding effort: 'After a while I *got to know* him better.' 'I was so excited that it was morning before I *got to sleep.*' 'I finally *got* the machine *running.*' 'When he'*s* (= he *has*) once *got going* there is no stopping him.' 'His prediction *came* true.' 'He finally *came to see* the error of his ways.' 'We finally *got to understand* each other better than before.'

An effective adverb gives to the expanded form of a durative verb progressive-durative-effective force: 'He *is fighting* it *out* with him.' 'They *are sitting out* the dance.' 'They *are working out* the problem.' The common form of such verbs represents the durative-effective idea as attained, as a fact: 'We often *sit out* a dance.' 'We *work out* our problems by ourselves.'

3. **Meaning of Auxiliary 'Be' and Participle in Aspect Forms.** In the course of the centuries a useful group of point-action (**52** 2) copulas have sprung up in English: *be, become, grow, turn, get,* etc. The oldest of these, *be,* differs from the others in that it has durative as well as point-action force. This came about through the fusion of the two originally different verbs *is* and *be.* The former was a durative, the latter a point-action verb with the force of *become.* Thus *be* now may indicate a continuing action or the beginning or the end of an action: Continuing action: 'He *is* working in the garden.' Beginning of an action: 'We must *be* going.' 'I will not interrupt you any longer. You want to *be* reading.' 'He intimated that they had better *be* dressing.' End of a development: 'This bright little boy is going to *be* (= *become*) a great man some day.' The double meaning of *be* is apparent in the passive: 'Our house *is painted*' (present state). 'Our house *is* (= *becomes*) *painted* every year' (an act). The effective force (**52** 2 *c*) of *is* in the last example indicates that *painted* is a verb; but as *is* indicates also a state, as in 'The house *is* painted,' it is not a clear effective form. In colloquial language we often employ *get* instead of *be* as it is a clearer effective form: 'He *got* (clearer than *was*) married yesterday.'

In duratives, ingressives, effectives, and iteratives the present participle represents the act as incomplete, while in terminates it represents the act as a whole, as a fact. Incomplete act with durative force: 'He *is working* in the garden.' Incomplete act with ingressive force: 'He *is* just *getting* up.' Incomplete act with effective force: 'His strength *is giving* out.' Incomplete act with iterative force: 'The girls *are giggling.*' Complete act with terminate force: 'In honoring him you *are honoring* (= *honor*) yourselves,' representing the act as a whole, as a fact. Compare **47** 2 *b.* This double use of the participle corresponds to usage elsewhere: 'From here I see the waves *beating* (act going on) on the shore.' 'I was proud of him *acting* (act as a whole = *since he acted*) so unselfishly.'

NUMBER AND PERSON

53. There are two numbers, singular and plural: *thou singĕst, ye sing; thou sangĕst, ye sang; he sings* (or *singĕth*), *they sing.* In poetry we can in the indicative distinguish between singular and plural in the second and third persons of the present tense and in the second person of the past tense, but in ordinary language only the third person indicative of a present tense form can indicate the number, as in the last example. The one verb *be* can go a little farther in indicating the number — a survival of the older usage which in verbs carefully distinguished the singular and the plural in all tenses and moods. *Be* still keeps the numbers distinct in the first and third persons indicative in both the present and the past tense: I *am*, he *is*, we *are*, they *are;* I *was*, he *was*, we *were*, they *were*. In poetic and biblical style we can always distinguish between singular and plural in the second person: *thou givĕst, ye give; thou gavĕst, ye gave.*

Elsewhere we do not distinguish singular and plural. We now feel that the subject makes the idea of number clear: *I sing, we sing; you* (speaking to a definite person) *sing, you boys sing, I sang, you* (speaking to a definite person) *sang, he sang, we sang, you boys sang, they sang, if he sing, if they sing.* The subject here makes also the idea of person clear.

As can be seen by the examples given above, the few endings that verbs now have indicate not only the number but also the person and the mood. The absence of an ending in the third person singular of any present tense form usually marks it as a subjunctive: he *comes* (indicative), if he *come* (subjunctive). Only two verbs have here an especial subjunctive form: if he *be*, if he *have* (regularly formed from *have*, while the indicative *has* is an irregular, contracted form).

a. Agreement of Verb with Subject in Number and Person. The English verb — except in the case of the copula *be* — has no endings in ordinary speech for the past tense and the first and second persons of the present tense. It distinguishes the numbers only in the third person of the present tense: 'Our *dog barks* too much.' 'Our *dogs bark* too much.' The verbal ending *-s* indicates the singular, and the lack of an ending indicates the plural. These forms for showing the singular and the plural of the third person of the present tense are very simple, but they afford us at this point means of expressing our thought accurately and of making fine shades of meaning: 'Three-fourths of the surface of the earth *is* (referring to a mass) sea,' but 'Three-fourths of our old college class *are* (referring to individuals) married.' Sometimes there is fluctuation of usage as people look at the matter from different points of view: 'Three times 3 *is*, or *are*, 9.'

The point of view sometimes shifts from century to century. In older English it was quite common to put the verb in the plural after the subjects *each one, everyone:* '*Everyone* in the house *were* in *their* beds' (Fielding, *Tom Jones*, VII, Ch. XIV). The singular of the verb is now required here in the literary language: '*Everyone* in the house *was* in *his* bed.' The old plural idea survives in part in popular speech: '*Everyone* in the house was in *their* beds.' Thus in earlier periods even educated people felt the plural idea in *every* and *each*, while today they feel in these words the conception of separate individuals. But in colloquial language most people still say, '*Everyone* was here, but *they* all went home early' (*Current English Usage*, p. 104), as there is no appropriate singular pronoun available. We say today 'The island of Australia with Tasmania *constitutes* the commonwealth of Australia.' In older English the verb was generally in the plural. Present-day popular speech preserves this older usage, while the singular prevails in the literary language. We now place the verb in agreement with the formal subject *the island of Australia* although there is a plural idea present. In many other expressions we follow the meaning: 'There *is* lots of fun in it.' 'The white and the red *rose are* both beautiful.' 'The *multitude*, unacquainted with the best models, *are* captivated by whatever stuns or dazzles them.'

Sometimes the little bit of verbal inflection we have left here causes us untold worry and drives us to dodge the questions of form that arise. One, remembering that he has been told to make the verb agree with the nearest subject, says 'Either he or I *am* in the wrong,' while another says 'Either, he or I, *is* in the wrong,' construing *either* as a pronoun in the subject relation with *he* and *I* as explanatory appositives. Still another, terrified by the possibilities of construction here, dodges the issue by giving each subject a separate verb: 'Either he *is* in the wrong or I *am*.' For fuller treatment see *Syntax*, **8**.

54. Number and Person in Older English. A glance at the Old and Middle English inflections in **56** 3 *a*, *b*, 4, **59** 1, 2, **61** 2, 3 will indicate how much more importance was attached to endings for number and person in older English. Even in the Old English period, however, changes had taken place that resulted in greater simplicity. The oldest ending of the second person singular was *-s*. The regular ending of the third person singular and the entire plural was þ (*th*), but in the North *s* was often employed here. This northern *s* is explained by some as a simple sound-change from þ, by others as an analogical spreading of the ending *-s* of the second person singular to the plural and the third person singular. Whatever may have been the cause of these changes the result was that all the persons of the singular and the plural now ended in *-s* except the first person singular. In Middle English in the North the *s* sometimes spread to the first person singular, so that at this time all persons single and plural could end in *-s:* 'as I before you *has* talde' (*Cursor Mundi*, 14,135, about A.D. 1300), now 'as I *have* told you before.' 'That *sais* the men that thar *has* ben' (*ib.*, 8854), now 'That *say* the men who *have* been there.'

This dialectic northern *s* was destined to play an important part in the literary language. In Middle English, as can be seen by the inflections in **56** 4, it spread southward to the northern part of the Midland and was used there in the East in the third person singular alongside of older *–th*. In the West it was often used also in the plural. In Chaucer's time it had not yet reached London, for Chaucer usually employed here the older *–th*. But the poet was acquainted with it, for in three instances he employed it for the sake of the rime and in his *Reves Tale* he let the two northern clerks use it. Later, it became established in London and the South generally. Many people from the North and the northern Midland came to the growing national capital to live and of course brought with them their handy *s*-ending, which by reason of its marked superiority in ease of utterance appealed to the people there as it had appealed previously to the people of the North. It affected at first only colloquial speech, while in literary prose the older and more stately *–th* maintained itself for a time. In Shakespeare's works *–s* prevails in the prose of his dramas, where the tone is colloquial, while in the serious style of the Bible *–th* is used throughout. The poets often employed *–s* on account of its warm tone or for the sake of rime or meter. After the time of Shakespeare *–s* gradually became established in all styles of the literary language, but only in the third person singular, not also in the other persons of the singular and throughout the plural, as in northern English. At the time of the landing of the Pilgrims on the eastern shore of America and in the early colonial days generally, *–th* was occasionally used, but it was ebbing. It occurred most frequently in *hath* and *doth*, which by reason of their frequent use were most firmly fixed and lingered longest. They often occurred where all the other verbs had *–s:* 'But he *perverts* the truth in this as in other things, for the Lord *hath* as well appoynted them (i.e. the pastors) to converte as to feed in their several charges; and he *wrongs* the church to say otherwise' (Bradford, *History of Plymouth Plantation*, p. 193, A.D. 1630–1640). The ending *–s* is now in the literary language restricted to the third person singular, but in older literary English was not infrequently used for any person or number, as described in the preceding paragraph for northern usage: 'Ffreinde, *does* not *thou* (or *thee*) discerne an exhortation from a Judgement?' (George Fox, *Journal*, p. 111, A.D. 1653). 'And, in a word, far behind his worth *Comes* the praises that I now bestow' (Shakespeare, *The Two Gentlemen of Verona*, II, IV, 71).

This tendency to employ the ending *–s* for all persons and numbers is only one manifestation among others of a general tendency to simplify verbal inflection in the present indicative. This was the strongest of these tendencies and survives in popular speech. Compare *Syntax*, **8** I 1 *h*. In early Modern English there was a tendency in the literary language for those who employed the ending *–th* in the third person singular to use it also in the plural. See **56** 2 and **56** 4 *c*. At the close of the Middle English period there arose in the east Midland a tendency to suppress the ending in the third person singular, so that the uninflected form was used in the third person for singular and plural. See **56** 4 *b*. This usage survives in the dialect of the east Midland, also in American dialect, as described in *Syntax*, **8** I 1 *h Note* (next to last par.).

The most important change in the literary language in the direction of greater simplification was the dropping of the Middle English endings *-e* and *-en*. This affected both the present (**56** 4) and the past (**59** 2 and **61** 3) tense. In the early part of the period the ending *-e* of the first person singular in the present tense and of the first and third persons singular in the weak past and the plural ending *-en* of the present and the past tense disappeared in the North. In the literary language of the Midland and South these endings did not disappear until near the close of the fifteenth century.

TENSE FORMATION

55. English originally had only two tenses — the present and the past — and in one sense still has only two tenses, for the four additional tenses — present perfect, past perfect, future, future perfect — have been formed by combining a present or a past tense with a participle or an infinitive, so that every tense in our language contains a present or a past tense.

PRESENT TENSE

56. The formation of this tense is simple and there are comparatively few irregularities. The common form for the second person singular is the second person plural form, which is now used also for the singular. Compare **33** *f*. The use and omission of the endings are treated in **53**. There were once two types of inflection — strong and weak — but in the present tense the differences have disappeared, so that almost any verb may now serve as a model of inflection of this tense.

	Indicative	Subjunctive
	Singular	
1.	I walk	I walk
2.	you walk (old form, thou walk*ĕst*)	you walk (thou walk)
3.	he walk*s* (old form, walk*ĕth*)	he walk
	Plural	
1.	we walk	we walk
2.	you walk (old form, ye walk)	you walk (ye walk)
3.	they walk	they walk

Imperative

walk (old forms, walk thou, walk ye)

Present Participle walking   Present Infinitive (to) walk

Present Gerund walking

1. Remarks on Present Tense Forms:

a. Ending of Third Person Singular and Change of Final 'Y' to 'IE' before an Ending. After a sibilant (*s, ss, c, sh, tch, ch, g, dg, x, z*) or a vowel not preceded by a vowel, *–es* is added instead of *–s:* (*e* pronounced) pass*es*, push*es*, lunch*es*, rag*es*, dodg*es*, relax*es*, doz*es;* (*e* silent) go*es*, do*es*, but tipto*es*, taboo*s*. Final *y* remains *y* after a vowel before the ending, but when preceded by a consonant becomes *ie:* 'He pla*y*s,' but 'He cr*ie*s.' Before the participial ending *–ing*, however, final *y* always remains *y:* cr*y*ing.

In words in which a silent *e* follows a sibilant, as in *splice, singe, pledge,* we add only *–s,* but we pronounce *–es:* splic*es*, sing*es*, pledg*es*.

b. Dropping of 'E.' An *e* at the end of a verb is dropped before a vowel in the ending: *love,* but *loving.* Notice, however, that we irregularly write *dyeing* (from *dye* to distinguish it from *dying,* from *die*), *singeing* (from *singe* to distinguish it from *singing,* from *sing*), *tingeing* (from *tinge* to distinguish it from *tinging,* from *ting*), *canoeing, hoeing, shoeing,* etc.

Verbs in *–ie* drop *e* and change *i* to *y* before *–ing: tying* from *tie; lying* from *lie.*

c. Doubling of Consonants. A final consonant preceded by an accented short vowel is doubled before a vowel in the ending: *shop,* but *shopping, shopped; gas,* but *gassing, gasses, gassed; quiz,* but *quizzing, quizzes, quizzed; whiz,* but *whizzing, whizzes, whizzed.*

d. Time Relations Indicated by Present Tense Form of Participle, Infinitive, and Gerund. The present participle, infinitive, and gerund are not confined to reference to present time. The situation indicates the time: 'the *rising* sun' (present time). 'My train starts at six, *arriving* (future time) in Chicago at ten.' '*Hearing* (past time) voices I stopped and listened.' 'I came late, *arriving* (past time) after all the others.' 'I expect *to arrive* (future) late.' 'He was very foolish *to do* (past time) it' (= It was very foolish that he *did* it). 'After *finishing* (with the force of a present tense = After I finish) my work, I go to bed.' 'After *finishing* (or *having finished* = After I had finished) my work, I went to bed.' Compare *Syntax,* **48** 2 (2nd par.), **49** 3, **50** 2.

e. The Old Present Tense Forms. The old forms for the second and third persons are now used only in poetry and biblical language. The usual old ending for the second person singular is *–est* for full verbs and *–st* for auxiliaries: 'thou help*est,*' 'thou walk*ĕst,*' 'thou ru*nnĕst*' (doubling a final consonant after a short vowel); 'thou may*st*' (**57** 4 B), 'thou can*st*' (**57** 4 B), 'thou ha*st*' (**57** 2), 'thou do*st*' (**57** 3), etc. But *be, shall, will,* have the old ending *–t:* 'thou ar*t*' (**57** 1), 'thou shal*t*' (**57** 4 B), 'thou wil*t*'

(**57** 4 B). For the use of the old forms for the second person see **33** *f*.

The old ending for the third person, *-th*, is discussed in **54** (2nd par.), **56** 2, **56** 4 *c*.

f. Assimilation in Popular Speech. In popular speech, the last consonant in the stem of the imperative is often assimilated to the *m* of the following *me:* 'Gi*m*me (for *give me*) a bite.' 'Le*m*me (for *let me*) see it.'

2. **Early Modern English Forms.** In the early part of the present period the old third person singular ending *-eth* was still widely used in the South and the Midland, also in the literary language, which was based upon the speech of this part of England. For the origin and spread of the new northern ending *-s* see **54.**

In early Modern English, *-th* is often used also as a plural ending: 'Blessed are they that heare the word of God and *keepeth* it' (Latimer, *Seven Sermons before Edward VI*, p. 129, A.D. 1549). Compare 4 *c* below and **54.**

3. **Old English Forms.** Contrasting with the simplicity of Modern English, the Old English forms were many and complicated without any corresponding gain in expressive power.

There were two conjugations — the strong and the weak. In both of these conjugations there was at this time in the North alongside of the regular ending *-þ* in both singular and plural the ending *-s*, so that in the North the second and third persons in the singular and all the persons in the plural often ended in *-s*, the second person singular always. For fuller information see **54.** This dialectic *-s* was destined to play an important rôle in the language later, and in Middle English will appear in the regular inflection. For fuller account of the part it has played in the language, see **54.**

a. Strong Present. In the second and third persons singular indicative, there was in many verbs a change of vowel; in others the vowel remained unchanged. In the inflections given below, where there are two forms, the first is older, i.e. is found chiefly in the early part of the period.

	bind	*help*	*fare*	*bind*	*help*	*fare*
		INDICATIVE			SUBJUNCTIVE	
		Singular			*Singular*, 1, 2, 3	
1.	binde	helpe	fare			
2.	bindes bintst	hilpst	fær(e)st	binde	helpe	fare
3.	bindeþ bint	hilpþ	fær(e)þ			
		Plural, 1, 2, 3			*Plural*, 1, 2, 3	
	bindaþ	helpaþ	faraþ	binden	helpen	faren

Imperative			Infinitive		
	Singular				
bind	help	far	bindan	helpan	faran
	Plural			Participle	
bindaþ	helpaþ	faraþ	bindende	helpende	farende

b. Weak Present. There are three classes of weak verbs, which, however, do not differ much in the present tense. The differences are more marked in the past tense, as is seen in **59** 1, where the past tense forms are given.

The present tense forms of three representative weak verbs are:

	defend	*love*	*have*	*defend*	*love*	*have*
		Indicative			Subjunctive	
		Singular			*Singular*, 1, 2, 3	
	I	II	III	I	II	III
1.	wĕrie	lŭfie	hǣbbe			
2.	wĕres(t)	lŭfas(t)	hăfas(t)	wĕrie	lŭfie	hǣbbe
			hǣfst			
3.	wĕreþ	lŭfaþ	hăfaþ			
			hǣfþ			
		Plural, 1, 2, 3			*Plural*, 1, 2, 3	
	wĕriaþ	lŭfiaþ	hăbbaþ	wĕrien	lŭfien	hǣbben
		Imperative			Infinitive	
		Singular			*Singular*	
	wĕre	lŭfa	hăfa	wĕrian	lŭfian	hăbban
		Plural			Participle	
	wĕriaþ	lŭfiaþ	hăbbaþ	wĕriende	lŭfiende	hǣbbende

c. Gerund in Old English and Its Later Development. In Old English, there was in use a verbal noun ending in *–ung* or *–ing*, which later developed into our gerund in *–ing*. At this time it was still a mere noun, with the inflection of a strong feminine, as *talu* in **29** I B, except that final *u* in the nominative had disappeared: Gyrstandæg ic wæs on *huntunge* (dative) = Yesterday I *was hunting*, lit. *on hunting*. The Old English gerund, like other verbal nouns, usually took a genitive object. When used merely as a noun, it still takes a genitive object: '*The overcoming of a besetting weakness* is an important victory.' The infinitive, though also originally a noun, was in Old English farther developed toward the estate of a verb than the gerund was. It took an accusative object, like a transitive verb, and was developing a passive form. In Middle English, it developed a perfect tense. The gerund was soon to develop in the same direction. In Middle English, it began to take an accusative object, like a transitive verb, and in early Modern English it developed forms for tense and voice. (Compare **47** 6 *b*.) Today, the verbal gerund is a very common construction, but in certain expressions older gerunds have been replaced by present participles. In the Old English expression '*on huntunge*' given above, the gerund has been replaced by the present participle, i.e. we now say 'Yesterday I was *hunting*,' but in popular speech the old gerund has been preserved: 'Yesterday I was *a-hunting*' (contracted from *on hunting*).

4. **Middle English Present.** In Middle English, the vowel change in the second and third persons singular of the strong present disappeared, as the vowel had by the process of leveling been conformed to that of the first person. Also other simplifications had taken place, so that any regular strong or weak verb may serve as a model for the inflection of the present tense, although the formation of strong and weak verbs differs radically in the past tense and must be treated separately there.

The Middle English present tense is characterized also by a change in the endings. The northern ending *–s* for the third person singular spread to the northern part of the Midland and was used there alongside of the old *–þ*. For an account of the origin of this *–s* see **54.** In the North and often also in the West Midland this *s*-ending was used also in the plural.

Another characteristic Middle English change of ending is the replacing of the old plural ending *–eþ* by *–en*, which spread from the past indicative and subjunctive and the present subjunctive to the present indicative, since this ending had become intimately associated with the plural and had come to be felt as a sign for the plural in general. This development was confined to the Midland, but is of importance on account of the high rank of some of the writers of this part of England. Chaucer employed the *en*-plural or its reduced *e*-form.

In the examples of inflection given below, if there are two or three forms the second form or the second and third forms are usually reduced or contracted forms, but in the case of the Midland forms those with the ending *–s* occur only in the northern part of the territory where they are used alongside of the regular forms. The forms of *binde(n)* 'bind' represent the regular Middle English inflection of the present tense. Alongside of it are given the forms of the present tense of *have(n)* 'have' to show how certain auxiliaries and very common verbs of complete predication by reason of their loss of stress had already in Middle English begun to suffer a marked reduction of form.

	INDICATIVE	
	Singular	
1.	binde	hăbbe, hā̆ve, hă
2.	bindest, bintst	hā̆vest, hăst, hĕst
3.	(Southern)	(Southern)
	bindth, bint	hăth, hĕth
	(East Midland)	(East Midland)
	bindeth, bindes	hā̆veth, hăth
	(West Midland)	(West Midland)
	bindeth, bindes	hā̆(ve)th, hăs
	(Northern)	(Northern)
	bindes	hā̆ues, hăs

SUBJUNCTIVE, 1, 2, 3	
Singular	
binde	hăbbe, hā̆ve
Plural	
binden, binde	hăbben, hā̆ve(n)
IMPERATIVE	
Singular	
bind	hā̆ve, hā̆, hā̆f

	Plural, 1, 2, 3		*Plural*, 1, 2, 3
	(Southern)	(Southern)	bindeth, binde, bind;
	bindeth	hăbbeth, hā̆veth	(Northern) bindes
	(East Midland)	(East Midland)	hā̆veth, hā̆ve, hă;
	binden, binde	hā̆ve(n), han	(Northern) hā̆ues, hăs
	(West Midland)	(West Midland)	
	binde(n), bindes	hā̆ve(n), has	
	(Northern)	(Northern)	
	bindes, bind	hā̆ues, hăs	
INFINITIVE	binden, binde	hăbben, hā̆ve(n)	hăn, hă
PARTICIPLE	(Southern)	(East Midland)	(Northern)
	bind*i*nd(e)	bind*e*nd(e)	bind*a*nd(e)
	(Southern)	(East Midland)	(Northern)
	hā̆v*i*nde	hā̆v*e*nde	hā̆v*a*nd(e)

in the 14th century becoming *binding*(*e*), *having*(*e*), except in Northern dialect where *bindand*, *hā̆vand* survived.

GERUND bindinge, hā̆vinge

a. The different variants of the same form for different sections of the country or for the same section are characteristic of the fluctuating usage of the Middle English period.

b. The Midland dialects are influenced by their position. Those to the North often have northern characteristics, i.e. *–s* in the singular and plural instead of *–th* or *–e*(*n*). Those to the South have southern characteristics, i.e. *–th* in the singular and plural.

The east Midland developed in the fifteenth century a peculiarity of its own — the suppression of the ending in the third person singular indicative: as 'John Dam *kno*' (Agnes Paston, *Paston Letters*, 183, A.D. 1452), instead of *knows*. Shakespeare has observed this peculiarity of dialect, but in *Henry the Fifth*, III, II, 116, he erroneously puts it into the mouth of an Irishman: 'The town is beseech'd, and the trumpet *call* (for *calls*) us to the breach.' Traces of the east Midland peculiarity are found in our early American documents written by people from this part of England. This is a trend toward simplicity as in the use of the ending *–s* for all persons and numbers, described in **54.** This older east Midland usage survives in England in the east Midland dialect. It is still found also in American dialect. Compare *Syntax*, **8** I 1 *h Note* (next to last par.). In the use of the auxiliary *do* for all persons and numbers this popular usage is much more widespread, but it is not due to the influence of the east Midland dialect. See *Syntax*, **8** I 1 *h Note* (next to last par.).

c. In the sixteenth century *–th* was frequently used in the plural in the literary language, which was usually without an ending here, as the old Middle English *–e*(*n*) had disappeared in the course of the fifteenth century: 'them that *seruyth* hym' (Lord Berners, *Huon*, I, p. 62, A.D. 1534). This use of plural *–th* is not a spreading of southern plural *-th* to the literary language, but the use of the common singular *–th* in plural function, i.e. a spreading of Middle English singular *–th* to the plural, a Midland development corresponding to the spreading of singular *–s* to the plural in the North, as described in **54.** The common use of plural *beth* (= *are*) and *hath* in Midland texts, however, may be explained differently. In these very common words the *–th* is probably the old original plural *–th,* which in the Midland was preserved in these forms by reason of their frequent and constant use from the earliest times. Elsewhere, it was preserved only in the South.

d. The northern plural in –(*e*)*s* was the more common form. The plural without an ending, as *bind,* had the ending *–en* at the beginning of the Middle English period. Early in the period the *n* of the ending dropped out and soon the vowel itself disappeared. The Midland plural ending *–en* met the same fate in the fifteenth century. The development began early in the North. The northern plural without an ending is only used when it has preceding it immediately a single plural personal pronoun as subject: 'Men *bindes,*' 'We that *bindes,*' but 'We *bind.*' This usage survives in northern British dialect, as illustrated by the following examples from Scotch dialect: 'Weemin *kenz* dhawt fein' (Women know that well). 'Mee un yoo *kenz* dhawt fein.' But 'Wee *ken* dhawt fein.'

e. The participial ending *–ing* arose in the South early in the Middle English period as a corruption of *–inde.* It was later adopted by Chaucer and gradually supplanted the old *–ind* or *–end* form. This is one of the most unfortunate developments in the history of our language, as it gave the present participle the same form as the gerund and sometimes makes English expression unclear.

f. The long *a* in *behāve* goes back to Middle English *hāve. Have* had *ā* when accented and *ă* when unaccented. As the auxiliary *have* was usually unstressed, *ă* became established with simple *have.*

Irregularities in Modern Present Tense

57. In a number of English verbs there have developed irregularities in inflection.

1. **Inflection of Present Tense of 'Be':**

	Indicative	Subjunctive
	Singular	
1.	I am	I be
2.	you are (old form, thou art)	you (thou) be
3.	he is	he be
	Plural	
1.	we are	we be
2.	you are (old form, ye are)	you (ye) be
3.	they are	they be

Imperative

be (old forms, be thou, be ye)

Present Participle being   Present Infinitive (to) be

Present Gerund being

a. Contractions: 'He *isn't* rich,' 'we, you, they *aren't* rich.' As can be seen by the examples, there is in the literary language no contraction with *n't* after *am.* In the declarative form, however, we can contract *am* to *'m:* '*I'm* not rich.' In interrogative form contraction does not take place here in the literary language at all. In colloquial speech *am I not?* or *am not I?* often becomes *ain't I?* or *aren't I?* — the latter regarded as choicer by many in England and by some in America: 'I'm such a catch, *ain't I?*' (A. Marshall, *Exton Manor,* Ch. V). 'Well, man alive, I'm bound to know, *aren't I?*' (Hutchinson, *If Winter Comes,* p. 101). '*Aren't I* silly to weep?' (Francis R. Bellamy, *The Balance,* Ch. XX). The first person singular form *aren't* is a leveled form, after the analogy of *we aren't, you aren't, they aren't.* Similarly, the first person singular *ain't* is after the analogy of *we ain't, you ain't, they ain't,* where *ain't* is corrupted from *aren't.* Colloquially *ain't* is often felt as a useful contraction in *ain't I?,* but it is elsewhere shunned. As the *r* in *aren't* is not pronounced in England before a consonant, we often find this form written *an't,* especially a little earlier in the period, as in Smollett and Dickens. Of course, the *r* is still silent in England, but it is now usually written. In Ireland the contraction *amn't* is sometimes used instead of *ain't* in the first person singular: '*Amn't I* after telling you she's a great help to her mother?' (Lennox Robinson, *The Whiteheaded Boy,* Act I, p. 9).

In older English, the usual contraction of *is* with the subject *it* was *'tis,* which is still used, but now the common contraction is *it's.*

b. Indicative 'Be.' In early Modern English, the form *be* was sometimes used also as a plural indicative: 'Here *be* my keys' (Shakespeare, *Merry Wives,* III, iii, 172). 'It is true, there *be* large estates in the kingdom, but not in this county' (Fielding, *Tom Jones,* Book VI, Ch. II). This older usage survives in popular speech. Also in the literary language in certain set expressions: 'The public is suspicious of *the powers that be*' (*Chicago Tribune,* Apr. 20, 1926). Compare *d* below.

c. Subjunctive 'Beest.' In the sixteenth and seventeenth centuries the form *beest,* though properly an indicative, was much used as the second person singular present subjunctive: '*Be'st* thou sad or merry, The violence of either thee becomes' (Shakespeare, *Antony and Cleopatra,* I, v, 59).

d. Older Inflection of Present Tense of 'Be.' The present tense of *be* is made up of three different roots — in older English with different variants, so that the present forms are the result of a long period of development and differentiation:

Old English	Middle English	Old English	Middle English
INDICATIVE	INDICATIVE	SUBJUNCTIVE	SUBJUNCTIVE
Singular	*Singular*	*Singular*	*Singular*
		1, 2, 3	1, 2, 3
1. eom, bīo, bēo	am, bē, es		
2. eart, bist	art { bist, bēst; es or bēs (North)	sīe, sī, bīo, bēo	bē
3. is, biþ	is { bith, bēth; es or bēs (North)		
Plural	*Plural*	*Plural*	*Plural*
1, 2, 3	1, 2, 3	1, 2, 3	1, 2, 3
aron (North) sint, sindon bīoþ, bēoþ	arn, are bēth, bē(n), es or bēs (North)	sī(e)n, bīon, bēon	bēn, bē

IMPERATIVE

Old English

Singular

bīo, bēo, wes

Plural

bīoþ, bēoþ, wesaþ

Middle English

Singular

bē
bēs (North)

Plural

bēth
bēs (North)

INFINITIVE

Old English

bīon, bēon, wesan

Middle English

bēn, bē

PARTICIPLE

Old English

bīonde, bēonde, wesende

Middle English

bēinge
bēand (North)

GERUND

Middle English

bēinge

In oldest English, the *be*-forms were used as indicatives and subjunctives, but later, in the Middle English period, *be* began to be felt as a subjunctive. In Shakespeare's day, and even later in Fielding's time, this differentiation was not yet complete, as *be* was still used as a plural indicative, as illustrated in *b* above. In England, the dialects of the South and the East still employ *be* in the singular and the plural indicative, so that *be* is not differentiated here as a subjunctive form. *Be* is used here and there also in American dialect as a singular or plural indicative, especially in the second part of a double question and in subordinate clauses, rarely however in the third person singular: 'You ain't tired, *be* you?' (Susan Warner, *The Wide, Wide World*, Ch. XIII). 'Now, Hiram, you ain't agoin' t' the store tonight!' — 'I say I *be* agoin' tew!' (*Dialect Notes*, I, p. 340).

Our plural form *are* was long a dialect word confined to the North of England. For centuries before the Modern English period the standard words for the South and the Midland were *beth, ben, be*. But *are* was all this time spreading southward in colloquial speech. In the early part of the sixteenth century it began to appear in standard English alongside of *be*, later gradually supplanting it.

2. Inflection of Present Tense of 'Have':

INDICATIVE	SUBJUNCTIVE
Singular	
1. I have	I have
2. you have (old form, thou hast)	you (thou) have
3. he has (old form, hath)	he have
Plural	
1. we have	we have
2. you have (old form, ye have)	you (ye) have
3. they have	they have

IMPERATIVE

have (old forms, have thou, have ye)

PRESENT PARTICIPLE having — PRESENT INFINITIVE (to) have

PRESENT GERUND having

Contractions:

a. The forms *hath* and *has* (formerly often written *ha's*) are contractions of older forms once in use — *hafeþ, haves.* In early Modern English the first person singular *have* was often contracted to *ha:* 'I *ha* but two hands' (Middleton-Rowley, *The Spanish Gipsie*, III, II, 128, A.D. 1661). In older English, the negative form was *ha'n't.* It still lingers in dialect: 'I *ha'n't* seen him' (Susan Warner, *The Wide, Wide World*, Ch. IX). The dialectic form *hain't* (or less commonly *ain't* with the *h* dropped) is used for all persons and numbers: 'Caleb (name) *hain't* no monopoly' (J. R. Lowell, *Biglow Papers*, No. II). 'Bein' they *hain't* no lead, they make their bullets out o' copper' (*ib.*). 'Oh! Then you *ain't* the money?' (Lynn Riggs, *A Lantern To See By*, III). The usual colloquial contractions are 'I, you, we, they *haven't,*' 'he *hasn't.*'

On the other hand, *hain't* is used in dialect for all persons and numbers as a contraction of the forms of *be* with *not:* 'I *hain't* bad nor mean' (Eugene O'Neill, *Desire under the Elms,* I, IV). 'Sun's a-rizin'. Purty, *hain't* it?' (*ib.*, last page).

b. In early Modern English, there were three other plural forms in use — *hath, han* (a contraction of the Middle English plural *haven*), and *ha:* 'The rulers in this realm *hath* no better a God than the poorest in this world' (Latimer, *Serm. and Rem.*, 201, A.D. 1555). 'When shepheardes groomes *han* leave to playe' (Spenser, *Shep. Cal.*, Mar. 62, A.D. 1579). The plural *ha* was very common as an auxiliary: 'Till we *ha* dined' (Middleton-Rowley, *The Spanish Gipsie,* II, I, 145, A.D. 1661), 'now 'till *we've* dined.' The negative form of *ha* was *ha'n't.* It still lingers in dialect: 'You *ha'n't* had supper, have yous?' (Susan Warner, *The Wide, Wide World,* Ch. XII).

For an explanation of the plural form *hath* see **56** 4 *c.*

c. In early Modern English, the infinitive *have* was often contracted to *ha,* especially in its use as an auxiliary: 'It should *ha* been so' (Beaumont and Fletcher, *The Maids Tragedie,* II, II, 49, A.D. 1622). This contraction is still common here, but we write it 'a.' We now use also the contraction 'of' here. Although in rapid speech we often use both contractions, we usually write *have.* In realistic literature, however, 'a' and 'of' are sometimes written: 'It should *a* (or *of*) been so.'

d. The contractions in *a, b, c* are the result of the weak stress that *have* often has as an auxiliary and as a verb of complete predication. The fuller Old and Middle English forms are given in **56** 3 *b* and 4.

3. **Inflection of Present Tense of 'Do':**

INDICATIVE	SUBJUNCTIVE
Singular	
1. I do	I do
2. you do (old forms, thou doest [full verb], dost [auxiliary])	you (thou) do
3. he does (old forms, doeth, doth)	he do
Plural	
1. we do	we do
2. you do (old form, ye do)	you (ye) do
3. they do	they do

IMPERATIVE

do

PRESENT PARTICIPLE doing   PRESENT INFINITIVE (to) do

PRESENT GERUND doing

a. The old forms in the second and third persons are used only in poetry and biblical language. In early Modern English, the plural ending *-th* was sometimes used: 'as wild horses *doth* race' (Ascham, *Toxophilus*, 8, A.D. 1545). For explanation of this form see **56** 4 *c*.

b. The contractions of *do* with a following *not* are: *I, you, we, they don't; he* (*she, it*) *doesn't.* In colloquial speech, *he, she, it don't* are much used instead of the literary *he, she, it doesn't.* Compare *Syntax,* **8** I 1 *h* *Note* (next to last par.).

4. **Present and Past Tense of Past-Present Verbs.** There is a group of strong verbal forms which were originally past tenses, but have come to have the meaning of the present tense. Originally the past tense had close relations to the present, much as the present perfect (**65** *b*) today, so that it pointed not only to the past but also to the present. In course of time the past tense became the tense of narrative, pointing purely and simply to the past without reference to the present. Thus in the course of the development of most verbs the past idea in the past tense form overshadowed that of the present, which was once also present there. In a few verbs, however, the opposite development took place — the idea of the present in the past tense form overshadowed that of the past, which was once also present there, so that these forms are now felt as present tenses. A comparatively recent case of this development is seen in *have got:* 'I*'ve got* a cold.' Here the present perfect tense form now has the force of a present tense. Similarly, in the prehistoric period the old past tense forms *can, dare, may, shall,* and the archaic *wot* (= *know*) developed the force of the present tense. Although we now use them as present tenses, their form still shows that they were originally past tenses. They all have a third person singular without the ending *-s:* 'In summer Mother *cans* as much fruit as she *can.*' The first *can* is a real present tense. The second *can* is a present tense with the form of the past tense — a past-present verb. In the prehistoric period after these old strong past tenses had come to be felt as present tenses, new weak past tense forms were coined for reference to the past: *could, durst, might, should, wist.* In early Modern English, another verb belonged to the list of past-present verbs — *mote.* It survives in its past subjunctive form *must.* This past subjunctive is now felt as a present tense. This development is an easy and natural one, as every past subjunctive may refer to present time, differing from the present indicative only in expressing the thought more modestly: 'I *should prefer* to stay at home,' a modest way of saying 'I prefer to stay at home.' Similarly, *ought,* old past subjunctive of *owe,* is now felt as a present tense: 'I

ought to do it,' originally = 'I *should owe* the doing of it.' Thus in comparatively recent times two past subjunctives — *must* and *ought* — have joined the list of past present verbs. This development has a counterpart in very early times. *Will,* now for many centuries felt as a present tense, was originally a past subjunctive.

A. *Historical Remarks.* These verbs, like other verbs, once belonged to regular inflectional systems, but have come down to us as shattered fragments.

a. Can, dare, may, shall, wot, are old past indicatives; *will, must, ought,* old past subjunctives. They are now all felt as present tenses.

b. Will once had a variant form, *wol,* which survives in *won't* (= *wol not*). In early Modern English, the full form of *wol* was still in use: 'God, I say, *woll* judge such Judges as ye are' (Thomas Cromwell, *Letter to the Bishop of Salisbury,* March, 1538).

In older English, the old negative *ne* (= *not*) and a following *will* were often contracted to *nill:* 'If I may rest, I *nill* live in sorrowe' (Spenser, *The Shepheards Calender,* May, 151, A.D. 1579). The old form survives in the expression *willy-nilly,* from *will he, nill he* = *Let him like it or not.* It is now a mere adverb referring to all persons and numbers: '*I, you, we, they,* must go, *willy-nilly.*' In older English, the proper person could be used: 'And, *will you, nill you,* I will marry you' (Shakespeare, *Taming of the Shrew,* II, 173).

c. Ought is an old past subjunctive of *owe.* In early Modern English, it was used also as a past indicative alongside of the newer past indicative *owed.* The original meaning of *owe* is *have, own, possess* — words which in the seventeenth century entirely replaced *owe* in this meaning. In early Modern English, the past indicatives *ought* and *owed* were still used with this meaning: 'Who *ought* (now *owned*) your castel thre thousande yere agoe?' (More, *Comfort against Tribulation,* III, Wrks., 1219, A.D. 1534). 'For several virtues Have I liked several women, never any with so full soul but some defect in her Did quarrel with the noblest grace she *ow'd*' (Shakespeare, *The Tempest,* III, I, 43), now *possessed. Ought* and *owed* served also as past participle. The past participle was originally strong. This old past participle with the original meaning survives in our present adjective *own,* literally *possessed.*

In Old English, the original meaning of *having* often went over into that of *having to pay, owing.* In this meaning *owe* has become a regular verb — *owe, owed, owed.* In early Modern English, the old past indicative *ought* was still in use in this meaning: 'He said . . . you *ought* (now *owed*) him a thousand pound' (Shakespeare, *Henry the Fourth,* First Part, III, II, 152). Also the newer past *owed* was in use at this time in this meaning. *Ought* was once employed here also as a past participle: 'a gentleman who had *ought* (now *owed*) us money a long time' (A.D. 1639, quoted from the *Oxford Dictionary*).

In older English, the old meaning of *having* often went over into that of *having to do as a duty*. In this meaning the present indicative *owe* was frequently employed, often alongside of the past subjunctive *ought*, which here, as the past subjunctive in general, had the force of the present indicative, only with a touch of modesty and cautiousness not found in the indicative: 'Y haue herd summe men seie (say) þat a man *owith* to lyue (live) in þis world moraly, vertuosely. And summe men Y haue herd seie þat a man in þis world *owȝt* to lyue aftir þe lawe of god' (Pecock, *The Donet*, p. 14, about A.D. 1449). Later, the present indicative in this meaning entirely disappeared.

The common people, however, did not give up the old literary distinction between the present indicative and the past subjunctive of *owe* in the sense of *ought*. They created new forms to bring out the idea clearly. They employ the unclear past subjunctive *ought* as an infinitive and place before it a clear present indicative or a clear past subjunctive auxiliary: 'He *don't ought* to do it.' 'He *shouldn't* (or *hadn't* or *didn't*) *ought* to do it.' When the reference is to the past, the infinitive dependent upon *ought* is usually in the perfect tense: 'You *shouldn't ought to have done* it.' Also *ought* itself is sometimes in the perfect tense: 'You *shouldn't have ought to have done* it.' Compare *Syntax*, **44** I *a* (last par.). Similarly, in the case of other past-present verbs the past subjunctive is often in popular speech treated as an infinitive: 'Better not tell me de bad news; ef it is terrible, I might not *could* stan' to hear 'em' (Julia Peterkin, *Green Thursday*, p. 183). *Could* is now used as an infinitive also in other constructions: 'I can't do it now like I used *to could*' (Gepp, *Essex Dialect Dictionary*, p. 183). Also *used* and *was* are now employed as infinitives: 'He didn't *used* to be so foolish' (*ib.*). 'That used *to was*' (*ib.*).

According to our English sequence a verb is attracted to the form of the past tense after a past indicative: 'He told me yesterday that he *would* (instead of *will*) help me.' That *must* and *ought*, originally past subjunctives, can stand after a past indicative shows that we still have a vague feeling that they are here past subjunctives, although we elsewhere regard these forms more commonly as present tenses: 'I thought it *must* kill him' (Meredith, *The Ordeal of Richard Feverel*, Ch. XLV). 'I thought he *ought* to do it and told him so.' Under the influence of *must* and *ought* we sometimes employ *dare* and *need* as past subjunctives after a past indicative, although we elsewhere regard them more commonly as present tense forms: 'He felt he *dare* not reply.' 'He had a good hour on his hands before he *need* go back.' Compare *Syntax*, **44** I *a*, **49** 4 C (1) *a* (4th par.).

d. The present subjunctive of *must* survives in archaic *mote* (in older English sometimes written *mought*): 'So *mote* (= *may*) it be!' In early Modern English, *mote* was still used as an ordinary present tense with the force of *may* (permission or possibility) or *must*. In early Modern English, *mote*, though a present tense, was sometimes, like *dare* and *need* in *c* (last par.), employed as a past tense form after a past indicative or a past subjunctive pointing to the past: 'Therefore he her did court, did serve, did wooe, With humblest suit that he imagine *mot*' (Spenser, *Faerie Queene*, IV, II, VIII, A.D. 1596), now *could*. 'However loth he *waere* his way to slake, Yet *mote* he algates now abide and answere make' (*ib.*, V, VIII, V) = 'However loath he was to slacken his pace, he *must* nevertheless stop and answer.'

e. *Wot*, an old past indicative used as a present: I *wot*, he *wot* = I know, he knows. It survives in the infinitive *to wit*, now with the meaning *namely*. The present participle survives in the adverb *unwittingly*. The new past *wist*, once common, was still in use in early Modern English, and is still found in the Bible (*Mark*, IX, 6): 'For he *wist* not what to say.' In early Modern English, the old forms for the present tense were still in use, but alongside of them appeared new, regular forms made from *wot* as a base: (present indicative) he *wotteth* or *wots*, (present participle) *wotting*. From this new base a new, regular past tense was formed, *wotted:* 'He stood still and *wotted* not what to do' (Bunyan, *Pilgrim's Progress*, I). The fact that new, regular forms could thus be made and used indicates clearly that *wot* was felt as no longer belonging to past-present verbs, which had now come to be modal auxiliaries, subjunctive forms. Later, *wot* disappeared for the most part from the language, since it was not in any way differentiated in meaning from *know* and hence was not needed.

In early Modern English, the old negative form *not* (or *note*) — contracted from *ne wot* — was still used. The old negative *ne* was employed here as in *b* above. *Not*(*e*), though a present tense, was sometimes, like *dare* and *need* in *c* (last par.), employed as a past tense form after a past indicative: 'Ere long so weake of limbe and sicke of love He woxe, that lenger he *note* (= *couldn't*, literally *didn't know how to*) stand upright' (Spenser, *Faerie Queene*, IV, XII, XX, A.D. 1596) = 'he *couldn't* stand upright any longer.'

f. The verb *need* has been drawn into this group under the influence of its meaning, which is similar to that of *must.* In the meaning *to be without, want,* it is always a regular verb: 'He *needs, needed,* men and money.' Elsewhere, there is fluctuation between the regular inflection of the different tenses and that of past-present verbs: 'He *doesn't need to* (or *need not*) go.' Compare *Syntax,* **49** 4 C (1) *a.*

g. Dare, on the other hand, is manifesting a tendency to leave this group. It is always a regular verb throughout in the sense of *challenge:* 'He *dares, dared,* me to do it.' Elsewhere, there is fluctuation between the regular inflection of the different tenses and that of past-present verbs: 'He *doesn't dare to* (or *dare not*) reply.' Compare *Syntax,* **49** 4 C (1) *a.* Also *will* is a regular verb when we feel its meaning as related to the noun *will:* 'God *wills, willed,* that man should be happy.'

h. What has drawn verbs of such different origin together? They are all verbs that do not state facts, but merely present conceptions, representing something as possible, necessary, desirable, befitting. These are ideas closely related to those expressed by the subjunctive, so that they have come to be felt as modal auxiliaries, as subjunctives, and, as subjunctives, naturally take no *-s* in the third person singular. The oldest of these forms once had an indicative alongside of the subjunctive in both the present and the past tense, the indicative with more positive force than the subjunctive. The old past indicatives could refer to the past, while our present past tenses, *could, durst, might, should, would,* prevailingly point to the present or the future, differing from the present tenses only in the *manner* of the conception, as described in **50** 2 *d:* 'It *might* rain,' indicating only a faint prospect of rain, but 'It *may* rain,' indicating a greater possibility. The past is often milder than the present: 'You *should* go,' but in a harsh tone 'You *shall* go!' '*Will* you do it for me?' but in a politer tone '*Would* you do it for me?' When a past tense that does not depend upon a past indicative points to the present or the future, as *might, could, should, would,* in these examples, it must be a subjunctive. Thus the past tenses of these verbs are losing their power to point to the past and are gradually becoming inflectional forms used in connection with an infinitive to express subjunctive ideas, modal auxiliary and infinitive together having the force of a simple subjunctive, pointing to the present or the future: 'You *might post* this for me.' 'We *must do* what we can for him.' 'We *ought to go* at once!' 'If it *should rain,* I *would stay* at home.' 'I *could do* it if I had time.' *Could* and *would,* however, are still, not infrequently, used as past indicatives, referring to the past. But this can be done only when the context clearly indicates that the reference is to past time, for these forms cannot of themselves point to the past: 'I *couldn't* find him yesterday.' 'This morning I tried to persuade him, but he *wouldn't* listen to me.' The *must* that is now used comes for the most part from the old past subjunctive and points to the present or the future, but it is sometimes the old past indicative, and hence points to the past: 'In those days he could not bear to be idle. He *must* always be doing something.' In early Modern English, also, *should* could thus point to the past, often being used with the infinitive with the force of a past indicative: 'When the priest *Should ask* (= *asked*), if Katherine should be his wife, "Ay, by gogswouns" (= *God's* wounds), quoth he' (Shakespeare, *The Taming of the Shrew*, III, ii, 160). The perfect infinitive was often used here to bring out more clearly the idea of past time: 'There are some rumors that the conspirators *should have taken* some other places' (Andrew Marvell, *Correspondence*, Works, II, 92, A.D. 1663). This older usage survives in dialect: 'They tell me so-and-so *should say*' (= *said*), etc. (Edward Gepp, *Essex Dialect Dictionary*, p. 137). ''Cordin' t' Bill, Sam *sh'd a said* (= *said*) I was a liar' (Ozark Dialect, *American Speech*, III, p. 4).

Must and *ought* were originally past subjunctives expressing a mild tone or a cautious statement, and this old meaning is still common: 'In such a trying situation you *must* (or *ought to*) think things over carefully before you act.' 'He *must* (or *ought to*) be there by this time.' As the past subjunctive often refers to present time these forms are often construed as present tenses, and as present subjunctives they express a more positive tone: 'You *must* (or *ought to*) go at once!' Unfortunately there are not two forms here for the differentiation of the thought, as in the case of *may-might*, *can-could*, *shall-should*, *will-would*. One form must serve for the two meanings. After the analogy of this usage *dare* and *need* are sometimes in questions and negative statements employed as subjunctive forms with a twofold force — with the force of a past subjunctive imparting a mild tone or with the force of the present subjunctive imparting a more positive tone: '*Dare* she now hope for a favorable turn of things?' '*Need* she worry so?' In a more positive tone: 'She *dare* not say that again!' 'He *need* not ask me for help again!' Compare *Syntax*, **49** 4 C (1) *a* (4th par.).

That all the verbs in this article (*h*) have for the most part lost their power to mark the time relations indicates that they are developing into subjunctive forms, mere coloring particles to tint thought and feeling. As can be seen by the examples in the preceding paragraph, the development here is uneven. Some of these verbs do not have the usual complement of two tenses — the present and the past — which most subjunctives have for the differentiation of thought and feeling. Compare **50** 2 *d.*

i. Although these verbs now for the most part have the force of subjunctives, they have in poetry and in biblical language an ending in the second person singular of the present tense, 'thou may*st*,' 'thou shal*t*,' etc., which is contrary to the usage observed in other subjunctives. Originally the indicative and the subjunctive of the modal auxiliaries were differentiated in form, but by the end of the Middle English period they had for the most part become identical. Occasionally, however, in early Modern English we still find the old subjunctive form for the old second person singular to the present tense: 'Saue thy head if thou *may*' (Udall, *Royster D.*, IV, VII, 72, A.D. 1553). The indicative form has replaced here the subjunctive. *Must,* which is now felt as a present tense, although historically a past subjunctive, has not followed the analogy of the present tense forms in this group. It is uninflected throughout.

B. *Inflection.* These verbs inflect in the present and the past tense as follows:

PRESENT TENSE

Singular

1.	can	dare	may
2.	can (canst)	dare (darest)	may (mayst)
3.	can	dares, dare	may

Plural for All Persons

can	dare	may

Singular

1.	shall	will	must
2.	shall (shalt)	will (wilt)	must (must)
3.	shall	will	must

Plural for All Persons

shall	will	must

Singular

1.	ought	need	wot
2.	ought (oughtest)	need (needest)	wot (wottest)
3.	ought	needs, need	wot (wotteth, wots)

Plural for All Persons

ought	need	wot

PAST TENSE

Singular

1.	could	dared, dare (durst [1])	might, *mought* † [2]
2.	could (couldst)	dared, dare (daredst, durst)	might, *mought* † [2] (might(e)st, *mought(e)st* † [2])
3.	could	dared, dare (durst)	might, *mought* † [2]

Plural for All Persons

	could	dared, dare (durst)	might, *mought* † [2]

Singular

1.	should	would	must
2.	should (shouldst)	would (wouldst)	must (must)
3.	should	would	must

Plural for All Persons

	should	would	must

Singular

1.	ought	needed, need
2.	ought (oughtest)	needed, need (neededst)
3.	ought	needed, need

Plural for All Persons

	ought	needed, need

[1] The past *durst* is often in older English, as the past subjunctive in general, used with the force of the present indicative, only expressing more caution, modesty: 'I have no desire, and besides, if I had, I *durst* not for my soul touch upon the subject' (Sterne, *Tristram Shandy*, III, xx). This usage is still very common in popular speech: 'He put (= puts) on mo' a'rs dan w'at I *dast* ter do' (Joel Chandler Harris, *Nights with Uncle Remus*, p. 307). 'I *durstn't* (or *dasn't* or *darsn't*) do it.' In older English, the past tense form *durst* was used also as a past indicative. In connection with a past indicative this form is sometimes in popular speech still used as a past indicative: 'I wasn't allowed to come into the house unless I changed my boots for slippers at the door. I *darsn't* smoke a pipe for my life unless I went to the barn' (L. M. Montgomery, *Anne of Avonlea*, Ch. XXV).

In popular speech the past subjunctive *dast*, like the past subjunctive *ought* (see A *c*, p. 254), is used as an infinitive: 'He wouldn't *dast* put in an appearance' (Lucy Furman, *Mothering on Perilous*, Ch. XV).

[2] In early Modern English widely used in the literary language, now replaced by *might* in literary usage, but still employed in dialect: 'He *mought* have done it and then again he *moughtn't*' (*Dialect Notes*, II, p. 231).

a. The inflection of *shall* and *will,* as given above, holds only for the use of these forms as modal auxiliaries. For their use in the future tense see **67** 2.

FORMATION OF THE PAST TENSE

58. There are two types of inflection — the weak and the strong. The two types were originally quite distinct in form and for the most part still are, but in a number of words do not now have distinctive forms. Compare **60** A *f.*

Formation of the Regular Weak Past

59. This type of inflection forms the past tense and past participle with the suffix *-ed,* in which *e* is silent except after *d* and *t.* With silent *e:* work, *worked* (past tense and past participle); taboo, *tabooed;* boo, *booed;* stew, *stewed;* flow, *flowed.* With pronounced *e:* hand, *handed;* hunt, *hunted.* Contrary to this principle, however, the *e* in a number of distinctively *adjective* participles is pronounced: *learnĕd, belovĕd, blessĕd, accursĕd,* etc. In 'on *bended* knees' the old adjective form is still used, while we elsewhere use the newer contracted form, even in adjective function, as in 'a *bent* twig.' We say 'a man *aged* (*ājd*) sixty-five,' but 'an *agĕd* (*ājid*) man.' The old full form with pronounced *e* is also preserved in derivative adverbs, *assurĕdly, avowĕdly,* etc. In all the cases where the *e* is silent, whether in past tense or past participle, the *d* is sounded as *d* only after vowel sounds or voiced consonants, as in *snowed, delayed, warmed, oiled, feared, robbed, raised,* elsewhere being pronounced *t,* as in *crossed, watched, locked, jumped, scoffed.* In earlier Modern English, the apostrophe often took the place of silent *e: fear'd,* etc.

A final consonant, preceded by an accented short vowel, is doubled before *e* of the ending *-ed:* drop, dro*pped;* rebel, rebe*lled.* But: travel, trave*led;* devil, devi*led;* develop, develo*ped;* nónplus, nónplus*ed,* but nonplús, nonplú*ssed.* The doubling of the *l* in 'rebe*ll*ed' shows that the second syllable is stressed, while the single *l* in 'trave*l*ed' indicates that the second syllable is unstressed. British orthography differs from American in that final *l* is doubled also after an unstressed vowel: travel, trave*lled;* devil, devi*lled.* In both American and British orthography a *k* (which virtually doubles *c*) is placed after an unstressed *c,* for it is necessary here to mark *c* as hard: picnic, picnic*ked;* bivouac, bivouac*ked.*

After a consonant, *y* becomes *ie* before *-ed:* rel*y,* rel*ied;* but pla*y,* pla*yed.*

Final silent *e* is dropped before *-ed:* love, lov*ed.*

After un-English vowel terminations (*a*, *i*, *o*, etc.) the contracted suffix *–'d* sometimes makes the grammatical relations clearer than does the full suffix *–ed:* one-idea'*d*, ski'*d*, mustachio'*d* (more commonly *mustached*), etc. In the case of the verb O.K. the contracted suffix is always employed: O.K., O.K.'*d*.

This class of verbs — regular weak verbs — is the largest in the language. There are, moreover, many irregular weak verbs, which are treated in **60.** These irregular weak verbs fall into certain definite groups described in 2 B below. There are also a few very irregular weak auxiliaries, treated in **57** 4. The weak class along with its irregular verbs comprises all the verbs in the language except about one hundred — the strong class described in **61, 62, 63.** Many verbs, once strong, have become wholly or partially weak. The regular weak class is the only living type. All new verbs enter this class.

Regular Weak Past

	Indicative	Subjunctive
	Singular	
1.	I loved	I loved
2.	you loved (thou lovĕdst)	you loved (thou lovĕdst)
3.	he loved	he loved
	Plural	
1.	we loved	we loved
2.	you loved (old form, ye loved)	you (ye) loved
3.	they loved	they loved

In early Modern English, the ending *–st* of the old *thou*-form was sometimes dropped: 'Thou *made* answere vnto the prophete,' etc. (John Fisher, *E.E.T.S.*, Ex. ser. XXVII, p. 172, early 16th century). Poets still employ this form occasionally: 'Where thou once *formed* thy paradise' (Byron). This form without *–st* served both as an indicative and a subjunctive. In accordance with older usage, the *thou*-form is still the same for the indicative and the subjunctive in the past tense, but it now has the ending *–st.* Compare **61** (last par.), where the absence of *–st* is explained and a fuller treatment of the old second person singular form is given.

1. **Old English Weak Past.** The three representative Old English weak verbs *werian* 'defend,' *lufian* 'love,' *habban* 'have,' inflected in the present tense in **56** 3 *b*, are here given with their Old English past tense forms:

	defend	*love*	*have*	*defend*	*love*	*have*
	INDICATIVE			SUBJUNCTIVE		
	Singular			*Singular*, 1, 2, 3		
	I	II	III	I	II	III
1.	wĕrede	lŭfode	hǣfde	wĕrede	lŭfode	hǣfde
2.	wĕredes(t)	lŭfodes(t)	hǣfdes(t)			
3.	wĕrede	lŭfode	hǣfde			
	Plural, 1, 2, 3			*Plural*, 1, 2, 3		
	wĕredon	lŭfodon	hǣfdon	wĕreden	lŭfoden	hǣfden

PAST PARTICIPLE gewĕred, gelŭfod, gehǣfd

a. Verbs without a Medial Vowel. In the examples of inflection given above 'were*d*e' represents the first class. It has the medial vowel *e*. A large number of verbs in this class, however, did not have this medial *e*. The medial *e* of the past tense was regularly dropped if the stem syllable had a long vowel or ended in *–dd, –tt, –ll, –ss*, or two different consonants: *dēman* 'judge,' 'deem,' past *dēmde*. A double consonant was simplified before *–de: fyllan* 'fill,' past *fylde*. A final *d* in the stem syllable preceded by a consonant disappeared before *–de: sendan* 'send,' past *sende*. The suffix *–de* became *–te* after a voiceless consonant: *grētan* 'greet,' past *grētte*. A double consonant was simplified before *–te: cyssan* 'kiss,' past *cyste*. A final *t* in the stem syllable preceded by a consonant disappeared before *–te: fæstan* 'make fast,' past *fæste*. A few verbs, however, that have at the end of their stem syllable a combination of consonants difficult to pronounce together with a following *–de* always took the medial *e: hyngran* 'hunger,' past *hyngrede;* etc. The past participle in all these verbs usually ended in *–ed: gedēmed, gefylled*, etc. But in verbs whose stem syllable ended in *–d* or *–t* the *e* of the suffix *–ed* was often suppressed and the final *dd* or *tt* then simplified: *gesend, gegrēt(t)*, etc. instead of *gesended, gegrēted*, etc.

There is another large group of verbs in the first class that have no medial *e*. They differ from the verbs in this group in that the vowel of the past tense and past participle is not identical with that of the present tense, while this group has the same vowel throughout. The group with the change of vowel is described in *b* (3) below.

b. Mutation. In Old English, many verbs of the first class experienced in all or some of their principal parts a change in the stem vowel called mutation. The cause of this change was the presence once of a *j* after the stem syllable in the present tense and the presence of an *i* after the stem syllable in the past tense and past participle. There are three groups of these verbs:

(1). This small group of verbs has a short stem syllable: *wĕrian* (Gothic *wărjan*) 'defend,' past *wĕrede* (Gothic *wărida*), past participle *gewered* (Gothic *wăriþs*). As in this example the old *j* of the present tense is preserved as *i* in all the verbs of this group ending in *–r*, and the old *i* of the past tense and past participle is preserved in the reduced form of *e* in all the verbs of this group. The older Gothic forms in parentheses show that the old *j* and *i* have mutated the old stem vowel *a* of the English verb to *e*. The vowel was not mutated in Gothic because mutation had not yet begun to operate. Mutation took place in English in the prehistoric period, probably in the sixth century.

(2). This large group of verbs has a long stem syllable, as described in *a* above. In most of these verbs every trace of *j* and *i* had disappeared except the reduced *e* of the participial suffix *-ed: dēman* (Gothic *dōmjan*) 'judge,' 'deem,' past *dēmde* (Gothic *dōmida*), past participle *gedēmed* (Gothic *dōmiþs*). Although there is here no medial vowel in the present and the past tense, the mutated stem vowel *e* — mutated form of *o* — in all the principal parts of this verb tells the story of the presence here formerly of *j* and *i*. The Gothic forms with their *j* and *i* show the older principal parts. Out of this large group of Old English verbs, described more fully in *a* above, have come the three Middle English groups described in 2 B *b*, *c*, *d* below.

(3). There is in Old English another large group of verbs in the first class, which are like the verbs in (2) in that they have no medial *e*, but which are unlike them in that there is a change of vowel in the different parts: t*e*llan 'tell,' past t*ea*lde, past participle get*ea*ld. In some verbs of this class the final consonant of the stem syllable was affected in prehistoric times by the suffixes of the past tense and past participle, so that there is in the different parts a difference of consonants as well as a difference of vowels: *by*cgan 'buy,' b*oh*te, geb*oh*t; s*ē*can 'seek,' s*ōh*te, ges*ōh*t. These verbs represent an old type of inflection which had no medial vowel in the past tense and past participle, but had once a *j* after the stem syllable of the present tense. In the period of mutation the *j* in the present tense mutated the stem vowel, but there was no medial *i* in the past tense and past participle to cause mutation there, so that there arose a difference of vowels in the different parts. The *j* that once stood after the stem of the present tense has disappeared, but the mutated stem vowel tells of its former existence. From this group of verbs comes the Middle English group described in 2 B *a* below.

c. *Size and Importance of the Different Classes*. In the Old English period, the verbs in the first class were numerous, but their inflection lacked simplicity, falling into three different types described in *b* above, from which four types were formed in Middle English, described in 2 B *a*, *b*, *c*, *d* below. The verbs in the second class were far more numerous than those in the first class and at the close of the period were growing in numbers at their expense. Moreover, they had a uniform inflection. In Middle English, this class developed the new past tense suffix *-ed*, which was to become the usual suffix for all regular weak verbs. In late Middle English the new type with the suffix *-ed* must be considered the regular weak inflection, while the four types developed in verbs of the first class, described in 2 B *a*, *b*, *c*, *d* below must be considered as irregularities of weak inflection. The third class was small in the Old English period, but it possessed the common verb *habban*, which in its modern form *have* is still playing an important part in the language. The third class as a class has disappeared.

2. **Middle English Weak Past:**

	defend	*love*	*have*	*defend*	*love*	*have*
		INDICATIVE			SUBJUNCTIVE	
		Singular			*Singular*, 1, 2, 3	
	I	II	III	I	II	III
1	wēred(e) / wēr(e)de	lŏv(e)de / lŏved(e)	hăfde / hăd(d)e	wēred(e)	lŏv(e)de / lŏved(e)	hăd(d)e
2.	wēredest	lŏvedest	hăd(d)est			
3.	wēred(e) / wēr(e)de	lŏv(e)de / lŏved(e)	hăfde / hăd(d)e			
		Plural, 1, 2, 3			*Plural*, 1, 2, 3	
	wēred(en) / wēr(e)de(n)	lŏv(e)de(n) / lŏved(en)	hăfde(n) / hădde(n)	wēred(en)	lŏv(e)de(n) / lŏved(en)	hăd(d)en

PAST PARTICIPLE (y)wēred, (y)lŏved, (y)hă̆ved, (y)hădde, (y)hăd

The participial prefix *y*–, Old English *ge*–, is cognate with German *ge*–. It was at this time in general characteristic of southern English.

The inflections given above in 1 (p. 262) and 2 (p. 264) and the important notes *a* and *b* under 1 serve as the basis of the following detailed description of the Middle English inflection of weak verbs. Middle English inflection here rests upon Old English inflection, and Modern English inflection with its numerous irregularities cannot be understood as a system without a careful study of Middle English inflection. If the Middle English categories given below be mastered, the Modern English weak inflection will seem a fairly consistent system instead of a mass of inconsistencies. In looking back at the changes of the Middle English period it is interesting to note how Englishmen were struggling with the weak verb. This activity in the field of verbal expression was followed by a still greater activity there in the modern period. In Middle English the main effort in the field of the verb was in the direction of simplifying the inflection. In the modern period the main effort here has been in the direction of creating new verbal forms for the needs of an unfolding intellectual life. Compare **45** (2nd par.).

A. The endings in the singular and the plural of the weak past disappeared early in the period in the North. As can be seen in the paradigms in 2, above, the singular ending –*e* and the plural ending –*e*(*n*) began early in the period to disappear also in the Midland and the South in trisyllabic forms. There was for a while a tendency here to suppress final *e* or *e*(*n*) when the stem syllable was long and to retain final *e* and suppress medial *e* when the stem syllable was short: *wēred*(*e*), but *lŏv*(*e*)*de*. This tendency was not strong, for also *wēr*(*e*)*de* and *lŏved*(*e*) were used. Later, the tendency to suppress uniformly final *e* became strong, utterly destroying the older tendency and creating the new past tense suffix *-ed.* This new past tense ending developed in trisyllabic past tense forms like *lŏved(e)*, *hāted(e)* by the suppression of final *e*, whether the stem syllable was long or short. These words belonged for the most part to the second class of weak verbs, of which *lovede* is given above as a model. This was a powerful, growing group of words capable of exerting a strong influence in the language, so that the new suffix *-ed* was destined to spread to other verbs and in the course of the Middle English period become the usual suffix of regular weak verbs. This new development brought into our language at this point great simplicity where there had been great complexity. All the trisyllabic past tense forms in the first class, like *wēred(e)* in the paradigm given above, went over into the new class, but there weren't many of them. On the other hand, there was a very large group of dissyllabic past tense forms in the first class that on account of the peculiarity of their form could not easily fit into the new class. As described in 1 *a* and *b* (2), (3), pp. 262–263, they had already in Old English lost their medial *e* or had never had one, so that it was unnatural for them to take an *e* before the suffix *-d*. This large group of words developed in a manner natural to their form, falling into four distinct groups described in B *a*, *b*, *c*, *d* below. But even here the new regular type with the suffix *-ed* made itself felt from the start and began early to influence the inflection of a number of verbs in each group. In the course of the Middle English period a large number of the verbs in these four groups went over into the regular class. A number of the Old English verbs in 1 *a* above never went over into one of these four groups, but after retaining their Old English form for a while became regular: *kysse* 'kiss,' past *kyste*, later *kyssede*, *kissed*. Some were in one or other of the four groups and at the same time had a regular form, which later prevailed: *dēme* 'judge,' 'deem,' past *dēmde*, later *dĕmpte* (see B *c* below) and alongside of it the new regular form *dēmed*, later *deemed*. With the exception of a few isolated cases the very large number of foreign verbs that were introduced in the Middle English period joined the new regular class. It continued to grow in early Modern English, and is still, in the literary language, the only class that is growing.

The suffix *-ed* has become in many words a form without a real meaning, as in the case of *kissed*, where *-ed* is pronounced *t*. Compare **59**.

B. A large number of Middle English verbs did not follow the general development described in A above, but formed four distinct groups, each preserving certain Old English features of inflection curiously mingled with new, Middle English characteristics. The common feature to all these groups is that there is no vowel before the suffix of the past tense and past participle, as explained in 1 *a*, *b* (3), pp. 262–263. In early Middle English, the suffix was *-de* or *-te*, which later in the period were reduced to *-d* or *-t*, which in some verbs survives, in others has disappeared.

a. As a result of phonetic developments in older periods, described in 1 *b* (3), p. 263, there was in Middle English in a large group of words a difference of vowels, and in some words also a difference of consonants, in the different principal parts: selle 'sell,' sōlde, sōld; telle 'tell,' tōlde, tōld; bye 'buy,' boughte, bought; sēke 'seek,' soughte, sought. In the course of the Middle English period final *e* disappeared in the spoken language, though it often lingered longer in the written language. The parts now are: sell, sōld, sōld; tell, tōld, tōld; *buy*, bought, bought; *seek*, sought, sought. In the course of this development the suffixes *-de*, *-te* have become *-d*, *-t*, and certain phonetical changes have taken place, but the peculiar difference of vowels in the principal parts has been preserved. Also the old difference of consonants has been preserved in the written language, but in the spoken language *gh* has become silent: buy, bought, bought; seek, sought, sought; teach, taught, taught.

b. From the Old English verbs described in 1 *a* (p. 262), there was in earlier Middle English a large group ending in *-t* or *-d* with the past tense suffix *-te* after *t* and *-de* after *d*, and in the past participle with the suffix *-t* after *t* and *-d* after *d: sĕtte* 'set,' *sĕtte, sĕtt; shēde* 'shed,' *shĕdde, shĕdd.* In adding the suffixes to the stem syllable the final *tt* of the stem syllable was simplified to *t*. The early Middle English verbs had, in general, the same type of inflection as the Old English verbs, but in the course of the Middle English period they experienced a further development that radically changed the old type. The vowel of the present tense in this group was shortened wherever it was long, so that the vowel throughout the parts was short. Through the suppression of final *e* and the simplification of *tt* or *dd* to *t* or *d* there resulted the simplest and most modern type of verbal inflection in our language: *sĕt, sĕt, sĕt; shĕd, shĕd, shĕd.* In late Middle English the list of these verbs was large, and today after considerable reduction the list is still large. They are given in **60** A *c*. Though the list is decreasing in the literary language, a few strong verbs are joining it in popular American: *begin—begin; sing—sing; sit—sit; win—win,* the present and the past tense having the same form after the analogy of *set—set.* See the separate treatment of these verbs in **63**.

In Middle English, as a result of peculiar developments, some of these verbs with the stem vowel *e* had a double past tense and past participle: *sprēde* 'spread,' *sprĕdde* or *sprădde, sprĕdd* or *sprădd; drēde* 'dread,' *drĕdde* or *drădde, drĕdd* or *drădd.* In the course of the Middle English and the early Modern English period final *e* was dropped, the final double consonants were simplified, and the vowel of the present was shortened so that all the parts had the same vowel: *sprĕd, sprĕd, sprĕd;* later *spread, spread, spread.* In the sixteenth century *dread* became regular: *dread, dreaded, dreaded.*

c. There is another group of Middle English verbs which come from the same Old English source (1 *a*, p. 262) as the verbs in *b*, but have a different development. They all have a long vowel, which in late Old English or early Middle English was shortened before the combination of consonants arising in the past tense and past participle from the addition of the suffixes. Thus they all have a long vowel in the present tense and a short one in the past tense and the past participle. In Old English, the suffixes here were for the past tense *-de* after voiced consonants and *-te* after voiceless consonants, and for the past participle *-ed* for all verbs. In

Middle English, *-te* was used for the past tense and *-t* for the past participle, not only after voiceless consonants but also after the voiced consonants *l*, *m*, *n*, and *v*: *kēpe* 'keep,' *kĕpte*, *kĕpt*; *mēte* 'meet,' *mĕtte*, *mĕt*; *fēle*, 'feel,' *fĕlte*, *fĕlt*; *dēme* 'judge,' 'deem,' *dĕmpte*, *dĕmpt*; *drēme* 'dream,' *drĕmpte*, *drĕmpt*; *lēne* 'lean,' *lĕnte*, *lĕnt*; *lēne* 'lend,' *lĕnte*, *lĕnt*; *mēne* 'mean,' *mĕnte*, *mĕnt*; *lēve* 'leave,' *lĕfte*, *lĕft*. After the voiced consonants *d* and *r* the suffixes were *-de* and *-d*; *blēde* 'bleed,' *blĕdde*, *blĕdd*; *brēde* 'breed, *brĕdde*, *brĕdd*; *chīde* 'chide,' *chĭdde*, *chĭdd*; *fēde* 'feed,' *fĕdde*, *fĕdd*; *hide* 'hīde,' *hĭdde*, *hĭdd*; *spēde* 'speed,' *spĕdde*, *spĕdd*; *hēre* 'hear,' *hĕrde*, *hĕrd*; *shō͞o* 'shoe,' *shodde*, *shodd*. The last word *shō͞o* was attracted into this group by its long stem vowel. As there is here no final *d* in the stem of the present tense the first of the two *d*'s in the past tense and the past participle is not a stem ending, but a *d* that was inserted to make the vowel of the past tense and the past participle short. The long vowel of the present tense led to the idea that the vowel of the past tense and the past participle must be made short. Similarly the strong verb *flee* 'flee' was attracted into this group by the long vowel of its present tense. A *d* was inserted into the past tense and the past participle and an *e* of the stem there was dropped to make the stem vowel short: *flee*, *fledde*, *fledd*. In the course of the Middle English period final *e* disappeared, so that the past tense suffix *-de* or *-te* became *-d* or *-t*: *blēde* (silent final *e*), *blĕdd*, *blĕdd*; *mēte* (silent final *e*), *mĕtt*, *mĕtt*; *kēpe* (silent final *e*), *kĕpt*, *kĕpt*; etc. Also in the course of the period final *dd* and *tt* were simplified: *blede*, *bled*, *bled*; *mete*, *met*, *met*; etc. Now *bleed*, *bled*, *bled*; *meet*, *met*, *met*; etc. In the course of the Middle English and the early Modern English period *dēme* and a number of other verbs that used to belong here, such as *sēme* 'seem,' *belēue* 'believe,' *hēde* 'heed,' went over into the regular weak class: *deem*, *deemed*, *deemed*; *seem*, *seemed*, *seemed*; *believe*, *believed*, *believed*; *heed*, *heeded*, *heeded*. Some verbs, like *drēme*, fluctuated between their old inflection and that of the regular weak verbs, and some still fluctuate: *dream*, *dreamed* or *dreamt*, *dreamed* or *dreamt*; *leap*, *leaped* or *leapt*, *leaped* or *leapt*. In early Modern English, *chide* and *hide* were under the influence of the strong verb *ride*, *rode* or *rid* †, *ridden*, so that strong forms were used alongside of the original weak ones: *chide*, *chid* or *chode* †, *chid* or *chidden*; *hide*, *hid*, *hid* or *hidden*. The strong past *chode* has disappeared, but the strong past participle *hidden* is still used and is even more common than the old weak form *hid*. The strong past participle *chidden* is still in use alongside of the perhaps more common weak form *chid*. Still more common, at least in America, are the regular weak forms *chide*, *chided*, *chided*. Alongside of Middle English *lēne* (Old English *hlǣnan*) 'lean,' *lĕnte*, *lĕnt* were regular forms going back to the Old English variant *hleonian*, a verb of the second class: *lēne*, *lēnede*, *lēned*. The present parts of these verbs are *lēăn*, *lĕănt*, *lĕănt* and *lēăn*, *lēăned*, *lēăned*, the former more common in England, the latter in America. Compare *lean*, **60** B.

The natural tendency for verbs in this group is to leave it and join the regular verbs, as in the case of *greet* (**60** B), *heat* (**60** B), *mete* (**60** B), etc., but some strong verbs and some weak verbs from other groups have been drawn into it by virtue of their long stem vowel. In the Middle English period five strong verbs with the long stem vowel *e* joined this group and have remained in it: *creep, crept, crept; flee, fled, fled; leap, leaped* or *leapt, leaped* or *leapt; sleep, slept, slept; weep, wept, wept. Leap* did not come over into this group entirely but often has regular weak forms: *leap, leaped, leaped.* Compare **60** B. Three other strong verbs on account of their long stem vowel have been attracted into the Middle English group with long present and short past and past participle: *cleave, cleft* (or *clove*), *cleft* (or *cloven*); *lose, lost, lost; shoot, shot, shot.* Compare *cleave* and *shoot* in **60** B and *lose* in **63.** Two weak verbs with a long stem vowel have joined this group: *kneel, knelt* (or *kneeled*), *knelt* (or *kneeled*); *say, said* (pronouned *sĕd*), *said* (pronounced *sĕd*). In popular speech still other weak verbs now follow this type of inflection: *clean, clent, clent; peel, pelt, pelt.* These forms are common in the British dialect of Essex.

As a result of peculiar developments several verbs in this group with the stem vowel *ē* had in Middle English a double past tense and past participle: *rēde* 'read,' *rĕdde* or *rădde, rĕdd* or *rădd; clēþe* 'clothe,' *clĕdde* or *clădde, clĕdd* or *clădd; lēde* 'lead,' *lĕdde* or *lădde, lĕdd* or *lădd; spēte* 'spit,' *spĕtte* or *spătte, spĕtt* or *spătt.* Later, final *e* disappeared and *dd* or *tt* was simplified: *rēde* (silent *e*), *rĕd* or *răd, rĕd* or *răd;* later *read, read, read,* the form *rad* disappearing. *Lēde* had the same development. The parts now are *lead, led, led,* the form *lad* disappearing. *Clēþe* had the same development, only that the form *cled* disappeared. In Middle English, there was alongside of *clēþe* a regular verb with the same meaning: *clothe, clothed, clothed.* Today, there is here in the present tense only one verb, *clothe,* but both verbs are represented in the past tense and past participle: *clothe, clothed* or *clad, clothed* or *clad.* Similarly, alongside of the Middle English *spēte* was another verb, *spitte,* with the same meaning. *Spitte* was inflected according to *b* above, so that in the course of the Middle English period its parts became *spit, spit, spit.* Americans still often employ here *spit, spit, spit.* Britishers say *spit, spat, spat,* the form *spit* being the present tense of *spit,* the form *spat* being the past tense and past participle of *spēte.* The present tense of *spēte* disappeared in the fifteenth century. Compare *spit,* **60** B.

d. A few verbs coming from the same Old English source (1 *a*, p. 262) as the verbs in *b* and *c* have retained more of their Old English forms. They have a stem syllable ending in *-nd* and retain their stem vowel throughout the principal parts. In early Middle English they had almost the same form as in Old English: *sende* 'send,' *sende, send.* The final *d* of the stem here is suppressed before the *-d* of the suffix. The *-d* of the suffixes soon developed into *-t*: *sende, sente, sent.* In the course of the Middle English period final *e* disappeared: *send, sent, sent.* The following verbs have had the same development: *bend, blend, rend, spend, wend. Blend* is now more commonly regular: *blend, blended* or *blent, blended* or *blent.* The development of *wend* is peculiarly interesting. In older English it had the meanings *wend, turn, go.* At the close of the Middle English period *went,* past tense of *wend,* became the past tense of *go.* Compare **63**, close of first paragraph and footnote under *go.* In its other meanings *wend* became regular: *wend, wended, wended.* In the Middle

English period *lēne* 'lend,' belonging to *c* above and thus having the same form of the past tense and the past participle as the *send* group of words, was often drawn into the *send* group, the present tense stem ending in *-d*, as in the other words of this group: *lĕnde, lĕnte, lĕnt.* It now always belongs to this group: *lend, lent, lent.*

The verbs *build, gild, gird,* have had a development similar to that of the verbs in the preceding paragraph. The final *d* of the stem syllable disappears in the past tense and past participle before the suffix, which is here *-t* as in the verbs in the preceding paragraph: *build, built, built; gild, gilt, gilt; gird, girt, girt.* Alongside of these forms are regular ones, which are now more common except in the case of those of *build: gild, gilded, gilded; gird, girded, girded. Build, builded, builded* were in use earlier in the present period. In pure adjective function the common form for the past participle is still *gilt:* 'a book with *gilt* edges,' but in figurative use 'the *gilded* youth,' i.e. the young men of wealth and fashion. In England the House of Lords is called 'the *Gilded* Chamber.'

With another group of verbs — *burn, learn, smell, spell, spill, spoil* — there is an inclination to employ *-t* as suffix in past tense and past participle, especially in England: *burn, burnt, burnt; learn, learnt, learnt; smell, smelt, smelt; spell, spelt, spelt; spill, spilt, spilt; spoil, spoilt, spoilt.* Americans prefer, in general, here the regular forms: *burn, burned, burned,* etc. See the separate treatment of these words in **60** B.

IRREGULARITIES IN THE WEAK PAST IN MODERN ENGLISH

60. The weak type of inflection is much simpler than it once was, but older conditions have left traces behind, so that there are still a number of irregularities. These irregularities are survivals of once widely used regular types of inflection, which in the struggle for greater simplicity have for the most part been abandoned for one regular type for all weak verbs. Only the commonest words formed on the older regular types have survived, protected by the frequency of their use. The study of the Old and Middle English types in **59** 1 and 2 will explain the irregular forms of today.

A. **General and Special Remarks:**

a. A number of verbs having a long stem vowel suffer in the past tense and past participle a shortening of their stem vowel and take as suffix *-t* or *-d*, except in the case of verbs whose stem ends in *-t* or *-d*, where the *-t* or *-d* of the suffix has disappeared, as being identical with the final *t* or *d* of the stem: *kēēp, kĕpt, kĕpt; lēāve, lĕft, lĕft; shōē, shŏd, shŏd;* etc. But *mēēt, mĕt, mĕt; blēēd, blĕd, blĕd;* etc. A historical explanation of this development is given in **59** 2 B *c*.

b. In a number of verbs ending in *-nd* or *-ld* the stem ending *-d* disappears in the past tense and past participle before the suffix, which is here regularly *-t: bend, bent, bent; build, built, built;* etc. Compare **59** 2 B *d.*

c. A number of verbs ending in *-d* or *-t* now have no suffix whatever for the past tense and past participle, the older suffix having disappeared, leaving the present and the past tense and past participle alike: *cut* (present), *cut* (past), *cut* (past participle). The peculiar historical development of these forms is given in **59** 2 B *b.* There are a large number of such verbs: *bid* (make an offer), *burst, cast, cost, cut, hight* (**60** B), *hit, hurt, let, put, rid, set, shed, shut, slit, split, spread, thrust.* Some of these verbs: *bid, burst, hight, let,* are strong verbs which have been drawn into this class under the influence of their final *d* or *t.* Alongside of the literary forms *burst, burst, burst* are the colloquial and popular forms *bust, busted, busted,* which have become especially common in the meaning *to break.* In a few cases we use either the full or the contracted form: *bet, bet* or *betted, bet* or *betted; knit, knitted* or *knit, knitted* or *knit; quit, quit* or *quitted, quit* or *quitted; rid, rid* or *ridded, rid* or *ridded; shred, shredded* or *shred, shredded* or *shred; sweat, sweat* or *sweated, sweat* or *sweated; wed, wed* or *wedded, wed* or *wedded; wet, wet* or *wetted, wet* or *wetted.* In America we usually say *spit, spit* or *spat, spit* or *spat,* but in England the parts are uniformly *spit, spat, spat.* In older English the list of the short weak forms was longer, as can be seen by examining the alphabetical list of irregular weak verbs given below, in which the short forms once in use but now obsolete are marked by a dagger. This is also attested by their survival in certain adjective participles: 'a *dread* foe,' but 'The foe was *dreaded*'; '*roast* beef' but 'The meat was *roasted.*' The extensive use of these short forms in older English and in the language of our own time is in part explained by the fact that in the third person singular the *-s* of the present tense distinguishes the two tenses: he *hits* (present) hard; he *hit* (past) hard. Elsewhere we gather the meaning from the situation. As the past tense is the tense of description, there is here usually something in the situation that makes the thought clear.

In older English, there were in use a number of short past participles — *addict, alienate, associate, attribute, celebrate, communicate, compact, consecrate, consolidate, consummate, contaminate, contract, convict, correct, create, decoct, dedicate, degenerate, deject, designate, detect, devote, disjoint, distract, elect, erect, exasperate, excommunicate, exhaust, exhibit, incorporate, indurate, infect, inflict, initiate, institute, instruct, mitigate, prostrate, redintegrate, reject, satiate, separate, situate, suffocate, suspect,* etc. — which were borrowed directly from the Latin or Old French and hence did not arise from contraction, as in the weak verbs described above: 'Obserue wherin and how they haue *degenerate*' (Bacon, *Ess. Great Place,* Arber, 285, A.D. 1625), now *degenerated.* 'And this report Hath so *exasperate* their king, that he Prepares for some attempt of war' (Shakespeare, *Macbeth,* III, II, 38), now *exasperated.* In older English these short forms were supported by the analogy of the English short forms, but later were replaced by the regular long forms just as many of the short forms resulting from contraction were later replaced by the regular long forms. Historically speaking, the regular weak verbs *addict, alienate, associate, attribute, celebrate, communicate, compact, consecrate, consolidate, consummate, contaminate, contract, convict, correct, create, decoct, dedicate, degenerate, deject, designate, detect, devote, disjoint, distract, elect, erect, exasperate, excommunicate, exhaust, exhibit, incorporate, indurate, infect, inflict, initiate, institute, instruct, mitigate, prostrate, redintegrate, reject, satiate, separate, situate, suffocate, suspect,* etc., are derived from the old borrowed short past participles. This list is not complete. Other verbs are added in B below, but also this larger list is incomplete. The use of the short past participle with borrowed verbs in *-t* or *-te* (from Latin participle in *-tus* or *-atus*) is a marked feature of early Modern English. As these old participles, when still used as adjectives or nouns, are no longer vividly felt as participles of these verbs, they are now in certain cases distinguished from them by a difference of accent or by the obscuring of the last pronounced vowel: (verbs) *attríbute, cónsummate, convíct, delíberate* (with long *a*), *séparate* (2nd *a* long); but *áttribute* (noun), *consúmmate* (adjective), *cónvict* (noun), *delíberate* (adjective; with obscured *a*), *séparate* (adjective; with 2nd *a* obscured).

d. In a number of words ending in *-l* or *-n* the ending is either *-ed* or *-t,* the latter especially in England: *spell, spelled* or *spelt; learn, learned* or *learnt;* etc. Compare **59** 2 B *d* (3rd par.).

e. Had and *made* are contracted from *haved* and *maked.*

f. In a large number of words the difference of vowel between the present and the past gives them the appearance of strong verbs, but the past tense ending *-t* or *-d* marks them as weak: *bring, brought; tell, told;* etc. But in the forms *hide — hid, bleed — bled, breed — bred, feed — fed, lead — led, meet — met, shoot — shot,* there is nothing that clearly marks them as weak. Upon the basis of their present forms these and other words of this group might be classed as strong, but their older forms reveal them as weak verbs that have had a peculiar development. Compare **59** 2 B *c* and footnote under *shoot* in **60** B.

g. The ending of the second person singular of the old form is

–est or *–st.* The former is used with full verbs, the latter with the auxiliary *had:* 'thou left*est*'; 'thou had*st.*'

B. **Alphabetical List.** In a number of cases the irregularities are only orthographical, as in *dressed* or *drest.* Where there is fluctuation in usage the more common form is given first. Sometimes the variant (i.e. the second form) is an old strong form, retiring from general service, now serving preferably in figurative use, as in the case of *shorn,* or, in the case of others now employed only in poetic style; sometimes, on the other hand, it is a vigorous, new, more regular form which is working its way to the front. Wherever the form is obsolete in plain prose or now used only in poetry, it is marked by a dagger. On the other hand, in older English these words were in common use. By older usage is here meant the usage of the earlier part of the Modern English period. This older usage, in certain words, survives in popular speech or in certain dialects. Wherever the form is used only in adjective function, there is an asterisk after it. In most cases these forms once had verbal force. Some of the verbs in the list were once strong and still have strong forms. The forms now employed in the literary language and good colloquial speech are given in roman type. Dialectic and popular forms are given in italics. A dagger after a word in italics indicates an older literary form. In early Modern English there were in a large number of cases, even in the literary language, two or more forms for past tense and past participle. Besides the list given below there are a few very irregular auxiliaries, treated at length in **57 4.**

Present	*Past*	*Past Participle*
accurse †	*accursed* †	accursĕd *
		accurst *
acquit	acquitted	acquitted
		acquit †
addict	addicted	addicted
		addict †
admit	admitted	admitted
	admit †	*admit* †
aggregate	aggregated	aggregated
		aggregate *
agitate	agitated	agitated
		agitate †
alienate	alienated	alienated
		alienate †
animate	animated	animated
		animate *
apocopate	apocopated	apocopated
		apocopate *

Present	*Past*	*Past Participle*
articulate	articulated	articulated articulate * *articulate* †
ask *ax* † [1], *ass* [1], *ast* [1]	asked *axed* † [1], *ast* [1]	asked *axed* † [1], *ast* [1]
associate	associated *associate* †	associated associate * [2]
attack, *attackt* [3]	attacked *attackted* [3]	attacked *attackted* [3]
attríbute	attríbuted	attríbuted *attríbute* † [4]
bake	baked	baked *baken*,† *bake* †
bedight †	*bedight* †	bedight [5] *bedighted* †
behave	behaved *behad* †	behaved
believe	believed *beleft* † (**59** 2 B *c*)	believed *beleft* † (**59** 2 B *c*)
bend	bent *bended* †	bent, bent * [6] benděd * [6]
bereave	bereaved [7] bereft [7]	bereaved,[7] bereft [7] *bereaven* †
beseech	besought beseeched [8]	besought beseeched [8]
———	———	besprent [9]
bet	bet [10] bettěd [10]	bet [10] bettěd [10]

[1] Heard in dialect. *Ax, axed* were once used also in the literary language.

[2] Now used only in adjective function: 'an *associate* professor.' In older English it could have pure verbal force: 'I chaunsed to be *assocyat* (now *associated*) with a doctor of Physik' (Barnes, *Defence of the Berde*, E.E.T.S., Ex. Ser. 10, p. 307, 16th century).

[3] Heard in American popular speech.

[4] Survives in the noun *áttribute*, which has been made from the old past participle. For the difference of stress here see **60** A *c* (close of 2nd par.).

[5] Lingering in poetry. Compare footnote to *dight* below.

[6] Compare **59**.

[7] 'A man *bereft* of consciousness by a blow,' 'a *bereaved* mother.' 'The blow *bereft* him of consciousness.' 'Death has *bereaved*, or *bereft*, her of her children.' *Bereave, bereft, bereft* follow the old type described in **59** 2 B *c*.

[8] Survives in American speech, where it is often still heard. Obsolete in England.

[9] Lingering in poetry: 'his boots with dust and mire *besprent*' (Longfellow, *Sir Christopher*, 133). It is the past participle of obsolete *bespreng* 'besprinkle,' *besprent, besprent*.

[10] Fowler in his *Modern English Usage* says that in England the shorter form is used of a definite transaction, while *betted* is employed when the sense

Present	*Past*	*Past Participle*
betide	betided	betided
	betid †	*betid* †
beware	*bewared* † [1]	*bewared* † [1]
bid ('offer')	bid	bid
(see also *bid*, **63**)	*bǎd*,† *bāde* †	
bide [2]	bided	bided
	bode,† [2] *bid* † [2]	*bidden*,† *bid* † [2]
bleed	bled (**60** A *f*)	bled
blend	blended	blended
	blent [3]	blent [3]
bless	blessed	blessed, blessĕd * [4]
	blest	blest, blest * [4]
bolt	bolted, *bolt* †	bolted, *bolt* †
breed, *brede* †	bred (**60** A *f*)	bred
	breded †	*breded* †
bring	brought (**59** 2 B *a*)	brought
	brung,[5] *brang* [5]	*brung* [5]
broadcast	broadcast	broadcast
	broadcasted [6]	*broadcasted* [6]
build	built (**59** 2 B *d*)	built
	builded †	*builded* †
burn	burned [7]	burned [7]
	burnt [7]	burnt [7]

is more general: 'I have *bet* £500 against it,' but 'They *betted* a good deal in those days.' American English prefers *bet* in both senses.

[1] In use in older English: 'I had *bewar'd* if I had foreseen' (Milton). *Beware* is now confined to the imperative and the infinitive, is hence a defective verb: '*Beware* of self-deception.' 'Let us *beware* of self-deception.' We now feel *ware* as a predicate adjective, as it once was, and hence hesitate to use it except where the *be* before it can be construed as a form of the verb *be.*

[2] Now little used except in the expression '*bide* one's time' (await one's opportunity): 'He held his peace and *bided* his time.' Tennyson employs the old past tense *bode* in the meaning *remained:* 'And thither wending there that night they *bode*' (*Lancelot and Elaine*, 410). 'And there awhile it (i.e. the cup) *bode*' (*Holy Grail*, 54). Compare footnote under *abide* in **63.** The explanation for the old parts *bide, bode* or *bid, bidden* or *bid* is the same as that given for the old parts of *bite* in **62** (p. 302).

[3] Compare **59** 2 B *d.*

[4] According to **59** the *e* in the suffix *-ed* is still pronounced in *blessĕd* when used as an adjective. This is still the usual adjective form: 'the *blessĕd* unconsciousness and ignorance of childhood.' Often used ironically: 'We were interrupted every *blessĕd* night.' 'There wasn't a *blessĕd* one there.' The adjective and noun form *blest* is now confined to a few set expressions: 'that *blest* abode,' 'the mansions of the *blest*,' etc.

[5] Common in popular speech.

[6] Common in popular and colloquial speech.

[7] *Burnt* is the more common form in England. In America *burned* is the more common form, although *burnt* is also widely used, especially in adjective use, as in 'a *burnt* match.' Compare **59** 2 B *d* (3rd par.).

Present	*Past*	*Past Participle*
burst, *bust* [1] *brest*,† *brast* †	burst, *busted* [1] *bursted*,† *brest* † *brast* †	burst, *busted* [1] *bursted*,† *brost*(*en*) † *bursten*,† *brast*(*en*) †
buy	bought (**59** 2 B *a*)	bought *boughten* [2]
carve	carved	carved carven * (arch.)
cast	cast, *kest* † *casted* †	cast, *kest* † *casted* †
catch, *ketch* † [3]	caught, *catched* † [4] *kotch*,[3] *kotched* [3] *ketched* [3]	caught, *catched* † [4] *kotch*,[3] *kotched* [3] *ketched* [3]
celebrate	celebrated	celebrated *celebrate* †
chide	chided, chid *chode* † [5]	chided, chid chidden [5]
cleave ('split')	clove,[6] cleft [6] cleaved, *clave* †	cloven,[6] cleft [6] cleaved, *clove* †
cleave ('adhere')	cleaved *clave*,† *clove* †	cleaved *clave* †
climb, *clime*,† *clim*(*me*) †	climbed, *clōmb* † [7] *clam*(*me*),† *clamb* † *clame*,† *clum*,[7] *clome*,[7] *clim* [7]	climbed, *clōmb* † [7] *clum*,† [7] *clome* [7]

[1] Common in colloquial and popular speech.

[2] Popular and colloquial form used in adjective function: '*boughten* stockings, bread, cake,' etc. Sometimes found in poetry for the sake of meter.

[3] The parts in dialect are often strong, *ketch, kotch, kotch*, after the analogy of *get, got, got:* 'Paw got wind of it and *kotch* 'em a-hanging around one day' (Lucy Furman, *Mothering on Perilous*, Ch. XX). Sometimes the weak ending *-ed* (*t*) is added to the strong form: *ketch, kotched, kotched.* Compare footnote to *fetch.* The parts are often weak throughout: *ketch, ketched, ketched.*

[4] 'Our straw *catch'd* a Fire' (George Washington, *Diary*, Apr. 2, 1748). 'On every side new prospects *catch'd* the eye' (Freneau, *The American Village*, about A.D. 1772).

[5] The forms *chode, chidden* are after the analogy of *rode, ridden.* Compare **59** 2 B *c*. The most common parts are *chide, chided, chided* for America, *chide, chid, chid* or *chidden* for England.

[6] In American authorities *cleft* is usually represented as more common than *clove*, but according to the author's observation *clove* occurs more frequently, and in England it is surely the leading form. Likewise in the past participle *cloven* seems to be more common than *cleft*. In certain expressions, however, the one or the other form has become fixed: 'a *cloven* hoof,' 'a *cleft* palate,' 'in a *cleft* stick' (in a tight place). The originally strong inflection is now represented by the parts *cleave, clove, cloven.* In Middle English arose the weak forms *cleft* (**59** 2 B *c*) and *cleaved*. Thus there has been fluctuation of usage for a long while, and this fluctuation still continues, for the word is little used and there is hence no firm impression on our minds as to the proper parts.

[7] Strong forms heard in dialect. *Clome* is a recent dialectic spelling for

Present	*Past*	*Past Participle*
clothe	clothed	clothed
	clad (**59** 2 B *c*)	clad (**59** 2 B *c*)
communicate	communicated	communicated
		communicate †
compact	compacted	compacted
		compact *
		compact †
confiscate	confiscated	confiscated
		confiscate *
consecrate	consecrated	consecrated
		consecrate †
consolidate	consolidated	consolidated
		consolidate †
construct	constructed	constructed
		construct * [1]
		construct †
consummate	consummated	consummated
		consummate *
		consummate †
contaminate	contaminated	contaminated
		contaminate †
contract	contracted	contracted
	contract †	*contract* †
convíct	convícted	convícted
		convíct † [2]
correct	corrected	corrected
		correct *
cost	cost (**60** A *c*)	cost
create	created	created
	create †	*create* †
creep	crept, *creeped* † [3]	crept, *creeped* † [3]
	crep [3]	*crep* [3]
	crope † [3]	*cropen*,† [3] *crope* † [3]

---

clōmb, which was once a literary form. *Clōmb* survives in the literary language in poetry: 'Hither . . . she *clōmb*' (Tennyson), riming with *dome*. In northern British dialect are heard the parts *clim, clam, clum* — after the analogy of *swim, swam, swum*. In certain dialects, especially American, *climb* (present), *clim* (past) are heard — after the analogy of *ride, rid*. The dialectic past participle *clum* often serves also as a past tense. The past participle *clum* (once also with the spelling *clom*) was in the sixteenth century a literary form.

[1] This old participle survives in adjective function in the technical language of Semitic grammar: 'a noun in the *construct* (or sometimes *constructed*) state,' or 'a noun in the state *construct*,' or 'a noun in the *construct*.'

[2] Survives in the noun *cónvict*, which has been made from the old participle. For the difference of stress here see **60** A *c* (close of last par.).

[3] In Middle English, the strong past tense of *crepen* 'creep' was *creep*, the regular form of the second class (**62**): 'He *creep*' (Chaucer, *The Reues Tale*,

Present	*Past*	*Past Participle*
crow	crowed [1]	crowed
	crew [1]	*crown* † [1]
curse, *cuss* [2]	cursed	cursed
	curst, *cussed* [2]	curst,* *cussed* [2]
cut	cut (**60** A *c*)	cut
deal	dealt, *dalt* †	dealt, *dalt* †
	dealed †	*dealed* †
decoct	decocted	decocted
		decoct †
dedicate	dedicated	dedicated
	dedicate †	*dedicate* †
deduct	deducted	deducted
		deduct †
deem	deemed	deemed
	dem(p)t † (**59** 2 B *c*)	*dem(p)t* †
defeat	defeated	defeated
	defeat †	*defeat* †
degenerate	degenerated	degenerated
		degenerate * [3]
delete	deleted	deleted
		delete †
deliberate	deliberated	deliberated
		deliberate * [4]
		deliberate †
delve	delved	delved
	dolve †	*dolve,*† *dolven* †
designate	designated	designated
		designate *
detect	detected	detected
		detect †
devote	devoted	devoted
		devote †

339). This old form survives in dialect, only the vowel is now short: *crĕp*, now used also as a past participle. Compare footnote to *leap*. The old strong past participle was *cropen*. The vowel of this form spread to the past, so that the past tense was often *crope*, which was used also as a past participle. *Crope* survives in dialect as past tense and past participle. In the literary language the weak forms *creep*, *creeped*, *creeped* were once in use. They are still heard in dialect. In the literary language all these forms have been gradually supplanted by the weak forms *creep*, *crept*, *crept*. Compare **59** 2 B *c*.

[1] 'He *crowed* over me.' 'The baby *crowed* with delight.' 'The cock *crowed* (in America, but in England also *crew*, as in older English) at five.' All the older parts, *crow*, *crew*, *crown*, are still heard in northern British dialects.

[2] Common in colloquial and popular speech.

[3] Formerly used as a verbal participle. See **60** A *c* (last par.). It is still used as an adjective participle: 'a *degenerate* family.' For pronunciation see **60** A *c* (close of last par.).

[4] For pronunciation see **60** A *c* (close of last par.).

Present	*Past*	*Past Participle*
digest	digested	digested
		digest †
dight †	*dight* †	dight [1]
	dighted †	*dighted* †
dilate	dilated	dilated
		dilate * †
dilute	diluted	diluted
		dilute *
dip	dipped	dipped
	dipt	dipt
disjoint	disjointed	disjointed
		disjoint †
distract	distracted	distracted
		distract †
		distraught † [2]
distribute	distributed	distributed
	distribute †	*distribute* †
dive	dived	dived
	dove,[3] *div* [3]	*dove*,[3] *div* [3]
drag	dragged	dragged
	drug [4]	*drug* [4]
dread, *dred* †	dreaded	dreaded, dread *
	drad,† *dred* †	*drad*,† *dred* †
dream	dreamed [5]	dreamed
	dreamt	dreamt
dress	dressed	dressed
	drest	drest
drop	dropped	dropped
	dropt	dropt
drown, *drownd* † [6]	drowned	drowned
	drownded † [6]	*drownded* † [6]

[1] Lingering in poetry: 'the clouds in thousand liveries *dight*' (Milton). 'Why do these steeds stand ready *dight?*' (Scott, *The Lay of the Last Minstrel*, I, 42). 'Many a rare and sumptuous tome, In vellum bound, with gold *bedight*' (Longfellow, *Tales of a Wayside Inn*, Prelude, 1, 128).

[2] Sometimes still used as predicate adjective participle instead of the more common *distracted:* 'Her mind was *distraught* with her misfortunes.' 'I lay awake *distraught* with warring thoughts.' Sometimes still used attributively: 'He knelt down beside the *distraught* woman and tried to take her hand.' It was earlier in the period employed also with pure verbal force.

[3] *Dove* is widely used in colloquial and popular speech, *div* has a much narrower territory. These forms follow the analogy of the parts of *drive* (**63**).

[4] Common locally in popular speech.

[5] In England *dreamt* is more common, in America *dreamed.* Compare **59** 2 B *c.*

[6] In older English these forms occur in the literary language: 'Take Pity on poor Miss; don't throw water on a *drownded* Rat' (Swift, *Polite Convers.*, 17, A.D. 1738). *Drownd, drownded, drownded* survive in popular speech.

Present	*Past*	*Past Participle*
dwell	dwelt *dwelled* †	dwelt *dwelled* †
elaborate	elaborated	elaborated *elaborate* *
elect	elected	elected elect *
enshield	enshielded	enshielded *enshield* †
erect	erected	erected, *erect* † erect *
estimate	estimated	estimated *estimate* †
exasperate	exasperated	exasperated *exasperate* †
excommunicate	excommunicated	excommunicated *excommunicate* †
exhaust	exhausted	exhausted *exhaust* †
exhibit	exhibited	exhibited *exhibit* †
extinct †	*extincted* † *extinct* †	*extincted* † extinct *
extract	extracted	extracted *extract* †
fare	fared *foore*,† *fure* †	fared
feed	fed (**60** A *f*)	fed
feel	felt (**59** 2 B *c*) *feeled* †	felt *feeled* †
fetch	fetched, *faught* † [1] *fotch*,[1] *fotched* [1]	fetched, *faught* † [1] *fotch*,[1] *fotched* [1]
flay, *flea* † [2]	flayed *flea'd* †	flayed *flain*,† *flea'd* †
flee, fly [3]	fled *flew* † [3]	fled flown * [3]
flow	flowed	flowed, *flown* †
fold	folded	folded *folden* †

[1] Earlier in the period the parts *fetch, faught, faught* (as in *stretch, straught* †, *straught* †) were in limited use: 'He *fetched*, or *faught* (now *took*), a walk.' The parts in dialect are often strong, *fetch, fotch, fotch*, after the analogy of *get, got, got:* 'Trojan *fotch* him his revolver' (Lucy Furman, *Mothering on Perilous*, Ch. XXVIII). Sometimes the weak ending *-ed* (*t*) is added to the strong form: 'They *fotched* me here' (S. V. Benét, *John Brown's Body*, p. 227).

[2] The regular present tense form, still in use earlier in the period, from the sixteenth century on gradually replaced by the irregular form *flay* with the vowel of the old past participle *flain*.

[3] Examples are given in **63** under *fly*.

Present	*Past*	*Past Participle*
force, *forst* (pop.)	forced	forced
	forsted (pop.)	*forsted* (pop.)
forecast	forecast	forecast
	forecasted †	*forecasted* †
fraught †	*fraught* †	fraught [1]
	fraughted †	*fraughted* †
freight	freighted	freighted
		freight * †
fret [2]	fretted	fretted
	fret †	*fret* †
frustrate	frustrated	frustrated
		frustrate *
		frustrate †
geld	gelded	gelded
	gelt †	*gelt* †
gild	gilded	gilded
	gilt (**59** 2 B *d*)	gilt (**59** 2 B *d*)
gird	girded	girded
	girt (**59** 2 B *d*)	girt
glide	glided	glided
	glid,† *glode* †	*glid*,† *glode* †
gnaw	gnawed	gnawed
		gnawn †
graduate	graduated	graduated
		graduate *
grave	graved	graven, graved
		graven *
greet	greeted	greeted
	gret † (**59** 2 B *c*)	*gret* †
hăve (**57** 2)	hăd (**60** A *e*)	hăd
(but behāve; **56** 4 *f*)	(but behāved)	(but behāved)
hear	heard, *hearn* [3]	heard, *hearn* [3]
	heerd,[3] *heern* [3]	*heerd*,[3] *heern* [3]
	hard † [3]	*hard* [3]
heat	heated	heated
	het † [4]	*het* † [4]
	heat †	*heat* †

[1] 'This measure is *fraught* with danger.'

[2] This verb was originally strong. It is a derivative made up of the prefix *fra* (= *away*) and the verb *eat*.

[3] In popular speech the parts of *hear* are *heer*, past *heerd, heard, heern, hearn*, past participle *heerd, heard, heern, hearn*. The past participles *heern, hearn* are formed after the analogy of strong verbs, as explained in the footnote to *shut*. The past participles *heern, hearn* are sometimes used by the common people as past tense forms, just as the past participle *seen* is used by them as a past tense. *Hard* is still employed in northern British dialect as past tense and past participle.

[4] Used in older English and still in popular speech or dialect. The form is explained in **59** 2 B *c*.

Present	*Past*	*Past Participle*
heave	heaved,[1] hove [1]	heaved
	heft †	hove, *hoven* †
help	helped	helped
	holp † [2]	*holpen*,† *holp* † [2]
hew	hewed	hewed
		hewn
hide	hid	hidden,[3] hid
hight †	*hight*,† [4] *highted* †	*hight*,† [4] *highted* †
		hoten,† *hote* †
hit	hit (**60** A *c*)	hit
	hot † [5]	*hot* † [5]
hoise	*hoist* †	hoist [6]
	hoised †	*hoised* †
hurt	hurt (**60** A *c*)	hurt
	hurted † [7]	*hurted* † [7]
incorporate	incorporated	incorporated
		incorporate †
indurate	indurated	indurated
		indurate †
infect	infected	infected
	infect †	*infect* †
inflict	inflicted	inflicted
		inflict †
initiate	initiated	initiated
		initiate * [8]

[1] 'The frost *heaved* the young plants out of the ground.' 'She *heaved* a heavy sigh.' 'Her face lit up and her bosom *heaved*.' 'We *hove* up the anchor. The sailors *hove* the bodies overboard.' 'A ship *hove* in sight.' 'The steamer *hove* to a little.'

[2] Old strong form; still used in dialect.

[3] In verbal function more common than *hid*, in adjective function the usual form. 'He has *hidden*, or *hid*, my hat,' but 'a *hidden* treasure.' Compare **59** 2 B *c*.

[4] Archaic forms. In older English, the third person singular of the present tense often had no ending, as it was in fact a past tense used as a present: 'that shallow vassal, which, as I remember *hight* Costard' (Shakespeare, *Love's Labor's Lost*, I, 258). The old past tense *hight* was used also as a past participle.

[5] In older English, the parts were sometimes *hit, hot, hot* after the analogy of *git* † (now *get*) *got, got*. *Hot* survives in dialect. In northern British dialect this verb is usually strong: *hit, hat, hutten* or *hitten*. Compare footnote to *shut*.

[6] Sometimes still used: 'The gentlemen may sit tight as long as they please, but they will be *hoist* by powers they cannot control' (Woodrow Wilson, Feb. 24, 1912). From *hoist* has been formed a regular weak verb — *hoist, hoisted, hoisted* — now in common use.

[7] Still used in dialect.

[8] Earlier in the period employed in adjective function: '*Initiate* in the secrets of the skies' (Young, *Night Thoughts*, VI, 95). The old adjective participle is still used as a noun: the *initiate*, the *uninitiate*.

Present	*Past*	*Past Participle*
instigate	instigated	instigated *instigate* †
institute	instituted	instituted *institute* †
instruct	instructed *instruct* †	instructed *instruct* †
keep	kept (**59** 2 B *c*) *keeped*,† *kep* [1]	kept *keeped*,† *kep* [1]
kemb †	*kempt* † *kembed* †	*kempt*,† unkempt * *kembed* †
knead	kneaded	kneaded *kned(d)en*,† *knod(d)en* †
kneel	knelt [2] kneeled	knelt kneeled
knit [3]	knitted knit	knitted knit, *knitten* † close-knit *
lade † [4]	*laded* †	laden *laded* †
laugh	laughed, *lough* †	laughed
lay [5]	laid (but belayed)	laid (belayed)
lead	led (**60** A *f*) *lad* † (**59** 2 B *c*)	led *lad* † (**59** 2 B *c*)

[1] The dialectic parts *keep, kĕp, kĕp* are strong after the analogy of dialectic *leap, lĕp, lĕp*. Compare footnote to *leap*.

[2] At present *knelt* seems to be more common than *kneeled* in both England and America. For the history of this interesting form see **59** 2 B *c* (2nd par.).

[3] Older *knit, knit, knit* are slowly yielding to newer *knit, knitted, knitted*. The older forms, however, are still favorites in figurative use: '*knitted* (also *knit*) goods.' 'Her mother *knitted* (or *knit*) quietly beside a shaded lamp.' But: 'The two were *knit* in friendship together.' 'She *knit* (or *knitted*) her brows angrily.' 'A well-*knit* frame.' The past participle used as a noun always has the old short form: 'stunning *knits*' (advertisement). Compare **60** A *c*.

[4] In the sense *to load* the parts in early Modern English were *lade, laded, laden* or *laded*, but *lade* is now usually replaced in the present and the past tense by *load*, a derivative from the noun *load:* 'They *load* the wagons every morning.' 'They *loaded* the wagons early this morning.' The past participle *laden* is still widely used in poetic style, but it is elsewhere more commonly replaced by *loaded*, except in adjective function in figurative use and in compounds in literal and in figurative meaning, where *laden* is the usual form: 'heavily *loaded* trucks,' 'a wagon *loaded* with hay,' 'a ship *loaded* with wheat,' but 'a soul *laden* with sin,' 'a sin-*laden* soul,' 'a hay-*laden* wagon.'

In the sense *to dip out with a ladle, bail*, the parts are *lade, laded, laded*. The word is now little used in this meaning.

[5] In the literary language always transitive, but in British and American popular speech used also intransitively corresponding to literary *lie, lay, lain*. In older English this usage sometimes occurs in the literary language: 'And dashest him again to earth — there let him *lay*' (Byron, *Childe Harold*, IV, CLXXX).

Present	*Past*	*Past Participle*
lean	leaned [1]	leaned
	leant [1]	leant
leap, *lepe* † [2]	leaped, *leped* † [2]	leaped, *leped* † [2]
	leapt, *lept* † [2]	leapt, *lept* † [2]
	lope,† [2] *lep* [2]	*lopen*,† [2] *lep* [2]
learn	learned [3]	learned,[3] learnĕd *
	learnt [3]	learnt [3]
leave	left (**59** 2 B *c*)	left
lend	lent (**59** 2 B *d*)	lent
let	let	let
	letted †	*letten* † [4]
let (arch.)	letted	letted, let
('hinder')		*letten* †
lift	lifted	lifted
	lift †	*lift* †
līght	līghted,[5] *līght* †	līghted,[5] *līght* †
('set fire to')	lĭt [5]	lĭt,[5] –lĭtten * [5]
līght	līghted,[5] *light* †	līghted, *līght* †
('descend')	lĭt [5]	lĭt [5]

[1] *Leaned* is more common than *leant* in the written language, but it is often pronounced *leant* (i.e. *lĕnt*). In general, the more common pronunciation of the past tense and past participle is *leant* (i.e. *lĕnt*) in England and *leand* (i.e. *leend*) in America. Compare **59** 2 B *c*.

[2] *Lepe* †, *leped* †, *leped* † are older spelling variants of *leap, leaped, leaped. Leapt* (= *lĕpt*) and *lept* † are spelling variants. The more common form for past tense and past participle is *leaped* in America. In England, both *leapt* and *leaped* are widely used, the former leading in frequency. Compare **59** 2 B *c*. The old literary strong forms *lope* and *lopen* survive in dialect. The dialectic past tense *lĕp* is the shortened form of the Middle English literary strong past tense. It is now used also as a past participle, so that the parts are: *leap, lĕp, lĕp. Creep, sleep, weep,* also originally strong verbs, have had in dialect the same development: *creep, crĕp, crĕp; sleep, slĕp, slĕp; weep, wĕp, wĕp.* In comparatively recent times three weak verbs have joined in dialect this strong group: *keep, kĕp, kĕp; reap, rĕp, rĕp; sweep, swĕp, swĕp.* Compare *creep.*

[3] *Learned* is more common than *learnt* in the written language, but it is often pronounced *learnt.* In general, the more common pronunciation of the past tense and past participle is *learnt* in England and *learnd* in America. Compare **59** 2 B *d* (3rd par.). The adjective form *learnĕd* (*learnĕd* men) is in universal use. For the pronunciation of *e* in *–ed* here see **59**.

[4] Still heard in northern British dialect. *Let* was originally strong. In the literary language it has become weak, following the analogy of *set;* but in northern British dialect the old strong past participle is preserved, as the past participle in *–en* is a favorite, being often used even with weak verbs. Compare footnote to *shut.*

[5] In the sense 'set fire to' *lighted* or *lit* are both common in verbal function and in the predicate, while in attributive adjective use *lighted* is the usual form: 'He *lighted,* or *lit,* a cigar.' 'Even at a distance I could see that the house was all *lighted,* or *lit,* up,' but 'a *lighted* cigar,' 'a well-*lighted* room.'

Present	*Past*	*Past Participle*
limit	limited	limited
	limit †	*limit* †
list[1]	*listed*[1]	*listed*[1]
	list[1]	
load	loaded	loaded
		lo(a)den †[2]
lose[3]	lost	lost
make	made (**60** A *e*)	made
manifest	manifested	manifested
	manifest †	*manifest* †
mean	meant	meant
	meaned †	*meaned* †
meet	met (**60** A *f*)	met
melt	melted	melted
	molt(e) †	molten,*[4] *melten* †
mete, *met* †	meted, *met* † (**59** 2 B *c*)	meted, *met(t)en* †
	mete,†[5] *mot* †[5]	met,† *mot(t)en* †[5]

In figurative use *lit* is the more common form: 'Her eyes *lit* up.' 'A star-*lit* night,' 'a mirth-*lit* face.' In compounds instead of *lighted* we sometimes find the irregular adjective form *-litten:* 'red-*litten* windows' (Poe, *Haunted Palace,* VI), 'dim-*litten* chamber' (Morris, *Earthly Paradise,* III, 9). In this sense the derivative verb *alīght* has become obsolete, except the past participle *alīght* in adjective function in the predicate relation: 'Mine's (my candle is) *alīght*' (Browning, *The Ring and the Book,* XII, 581). 'Having the little brazen lamp *alight*' (Shelley, *Julian,* 553). 'But, then, evening came, and the stars sprang *alīght*' (S. G. Millin, *God's Stepchildren,* Ch. II, I).

In the sense 'descend' the derivative verb *alight* is common. The regular weak forms are more common than the strong: 'We *alighted* and walked a little way.' 'They *alighted* from their car.' 'The aviator has just *alighted* from his airplane.' We do not use *lit* or *lighted* of persons getting down from a horse, car, or airplane, as in these examples, but we use these forms freely of persons, animals, and things in other applications of the meaning 'descend': 'He fell from the tree, and *lit,* or *lighted,* on his head.' 'The bird came down, and *lit,* or *lighted,* on a limb of a tree.' 'A snowflake *lit,* or *lighted,* on his nose.' 'A curse *lit,* or *lighted,* upon the land.' 'I have never *lit,* or *lighted,* upon this meaning of the word before.'

The parts *light, lit, lit* follow the analogy of *bite, bit, bit.* See **62** (p. 302).

[1] Archaic forms. The third person singular of the present tense has three forms: *listeth, list,* (contracted from *listth*), *lists.* 'The wind bloweth where it *listeth.*' 'Let him come when him *list.*'

[2] After the analogy of *laden:* '*loaden* with heavy news' (Shakespeare, *Henry the Fourth,* First Part, I, I, 37).

[3] In older English, *loose* was employed as a variant spelling of *lose.* Although we now feel *lose* as a weak form, it is historically an old strong present. See *lose* in **63**.

[4] Of metals and other things difficult to liquefy we say '*melted* or *molten* gold, lava, glass,' etc., but always '*melted* butter, snow,' etc.

[5] In older English, *mete* was a strong verb in the same class as *eat,* and

Present	*Past*	*Past Participle*
mitigate	mitigated	mitigated
		mitigate †
mow	mowed	mowed
	mew †	mown
mulct	mulcted	mulcted
	mulct †	*mulct* †
obligate	obligated	obligated
		obligate *
		obligate †
owe (**57** 4 A *c*)	owed, *ought* †	owed, own *
	ought (subj.; **57** 4 A *c*)	*owen*,† *ought* †
pave	paved	paved
		paven * [1]
pay	paid	paid
	payed ('let out rope')	payed
pen, *pend* † ('confine')	penned	penned
		pent [2]
pitch	pitched	pitched
	pight †	*pight* †
plead, *plede* †	pleaded	pleaded
	plead [3]	plead [3]
plight	plighted	plighted
	plight †	*plight* †
prostrate	prostrated	prostrated
	prostrate †	prostrate *
		prostrate †
protect	protected	protected
		protect †
prove	proved	proved
		proven [4]

formed its parts in the same way: *mete, mete, mete(n)*, as in *ete, ete, ete(n)*. These parts have disappeared from the literary language, but, in the case of *eat*, they survive in dialect. See *eat* in **63**. At this time *mete* was associated also with *get*, and sometimes formed its parts in the same way: *met, mot, motten*. It was also under the influence of *meet*, as can be seen by its older parts: *mete, met, met*. It is now entirely regular.

[1] After the analogy of *shaven*, now little used outside of poetry.

[2] An adjective participle of the obsolete *pend* (once a variant of *pen*): 'his *pent-up* fury,' '*pent-up* emotions.'

[3] Pronounced *pled* and in older English often written so. It was once used in choice language: 'And with him . . . came Many grave persons that against her *pled*.' (Spenser, *The Faerie Queene*, V, IX, XLIII, A.D. 1596). It is now little used in England, but lingers in American colloquial speech: 'They *plead* so hard that I finally gave in' (Theodore Roosevelt, *Letter to Miss Emily T. Carow*, Aug. 6, 1903).

[4] A northern British participle that is sometimes used in the literary language. There is a trend in northern British dialects toward the past

Present	*Past*	*Past Participle*
put	put (**60** A *c*)	put
	putted,† *pat*[1]	*putted*,† *putten*[1]
quake	quaked	quaked
	quook †[2]	
quit	quit, quitted[3]	quit, quitted[3]
rap ('strike')	rapped	rapped
rap † ('carry away')	*rapt* †	rapt[4]
reach	reached	reached
	raught †	*raught* †
read, *rede*,†[5] *reed* †[5]	read, *red* †[5]	read, *red* †[5]
	rad †	*readen* †
reap	reaped	reaped
	reapt †	*reapt* †
	rep (see footnote to *leap*)	*rep* (dial.)
reave	reft	reft
	reaved	reaved
redd †[6] (now pop.) ('put in order')	*redd*[6]	*redd*[6]
	redded	*redded*
redintegrate	redintegrated	redintegrated
		redintegrate †

participle in *-en*. Even a number of weak verbs take this strong participial ending in these dialects: *proven, shutten* (see *shut*), etc. In the eighteenth century, under Scotch influence, *proven* began to appear in the literary language of the South of England. It is still occasionally used in the literary language. It is most common with passive force in the predicate relation: 'That is not yet *proven*.' But the regular form *proved* is more common even here.

[1] In northern British dialect this verb is strong: *put* or *pit, pat, putten* or *pitten*.

[2] After the analogy of *shook*.

[3] The ordinary form in England. American English preserves the older form *quit*. In the meaning *cease* this word is very common in America but in this sense is not used at all in England: 'He has *quit* smoking.' This meaning is a survival of older British usage. It survives also in Scotch and Irish English, which may have strengthened the American tendency. The form in *-ed* is regularly used also in American English with *acquit*, also with simple *quit* when used in archaic language with the meaning of *acquit*. Compare **60** A *c*.

[4] 'The *rapt* saint is found the only logician' (Emerson). 'It is not the poetry of deep meditation or of *rapt* enthusiasm.' In older English a present and a past tense were formed from this participle, but they have gone out of use. The participle itself comes from Latin *raptus*.

[5] Older spelling variants of *read, read, read* are *rede* or *reed, red, red*, which indicate the pronunciation more accurately than *read, read, read*, but have not become established in the language.

[6] Often written *red:* 'I *red(d) up* the house before they came.' *Rid* has the same force, but it is usually associated with *out:* 'I *rid* the closets *out* while you were gone.' But we hear also: 'I *rid up* the house before they came.'

Present	*Past*	*Past Participle*
reeve	rove	rove
	reeved	reeved
		roven
reject	rejected	rejected
		reject †
rend	rent	rent
		rended †
rid	rid	rid
	ridded [1]	ridded [1]
ring (cattle)	ringed	ringed
	rung †	*rung* †
rive	rived	riven
	rove,† *rave* †	rived
roast	roasted	roasted
	roast †	roast * [2]
rot	rotted	rotted [3]
		rotten * [3]
row	rowed	rowed
		rown †
satiate	satiated	satiated
		satiate *
saw	sawed	sawed
	sew †	sawn [4]
say [5]	said [5]	said [5]
seek	sought (**59** 2 B *a*)	sought
seem	seemed	seemed
	sem(p)t † (**59** 2 B *c*)	

[1] In the active now the more common form in England: 'We *ridded, have ridded* (or *rid*), the land of robbers,' but 'I thought myself well *rid* (passive) of him.' In America *rid* is the usual form for past tense and past participle, active and passive. Compare **60** A *c*.

[2] 'He prefers *roast* beef,' but 'He prefers his meat *roasted.*' Compare **60** A *c*.

[3] *Rotted* is used both in verbal and adjective function. *Rotten* is the old strong Danish form of the participle, used only in adjective function. The two adjective participles differ in meaning in that *rotten* always contains the idea of the undesirable, unpleasant, bad, disgusting: '*Rotted* leaf-mould is a good fertilizer,' but only unpleasant ideas are associated with '*rotten* eggs,' '*rotten* politician,' etc.

[4] In the fifteenth century *saw* had besides the old regular weak forms also new strong ones: past *sew*, past participle *sawn*, after the analogy of *draw, drew, drawn*. The strong participle survives. In England it is now the more common form, and is the decided favorite in adjective function, as in '*sawn* wood.' In America the old weak form is preferred.

[5] The vowel is long in the present tense except in the 3rd pers. sing. form *says* (= *sĕz*): It is short in *says* and in the past tense and the past participle, but the vowel of *said* is often long in *gainsaid*, past tense and past participle. Compare **59** 2 B *c*.

Present	*Past*	*Past Participle*
seethe	seethed	seethed, sodden *[1]
	sod †	*sod* †
sell	sold (**59** 2 B *a*)	sold
	selled †	*selled* †
send	sent (**59** 2 B *d*)	sent
separate	separated	separated
		separate *[2]
set	set[3] (**60** A *c*)	set, *setten*[3]
	sot[3]	*sot*[3]
sew,[4] *sow* †	sewed	sewed, sewn[4]
	sowed †	*sowed*,† *sown* †
shape	shaped	shaped
	shoope,† *shope* †	shapen[5]
shave	shaved	shaved
	shove †	shaven *[6]

[1] Now usually employed as a pure adjective without any feeling of its relation to *seethe:* 'The cake was *sodden*' (= doughy). From this adjective a verb *sodden* has been coined: 'The rains have *soddened* the earth.' Earlier in the period the participle *sodden* could have pure verbal force and its relation to *seethe* in its old meaning *boil* was still clearly felt: 'We saw crabs swimming on the water that were red as though they had bene *sodden*' (T. Stevens, *Hakluyt's Voy.*, II, II, 101, A.D. 1579). *Sod* was used here alongside of *sodden:* 'Fysshe may be *sod*, rostyd, and baken' (Andrew Boorde, *E.E.T.S.*, Ex. Ser. 10, p. 277, A.D. 1542).

[2] Now employed only in adjective function. Earlier in the period it could have pure verbal force: 'After they have *separate* from all other Churches' (R. Baillie, *Anabaptism*, 51, A.D. 1646). For the difference of pronunciation between verbal *separate* and adjective *separate* see **60** A *c* (close of last par.).

[3] In many dialects the parts are strong, *set, sot, sot,* after the analogy of *get, got, got.* In northern British dialects the past participle *setten* is widespread. Compare footnote to *shut.* In older English *set* sometimes replaced *sit,* even in the literary language: 'It is very possible that the President and the new Congress are *setting* at New York' (Jefferson, *Writings*, II, 385, A.D. 1788). This usage survives in popular speech: 'He *set*, or *sot*, down on the bench.' On the other hand, in older literary English *sit* sometimes replaced *set:* 'The foremost *sat* (now *set*) down his load (B. Church, *Hist. Philip's War*, I, 119, A.D. 1716). Compare **63** footnote to *sit.*

[4] Of the two verbs *sew* and *sow* † the form *sew* alone survives, but it has the pronunciation of *sow.* The strong past participles *sown* †, *sewn* show the influence of the strong participle *blown.* The form *sewn* is little used in America, but is common in England, where it is competing with the old original weak form *sewed.* In America the old weak form is still the usual one.

[5] Now obsolete or archaic except in the adjective participle *misshapen.* The adjective participle *well-shapen* is somewhat archaic, *well-shaped* being now more common. The older strong form was in early Modern English still used also in the past tense, where *shoope* (also spelled *shope*) was employed alongside of the more common *shaped.*

[6] Now employed only in adjective use, but in early Modern English employed also with verbal force.

Present	*Past*	*Past Participle*
shear	sheared	sheared, shorn [1]
	share,† *shore* †	*shore* †
shed, *shode* † [2]	shed (**60** A *c*)	shed
	shod † [2]	
shend	*shent* †	*shent* †
shoe	shod,[3] *shoed* [3]	shod, *shoed* [3]
shoot [4]	shot, *shotte* †	shot
	shotted,† *shooted* †	*shotten* †

[1] This form is the common one in figurative use and in poetical style: '*Shorn* of one's authority, one's privileges.' 'These are the *unshorn* fields, boundless and beautiful' (Bryant, *Prairies*, 2). In England, however, it is still quite common in its old concrete meaning: 'The sheep are being *shorn*' (in America usually *sheared*). When employed as an adjective, it is often used in England of human hair, and is sometimes indispensable here, as it cannot be replaced by another word: 'the caresses of the old gentleman *unshorn* and perfumed by tobacco' (Thackeray, *Vanity Fair*, Ch. XXXIX). In America we avoid this use of the word wherever we can: 'a *neglected* beard,' 'a neatly *trimmed* beard,' etc.

[2] Old weak forms once used in the literary language: 'Who can recounte what plentie of teares she *shodd* for her owne sinnes' (*Lives of Women Saints*, 102, 9, A.D. 1610). This form survives in dialect. Older *shode* † — *shod* † shows the same development as *shoot* — *shot*, i.e. long present, short past. See **59** 2 B *c*.

[3] In the modern period there has been a tendency towards the regular parts *shoe, shoed, shoed,* but it has not become strong in either dialect or the literary language. For an explanation of the short vowel in *shod* see **59** 2 B *c*.

[4] In older English, *shote, shoote, shoute, shute,* were employed as variant spellings of *shoot*. *Shute*, however, had a little different pronunciation. There was an *i* sound before the vowel, as in *chuse* (**63** under *choose*). The past form *shotte* is an older spelling variant of *shot*. In Middle English, the final *e* was sounded. *Shotte* † is an old weak past, later shortened to *shott*, still later entirely replaced by the spelling *shot*. The older spelling *shotte* continued to be used for a while in early Modern English, but the final *e* was no longer pronounced. Instead of *shoot* there were in Old English two verbs, one strong, one weak, with different forms throughout — the strong verb of the second class (**62**) *sceotan* and the weak verb *scotian*. The strong form survives in the present tense *shoot* and the weak in *shot*, past tense and past participle. As the vowel is long in *shoot* and short in *shot*, the feeling arose that the short past belonged to the long present, as in the large group in **59** 2 B *c*. We see the same development in *lose, lost, lost* as explained in **63** under *lose*. In early Modern English there was in limited use the old strong past participle *shotten*, which has since disappeared in the literary language, but survives in northern British dialect, also here and there in American dialect. In northern British English it is still employed with verbal force, in America it survives widely only in adjective function: 'You are as lean as a *shotten* herring.' Compare 'If manhood, good manhood, be not forgot upon the face of the earth, then am I a *shotten* herring' (Shakespeare, I *Henry the Fourth*, II, IV, 143). The *Santa Ana* (Calif.) *Register* (Mar. 3, 1931) reports a Negro as using this form with verbal force: 'I has *shotten* craps for 45 years.'

Present	*Past*	*Past Participle*
show, *shew* †	showed, *shew* † [1]	shown
	shewed †	showed, *shewed* †
shred	shredded	shredded
	shred (**60** A *c*)	shred
shrive	shrived	shrived
	shrove	shriven
shut, *shit*,† *shet* †	shut (**60** A *c*)	shut, *shutten* [3]
	shit,† *shet* † [2]	*shit*,† *shet* †
sigh	sighed	sighed
	sight †	
situate	*situated* †	situated
		situate * †
skin	skinned	skinned
	skun [4]	*skun* [4]
sleep	slept (**59** 2 B *c*)	slept
	slep † (see footnote to *leap*)	*slep* (dial.)
slit	slit (**60** A *c*)	slit
	slitted †	*slitted* †
smart	smarted	smarted
	smart †	*smart* †
smell	smelled [5]	smelled [5]
	smelt	smelt
sneak	sneaked	sneaked
	snuck (pop.)	*snuck* (pop.)
snow	snowed	snowed
	snew † [6]	*snown* † [6]
sow	sowed	sowed
	sew †	sown
speed [7]	sped	sped
	speeded	speeded

[1] Popular strong past of *show*, earlier in the period employed also in the literary language. *Show*, *shew* †, *shown* were formed after the analogy of *blow*, *blew*, *blown*. The strong past participle, *shown*, is still the usual literary form.

[2] Survives in dialect: 'When we growed up, and they *shet* down on me and her a-runnin' roun' Together' (James Whitcomb Riley, *Marthy Ellen*).

[3] Heard in British dialect. In some dialects the past participle in *-en* is a favorite, especially in northern British. It is even used, as here, with weak verbs. Compare the footnote to *hear*, *let*, and *prove*.

[4] Heard in American dialect. These parts are formed after the analogy of popular *begin*, *begun*, *begun*.

[5] *Smelled* is the more common form in America, *smelt* the more common form in England. Compare **59** 2 B *d* (3rd par.).

[6] After the analogy of *blow*, *blew*, *blown*.

[7] In rather choice literary English we still use *speed* in the general sense of a rapid movement, now usually with the parts *speed*, *sped*, *sped*: 'I *sped* to meet them' (Keats, *A Galloway Song*, 14). 'In two autos they *sped* along

Present	*Past*	*Past Participle*
spell	spelled [1]	spelled [1]
	spelt [1]	spelt [1]
spend	spent	spent
spill	spilled [2]	spilled [2]
	spilt [2]	spilt [2]
spit, *spēte* †	spat, spit,[3] *spet* †	spat, spit, *spet* †
	spitted,† *spate* †	*spitted,*† *spitten* † [3]
		spetten †

the Lincoln Highway' (*Chicago Tribune*, Apr. 24, 1927). 'The bullet *sped* on its fatal course.' 'The glance he *sped* towards his betrothed was brimful of expectant love' (H. Herman, *His Angel*, XII, 236). In older English, also *speed, speeded, speeded* were used here: 'I have *speeded* (now *sped*) hither with the very extremest inch of possibility' (Shakespeare, II *Henry the Fourth*, IV, III, 37).

Where there is a reference to an engine or to mechanical or routine movement or work of any kind, the usual parts are *speed, speeded, speeded:* 'This engine is *speeded* to run 300 revolutions per minute.' 'I *speeded up*, or *speeded up* the motor, so as to arrive on time.' 'We *speeded up* the work on the house as much as we could.' 'Ship-construction is to be *speeded up* as much as possible.' 'He *speeded* through the main thoroughfare of the city and was fined for it,' i.e. he drove his car faster than the law permits. *Speeded* is often used of a high engine *speed* in general, where also *sped* might be employed: 'The machines *speeded* (or *sped*) on south and across the boulevard' (*Chicago Tribune*, Mar. 23, 1927).

[1] *Spelled* is the more common form in America, *spelt* the more common form in England. Compare **59** 2 B *d* (3rd par.).

[2] *Spilled* is the more common form in America, *spilt* the more common form in England. Compare **59** 2 B *d* (3rd par.).

[3] In American English the usual colloquial form for past tense and past participle is *spit*, but *spat* is coming into ever wider use in the literary language and will doubtless ultimately prevail: 'She *spat* in his face' (*The New York Times*, July 19, 1934). 'The boy took a gulp, choked, and *spat* it out' (Ralph Connor, *The Man from Glengarry*, Ch. I). 'Crooked Jack *spat* on his hand and resumed his work' (L. M. Montgomery, *The Chronicles of Avonlea*, Ch. II). 'As they passed, he *spat* tobacco juice on the dog' (E. T. Seton, *Rolph in the Woods*, Ch. XVII). 'The blood came, but the shiftless one merely *spat* it out' (J. A. Altsheler, *The Scouts of the Valley*, Ch. X). 'As Dar Mennou came into view, Madani turned back and *spat* on the new road' (Wythe Williams, *Saturday Evening Post*, Aug. 28, 1926). 'Jack *spat*' (S. V. Benét, *John Brown's Body*, p. 367). 'Now and then a wave *spat* in the faces of the passengers huddled aft' (Harry A. Franck, *A Vagabond Journey around the World*, Ch. III). In England *spat* is the more common form for past tense and past participle. In older English, two different verbs were in use here — *spit* and *spēte*. The principal parts of *spit* were *spit, spit, spit*. The parts of *spēte* were *spēte, spĕt* or *spăt, spĕt* or *spăt*. The form *spat* survives. The parts *spit, spat, spat* seem to be after the analogy of *sit, sat, sat*, which may have facilitated their establishment, but historically *spat* is past tense and past participle of *spēte*. For the weak past tense forms *spat* and *spet* † see **59** 2 B *c* (last par.). The influence of *sit* here can be seen also in the older past tense *spate* and in the older past participles *spitten* and *spetten*. Compare

Present	*Past*	*Past Participle*
split	split (**60** A *c*)	split
		splitted,† *splitten* * †
spoil	spoiled [1]	spoiled [1]
	spoilt [1]	spoilt [1]
spread	spread (**60** A *c*)	spread
start	started	started
	start †	*start* †
stave	staved [2]	staved [2]
	stove [2]	stove [2]
stay	stayed	stayed, staid * [3]
	staid	staid
stretch	stretched	stretched, straight * [4]
	straught †	*straught* †
strew,[5] *strow* †	strewed	strewed, strewn
	strowed †	*strown*,† *strowed* †
subject	subjected	subjected
	subject †	*subject* †
subjugate	subjugated	subjugated
		subjugate †
suffocate	suffocate	suffocated
		suffocate †
suspect	suspected	suspected
		suspect * [6]
		suspect †
sweat	sweat,[7] sweated	sweat,[7] sweated
	swat †	*swat*,† *sweaten* †

---

sit, **63**. In the meaning 'transfix' *spit* is regular: 'He *spitted* some meat and set it to roast.'

[1] *Spoiled* is the more common form in the written language, but the more common pronunciation of the past tense and past participle is *spoilt* in England and *spoild* in America. These forms, however, are pronounced *spoild* also in England in the sense of *despoil, plunder, deprive.* Compare **59** 2 B *d* (3rd par.).

[2] 'I *staved, have staved,* off a bad cold.' 'Two of his ribs were *stove,* or *staved,* in.' 'The fore compartment of the boat was *stove* (nautical term) in by the collision.'

[3] 'A *staid* elderly man.'

[4] 'A *straight* line,' '*straight* dealings.'

[5] The strong past participles *strown* †, *strewn* show that *strow* † and *strew* have been influenced by *blow* — *blown.* In pure verbal use the weak past participle *strewed* is more common than the strong form *strewn*, but in adjective use the strong form seems to be the favorite: 'They have *strewed* (or *strewn*) the floor with sand,' but 'a floor *strewn* (or *strewed*) with sand,' 'a pathway *strewn* (or *strewed*) with flowers.' 'The table was *strewn* (or *strewed*) with papers.'

[6] 'Enemy statements are *suspect.*' Compare **60** A *c* (2nd par.). This form has become established under French influence.

[7] Widely used in America though now obsolete in England, which prefers the newer form *sweated:* 'He *sweat* plentifully during the night.' As a causative the form in *-ed* is the usual one also in America: 'His physician *sweated*

Present	*Past*	*Past Participle*
sweat (caus.)	sweated	sweated
sweep	swept	swept
	swep [1]	*swep* [1]
swell	swelled	swelled
	swoll †	swollen [2]
taint	tainted	tainted
		taint †
teach	taught (**59** 2 B *a*)	taught
	teached †	*teached* †
tell	told (**59** 2 B *a*)	told
	telled † [3]	*telled* † [3]
thaw	thawed	thawed
	thew † [4]	*thawn* †
think	thought	thought
	thunk (dial.)	*thunk* (dial.)
threat †	*threated* †	*threated* †
	thrett †	*thrett* †
thresh, thrash [5]	threshed, thrashed	threshed, thrashed
		throshen,† *threshen* †

him.' This form is universal also in '*sweated* labor,' '*sweated* workman,' '*sweated* clothes,' etc. Compare **60** A *c*.

This word is avoided in refined speech in the ordinary physical senses, where it is replaced by *perspire:* 'He *perspired* plentifully during the night.' It is, however, still freely used of things, also of persons in figurative language: 'The place was so damp that the walls *sweat*.' 'They made him *sweat* for it.'

[1] The dialectic forms *sweep, swĕp, swĕp* are strong after the analogy of dialectic *leap, lĕp, lĕp*. Compare footnote to *leap*.

[2] *Swollen* is for the most part the usual form in adjective function: '*swollen* cheeks,' 'the *swollen* river,' '*swollen* estimates.' 'The cheeks are *swollen*.' 'The river is *swollen*.' *Swollen* and *swelled* are now differentiated in '*swollen* head' (swollen from physical causes) and '*swelled* head' (swelled by conceit). As a pure verb *swelled* is the more common form: 'The wood has *swelled* from moisture.' 'A creek that had been *swelled* by a spring freshet' (Victor Appleton, *Don Sturdy in the Port of Lost Ships*, Ch. I). 'Our hearts have often *swelled* with indignation at the sight of these conditions.' 'The crowd around the door had *swelled* to a considerable size.' 'The army had been *swelled* by large reinforcements.' 'A lively breeze has *swelled* our sails.' Even in pure verbal function, however, *swollen* is sometimes still used of a swelling arising from a diseased condition: 'My face has *swelled*, or *swollen*, considerably in the last two hours.' Figuratively: 'The river has *swelled*, or *swollen*, a good deal during the night.' The past participle *swollen* is used more widely in England than in America.

[3] Still used in popular speech.

[4] In popular speech the parts of *thaw* are sometimes *thaw, thew, thawn* after the analogy of *draw, drew, drawn*. In older English *thawn* was in limited use also in the literary language.

[5] *Thrash* was originally a mere variant of *thresh*, but it has become differentiated in meaning from it, now being used with the force of *flog soundly, conquer, surpass*, and, in a nautical sense, *make way against wind or tide*, as in 'We *thrashed* to windward.'

Present	*Past*	*Past Participle*
thrive	thrived,[1] throve [1]	thrived [1]
	thrave †	thriven [1]
thrust	thrust (**60** A *c*)	thrust
	thrusted †	*thrusted* †
toss	tossed	tossed
	tost †	*tost* †
touch, *tech* [2]	touched	touched
	toch [2]	*toch* [2]
use to † [3] (**52** 2 *b*, 2nd par.)	used to (*ūstu* or *ūste*)	used to (**52** 2 *b*, 2nd par.)
	usen to (dial. [3])	*usen to* (dial. [3])
waft	wafted	wafted
	waft †	*waft* †
wash	washed	washed
		washen † [4]
wax, *wex* † ('become')	waxed, *wexed* †	waxed, *wexed* †
	wox,† *wex* †	*waxen*,† *woxen* †
wed	wed [5]	wed [5]
	wedded	wedded [5]

[1] *Thrive, thrived, thrived* are the more common forms in America, while *thrive, throve, thriven* are preferred in England.

[2] The parts in popular speech are locally *tech, toch, toch:* 'Trojan fotch him his revolver and he wouldn't *tech* it' (Lucy Furman, *Mothering on Perilous*, Ch. XXVII). 'I haint *toch* my hand to a game of keeps this whole school' (*ib.*, Ch. XXVIII).

[3] In older English employed in the different tenses, but now confined to the past tense and the past participle: 'I *used* to do it.' 'I am *used* to doing it.' 'He *did not use*, or *used not*, to smoke,' or colloquially 'He *didn't use*, or *usedn't* (*usen't*), to smoke,' where Americans prefer the *do*-forms, Britishers the simple form. In America and England both constructions are often blended in colloquial and popular speech: 'I *didn't used* to mind your embarrassing me' (Sinclair Lewis, *Dodsworth*, last Ch.). Similarly in the positive form: 'It *did used* to be a willow' (Wells, *Mr. Britling Sees It Through*, p. 74). In questions we say: '*Did you use* to do such things?' or '*Used you* to do such things?'

In dialect the strong past participle *usen* is employed, which is used also as a past tense: 'Me and you ain't *usen ter* dese small-town slow ways' (DuBose Heyward, *Porgy*, p. 82). 'He *usen tuh* hate all dese children' (*ib.*, p. 64). Originally, of course, the verb was weak. In certain British dialects a weak suffix is added to the strong: 'I can't think as it *usened* to smell so' (George Eliot, *Silas Marner*, p. 268).

[4] A little earlier in the period still in use in adjective function: 'With *washen* hands They took the salted meal' (W. C. Bryant, *Iliad*, I, 563, A.D. 1870). In a recent poem of the English poet Rupert Brooke, *The Great Lover*, which appeared in 1914, we find '*Washen* stones gay for an hour.' Still earlier in the period it was employed with full verbal force: 'When you give her casting of flannel or cotton, take care to have them *washen* as clean as they can be' (J. Campbell, *Mod. Faulconry*, 199, A.D. 1773).

[5] The parts *wed, wedded, wedded* are the usual ones in England, while in America *wed, wed, wed* (**60** A *c*) are more common: 'MISS LUCIA B. PAGE TO BE *WED* ON SEPT. 9' (headlines in *The New York Times*, Aug. 31, 1933).

Present	*Past*	*Past Participle*
weed	weeded	weeded
	wed †	*wed* †
weep	wept (**59** 2 B *c*)	wept
	weeped †	*weeped* †
	wep (dial., see foot-note to *leap*)	*wep* (dial.)
wet	wet [1] (**60** A *c*)	wet [1]
	wetted	wetted
whet	whetted	whetted
	whet †	*whet* †
whist †	*whisted* †	*whisted* †
	whist †	*whist* †
won † [2]	*wonn'd* [2]	wont [2]
		wonted [2]
wont [2]	wonted [2]	———
	wont	———
work	worked	worked
	wrought [3]	wrought [3]

In adjective function, however, the past participle *wedded* is universal: '*wedded* life.' 'I am not *wedded* to this idea.' In the substantive relation we say 'newly *weds*,' but 'among the happily *wedded*.'

[1] The short form *wet* is little used in England for either the past tense or the past participle, but it is widely employed in America: 'He *wet* his lips.' 'The rain has *wet* the grass.' But the longer form *wetted* is used also in America in the passive to distinguish the participle from the adjective *wet*: 'The particles of copper sulphide become *wetted* by the oil' (Smith's *Intermediate Chemistry*, p. 511). It is used in America also with the objective predicate (**8**, 4th par.) adverb *down* to indicate the result of the action: 'He filled the ditch with earth and *wetted* it down.'

[2] *Wont*, the past participle of the obsolete verb *won* (= *dwell, be accustomed*), has an expanded form *wonted*, which is used principally as an adherent (**8**) adjective: 'He is (was, has been) *wont* to act with energy,' but 'He acted with his *wonted* energy.' From the past participle *wont*, used in the sense of *accustomed*, has been formed the verb *wont*, which has as past tense the forms *wonted* or *wont*: 'He *wonts* to act with energy.' 'In those days he *wonted*, or *wont*, to act with energy.' In older English, the third person singular of the present tense was sometimes without an ending, after the analogy of *list* and *hight*, which also end in *t*: 'I bear it on my shoulders as a beggar *wont* (= *wonts to bear*) her brat' (Shakespeare, *The Comedy of Errors*, IV, iv, 38). The verb *wont* has not yet developed an infinitive or a participle. It has also never become so common as *is* (*was*) *wont*, which itself is only used in poetry or choice prose. From the old participle *wont* has been formed the noun *wont*: 'He will, as is his *wont*, act with energy.'

Scott used archaically the old form *wonn'd* in the sense of *dwelt*: 'Up spoke the moody Elfin King, Who *wonn'd* within the hill' (*Alice Brand*, X).

[3] '*Wrought* iron,' '*overwrought* nerves.' It is used also in certain expressions as a verbal participle: 'a belief which has *wrought* much evil.' Also the past *wrought* is still used in certain expressions: 'She *wrought* upon his feelings.' 'This *wrought* infinite mischief.'

Present	*Past*	*Past Participle*
wrap	wrapped	wrapped
	wrapt	wrapt
wreak	wreaked	wreaked
		wroken †
wrīthe	wrīthed	wrīthed, wrĭthen [1]
		wreathen [1]
———	———	yclĕpt [2]
		yclēped [2]
yield	yielded	yielded
	yold †	*yold,*† *yolden* †

FORMATION OF THE STRONG PAST

61. Strong verbs form the past tense without a suffix, by changing the root vowel: eat, *a*te; know, kn*ew*.

They form the past participle with the suffix *–en* or *–n:* eat*en*, know*n*. The vowel of the past participle may be either the same as that of the past tense, or the same as that of the present tense, or it may be different from that of both: tread, tr*o*d, tr*o*dden; sh*a*ke, shook, sh*a*ken; drīve, dr*o*ve, drĭven.

In many verbs the suffix of the past participle has disappeared: bind, bound, *bound*. The older form of the participle in *–en* is often preserved in adjectives: 'The ship has *sunk*,' but 'a *sunken* ship.'

The past tense of *see* may serve as an example:

[1] These old forms, still found in poetic language, are old strong participles of the once strong verb *writhe*, which formerly had a wider meaning than now, namely, 'twist,' 'turn,' 'bind.' The old participles preserve the old meaning: 'The tawny stream . . . Of intertwining *writhen* snakes was full' (Morris, *Earthly Paradise*, Doom of King Acrisius, 72, A.D. 1868–1870). '"Red Injun stuff, hey?" scoffed Beemis from between *writhen* lips' (Albert Payson Terhune, *Treasure*, Ch. XIII, A.D. 1926). 'And they put the two *wreathen* chains of gold in two rings on the ends of the breastplate' (*Exodus*, XXXIX, 17). 'And all the scowling faces became *smile-wreathen*' (Annie Besant, *Autobiography*, 74, A.D. 1893). *Wreathen* arose in Middle English as *wrēthen*, a variant of *wrĭthen* (a regular past participle of the first class [**62**] of strong verbs). This Middle English development of *ĭ* into *ē* (later often written *ea*) was once a common feature of the past participles of this class. *Wreathen* is the only surviving participle with this form. In early Modern English, there were other participles with this form: 'I would have *wrēten* (now *written*) to you' (Seafield, *Letter*, A.D. 1685).

[2] Archaic past participle of the obsolete verb *clepe* (= *call*), sometimes still employed in poetical or serio-comical language: 'the sweet wood *yclept* sassafras' (Lamb, *Elia*, Series I, Praise of Chimney-Sweepers); 'the Associated South London Extended Gold Mines Corporation, *yclept* in the market Suds' (*Westminster Gazette*, Feb. 23, 1900). For the prefix *y–*, see **59** 2.

Indicative	Subjunctive
Singular	
1. I saw	I saw
2. you saw (old form, thou sawĕst)	you saw (thou sawĕst)
3. he saw	he saw
Plural	
1. we saw	we saw
2. you saw (old form, ye saw)	you (ye) saw
3. they saw	they saw

In Middle English, there was in strong verbs no *est*-ending in the second person singular of the *thou*-form as now. See Middle English past tense in 3 below. In early Modern English, the weak *est*-ending was extended to strong verbs, but in the early part of the period there was sometimes no *–est* here, as in older English: 'And nowe behold the thing that thou erewhile *Saw* only in thought' (Thomas Sackville, *Induction* to *Mirror to Magistrates*, LXXVI, A.D. 1563). This form without *–est* was sometimes extended to weak verbs. Compare **59** (last par.). This form served also as a subjunctive: 'If *thou saw* thyne enimie thus mangled and wounded, it might styrre thee to take compassion vpon him' (John Fisher, *Works*, E.E.T.S., Ex. Ser., p. 403, early sixteenth century). Later, the subjunctive here, differing from usage in the present, took –(*e*)*st*, as in the indicative. The ending –(*e*)*st* is now usually employed in all past indicatives and subjunctives, strong or weak, except in the case of *wast* and *wert* (1 *c* below). The regular ending of full verbs not ending in *–ĕd* is *–ĕst*, but it is *–st* for those ending in *–ĕd* and for the auxiliaries other than *wast* and *wert:* 'thou wrot*ĕst*,' 'thou slept*ĕst*,' but 'thou lovĕd*st*,' 'thou did*st*,' 'thou should*st*,' 'thou would*st*.' Sometimes, however, the ending is dropped, whether the form be indicative or subjunctive: 'I heard Thee when Thou *bade* me spurn destruction' (S. V. Benét, *John Brown's Body*, p. 32).

1. **Irregular Past Tense.** There is one irregular strong past tense form — that of the verb *be*. It preserves certain peculiarities of older inflection, as can be seen by comparing its forms with the Old English forms in 2 below. The vowel of the plural indicative is different from that of the singular. As the common form for the second person singular is historically the second person plural, as in **56,** its vowel is different from that of the first and third persons. The vowel of the subjunctive is uniform throughout, being the same as that of the indicative plural.

Past tense forms of *be:*

	Indicative	Subjunctive
	Singular	
1.	I was	I were
2.	you were (old forms, thou wast, wert, *wart*,† *werst*,† *were* †)	you were (thou wert, *werĕst*,† *werst*,† *were* †)
3.	he was	he were
	Plural	
1.	we were	we were
2.	you were (old form, ye were)	you (ye) were
3.	they were	they were

a. In older English, *war* was dialectically used instead of *was.* The singular form *war* or *were* is still heard here and there in British dialect. Also in American dialect: 'Robbins (name) *war* a good man' (DuBose Heyward, *Porgy,* p. 33). 'I follered singing when I *were* young' (Lucy Furman, *The Quare Women,* Ch. I). The contracted negative form *wa'n't* or *warn't* was once sometimes employed in the literary language: 'No, that *wa'n't* it' (Sheridan, *The Rivals,* II, I, A.D. 1775). This form survives in popular speech: 'I'm plumb sure it was a Swamp Hole boat. Reckon *'twan't* none of ourn' (Ralph Henry Barbour, *Pud Pringle Pirate,* Ch. XIX). 'When she *warn't* scoldin' Amos, she was scoldin' about him' (Amy Lowell, *East Wind,* p. 113). The contraction in the literary language is now, of course, *wasn't,* as it rests upon the literary past tense *was.*

b. In older English, in accordance with the general usage elsewhere of one form for singular and plural in the past tense, *was* was often used for *were* in the second person where the reference was to a single individual: 'And *was* you in company with this lawyer?' (Fielding, *Tom Jones,* Book XVIII, Ch. V). 'I conclude you *was* eased of that friendly apprehension' (Alexander Pope, *Letter to Swift,* Mar. 25, 1736). Compare *Syntax,* **8** I 1 *h Note.*

c. In the second person singular the indicative form *wert* occurs sometimes still as a variant of *wast:* 'Just now thou *wert* but a coward' (Kingsley, *Westward Ho!* Ch. XVIII). In early Modern English, the old forms *were, wart, werst,* were still in use here. *Were* is the old original form without a consonantal ending, as in **61** (last par.). The ending *–t* in *wert, wart,* and *wast* is after the analogy of the *–t* in *art* (thou ar*t*). The *–st* in *werst* is after the analogy of the usual modern ending *–st,* as in **61** (last par.). The corresponding early Modern English subjunctive forms were *were, wert,* and *werĕst* or *werst.* In the Bible of the seventeenth century the indicative and subjunctive were differentiated here by the employment of *thou wast* for the former and *thou wert* for the latter. This differentiation is in general still observed, but there is some fluctuation, *thou wert* sometimes being used instead of *thou wast.*

d. As the past subjunctive has become identical in form with the past indicative in all verbs except *be,* we often in colloquial speech find the past indicative singular *was* used as a past subjunctive singular instead of the regular *were,* after the analogy of other verbs in which the past subjunctive is identical in form with the past indicative: 'He looks as if he *was* sick.' In older English, this usage often occurs in the literary language: 'I shall act by her as tenderly as if I *was* her own mother' (Richardson, *Pamela,* II, p. 216). Compare *Syntax,* **44** II 5 C (2nd par.).

2. **Old English Past Tense.** The vowel of the plural indicative and the second person singular is, in most verbs, different from that of the first and third persons singular. The vowel of the subjunctive is uniform throughout, being the same as the vowel of the indicative plural.

The strong verbs *bind, help, fare,* inflected in the present tense in Old English form in **56** 3 *a,* are inflected in the past tense in Old English form as follows:

	bind	*help*	*fare*	*bind*	*help*	*fare*
	Indicative			Subjunctive		
	Singular			*Singular,* 1, 2, 3		
1.	band	healp	fōr			
2.	bunde	hulpe	fōre	bunde	hulpe	fōre
3.	band	healp	fōr			
	Plural, 1, 2, 3			*Plural,* 1, 2, 3		
	bundon	hulpon	fōron	bunden	hulpen	fōren

Past Participle (ge) bunden, holpen, faren

3. **Middle English Past Tense.** The past tense forms of the verbs in 2 above are as follows:

	Indicative			Subjunctive		
	Singular			*Singular*		
1.	band bond	halp	fōr	bounde	hulpe holpe	fōre
2.	bounde	hulpe holpe	fōre			
3.	band bond	halp	fōr			

Indicative			Subjunctive		
Plural, 1, 2, 3			*Plural*, 1, 2, 3		
bounde(n)	hulpe(n) holpe(n)	fōre(n)	bounde(n)	hulpe(n) holpe(n)	fōre(n)

Past Participle (y) bounde(n), holpe(n), fāre(n)

The participial prefix *-y* was at this time in general characteristic of southern English. The plural ending *-en*, as found in the inflections given above, was characteristic of the Midland and South. In the North it was dropped early in the period. In the literary language the *-e(n)* disappeared at the close of the fifteenth century.

CLASSES OF STRONG VERBS

62. There were in older English seven well-defined classes of these verbs, grouped together on the basis of the vowels of their present and past tense and their past participle, as illustrated by the following seven verbs, each of which represents its own class:

Old English Classes

	Present Infinitive		Past Tense: *Singular*	Past Tense: *Plural*	Past Participle
I.	wrītan	*write*	wrāt	writon	writen
II.	cḗosan[1]	*choose*	cēas	curon	coren
III.	singan	*sing*	sang	sungon	sungen
IV.	beran	*bear*	bǣr	bǣron	boren
V.	sittan	*sit*	sǣt	sǣton	seten
VI.	scacan	*shake*	scōc	scōcon	scacen
VII.	blāwan	*blow*	blēow	blēowon	blāwan

Middle English Classes

	Present Infinitive	Past Tense: *Singular*	Past Tense: *Plural*	Past Participle
I.	wrīte(n)	wroot	write(n)	writen
II.	cheese(n), chōse(n)	chees	curen, chōse(n)	coren chōsen
III.	singe(n)	sang	sunge(n)	sungen
IV.	bēre(n)	băr, bāre	bēre(n)	bōren
V.	sitte(n)	săt, sāte	sēte(n)	sēten
VI.	schāke(n)	schōk schook[2]	schōke(n) schooke(n)[2]	schāken
VII.	blowe(n)	blew	blewe(n)	blowen

[1] Alongside of this form was the variant *ceṓsan*, from which M.E. *chose(n)* and our present form *choose* come.

[2] Spelling variants of *schōk*, *schōke(n)*.

Modern English Classes

I. wrīte	wrote	wrote	written
II. choose	chose	chose	chosen
III. sing	sang	sang	sung
IV. bear	bare,[1] bore	bare,[1] bore	born, borne
V. sit	sat, sate[1]	sat, sate[1]	setten,[1] sitten[1] sat, sate[1]
VI. shake	shook	shook	shaken, shook[1]
VII. blow	blew	blew	blown

For many years there have been forces working upon the vowels of these verbs and upon the verbs themselves, affecting them in many ways and thus breaking up the old classes. Earlier in the present period, a number of words in the fourth class had *a* in their past tense and *o* in the perfect participle: bear, b*a*re, b*o*rn; break, br*a*ke, br*o*ken; speak, sp*a*ke, sp*o*ken; steal, st*a*le, st*o*len. Gradually the *o* of the past participle assimilated to itself the *a* of the past tense, so that *bare, brake, spake, stale,* became *bore, broke, spoke, stole.* In *choose, cleave, freeze* — verbs of the second class — a similar development has taken place, the Old English plural vowel *u* of the past tense conforming in Middle English to the *o* of the past participle, to which still later the singular vowel conformed. Thus the Old English past tense plurals *curon, clufon, fruron,* later in the Middle English period, following the analogy of the past participles *chosen, cloven, frosen,* became *chose(n), clove(n), frose(n).* Still later in early Modern English, the vowel of the singular was conformed to that of the plural, *chees — chose(n), cleef — clove(n), frees — frose(n),* becoming *chose — chose, clove — clove, froze — froze.* In the thirteenth century, *get* and *speak* were in the fifth class with the principal parts *gēten, gat, gēten; spēken, spack, spēken.* Later these verbs came under the influence of the fourth class (*bear, bar* or *bare, born*), their principal parts becoming *gĕt, gat* or *gate, gŏten; speak, spack* or *spake, spōken.* Then in the modern period *get* and *speak* developed along with *bear,* as described above, so that the parts became *gĕt, gŏt, gŏten; speak, spōke, spōken.* Thus certain verbs from the second, fourth, and fifth classes have been thrown together and the old organization has in part been broken up. In older English the vowels in the parts of *get* were long or short. The short vowels have prevailed: *get, got, gotten.*

In all these examples the common feature is that the vowel of the past participle has influenced the vowel of the past tense. Something similar and yet different has taken place in modern popular speech in a number of verbs — the past tense has assumed

[1] Now obsolete.

the form of the past participle: *seen, done, taken,* etc., serving both as a past tense and as a past participle. The monosyllabic forms, as *seen* and *done,* are widely used, but the dissyllabic forms, as *taken, written,* etc., are for the most part confined to popular southern American English, also *been* and *gone.* Earlier in the period, *gin,* contracted past participle of *give,* was widely employed as past tense, but it is now yielding to *give* (**63** under *give*), a present tense used as a past tense. The use of past participle as past tense originated in southeastern British, but now has its widest boundaries in southern American English. For examples see footnotes in **63** under *be, do, go, see, take, write.* In all these cases the past tense has not only the vowel of the past participle but also the -(*e*)*n* of the participial suffix.

On the other hand, the past tense, in a number of verbs, has assimilated to itself the form of the past participle: *abide — abode — abode* (in older English *abidden*); *bite — bit — bit* (or more commonly *bitten,* as in older English); *shine — shone — shone; get — got — got* (or in America still quite commonly *gotten,* as in older English); *sit — sat — sat* (in older English *setten* or *sitten*). Similarly, instead of *drive — drove — driven, ride — rode — ridden, write — wrote — written, shake — shook — shaken,* etc., we often find in older English *drive — drove — drove, ride — rode — rode, write — wrote — wrote, shake — shook — shook,* etc. These new forms, however have not become established. The older past participles are now always used in the literary language, but the newer ones survive in popular speech.

In a few cases the vowel of the past tense was in early Modern English influenced by the vowel of the past participle, and later the new past tense was used also as a past participle: *bite, bote,*† *bitten* becoming *bīte, bĭt, bĭt; slide, slode,*† *slidden* becoming *slīde, slĭd, slĭd.* The new past participle *slid* is more common than the older form *slidden,* but the new past participle *bit* is not so widely used as the older form *bitten.* There were once more verbs in this new class: *wrīte, wrĭt, wrĭt; rīde, rĭd, rĭd; strīde, strĭd, strĭd* (still lingering in England). For the most part these new forms survive only in popular speech. A weak verb has been attracted into this strong class: *light, lit, lit* after the analogy of *bite, bit, bit.* Compare *light* in **60** B. The formation of this new strong type was facilitated by the old weak type of the same form, *hide, hid, hid,* described in **59** 2 B *c.* It is characterized by a long vowel in the present tense and a short vowel in the past tense and the past participle.

The old classes have been disturbed, not only by analogies between the past tense and the past participle, but also by analogies between the singular and the plural of the past tense. In older English, there is often a different vowel in the singular and the plural of the past indicative, as can be seen by a glance at the classes given above. In modern English, the plural vowel has, in a number of verbs, especially in the third class, become assimilated to the vowel of the singular: (Middle English) *rang* — *runge(n)*, *sang* — *sunge(n)*, *schrank* — *schrunke(n)*, *sank* — *sunke(n)*, *sprang* — *sprunge(n)*, *stank* — *stunke(n)*, *swam* — *swumme(n)*; (Modern English) *rang* — *rang*, *sang* — *sang*, *shrank* — *shrank*, *sank* — *sank*, *sprang* — *sprang*, *stank* — *stank*, *swam* — *swam*. On the other hand, six words in this class now have in both singular and plural the old plural vowel, which has thus assimilated to itself the vowel of the singular: *slung* — *slung*, *slunk* — *slunk*, *spun* — *spun*, *strung* — *strung*, *swung* — *swung*, *wrung* — *wrung*.

In a number of verbs in the fourth class the quantity of the vowel in the plural of the past tense has influenced the quantity of the vowel in the singular of the same tense. In the fourteenth century the vowel of the singular was still usually short — *bar*, *brack*, *cam*, *spack*, *stal*, *tar*. Occasionally the singular vowel became long under the influence of the long plural vowel *e* in the same tense: *spaak* (Wyclif, *Sel. Wrks.*, III, 265, A.D. 1380). Later, long *a* was indicated by writing *e* after the final consonant: *spake* (*Paston Letters*, II, 14, A.D. 1461). The long past — *bare*, *brake*, *spake*, *stale*, *tare* — was the common form from the late fifteenth to the seventeenth century, although the older form with the short vowel still lingered on alongside of it. These new singular forms soon became established also in the plural, displacing the older forms with the stem vowel *e*. But, as described above, there arose in the sixteenth century a new type of past tense here — *bore*, *spoke*, *stole*, *tore*.

The long *a* of the past tense, described in the preceding paragraph, should not be confounded with the long *a* found in northern British dialect in the past tense of verbs of the first class — *drave*, *rade*, *rase* (or *raise*), *strade*, *strake*, *strave*, *thrave*, etc.: 'Where'er I gaed, where'er I *rade*' (Burns, *Mauchline Lady*). In Scotch this long *a* is often written *ai*. This long *a* is a development out of the long *a* found here in Old English. Earlier in the present period we find a long *a* in this same group of words also in the literary language, but it is an analogical formation following the example of *spake* and the other past tenses described in the preceding paragraph: 'Huon lyft up his sworde and *strake* therewith the admyrall' (Lord Berners, *Huon*, I, p. 153, A.D. 1534).

The verb *choose* in the second class has experienced a number of assimilations. By 1200 the consonants of the past participle *coren* had become assimilated to the consonants of the present tense and the singular of the past tense, becoming *chosen*. Later, this form assimilated to itself the old plural *cure(n)* of the past tense, which thus became *chose(n)*.

There is another force that has long been active in breaking up the old classes — a strong trend in the direction of the weak inflection, so that parts of certain verbs are now weak.

Consequently, what we have left of the old classes is merely scattered clusters of words which still cling together. Thus after the model of *write, wrote, written* in the first class we still inflect *drive, ride, rise, arise, shrive* (**60** B), *smite, stride, thrive* (**60** B), *strive*. There are also other groups of verbs which cling together, but there are so many irregularities that it is thought best to recognize that the old classes are definitely broken up and hence to put all the strong verbs into an alphabetical list (**63**) for convenient reference.

LIST OF STRONG VERBS

63. There are now less than one hundred strong verbs in our language. For many centuries there has been a steady loss in favor of the weak class. In only a few cases have weak or foreign verbs been drawn into the strong class. *Ring* was originally weak, but in Middle English became strong after the analogy of *sing*. Similarly, the originally weak verb *string* has become strong under the influence of *sling*. The weak verbs *chide, hide,* and the borrowed verb *strive* have been influenced by the strong verb *ride*, the first two following it frequently in the past participle, *strive* following it throughout. Similarly, *wear* has become strong under the influence of *tear*. In early Modern English, *stick* could still be inflected weak. Also *dig*, once regularly with the past tense and past participle *digged*, has, for the most part, become strong. After the analogy of *blow — blown* have arisen *show — shown*, *sow* † (now *sew*) — *sown* † (now *sewn* in England, but in America *sewed*), *strow* † (now *strew*) — *strown* † (now *strewn*). After the analogy of *blow, blew, blown* came into use *snow, snew* † (now *snowed*), *snown* † (now *snowed*). After the analogy of *draw, drew, drawn* arose *saw, sew* † (now *sawed*), *sawn* (used in England, but in America the original weak *sawed* is still the common form). As can be seen by the examples the development here is uneven. In some cases the new strong forms have become established, in others they have disappeared, yielding to the original weak forms. The new strong forms maintained themselves better in England than in America. The weak class has made another important contribution to the strong. The old weak verb *wend, went, went* with the transitive meaning *direct* (one's way, course) and the intransitive meaning *go* has furnished the old strong verb *go* with a past tense, relinquishing to it its past tense *went* for use as an intransitive and reforming its parts to *wend, wended, wended* for use in its old transitive meaning. Compare **59** 2 B *d*.

In the following list are given only such strong verbs as are still prevailingly strong. Old strong verbs that are now prevailingly weak but have strong forms alongside of the weak are given in **60** B with irregular weak verbs. Where there is fluctuation in usage, the more common form is given first. The variant (i.e. the different form) may be a less common strong form, or, on the other hand, a vigorous weak form, as in the case of *waked,* which is now widely used, especially in the past participle. Sometimes, as in the case of *weaved,* the weak form has not yet gained wide currency. The verb *shine* is strong only as an intransitive. The causative (**12** 1 *a*) *shine* is weak although the intransitive *shine* is strong, while in general causatives have the forms of the corresponding intransitives: 'The boy *swam* across the river' and 'The boy *swam* his horse across the river,' but 'The sun *shone* brightly all day,' while we say, 'He *shined* our shoes last night.' We now feel the causative *shine* as belonging to the noun *shine* rather than to the intransitive *shine.* Causative *shine* is an American verb. In the case of one old verb only the form for the first and the third person of the past tense survives, namely, *quoth* (= *said*), now only used archaically or in quoting contemptuously, always with the inverted word-order: *quoth he* (or *she,* etc.). Another old strong verb — *worth* 'be' — survives only in a few expressions in the third person singular of the subjunctive: Woe *worth* the day! = Woe *be* to the day! Compare *Syntax,* **6** B (last par.). Forms now used only as adjectives have an asterisk after them. In most cases these forms once had verbal force. Whenever a verbal form is obsolete in plain prose or now used only in poetry, it is marked by a dagger. On the other hand, in older English these words were in common use. By older usage is here meant the usage of the earlier part of the modern English period. This older usage, in many cases, survives in popular speech or in certain dialects. This is usually indicated in the case of widely used popular forms. Many other old literary forms, however, survive here and there in out-of-the-way places that are not in easy touch with the rest of the country. The forms now employed in the literary language and good colloquial speech are given in roman type. Dialect, popular speech, and older literary forms are given in italics. A dagger after a word in italics indicates an older literary form. In early Modern English there were in a large number of cases, even in the literary language, two or more forms for past tense and past participle. This older order of things survives in popular speech.

Present	*Past*	*Past Participle*
abide	abode [1]	abode,[1] *abidden* †
	abided [1]	abided [1]
arise	arose	arisen
awake [2]	awoke	awaked,
	awaked	awoke, awoken,
		awake *

[1] In the meaning 'dwell' the more common parts are *abide, abode, abode,* but in other meanings the parts *abide, abided, abided* now seem more natural: 'All the other thinkers *abided* by the conclusions to which they were led' (Lewes, *Hist. of Phil.*, p. 63).

[2] *Wake, awake, waken,* and *awaken* are closely related. They are now usually ingressives (**52** 2 *a*), i.e. indicate entrance into the waking state: 'I *awoke* early.' In older English, *wake* was often used also as a durative with the meaning *remain awake:* 'You promised to *wake* with me the night before my wedding' (C. Brontë, *Jane Eyre*, Ch. XXV). The first two of these verbs are often strong, the last two are always regular weak forms. *Wake* is often accompanied by the ingressive particle *up* to emphasize the moment of awaking. Examples: 'I *woke* (or *waked*) *up* early.' 'He *woke* (or *waked*) me *up* early.' 'I've just *waked up*.' 'I've just *waked* him *up*.' Likewise *awake:* 'I *awoke* early.' 'I've just *awaked*.' 'I *awoke* him early.' 'I've just *awaked* him.' In the passive *waken* and *awaken* are the favorites: 'I was *wakened* (or *awakened*) by the noise.' In figurative language *awake* and *awaken* are preferred, *awake* in intransitive and *awaken* in transitive or intransitive function: 'After that new ambitions *awoke* (or *awakened*) within him.' 'That *awakened* new ambitions within him.' *Awaken* is the proper form here in the passive: 'New ambitions were *awakened* within him.' In Middle English *(a)wake* belonged to the same strong class as *shake*, and if it had developed regularly, its parts would now be *(a)wake, (a)wook, (a)waken*. The shortened form of the past participle, namely, *awake*, survives as an adjective. In the fourteenth century weak forms began to appear alongside of the old strong ones, and in Shakespeare's day entirely displaced them. In the seventeenth century, however, new strong forms sprang up under the influence of *speak: (a)wake, (a)woke, (a)woke(n)*. In our own time the new strong form is quite a favorite in the past tense and the weak form a favorite in the past participle, but sometimes we hear *(a)waked* in the past tense. In British English the strong forms *awoke, awoken, woken, woke* still occur in the past participle: 'They had *woken* her from a very delightful sleep' (Walpole, *Fortitude*, I, Ch. III). 'It was seven years since Horace Walpole, sleeping beneath the crochets of Strawberry Hill, had seen the giant fist of mail lying on his banisters and *woken* to write "The Castle of Otranto"' (*London Times*, Sept. 15, 1932). 'An evil dream from which you had *awoken*' (*ib.*, July 5, 1925). 'Past *woke, waked*, past participle *waked, woken, woke*' (*Concise Oxford Dictionary*). In American English the past participle *(a)woke(n)* is confined to colloquial and popular speech.

Present	*Past*	*Past Participle*
be, *bee* † (**57** 1)	was (**61** 1) *been* (pop. [2])	been,[1] *bene* † *bin,*† *ben,*† *be* †
bear, *bere* † [3] ('bring forth')	bore *bare* †	born,[4] *borned* [4] *bore* †
bear, *bere* † [3] ('carry')	bore *bāre,*† *beared* †	borne [4] *bore* † [4]
beat, *bēte,*† [5] *bett* † [5]	beat, *bett* † [6] *beated* †	beaten, beat [7] *beated,*† *bett,*† *betten* † [6]
befall	befell	befallen *befell* † [8]
beget	begot *begăt,*† *begāte* †	begotten
begin	began, *begun* † [9] *begin* [10]	begun, *began* †

[1] In England 'been' is pronounced *been* or *bĭn,* more commonly the former. In America the usual pronunciation is *bĭn,* dialectically *bĕn.* In the period before the colonization of America 'been' was often pronounced and written *bin* by prominent English writers, so that *bin* is not an American creation: 'if it had *bin* possible' (Sir Walter Raleigh, *Discoverie of Guiana,* p. 6, A.D. 1596). In older English *bene* was sometimes employed as a spelling variant of *been.* *Bee* was a common spelling variant of the present tense form *be.*

[2] 'Dat ol' shu't o' you' own *been* (= *was*) too ol' fo' patch any mo'' (Julia Peterkin, *Green Thursday,* p. 59). This is popular southern American English. See **62** (p. 302).

[3] An older spelling, replaced in the sixteenth century by *bear.*

[4] 'He was *born* in Chicago.' But: 'She has never *borne* children.' 'He was the last child *borne* by her.' 'The tree has never *borne* fruit.' In many British and American dialects the weak *-ed* is added to the strong past participle *born:* 'He was *borned* in 1852.' This new past participle is sometimes used as a past tense: 'The mare *borned* a colt' (*Dialect Notes,* III, p. 537). The old literary past participle *bore* (= *borne*) is still widely used in popular speech: 'My trees ain't *bore* so good this year.'

[5] Older spelling, later in the sixteenth century replaced by *beat.* In early Modern English there was alongside of the long-voweled *bete* or *beat* the short-voweled *bett.*

[6] Survives in dialect.

[7] Often in the sense 'surpassed': 'In football we have always *beaten* (or often *beat*) them.' 'Well I [have] got you *beat,* I [have] been in leather longer than that' (John Herrmann, *The Big Short Trip*). In adjective function in the position before the noun the past participle is usually *beaten:* 'the *beaten* football team.' Used as a predicate adjective the past participle is now always *beat* in *dead-beat* (tired out): 'She sank down *dead-beat* on the door-step.' In this meaning this word is not now so common in America as in England, but it is widely used in America as a noun: a *deadbeat,* one who sponges on others.

[8] 'No such misfortune has *befell* me these douzen years' (Franklin, *Works,* I, 191, A.D. 1732).

[9] Survives in popular speech.

[10] Popular form after the analogy of *set — set:* 'Half ways back to camp, Smoky *begin* to notice big dusts on both sides of him' (Will James, *Smoky,* Ch. VIII). Compare **59** 2 B *b.*

Present	*Past*	*Past Participle*
behold	beheld	beheld
		beholden * [1]
bespeak	bespoke	bespoken
	bespake †	*bespoke*,† [2] bespoke * [2]
bid [3]	bă̆de (bāde), *bă̆d* †	bidden, unbidden *
	bid	bid, bă̆de
	bode,† *bod* †	*boden*,† *bodden* †

[1] 'I don't like to be *beholden* to anybody.' Earlier in the period it could have pure verbal force: 'Within a small distance we might perceiue a farre more cleere and radiant light than euer before till that present wee had *beholden*' (B. Rich, *Greenes Newes from Heauen and Hell*, p. 13, A.D. 1593).

[2] In the seventeenth and eighteenth centuries the past tense form *spoke* was often used also as a past participle alongside of *spoken*. In England *bespoke* is in adjective function still widely used as a past participle: '*bespoke* boots,' i.e. made to order in contrast to ready-made.

[3] *Bid* represents two verbs which in Old English were distinct in form and meanings — *biddan* (fifth class) 'pray,' 'beg,' 'ask,' 'bid' ('request') and *beodan* (second class) 'order,' 'command,' 'offer.' The forms of the two old verbs became confounded in Middle English. The forms in present use all belong to Old English *biddan*. The early Modern English forms *bode* and *bod* belong to Old English *beodan*. The past participle *bidden* is not a phonetical development of the Old English past participle *beden* but an analogical formation showing the influence of the vowel of the present tense. The shortened form *bid* serves also as a past tense.

Modern *bid* contains the meanings of the two old verbs and in addition the new meanings '*bid* at an auction,' '*bid* for votes, public favor,' '*bid* for the construction of a house,' etc., developments of the old meaning 'offer,' belonging to Old English *beodan*. The usual parts for all the old original meanings are *bid*, *bade* (or less commonly *bid*), *bidden* or *bid*: 'I *bade* him go.' 'A haggard man *bid* (more commonly *bade*) them depart' (Eden Phillpotts, *Eng. Rev.*, Oct., 1913, p. 344). 'I was *bidden* to go.' 'Do as you are *bid*.' 'I *bade* him welcome.' 'The proposed expedition *bade* fair to be successful.' 'For a long while they *bade* us defiance.' In Middle English, the idea of *bidding*, *requesting* led to that of *inviting*, which still survives but is not common: 'They were all *bidden*.' Earlier in the present period the old meaning of 'offer' was still found here: '(They) *bade* her half the price she asked' (Johnson, *The Rambler*, No. 161, 10, A.D. 1751). *Bade* is now replaced here by *bid* in British English and by *offered* in American English. The parts for the new meanings are *bid*, *bid*, *bid*: 'Someone *bid* five dollars.' 'He has often *bid* for public favor.' 'He *bid* too high and thus failed to get the contract.' These are weak forms after the analogy of *rid*, *rid*, *rid*, so that *bid* with these meanings is listed in **60** B among the weak verbs. These parts are used also for the modern meaning *invite to membership in a college fraternity or sorority*: 'He (or she) *had been bid*.'

The vowel *a* of the past tense is long or short, much more commonly, however, short, so that the present spelling *bade* is misleading. This past tense is not infrequently used by good authors also as a past participle, though not usually recorded as such by grammarians: 'Suppose Pauline had *bade* me sing!' (Robert Browning, *One Way*, 12).

In the meaning 'command' *bid* is now in colloquial speech replaced by *tell*. 'I *told* him to do it.'

Present	*Past*	*Past Participle*
bind	bound *band*,† [1] *bond* † [1]	bound bounden * [2]
bite	bit (**62**, p. 302) *bote* †	bitten bit
blow [3]	blew *blowed* †	blown *blowed*,† *blew* [3]
blow (poetic) ('bloom')	blew	blown
break, *breke* [4]	broke *brăck*,† *brāke* †	broken *broke* † [5]
chide (**59** 2 B *c*)	chided, chid *chode* †	chided, chid chidden
choose, *chose*,† [6] *chuse* † [6]	chose, *chase* † *choosed*,† *chused* †	chosen, *chose* † [7] *choosed*,† *chused* †
cling	clung, *clang* † *clong*,† *clinged* †	clung, *clong* † *clinged* †
come	came, *cōme* † [8] *cam*,† *come* [8]	come, *comen* † [9] *comed*,† [9] *came* [10]

[1] These old forms are preserved in the nouns *band, bond,* which were originally different forms of the same word, but later became differentiated in meaning.

[2] It is still used in attributive adjective function in 'It is my *bounden* duty.' Earlier in the period it was much used in the predicate: 'I am much *bounden* (now *obliged* or *indebted*) to your Majesty' (Shakespeare, *King John*, III, iii, 29). *Bound* is now the usual form also in adjective function: 'a *bound* volume.' 'I am not *bound* to do it.'

[3] Earlier in the period sometimes weak: *blow, blowed, blowed.* In loose colloquial and popular speech weak forms sometimes still occur: 'It *blowed* terribly.' 'He *blowed* in all the money he had.' 'He cheated in examinations, and even *blowed* about it.' 'He *blowed* (told) on me.' In slang: 'I'll be *blowed* (hanged) if,' etc. In popular speech the past tense *blew* is sometimes used as a past participle.

[4] An older spelling, replaced in the sixteenth century by *break.*

[5] In the seventeenth and eighteenth centuries the past tense form *broke* was often used also as a past participle alongside of *broken.* It survives in popular speech. It is still used also in colloquial language in the meaning *out of money:* 'I'm *broke.*'

[6] In older English, *chose* and *chuse* were employed as variant spellings of *choose. Chuse,* however, had a slightly different pronunciation. There was an *i*-sound before the vowel. This pronunciation survives in British dialects.

[7] Still heard in popular speech.

[8] In the sixteenth century *cōme* was still in use in the literary language. It was in Old English the usual past tense form. It survives in British dialect, now written *coom.* In popular speech there is another past tense form *come* with a different pronunciation, which is the past participle *cŏme* used for the past tense. The stem vowel is a short *u*-sound. The use of this past tense form is furthered by the fact that the present tense has the same form. Compare **59** 2 B *b*.

[9] Still heard in British dialects.

[10] Heard in American popular speech.

Present	*Past*	*Past Participle*
dig	dug (see footnote to *strike*)	dug
	digged	digged
do (**57**	did, *done* [1]	done, did [1]
draw	drew,[2] *drawed* † [3]	drawn, *drawed* [3] *drew* [4]
drink	drank	drunk, drunken * [7]
	drunk,† [5] *drinked* [6]	drunk,* [7] *drank* † [5]
drive	drove, *drāve* †	driven, *drove* †
	drived,† *driv*,[8] *druw* [8]	*drived*,† *driv*,[8] *druw* [8]
eat, *eate*,† *ete*,† *ette* †	ate,[9] *eat* † [9]	eaten, *eat* † [9]
	ete,† *eet* †	*ete*,† *etten*,† *ate* [9]

[1] Heard in popular speech or dialect. The past participle *done* is now widely used as a past tense, but usually only as an independent verb: 'I *done* my best,' but 'I *did*n't (auxiliary) go.' In southern American popular speech *done* is employed as a past tense auxiliary, but it is then usually followed by a past tense: ''Tain't so mighty long sence I *done tole* you 'bout old Mr. Benjermin Ram' (Joel Chandler Harris, *Nights with Uncle Remus*, p. 297). For explanation of this construction see **47** 3 (4). On the other hand, the past tense *did* is sometimes in American popular speech used also as a past participle.

[2] *Drew* arose in the fourteenth century after the analogy of *threw*, later gradually replacing older *drough* and *drow*.

[3] In older English used sometimes in the literary language. It is still sometimes heard in popular speech.

[4] Sometimes used in American popular speech.

[5] Forms sometimes used in older English in the literary language. They survive in popular speech.

[6] Sometimes heard in dialect.

[7] *Drunk* is not only used with pure verbal force but also as a predicate adjective: 'He has already *drunk* two cups of coffee.' 'He is *drunk*.' Also *drunken* is employed in adjective function, usually however only before a noun in the attributive relation: 'Before me reeled a *drunken* sailor.' In older English, *drunken* could be used with pure verbal force: 'Yf it (i.e. cider) be *dronken* (older spelling variant of *drunken*) in haruyst, it doth lytell harme' (Andrewe Boorde, *Dyetary of Helth*, *E.E.T.S.*, Ex. Ser. 10, p. 257, A.D. 1542).

[8] Forms heard in popular speech.

[9] The past tense form *āte* has two different pronunciations. In England, it is pronounced *ĕt*, less commonly *āte* (*a* as in *late*), in America *āte*, much less commonly *ĕt*, which for the most part is now confined to popular speech. The form *ĕt* (now written *ate* in England) has resulted from a shortening of Middle English *ēt* (*e* as in *there*). The long form *ēt* became in early Modern English *eet* (written *eat*, *ete*, *eet*). Since 1900 this form has been restricted to popular speech. In the language of the common people both *ĕt* and *eet* are used also as past participles, a usage which earlier in the present period obtained also in the literary language. The common American literary past tense *āte* (*a* as in *late*) is of the same origin as the less common British form *āte*. It arose in the thirteenth century as *at* (short *a*) after the analogy of *spăc*. Later, the *a* became long and developed into the sound of *a* in *late*: *spāke*, *āte*. *Spāke* has disappeared, but *āte* survives. In dialect *āte* is used also as a past participle.

Present	*Past*	*Past Participle*
fall	fell	fallen, *fell* †[1]
fight	fought	fought, foughten *[2]
	fit[3]	*fit*[3]
find	found	found
fling	flung, *flang* †	flung, *flang*
	flong †	*flong* †
fly[4]	flew	flown
		fline,† *flyen* †
forbear	forbore	forborne

[1] Survives in dialect and popular speech: 'But now I know I *have fell* short of what the Lord my God required of me' (Lucy Furman, *The Glass Window*, p. 284).

[2] Archaic attributive form: '*foughten* field' = 'battle field.' In older English, *foughten* was used also with pure verbal force.

[3] In popular speech *fight, fit, fit* are often used after the analogy of *bite, bit, bit.* The similar analogical development *light, lit, lit* has become established in the literary language. Compare **62** (p. 302).

[4] In Old English, *fly* had two different sets of meanings, as *fly* and *flee* had become confounded. On the one hand, it expressed the idea of a movement by means of wings or rapid movement in general. On the other hand, it was used in the sense of *flee* with its different shades of meaning. Today *fly* is still the usual word to express the idea of movement by means of wings or rapid movement in general: 'The bird *flies, flew,* has *flown.*' 'Fast the happy moments *flew*' (R. Browning). In England, *fly* is still the usual present tense form in the sense *flee,* so that the parts in this meaning are *fly, fled, fled:* 'the *flying* enemy.' 'When the enemy *flies,* the enemy is *flying,* the enemy will *fly,* the enemy *fled,* has *fled.*' Americans use *flee, fleeing, fled, fled* in this meaning. A little earlier in the present period, however, *fly* occurs in this meaning also in American English: 'When first seized with that indescribable terror which induces them (i.e. frightened horses) to *fly,* they seem to have been suddenly endowed with all the attributes of their original wild nature' (Kendall, *Narrative of the Texan Santa Fe Expedition,* A.D. 1844). Everywhere the past participle *flown* is still sometimes used instead of *fled:* 'It was to England he must have *flown* (now more commonly *fled*) for protection' (Jas. Mill, *British India,* III, V, VIII, 641). 'In all ages solitude has been called for, has been *flown* to' (Disraeli). 'O faith, where art thou *flown* from out the world?' (Browning, *The Ring and the Book,* IX, 1319). As *fled* is not a clear participial form distinct from the past tense *fled* and there is often need of such in adjective function, most writers avoid it in adjective function and employ the distinctive participial form *flown:* 'He had returned to Birmingham to find his lady-love *flown*' (Rider Haggard, *Mr. Meeson's Will,* Ch. XXII). 'Time fleets how fast, And opportunity, the irrevocable, Once *flown,* will flout him' (Browning, *The Ring and the Book,* IX, 1230). In the eighteenth century the past tense form *flew* could still be used instead of *fled* for sake of rime: 'And as a hare, whom hounds and horse pursue, Pants to the place from whence at first she *flew*' (Goldsmith, *Deserted Village,* 94), now *fled.*

The past tense form *flew* arose in the fifteenth century under the influence of *blew,* replacing older *fligh, flough,* and *flow.* The past participle *fline* † (also written *flyen*) was formed in the sixteenth century from the present tense and continued in limited use throughout the next century.

Present	*Past*	*Past Participle*
forbid	forbăde	forbidden, *forbid* † *forboden* †
forget	forgot *forgăt*,† *forgāte* †	forgotten *forgot* †
forsake	forsook	forsaken *forsook* †
freeze	froze, *fraze* † *freezed*,† *friz* [1]	frozen *froze*,† [2] *freezed* †
gĕt, *gēte*,† [3] *git* † [3]	got, *gote* † *găt*,† *gāte* †	got gotten,[4] *goten* † gotten * (ill-gotten)
give, *gēve*,† *gin* [5]	gave, *gived* † *give* [5] *gin*,[5] *gun* [5]	given, *gēven* † *give*,† [5] *gave* † [5] *gin*,[5] *gun* [5]
go	went,[6] *gone* [7] *yede*,† [6] *yode* [6]	gone, *go* † [6] *went*,† [6] *went* [6]

[1] Common in popular speech.

[2] Once a literary form, still used in popular speech.

[3] In older English the vowel *i* was sometimes used here instead of *e*, and *git* is still heard in certain British dialects, also in American popular speech. In the sixteenth century older *gēte* still lingered on. Compare **62** (p. 301).

[4] Very common in early American English and still common in the spoken and written language of America, though little used in Great Britain. At the time when the first English colonists left England for their new home in America, *gotten* was a common form also in the mother country. The colonists simply brought it along with them. The later form *got* — the past tense used as a past participle — began to be used in England in the sixteenth century and gradually displaced *gotten* there. It is now widely used also in America alongside of *gotten*. It is even the rule where the form is a mere auxiliary: 'He has never *got* punished enough.' It is always employed in the expression *has got* used as a present tense: 'He *has got* a black eye.'

[5] Used in popular speech. *Give*, shortened from *given*, is an old past participle once used in the literary language. In popular speech it is still employed as a past participle and now used also as a past tense: 'I had *give* my hand to the woman there would be no drinking' (Lucy Furman, *The Quare Women*, Ch. I). 'I *give* it to him yesterday.' The common use of *give* as a past tense is furthered by two tendencies — the tendency to employ the past participle also as a past tense and the tendency to use the present tense also as a past tense after the analogy of *set* — *set*. Compare **62** (toward end of 2nd par. under Modern English Classes, p. 302) and **59** 2 B *b*. The past tense form *gave* was once employed also as a past participle: 'O had she then *gave* over, Such nectar from his lips she had not suck'd' (Shakespeare, *Venus and Adonis*, 1. 571). This usage survives in popular speech. The popular past participle *gin*, shortened from *given*, is used also as past tense: 'His folks *gin* the letter to me' (James Russell Lowell, *The Biglow Papers*, No. II). This once common popular past is now largely replaced by *give*, as described above. *Gin* is sometimes used as a present: '*Gin* it to me.'

[6] In early Modern English, *yede* and *yode*, older past tense forms of *go*, were still lingering on. But some of those who used these old forms did not

Present	*Past*	*Past Participle*
grind	ground	ground
	grinded †	*grinded* †
grow	grew	grown
	growed † [1]	*growed* † [1]
hang (general sense)	hung	hung
	heng,† *hing* †	*hangen* †
hang [2] (narrower	hanged	hanged
sense of 'execute')	hung	hung
hold	held, *hild* †	held, *holden* [3]
	holded †	*holded* †

understand them, for they construed *yede* (also spelled *yeed*) as a present tense and *yode* as its past: 'On foot was forced for *to yeed*' (Spenser, *The Faerie Queene*, II, IV, 2, 3). 'Forth they *yode*' (*ib.*, IV, VIII, 34, 6). These two old past tense forms were gradually supplanted by another word which had a similar meaning. *Went* is the old past tense and past participle of the weak verb *wend*, which was once used intransitively in the sense of *go*. In early Modern English, it became established as the usual past tense of *go*. It was at this time sometimes used also as a past participle of *go*, but this usage later disappeared in the literary language. The present use of *went* in popular speech as the past participle of *go* has resulted from the spreading of the past tense form to the past participle. Compare **59** 2 B *d* and **63** (1st par.).

In early Modern English, *go*, the old shortened form of *gone*, was still in use. It survives in *ago*, past participle of the old derivative verb *ago* 'go by': 'Three days *ago* (lit. *gone by*) I became sick.' We now feel *ago* as an adverb, since we are no longer conscious that it has anything to do with *go*.

[7] 'I aint fo'git how good you been to me sence Bully *gone* off an' lef' me' (Julia Peterkin, *Green Thursday*, p. 154). *Gone* is common as past tense in popular southern American English. Compare **62** (toward end of 2nd par. under Modern English Classes), p. 302.

[1] In older English, sometimes used in the literary language, but now restricted to popular speech.

[2] In early Modern English, the parts *hang, hanged, hanged* had not yet become restricted to the narrower sense, but could be used also in the general sense: 'Also the chambre was *hangyd* with riche clothes' (Lord Berners, *Huon*, I, p. 102, A.D. 1534). In northern British at this time the parts were *hing, hang* (or *hung*), *hung*, in the general sense. These northern forms have influenced the literary language. As there is no such verb as *hing* in the literary language, the northern parts have been modified to *hang, hung, hung*, which have replaced the older literary forms *hang, heng* or *hing, hangen*. In the best literary usage these new parts are now employed in the general sense and *hang, hanged, hanged* are restricted to the narrower sense. There is a strong tendency in American and southern British colloquial speech to use *hang, hung, hung* in both senses. Northern British dialect now has here two verbs with different parts: (general sense) *hing, hang* (*hung*), *hung;* (narrower sense) *hang, hanged, hanged.*

[3] An old past participle that still lingers in archaic language, especially in formal reports of meetings, in legal expressions, and in poetry: 'O yester-day, you know, the fair Was *holden* at the town' (Tennyson, *The Talking Oak*, 101).

Present	*Past*	*Past Participle*
know	knew	known
	knowed [1]	*knowed*,[1] *knew* [2]
lie [3]	lay	lain, *lien* †
lose,[4] *loose* †		lorn *
leese †		forlorn *
ride	rode	ridden
	rid † [5]	*rode*,† *rid* † [5]
ring	rang, *rung* †	rung, *rang* † [6]
	rong,† *ringed* †	*rong* †
rise	rose, *rised* †	risen, *rose* †
	rise,† [7] *ris*,† [7] *riz* [7]	*rise*,† [7] *ris*,† [7] *riz* [7]
run, *rin*,† *ren* †	ran	run
	run,† [8] *runned* † [8]	*ran*,† [8] *runned* † [8]
see	saw, *seen* [9]	seen, *saw* [9]
	seed,[9] *see* † [10]	*seed* [9]

[1] In older English, sometimes used in the literary language, but now restricted to popular speech.

[2] Used in popular speech: 'If I'd 'a' only *knew!*' (Elmer L. Rice, *The Adding Machine*, p. 102).

[3] In popular speech intransitive *lie* is often confounded with transitive *lay*, so that the parts *lay, laid, laid* are used both intransitively and transitively: '*Lay* (instead of the correct *lie*) down.' '*Lay* it down.' 'She *laid* (instead of correct *lay*) down for a little rest.' 'She *laid* it down.' 'She has *laid* (instead of the correct *lain*) down for a little rest.' 'She has *laid* it down.' Compare *lay* in **60** B.

[4] A strong present tense of the same class as *shoot* and *choose*. Its past tense and past participle have been replaced by the weak form *lŏst*, past tense and past participle of a lost weak verb. As the vowel is long in *lōse* and short in *lŏst*, the feeling arose that the short past belonged to the long present, as in the large group in **59** 2 B *c*. The same development took place in *shōōt, shŏt, shŏt*. Compare **60** B, footnote under *shoot*. Though *lose* has lost its old strong participle in general use, the old strong forms *lorn* and *forlorn* are still employed in adjective function in the meaning 'forsaken.'

[5] Very common in Washington's Diary: '*Rid* to the Mill and returned to Dinner' (Dec. 7, 1770). It is still often heard in popular speech. It was earlier in the period used also as a past participle: 'He has *rid* out this morning with my father' (Jane Austen, *Northanger Abbey*, Ch. X). Also this form survives in popular speech: 'I would have *rid* to The Forks today, but I hain't got my strength good yet' (Lucy Furman, *The Glass Window*, p. 203). Compare **62** (p. 302).

[6] Once a literary form, still employed in popular speech or dialect.

[7] *Rise, ris,* and *riz* are variant spellings of the same form. The usual spelling now is *riz*, in older English *rise* or *ris*. This form for past tense and past participle was once used in the literary language, but is now confined to popular speech.

[8] Once literary forms, now confined to popular speech.

[9] Forms used in popular speech. For the use of *seen* as a past see **62** (2nd par. under Modern English Classes, p. 302). *Saw* as a past participle is a new form now heard in popular American English.

[10] An old past tense form once used in the literary language, but now confined to popular speech.

Present	*Past*	*Past Participle*
shake	shook	shaken
	shaked †	*shook*,† [1] *shaked* †
	shuck (pop.)	*shuck* (pop.)
shine	shone	shone
(intrans.)	*shined* †	*shined* †
shrink	shrank, shrunk	shrunk, shrunken *
	shronk,† *shrinked* †	*shrinked* †
sing	sang, *song* † [2]	sung
	sung, *sing* [3]	*song*
sink	sank	sunk, sunken *
	sunk	*sank* †
sit	săt, *sāte* †	sat, *sate* †
	sot,[4] *sit* [4]	*setten*,† *sitten* †
		sit(t),† *sot* [4]
slay, *slee*,† [5] *slea* † [5]	slew	slain
slide	slid (**62**, p. 302)	slid, slidden
	slode,† *slided* †	*slided* †
sling	slung, *slang* †	slung
	slong,† *slinged* †	*slinged* †
slink	slunk, *slank* †	slunk, *slunken* [6]
	slonk,† *slinked* †	*slinked* †
smite	smote, *smit* †	smitten, *smote* †
	smited †	*smit*

[1] An older literary form which survives in dialect.

[2] This form was a natural development out of older *sang*, and was used for a time alongside of it. It has survived in the noun *song*. But the verb was under the influence of other verbs, as *drink* (drink, *drank*, drunk), so that the older form *sang* finally prevailed.

[3] Popular form after the analogy of *set — set:* 'I set there and *sing* for an hour' (*Dialect Notes*, III, p. 448).

[4] In popular speech and dialect the parts are often *set, set* or *sot, set* or *sot*, i.e. *sit* is replaced by *set*. The latter is now often used here in all transitive and intransitive functions: 'He *set* or *sot* (in the literary language always *set*) it down.' 'He *set* or *sot* (in the literary language always *sat*) down.' 'He *set* or *sot* (in the literary language always *set*) out for home.' On the other hand, in older English *sit* was sometimes used in the literary language for intransitive *set* (*Syntax*, **46**, 4th par.): 'The coach being ready, the ladies *sate* (now *set*) out for the hall' (Toldervy, *Hist. 2 Orphans*, I, 109, A.D. 1756). Compare **60** B, footnote to *set*. In popular speech *sit* is sometimes used intransitively, as in the literary language, but with the popular parts *sit — sit*, after the analogy of *set — set*. Compare **59** 2 B *b*. The old literary past participles *setten* and *sitten* are still used in northern British dialects. Compare **60** B, *let*, footnote.

[5] *Slee* and *slea* are spelling variants of the old regular present tense, which was still used in early Modern English, but was replaced after the sixteenth century by the irregular form *slay* with the vowel of the past participle. The past tense form *slew* arose in the fourteenth century after the analogy of *threw*, later gradually replacing the older form *slough*.

[6] Used in dialect.

Present	*Past*	*Past Participle*
speak, *spēke* †[1]	spoke, *spăck*,† *spāke* †	spoken, *spoke*,†[2] *spāke* †
spin	spun	spun
	span,[3] *spinned* †	*spinned* †
spring	sprang, sprung	sprung
stand	stood, *stode* †[4]	stood,[5] *standed* †
		stand(*e*),† *stond*(*e*) †
steal, *stēle*[6]	stole, *stăl* †	stolen, *stole* †
	stāle,† *stealed* †	
stick[7]	stuck, *sticked* †	stuck, *sticked* †
	stack,† *stake* †	*stack*,† *stucken* †
sting	stung, *stang* †	stung, *stongen* †
	stong,† *stinged* †	*stong*,† *stinged* †
stink	stank, stunk	stunk, *stank* †
	stonk,† *stinked* †	*stonk*,† *stinked* †
stride	strode, *strided*[8]	stridden, *strided*[8]
	strid †	*strid* †[9]
strike,[10] *strick* †	struck, *stroke* †	struck, stricken
	strook,† *stroak* †	*stroken*,† *strooken* †
	strick,† *strāke* †	*strucken*,† *stroke* †
	striked †	*strick*,† *striked* †

[1] Older spelling, replaced in the sixteenth century by *speak*.

[2] Once a literary form, still used in popular speech.

[3] Still used in England though the less common form.

[4] In early Modern English *stood* and *stode* were different spellings for the same word.

[5] *Stood* is the past tense form used also as a past participle, replacing the older past participle *standen*, which was employed also in the shortened form *stand*(*e*). Similarly the old past participle *sitten* has been replaced by the past tense form *sat*. In older English, *shaken* was sometimes replaced by the past tense form *shook*. We feel *shook* today as plebeian when used as a past participle. There is nothing plebeian in the use of a past tense as a past participle when good authors so employ it, as in the case of *sat* and *stood*. There is often nothing good or bad in the form itself. The use of the best authors stamps it as good. Usage not in harmony with that of the best authors is bad usage. The common people often still use the forms of the great masters of earlier centuries, but these forms are now felt as plebeian because they are not now used by our best authors. Forms, like fashions, come and go. They find favor only when used in season.

[6] An older spelling, replaced in the sixteenth century by *steal*.

[7] *Stick* was originally a weak verb. In the first half of the sixteenth century it came under the influence of *sting, stung, stung*, and the new parts *stick, stuck, stuck* arose. The past tense *stack*, which was very common at this time alongside of *sticked*, shows that *stick* had been influenced in its inflection by the strong *steek* †, *stack* † (or *stake* † or *stoke* †), *stoken* †, a verb with the same meaning. Toward the end of the first half of the sixteenth century *stuck* began to be common and in the seventeenth century replaced both *sticked* and *stack*.

[8] Occurs occasionally in good authors.

[9] According to the *Concise Oxford Dictionary* a rare past participle, but it does not now occur at all in the literary language of America.

[10] In the first half of the sixteenth century it was still usual to employ the

Present	*Past*	*Past Participle*
string [1]	strung	strung
	stringed †	*stringed* †
strive	strove, *strave* †	striven,[2] *strove* † [2]
	strived [2]	strived [2]

old regular forms *strike, stroke, stricken* — a verb of the first class, like *write, wrote, written.* Instead of *stroke* the spelling *stroak* was in limited use. In the second half of the sixteenth century the two forms *strook* and *struck* began to compete with the old past *stroke.* Later, *struck* replaced both *stroke* and *strook.* The past tense forms *strook* and *struck* show that *strike* was being influenced by other verbs. The past tense *strook* was after the analogy of *shook,* past tense of *shake. Strook* survives in British dialects. The past tense *struck* was after the analogy of *stuck,* past tense of *stick. Stuck* itself was after the analogy of *stung,* past tense of *sting.* The development of *struck* was facilitated by the old present tense form *strick,* which had the same vowel as *sting* and *stick.* The old weak verb *dig* joined this group of verbs, the past tense becoming *dug.* After the analogy of *stung* the forms *stuck, struck,* and *dug* were used also as past participles.

In early Modern English, there were still other past tense forms — *strick* and *strake. Strick* had the short vowel of the past participle, as often other words of the same (i.e. the first) class: *strike, strick* †; *write, writ* †. The once common past tense *strake* was after the analogy of *spake,*† *stale,*† etc.

The old past participle *stricken* survives in the passive meaning *afflicted* and, in archaic language, in the old intransitive meaning *gone, advanced:* 'I was *stricken* with fever, paralysis, grief.' 'I am *stricken* in years.' Elsewhere the past participle is now *struck:* 'I was *struck* with a cane, with amazement.' But in pure adjective function *stricken* is still often used, especially in the position before the noun: 'They were *struck* with terror,' but 'the *terror-stricken* city.' The archaic expressions 'a *stricken* (i.e. full) hour' and 'a *stricken* field' (= a *pitched battle*) still linger on. In American English, *stricken* is still sometimes used with full verbal force in the expression '*stricken* out': 'The clause was objected to and was finally *struck* (or sometimes *stricken*) out.' The past participle *strucken* † is still heard in northern British dialect. Also in Negro speech: '*strucken* wid de palsy' (Joel Chandler Harris, *Nights with Uncle Remus,* p. 715).

Strick — an old present tense form with shortened vowel — survives in British dialect.

[1] Originally weak and still occasionally so earlier in the period. The parts are now, under the influence of *sling,* always strong, without regard to the meaning. A useful differentiation might be made here between strong forms and regular weak ones: The bow is *stringed* (provided with a string) and *strung* (bent to the *string*). But we now usually say *strung* in both meanings. As a pure adjective, however, *stringed* is the usual form: *stringed* instruments, a gut-*stringed* racket. We should say *hamstring, hamstringed, hamstringed,* for the verb is made from the noun *hamstring,* but some say *hamstring, hamstrung, hamstrung.*

[2] Originally strong or weak, now usually strong, but in America the weak forms sometimes still occur: 'to achieve a world state of peace, for which men *have strived* since the time of Alexander' (Edgar Snow in *The Saturday Evening Post,* Aug. 26, 1933, p. 69). In older English the past tense *strove* was used also as a past participle. This older usage survives in popular speech.

Present	*Past*	*Past Participle*
swear, *swere* † [1]	swore, *sware* † *sweared* †	sworn, *swore* † [2]
swim	swam, *swum* † *swimmed* †	swum, *swam* † *swimmed* †
swing	swung, *swang* † *swinged* †	swung, *swang* † *swinged* †
take	took, *toke* † [3] *taken* [4] *tuck* [6]	taken, *tane* † *took*,† [5] *toke* † *tuck* [6]
tear, *tēre* † [7]	tore, *tare* † *teared*,† [8] *tored* [9]	torn, *tore* † [9] *teared*,† [8] *tored* [9]
throw	threw *throwed* † [10]	thrown *throwed*, † [10] *threw* [11]
tread	trod, *trōde* † *trad(d)* †	trodden, trod *trōden*,† *trōde* † *tredden*,† *trad(d)* †
understand	understood	understood *understand(e)* † *understanded* *understond(e)*
wake (see awake)	woke waked	waked woken woke
wear, *wēre* † [12]	wore, *ware* † *weared* † [13]	worn, *wore* † [14]

[1] Older spelling, replaced in the sixteenth century by *swear*.

[2] Once literary, still common in popular speech.

[3] In early Modern English, *took* and *toke* are different spellings for the same word.

[4] 'He was working on the highway when I *taken* the order' (from the letter of a salesman, San Francisco, Aug. 12, 1927). *Taken* as past tense is most common in popular southern American English. Compare **62** (2nd par. under Modern English Classes, p. 302).

[5] Once literary, still used in popular speech.

[6] Heard in popular speech.

[7] Older spelling, replaced in the sixteenth century by *tear*.

[8] Once literary, still heard in popular speech.

[9] In older English the past tense form *tore* was often used also as a past participle. This usage survives in popular speech. The common people sometimes add the weak ending *-ed* to the strong past *tore* to form past tense and past participle: *tear, tored, tored*. Compare **60** B (footnote under *fetch*).

[10] Once literary, still used in popular speech.

[11] Heard in popular speech.

[12] Older spelling, replaced in the sixteenth century by *wear*.

[13] *Wear* was originally weak. Chaucer used the weak forms, and much later, in the eighteenth century, the weak past *weared* was still lingering alongside of the more common strong form *wore*. *Wear* has become strong under the influence of *tear*.

[14] Once a literary form, still common in popular speech.

Present	Past	Past Participle
wear (naut. term)	wore	wore
weave, *wēve* † [1]	wove	woven, wove
	weaved †	*weaved* †
win	won, *wun* † [2]	won
	wan,† *winned* †	*wonnen* †
	win [3]	
wīnd ('twine')	wound	wound
wīnd ('sound')	wound	wound
	wīnded [4]	wīnded [4]
withstand	withstood	withstood
		withstanded †
wring	wrung, *wrang* † [5]	wrung, *wrang* † [5]
	wrong,† *wringed* †	*wrong*,† *wringed* †
write	wrote, *writ* † [6]	written, *wrēten* † [8]
	wrat,† *wrāte* †	*writ*,† [6] *wrote* †
	written [7]	

FORMATION OF THE COMPOUND TENSES

64. A compound tense is formed by the use of a present or a past tense of an auxiliary in connection with a participle or an infinitive. The treatment of the different compound tenses follows.

[1] Older spelling, replaced in the sixteenth century by *weave.*

[2] Older variant spelling of *won.*

[3] Popular form after the analogy of *set — set.* Compare **59** 2 B *b.*

[4] In early Modern English, *wīnded* was the regular past tense and perfect participle of the weak verb *wīnd* (= *sound, blow*), which was formed from the noun *wind* in the fifteenth century at a time when it was pronounced *wīnd:* 'Horns wīnded within' (Shakespeare, *Midsummer-Night's Dream,* IV, I, 106). After the pronunciation of the noun became *wĭnd* in the course of the eighteenth century, the verb *wīnd* was no longer vividly felt as belonging to it and was gradually, by the likeness of sound, brought into relation to the strong verb *wīnd* 'coil,' 'twine,' 'turn about something' and finally assumed its parts. Today the old weak forms linger on alongside of the more common strong: 'And raised a bugle hanging from his neck, And *wīnded* it' (Tennyson, *Pelleas and Ettarre,* 364). 'Thither he made and *wound* the gateway horn' (*id., Elaine,* 169). 'The horn is *wound* faintly' (Whittier). 'The apostles of melancholy *wound* their faint horns' (*Athenæum*). The verb *wĭnd* 'get wind of,' 'exhaust wind of,' which is felt as belonging to the noun *wĭnd,* is always weak: 'The hounds *wĭnded* the fox.' 'I am *wĭnded* with the climb.'

[5] Still heard in popular speech.

[6] Still heard in popular speech. Compare **62** (p. 302).

[7] In popular southern American English: 'I *written* to him yesterday' (*Dialect Notes,* III, p. 164). Compare **62** (toward end of 2nd par. under Modern English Classes, p. 302).

[8] See *writhe* in **60** B, footnote.

65. Present Perfect. This tense is made up of the present tense of the auxiliary *have* and the past participle of the verb to be inflected.

	INDICATIVE	SUBJUNCTIVE
	Singular	
1.	I have taken	I have taken
2.	you have taken (thou hast taken)	you have taken (thou have taken)
3.	he has taken (he hath taken)	he have taken
	Plural	
1.	we have taken	we have taken
2.	you (ye) have taken	you (ye) have taken
3.	they have taken	they have taken

PARTICIPLE having taken INFINITIVE (to) have taken

GERUND having taken

a. Time Relations Indicated by Perfect Tense Form of Participle, Infinitive, and Gerund. As there are no participial, infinitival, or gerundial forms corresponding to the past perfect tense, the present perfect forms must serve both as a present perfect and a past perfect: '*Having been* (= *As I have been*) sick so much, I have learned to take good care of my health.' '*Having finished* (= *After I had finished*) my work, I went to bed.' 'I rejoice *to have finished* (= *that I have finished*) it so soon.' '*He is said to have spoken* (= *It is said that he had spoken*) to his brother about it before he did it.' 'After *having taken* (= *I have taken*) some exercise, I feel like studying.' 'After *having completed* (= *I had completed*) my work, I went to bed.' Compare *Syntax*, **48** 2 (6th par.), **49** 3, **50** 2.

b. Origin of Present Perfect and Its Present Nature. We now say 'I *have written* a letter.' The original form was 'I *have* a letter *written*,' so that the form was at the start a present tense. The present form arose from a slight change of the original word order: 'I *have written* a letter.' Back of this change, of course, was a desire to express an idea a little different from the original one — to express a past act but at the same time to bring it into relation to the present. Our name of this tense — present perfect — is a terse and apt characterization of the inner nature of the form. The original form and meaning, however, did not disappear, for we still often desire to use the words with the full force of the present tense: 'I *have* all my letters *written*.' 'I *have* my garden *spaded* and ready for planting.' 'Our football team *has* all the other teams *beaten* to a frazzle.'

Our present perfect tense was a natural, much-needed development. It arose in Old English, probably under the influence of the compound popular Latin perfect with the same formation. This Latin formation has become established in a number of other languages, but its original meaning has changed in most of them. In German and French it points not only to the immediate past — its original meaning — but also to a remote act without the slightest relation to the present, thus taking over the two meanings of the simple Latin perfect. In Italian, Spanish, and English it retains more of its original meaning, pointing for the most part to the immediate past. In English the person or thing referred to must be living or still existing and thus related to the present: 'My grandfather *has seen* a good deal in his lifetime,' but not 'Cæsar *has seen* a good deal in his lifetime.' 'England *has had* many able rulers,' but 'Assyria *had* many able rulers,' for Assyria does not now exist as an independent country. The English present perfect can refer to the remote past if the present is not excluded by the statement: 'Such epidemics *have occurred* in all ages.' Such statements are in English always indefinite. On the other hand, the passing of a single minute may make it impossible to employ the present perfect. A minute before 12 o'clock in the morning we may say 'I *have bought* a new hat this morning.' A minute later this morning is gone forever and the afternoon is ushered in. After the bell taps twelve we must say 'I *bought* a new hat this morning,' for the morning belongs to the past. Thus the present perfect distinguishes sharply between present and past. It can never be used for something past. We can say 'I *have been* in England twice,' for we are thinking of our life, which is not ended; but we cannot say 'I *have been* in England twice last year,' for last year is past forever.

In the above examples we have seen how closely the present perfect is associated with the present. Sometimes it seems to have the full force of the present: 'I *have got* a cold' = 'I *have* a cold.' In our southern American dialect the present perfect assumes the ending of the present tense — the *-s* that appears in all persons and numbers, as described in **54**: 'I [have] *gots* good news' (DuBose Heyward, *Porgy*, p. 54). Here, however, *have got* can take the place of *have* only with reference to the present moment. It can never, like the present of *have*, be used to express customary action. Thus it cannot replace *have* in 'We *have* a good deal of rain here in the fall.'

On the other hand, we often do not employ the present perfect of a past event closely connected with the present moment. If we think of the past event as past we use the past tense even though only a moment has passed since its occurrence: 'I am glad you *came*' (Hergesheimer, *Balisand*, p. 203). These words are spoken by a woman standing in the doorway of her house welcoming two visitors. The following examples are similar: '*Did* you *see* him do it?' (referring to something that has just taken place). 'I am sure he *did* it. I *saw* him do it.' '*Did* you ever *see* anything to beat it?' (Tarkington, *Napoleon Was a Little Man*). In referring to something that has taken place the speaker uses the past tense when he speaks in a lively tone with a vivid impression of the past in his mind, i.e. with his mind still turned to the past. He employs the present perfect when he speaks in a calmer, more detached tone, feeling clearly that he is standing in the present looking backward: '*Have* you ever *seen* anything to beat it?' Thus the present perfect is the tense of personal experience.

Earlier in the present period the auxiliary of the present perfect of intransitives was often *be* instead of *have*. In accordance with older usage *be* was used with verbs indicating a change of place or condition: 'The King himself *is rode* to view the battle' (Shakespeare, *Henry the Fifth*, IV, III, 2). 'I *am* this instant *arrived* here' (William Marsh, *Letter*, written at Albany, N. Y., Apr. 18, 1763). 'Nor do I know what *is become* of him' (Butler, *Hudibras*, I, III, 263, A.D. 1663). 'For this orphan I *am come* to you' (Tennyson, *Dora*, 89). We still use *be* when we think of a state pure and simple: 'My money *is* all *gone*.' 'Children, you must be good while I *am gone*.' 'He *is* so terribly *changed* that you wouldn't recognize him.' 'My children *are* all *grown*-up.' But where the idea of an action as a whole is in our mind, as in the example from Shakespeare, we now employ *have*, not *be*, for we now feel *have* as the more appropriate tense auxiliary to express the terminate (**52** 3) idea, i.e. an action as a whole: 'The King *has ridden* away to view the battle.' 'John *has grown* (an action as a whole) a good deal the last two years, but he *is* not yet fully *grown*' (state). This change has brought us more accurate expression. We can now distinguish action and state.

c. Use of 'Be' instead of 'Have' with Transitive Verbs. In certain British dialects the auxiliaries *have* and *be* are sometimes confounded, so that forms of *be* are used instead of forms of *have*. Also in certain American dialects: '*Is* (instead of *have*) you seed any sign er (of) my gran'son dis mawnin'?' (Joel Chandler Harris, *Nights with Uncle Remus*, p. 55).

66. Past Perfect. This tense is made up of the past tense of the auxiliary *have* and the past participle of the verb to be inflected.

	Indicative	Subjunctive
	Singular	
1.	I had taken	I had taken
2.	you had taken (thou hadst taken)	you had taken (thou hadst taken)
3.	he had taken	he had taken
	Plural	
1.	we had taken	we had taken
2.	you (ye) had taken	you (ye) had taken
3.	they had taken	they had taken

a. Origin of Past Perfect. This tense was originally a past tense just as the present perfect was originally a present tense. The description of the development of the present perfect, given in **65** *b*, will make the development of the past perfect clear.

b. 'Be' Used instead of 'Have' as Auxiliary in Older English. In older English *was* was often used instead of *had* as auxiliary in the past perfect, just as *is* was used instead of *has* as auxiliary in the present perfect, as described in **65** *b* (last par.).

67. Future Tense. There are two entirely different types of expression in English to indicate future time.

1. *Present and Past Used as Future Forms.* In oldest English the present tense was the usual form employed to express future time, and it is still commonly employed for this purpose where an adverb or conjunction of time or the situation makes the thought clear: 'The ship *sails* tomorrow.' 'Wait until I *come*.' For fuller statement see *Syntax*, **37** 1 *e*. As this old means of expression is not accurate enough for higher purposes, it has long been common to employ an especial form to express future time, the future tense described in 2 below.

This is true, however, only for the indicative. No especial future form for the subjunctive has developed, nor has there been any need for such, for the old type of expression had great possibilities of development.

In oldest English, the simple present subjunctive was much used to express future time, and it can often still be used in choice language: 'We shall have passed Dover tomorrow if the wind *keep* favorable.' The simple subjunctive has for the most part been gradually replaced by a compound form made up of a modal auxiliary (*may, might, shall, should, will, would*, etc.) and the infinitive of the verb to be conjugated. The newer compound subjunctive forms have by virtue of the fine expressive power of these various modal auxiliaries more shades of meaning than the old simple forms. The old type of expression, however, has been retained. In this old type there are two tenses of the subjunctive employed for reference to the future — the present and the past — which differ only in the *manner* of the conception, the present tense expressing a greater degree of probability. Thus the present tense in 'It *may* rain' expresses greater probability than the past tense in 'It *might* rain.' Compare **50** 2 *d*. As the uncertainty in the outcome of future events is great, the past tense form of the subjunctive is a pronounced favorite. In conditional sentences (**50** 2 *b*) when future events present themselves to our mind in only a vague, indefinite way, we employ a past subjunctive in the condition, and in the conclusion employ *should* in the first person and *would* in the second and third persons: 'If it *rained* (or *should rain* or *were to rain* — indicating decreasing grades of probability) tomorrow, I *should*, or he *would*, be very much disappointed.' *Would* here in the first person of the conclusion represents the future act as intended: 'If it *rained* (or *should* rain or *were* to rain) tomorrow, I *would* stay at home.' A modest opinion as to a future result is expressed by *should* in the third person: 'If everything goes right, the work *should* be done by tomorrow evening.' In wishing with the verb *like* we employ *should* in the first person and *would* in the second and third persons; but we use *should* in the second person in questions, for we expect the person addressed to answer in the first person with *should:* 'I *should like* to go.' 'I know he *would like* to go.' '*Should* you *like* to go?'

The use of the subjunctive forms is treated in **50** 2 and in *Syntax*, **41–44.**

2. *Future Indicative.* This form is made up of the present tense of the auxiliary *shall* or *will* and the simple infinitive of the verb to be inflected. In independent declarative sentences *shall* is employed in the first person and *will* in the second and the third:

Singular

1. I shall take
2. you will take — you'll take
   (thou wilt take)
3. he will take — he'll take

Plural

1. we shall take
2. you (ye) will take — you'll take
3. they will take — they'll take

There are peculiar difficulties connected with the use of the indicative of this tense, since the employment of *shall* and *will* in the different persons varies according to the form of the sentence and the meaning to be conveyed. To express the idea of pure futurity we employ for the declarative form *shall* in the first person and *will* in the second and third persons: 'We *shall be* very poor, at the start, but we feel sure that things *will improve* later.' 'I *shall be* nineteen years old on the third of July, and my brother *will be* twenty-two on the same day.' 'If he doesn't come tomorrow I *shall be* very sorry, and I know that you *will* [*be*], too.' If an element of will, desire, determination enters into the statement we employ *will* for the first person and *shall* for the second and third persons: '*I will* (or *I'll*) *help* you all I can,' but 'You *shall do* as I say.' '*We will* (or *we'll*) *do* our best,' but 'You *shall pay* for that.' 'I'*ll* (or *will*) never *give* my consent to that,' but 'I mean it; nothing *shall stop* me.' Thus *will* in the first person and *shall* in the second and third persons are not tense auxiliaries but modal auxiliaries. *Shall* in the first person is not always, however, a future tense auxiliary. Sometimes it is a modal auxiliary, clearly differentiated from modal *will* in meaning. Modal *will* represents something as sprung from the feeling of the moment. Modal *shall* represents the resolution as the result of previous deliberation, or deep conviction, or deeply rooted feeling, and represents the execution as assured: 'I *shall stand* my ground as firmly as I can.' 'Then, Patty, since you make me choose, I *shall* not *give* up the Lord even for you' (Eggleston, *Circuit Rider*, Ch. XIX). '"I *shall do* my share," said Unkerlarther sturdily' (J. B. Priestley, *The Good Companions*, p. 499).

In the second person in questions that auxiliary is used which is expected in the answer, so that also in questions we must carefully distinguish between *tense* and *modal* auxiliaries: '*Shall* (tense auxiliary) we have the pleasure of seeing you tomorrow?' '*Will* (tense auxiliary) he come tomorrow?' '*Shall* (tense auxiliary) you have time enough tomorrow to do this for me?' corresponding to the expected answer, 'I *shall* have time enough'; but '*Will* (modal auxiliary) you do this for me?' i.e. 'Are you willing to do this for me?' corresponding to the expected answer, 'I *will* do it for you.'

Will is used by some in the first person as a pure future when in a compound subject *I* or *we* is preceded by a pronoun in the second person, or by a noun or pronoun in the third person: 'you and I *will* get on excellently well' (Dickens, *Martin Chuzzlewit*, Ch. V). 'Eddie and I *will* be delighted to come on Monday' (A. Marshall, *The Greatest of These*, Ch. X). The preceding pronoun or noun in the second or third person here influences the selection of the auxiliary. But we employ *will* here also to express willingness, intention, so that the tone of the voice or the context must decide the meaning: 'John and I *will* assist you.' To express the pure future idea, however, others employ *shall* if one of the subjects is a pronoun in the first person: 'I hope Chattam and I *shall* (preferred by many to *will*) always be good friends' (George Eliot, *Middlemarch*, I, Ch. VI).

In dependent clauses the use of *shall* and *will* is the same as that found in independent statements except that instead of *will* in the third person *shall* is in British usage often employed where it corresponds to a *shall* in the direct statement: 'Sir Hugo says he *shall* (in the direct I *shall*) come to stay at Diplow' (George Eliot). 'He thinks himself that he *shall* (in the direct *I shall*) recover, but the doctor says that he will die soon.' In America we employ *will* here.

The use of *shall* and *should* (see 1 above) as future forms for the first person is literary usage. In our colloquial speech we employ *will* or *would* for all persons uniformly. The modal forms are the same for both literary and colloquial language. The literary pure future forms developed in the southeastern part of England, and in early colonial days were spoken and written in New England and in a general sense are still recognized as our literary standard. Our American colloquial speech has been influenced by heavy streams of immigration which have brought us large numbers of people from Ireland and other parts of Great Britain than the southeast. These immigrants brought with them *will* as a uniform pure future form. At the present time it is natural for most Americans to use this pure future form in colloquial language.

For a more detailed treatment of the future tense see *Syntax*, **57** 5 *a*.

a. Aspect Form instead of the Future Tense. The usual future tense (**67** 2) has terminate (**52** 1) force, i.e. represents the act as a whole. The expanded form of *go* often points to the future. In **52** 2 *c* we see that the expanded form is widely employed as an aspect form to call attention to the beginning or to the end of an act. Beginning: 'Look out! I *am going to shoot!*' Here the expanded form of *go* points to the preparations for the act, indicating that it will follow immediately. The expanded form of *go* is much used to make known that preparations are being made for some act, either one near at hand or one farther off: 'There *is going to be* a circus here next week.' 'I *am going to study* in Germany next year.' This form is much used to point also to the end of a development: 'This bright little chap *is going to be* a great man some day.' Again, it is widely employed to point to the outcome of events: 'The world *is going to look* at this differently some day.'

The expanded form of *go* is often called a future tense form, but two things — the expanded form and the peculiar meanings of the form — show that it is primarily an aspect form. It points, not to the future act as a whole, but to a preparing for or an outcome.

68. Future Perfect Tense. This tense is differently formed in the indicative and the subjunctive:

1. *Future Perfect Indicative.* This form is the same as the future indicative, described in **67** 2, with the exception that the present perfect infinitive is used instead of the present infinitive:

Singular	*Plural*
1. I shall have taken	1. we shall have taken
2. you will have taken (thou wilt have taken)	2. you (ye) will have taken
3. he will have taken	3. they will have taken

This form represents that an action or state will be completed at or before a certain time yet future: 'I *shall have completed* the task by evening.' 'He *will have completed* the task by evening.' For fuller treatment see *Syntax*, **37** 6.

2. *Future Perfect Subjunctive.* To express the probable completion of an act in the future we employ the past subjunctive *should* in the first person and the past subjunctive *would* in the second and third persons in connection with a perfect infinitive: '*I should have finished* (or *he would have finished*), the work by tomorrow evening if everything had gone right.' The use of *would* in the first person represents the completion of the future act as intended: 'I *would* have gone tomorrow evening if things had gone right.' A modest opinion as to a future result is expressed by *should* in the third person: 'If things should go right, they *should have completed* the work by tomorrow evening, or they *should complete* the work by tomorrow evening.'

FULL INFLECTION OF VERBS

Active

69. *Take* may serve as a model.

A. Common Form

Present

Indicative	Subjunctive
I take	take
you take	take
(thou takĕst)	(take)
he takes	take
(he takĕth)	

INDICATIVE	SUBJUNCTIVE
we take	take
you (ye) take	take
they take	take

IMPERATIVE take (old forms, take thou, take ye)

PARTICIPLE	INFINITIVE
taking (**56** 1 *d*)	to take (**56** 1 *d*)

GERUND taking (**56** 1 *d* and **47** 6 *b*)

Past

INDICATIVE	SUBJUNCTIVE
I took	took
you took	took
(thou tookĕst)	(tookĕst)
he took	took
we took	took
you (ye) took	took
they took	took

Present Perfect

INDICATIVE		SUBJUNCTIVE	
I have	taken	have	taken
you have		have	
(thou hast)		(have)	
he has		have	
(he hath)			
we have		have	
you (ye) have		have	
they have		have	

IMPERATIVE have done (**50** 3, next to last par.)

PARTICIPLE	INFINITIVE
having taken (**65** *a*)	(to) have taken (**47** 5 *b*)

GERUND having taken (**47** 6 *b*)

Past Perfect

INDICATIVE		SUBJUNCTIVE	
I had	taken	had	taken
you had		had	
(thou hadst)		(hadst)	
he had		had	
we had		had	
you (ye) had		had	
they had		had	

Future	*Future Perfect*
INDICATIVE	INDICATIVE
I shall take	shall have taken
you will take	will have taken
(thou wilt take)	(wilt have taken)
he will take	will have taken
we shall take	shall have taken
you (ye) will take	will have taken
they will take	will have taken
For SUBJUNCTIVE see **67** 1.	For SUBJUNCTIVE see **68** 2.

B. **Expanded Form** (**47** 2)

Present

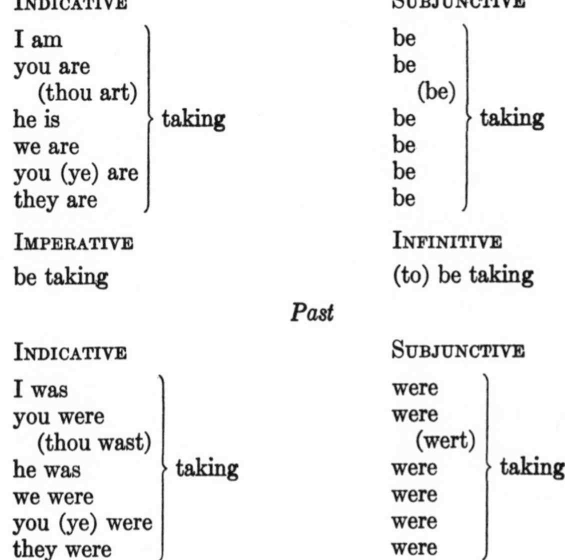

INDICATIVE	SUBJUNCTIVE
I am } taking	be } taking
you are	be
(thou art)	(be)
he is	be
we are	be
you (ye) are	be
they are	be

IMPERATIVE	INFINITIVE
be taking	(to) be taking

Past

INDICATIVE	SUBJUNCTIVE
I was } taking	were } taking
you were	were
(thou wast)	(wert)
he was	were
we were	were
you (ye) were	were
they were	were

Present Perfect

INDICATIVE	SUBJUNCTIVE
I have been } taking	have been } taking
you have been	have been
(thou hast been)	(have been)
he has been	have been
(he hath been)	
we have been	have been
you (ye) have been	have been
they have been	have been

PARTICIPLE	INFINITIVE
having been taking	(to) have been taking

GERUND having been taking

Past Perfect

INDICATIVE		SUBJUNCTIVE	
I had been	taking	had been	taking
you had been		had been	
(thou hadst been)		(hadst been)	
he had been		had been	
we had been		had been	
you (ye) had been		had been	
they had been		had been	

Future		*Future Perfect*	
INDICATIVE		INDICATIVE	
I shall be	taking	shall have been	taking
you will be		will have been	
(thou wilt be)		(wilt have been)	
he will be		will have been	
we shall be		shall have been	
you (ye) will be		will have been	
they will be		will have been	

The future and future perfect SUBJUNCTIVE forms are treated in **67** 1, **68** 2.

C. 'Do'-Form (**47** 3)

Present

INDICATIVE	SUBJUNCTIVE
I do take	do take
you do take	do take
(thou dost take)	(do take)
he does take	do take
(he doth take)	
we do take	do take
you (ye) do take	do take
they do take	do take

Past

INDICATIVE	SUBJUNCTIVE
I did take	did take
you did take	did take
(thou didst take)	(didst take)
he did take	did take

INDICATIVE	SUBJUNCTIVE
we did take	did take
you (ye) did take	did take
they did take	did take

PASSIVE

70. The full forms follow.

A. Common Form

Present

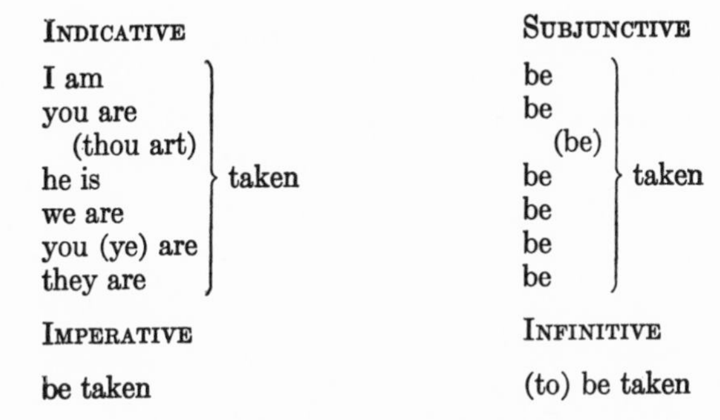

INDICATIVE		SUBJUNCTIVE	
I am	taken	be	taken
you are		be	
(thou art)		(be)	
he is		be	
we are		be	
you (ye) are		be	
they are		be	

IMPERATIVE	INFINITIVE
be taken	(to) be taken

GERUND being taken

PARTICIPLE being taken

Past

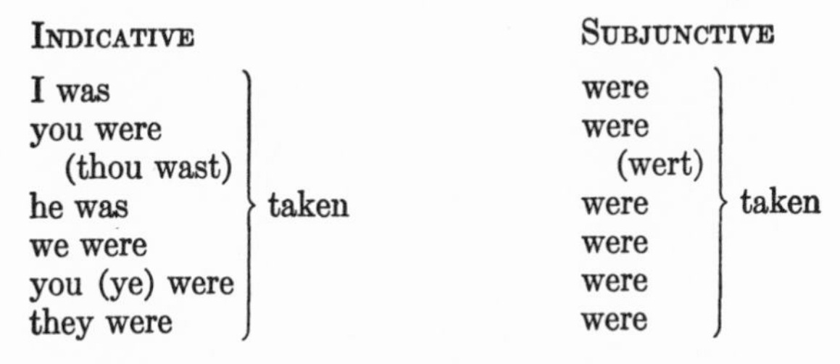

INDICATIVE		SUBJUNCTIVE	
I was	taken	were	taken
you were		were	
(thou wast)		(wert)	
he was		were	
we were		were	
you (ye) were		were	
they were		were	

Present Perfect

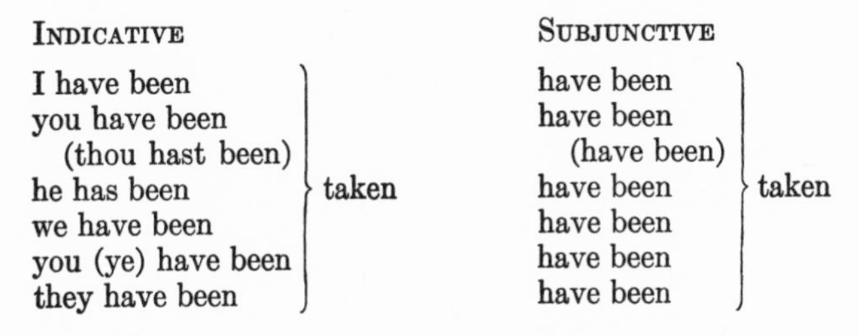

INDICATIVE		SUBJUNCTIVE	
I have been	taken	have been	taken
you have been		have been	
(thou hast been)		(have been)	
he has been		have been	
we have been		have been	
you (ye) have been		have been	
they have been		have been	

PARTICIPLE	INFINITIVE
having been taken	(to) have been taken

GERUND having been taken

In older English, the present perfect passive had the form of the present passive: I *am taken*, etc. See **49** 1.

Past Perfect

INDICATIVE		SUBJUNCTIVE	
I had been		had been	
you had been		had been	
(thou hadst been)		(hadst been)	
he had been	taken	had been	taken
we had been		had been	
you (ye) had been		had been	
they had been		had been	

In older English, the past perfect passive had the form of the past passive: I *was taken*, etc.

Future		*Future Perfect*	
INDICATIVE		INDICATIVE	
I shall be		shall have been	
you will be		will have been	
(thou wilt be)		(wilt have been)	
he will be	taken	will have been	taken
we shall be		shall have been	
you (ye) will be		will have been	
they will be		will have been	

a. Time Relations Indicated by the Passive Forms of the Participle. The different tenses of the verbal forms indicate accurately the time of the action, but in the case of the adjective forms the time relations are indicated only by the situation: this *broken* (a present state) chair; a man *respected* (= *who is respected*) by everybody; a bridge *destroyed* (past perfect = *which had been destroyed*) two hours before by the enemy; a feat often *performed* (present perfect = *which has often been performed*) by me. *Having been deceived* (= *Since I have been deceived*) so often, I am now on my guard. He is a man *broken* (= *who has been broken*) by misfortune. *Having been more strongly opposed* (= *Since they had been more strongly opposed*) than they expected, they retreated. 'His last novel, *written* (past = *which was written*) in 1925, is his best.' Compare *Syntax*, **48** 2 (2nd par.).

B. Expanded Form (49 3)

Present

INDICATIVE		SUBJUNCTIVE
I am being you are being (thou art being) he is being we are being you (ye) are being they are being	taken	(lacking)

IMPERATIVE, INFINITIVE, PARTICIPLE, GERUND, are lacking.

Past

INDICATIVE		SUBJUNCTIVE	
I was being you were being (thou wast being) he was being we were being you (ye) were being they were being	taken	were being were being (wert being) were being were being were being were being	taken

Present Perfect

INDICATIVE (**49** 3 *a*)

it has been building
they have been building

SUBJUNCTIVE

it have been building
they have been building

PARTICIPLE

having been building

INFINITIVE

(to) have been building

Past Perfect

INDICATIVE (**49** 3 *a*)

it had been building
they had been building

SUBJUNCTIVE

it had been building
they had been building

Future

INDICATIVE (**49** 3 *a*)

it will be building
they will be building

Future Perfect

INDICATIVE (**49** 3 *a*)

it will have been building
they will have been building

CHAPTER XIII

FORM AND COMPARISON OF ADVERBS

71. In the following articles are discussed matters pertaining to the form of adverbs in the positive, comparative, and superlative.

1. **Form of Simple Adverbs.** Adverbs have in part no distinctive form, as in the case of *here, there, then, when, where, why, late, straight, far, near, close, quick, slow, fast, high, low, much, little, very, right, wrong, cheap, just, well,* etc.; in part they have the distinctive suffix *-ly*, as in *rapidly, diligently, hurriedly, powerfully,* etc.; also often in the case of some of the words in the first group, which have a form in *-ly* alongside of their simple form, as in *slowly, quickly, highly, rightly, cheaply,* etc. Sometimes the two forms are differentiated in meaning: 'I'll go as *high* as a hundred dollars,' but 'The wood is *highly* polished.' 'He aimed *higher,*' but 'We ought to value our privileges more *highly.*' 'He sat up *late,*' but 'He died *lately.*' 'We are doing *fine*' (colloquial for *very well*), but 'These greenish tints contrast *finely* (= *splendidly*) with the moon's own soft white.' 'He works *hard,*' but 'I could *hardly* hear him.' 'He lives *near* (originally an adverb, as shown here by its comparative form *nearer*, but now widely felt as a preposition) us, *nearer* to us,' but 'It is *nearly* done.' 'He is *real* (colloquial for *very*) good,' but 'He is *really* (sentence adverb) good.' 'The bird is now flying quite *low,*' but 'He bowed *lowly* before the duchess,' i.e. bowed humbly and respectfully. 'You know *jolly* (slang for *very*) well,' but 'He smiled *jollily.*' 'Speak *loud* and distinctly,' but 'He boasted *loudly* of his power.' With certain adverbs we use the simple form after the modified word and the form with *-ly* before it: 'He guessed *right,*' but 'He

rightly guessed that it was safe.' 'He spelled the words *wrong*,' but 'the *wrongly* spelled words.' Earlier in the period the old simple form was often used where we now employ the form in *-ly:* 'to haue him stand in the raine till he was *through* (or *thorough*) wet' (Thomas Nashe, *The Vnfortvnate Traveller*, Works, II, p. 246, A.D. 1594), now '*thoroughly* wet'; but the old simple form is preserved in *thorough*bred, *thorough*going, etc. 'She is not *near* (now *nearly*) so small as I had expected' (Horace Walpole, *Letter to Miss Mary Berry*, Sept. 25, 1793). *Scarce* was widely used in early Modern English, but is now employed only in rather choice language, yielding to *scarcely* in normal speech.

In older English, many adverbs had the suffix *-e*, which distinguished them from the corresponding adjectives. In the fifteenth century, after this ending had disappeared, many adjectives and adverbs had the same form. For a long while there has been a tendency to distinguish the adverb from the adjective by giving it the suffix *-ly*, as indicated above. The old simple form, though often replaced by the new form in *-ly*, often remains firm before an adjective or participle: *líght yèllow, dárk blùe, déad drùnk, précious lìttle, míghty delìghtful, búrning hòt, réd hòt, stárk nàked, prétty brìght*; *néw làid* eggs, *módern bùilt* house, *fóreign bòrn* citizens, etc. These are in large measure modern formations, but we feel them as groups akin to our old compounds for which we still have a lively feeling. In the old compounds the modifying word always precedes the governing word, so that the word-order of itself makes the grammatical relations clear and hence the lack of a distinctive adverbial ending is not keenly felt. But here, as also elsewhere, distinctive grammatical forms are sometimes introduced: an *uncommon* or *uncommonly* fine fellow; *terrible* or *terribly* strong; an *exceeding* or *exceedingly* great joy; a *newly* married pair; the *newly* appointed chaplain; etc. We should distinguish between 'a *góod-nàtured* boy,' where the compound *gòod náture* has been converted into a derivative adjective by means of the suffix *-ed*, and 'a *wéll-behàved* boy,' where *behaved* is an adjective participle and *well* the modifying adverb. Similarly, we say 'a *hígh-tèmpered* man,' but '*híghly sèasoned* food.' In many cases we can construe a group of words according to either of these two types, hence we often find a difference of usage: *íll-mànnered*, 'the *most swéetly mànnered* gentleman alive' (Disraeli, *Endymion*, III, III, 25), but also *géntle-mànnered, símple-mannered.* In both constructions the stress shifts to the second component in the predicate: 'He is *gòod-nátured.*' 'He is *wèll beháved.*'

On the other hand, after verbs, where the word-order is always different from that required in compounds, the tendency is to give the adverb its distinctive suffix: '*wíde*- òpen,' but 'He àdvertises *wídely*'; '*tíght*-fìtting,' but 'He clàsped his hands *tíghtly* together.'

While in the literary language the form with *-ly* is becoming ever more firmly fixed, colloquial and popular speech still cling tenaciously to the older type of expression without *-ly*, especially in American and Irish English: 'I wánted to do it *bad* (instead of the usual literary form *badly*) enough, and if it was to do over again I wóuld' (Mark Twain, *Joan of Arc*, Book I, Ch. IV). 'He (a certain dog) isn't anyway *near* (instead of literary *nearly*) as full-blooded as Duke' (Tarkington, *Penrod Jashber*, Ch. I). 'I beat them *easy*' (instead of the literary form *easily*), but also in good English with the short form in 'to take it *easy*' and 'to let one off *easy*.' This conservative tendency in colloquial and popular speech to employ the old type is especially noticeable in the case of sentence adverbs (see **15 1** *b*), where in the literary language the form with *-ly* is most firmly established: 'It *sure* (in the literary language *surely*) will help.'

In older English, *-ly* was often added to adverbs formed from adjectives in *-ly*, and this older usage survives in a few adverbs: *holily, jollily* (see 1st par.), *sillily, wilily*. In general, *-ly* is now avoided here as awkward, although elsewhere there is a strong tendency toward it on account of its distinctiveness. The present tendency in this particular group is to employ the adjective also as an adverb, as in *early, daily, hourly, friendly, kindly, only*, etc. In many other words, however, we avoid such adverbs, as we feel their lack of distinctive form.

It is common to form an adverb out of a compound adjective provided the final element in the compound is an adjective form: *world-wide*, adv. *world-widely; high-minded*, adv. *high-mindedly*. If the final element is a noun we must employ the compound adjective also as an adverb: 'a *first-rate* (adj.) machine.' 'I am getting along *first-rate*' (adv.).

a. Genitive, Dative, and Accusative Used Adverbially. In oldest English, nouns in the genitive, dative, and accusative were often used adverbially. The old adverbial genitive survives in a few nouns and adverbs in the literary language and in a much larger number in popular speech: must *needs, nowadays, once* (i.e. *ones*, from *one*), *twice* (formerly *twies*), *thrice, unawares, afterward* (especially in America) or *afterwards, backward* or *backwards, forward* or *forwards, onward* or less commonly *onwards, seaward* or *seawards, sideways, always*, etc.; in popular speech *anywheres, somewheres, nowheres*, etc., instead of the literary forms *anywhere, somewhere, nowhere*, etc. In colloquial speech it is still common in a few nouns to indicate repeated occurrence, but is now felt as an accusative plural: 'returning *nights* to his home' (F. J. Mather, *Chaucer's Prologue*, p. vii). 'Farmer Spurrier could see the plow at work before he got out of bed *mornings*' (H. C. O'Neill, *Told in the Dimpses*, p. 28). After the analogy of such common expressions we now often use this plural accusative: 'The museum is open *Sundays*' (or *on Sundays*). The modern prepositional genitive is used in 'of a morning,' 'of an evening,' 'of a Sunday afternoon,' 'of late years,' 'of rainy afternoons,' etc. In popular speech an excrescent *t* is often added to the genitive form *once: wunst.* While the literary language rejects the genitive form with excrescent *t* here, it has adopted it in the case of *amongst* and *whilst*, adverbial genitive forms now used alongside of *among* and *while* as preposition and subordinate conjunction.

The old dative plural survives in *whilom* (= *formerly*), now used only in poetry or archaic language. It is the old dative plural form of the noun *while*, used adverbially: '*Whilom* she was a daughter of Locrine' (Milton, *Comus*, 827). It is sometimes, like certain other adverbs, used also as an adjective: 'his *whilom* associates.'

The old adverbial accusative of extent is well preserved in the case of nouns: 'They remained *a long while, three years.*' 'It is *a long way* off.' 'He went *the full length.*' 'That went *a long way* toward remedying the evil.' 'He walked *two miles.*' 'He will not swerve a hair's *breadth* from the truth.' 'The lake is *three miles* wide.' 'He is *fourteen years* old.' 'The garden is *one hundred and seventy feet* long.' 'He towers *head* and *shoulders* above his contemporaries.' 'The sober sense of the community are *heart* and *soul* with the Chief of Police in his crusade.' 'Vivisection must be abolished *root* and *branch.*' In early Modern English, the genitive was not infrequently used here instead of the accusative, and this older usage still lingers in popular speech, which here, as in the first paragraph, is quite fond of the genitive as a more distinctive form: 'He'd given up sea-faring and moved quite *a way's* inland' (Amy Lowell, *East Wind*, p. 188, A.D. 1926). 'It seems *a long ways* off.'

The adverbial accusative of extent is common also in the case of indefinite pronouns, especially *a bit, every bit, a lot, lots, a sight* (colloquial and popular), and *whatever* in the meaning *at all*, also with other indefinites when used in connection with *too* or a comparative: 'Wait *a bit.*' 'I am *every bit* as good as you.' 'I am not *a bit* tired.' 'I have *a lot* (or *lots*) more to tell you.' 'I have *lots* more things to show her' (Clyde Fitch, *Letter*, Feb. 10, 1903). 'It is *a long sight* better' (*Concise Oxford Dictionary*), or more commonly '*a darn sight* better.' 'There is no doubt *whatever.*' 'Is there any chance *whatever?*' 'I cannot see anyone *whatever.*' 'No one *whatever* would have anything to do with him.' '*What* (= *to what extent* or *in what way*) is he the better for it?' 'The help came *none* too soon.' 'It is *much* too large.' 'The triumphant people haven't *any* too much food' (*Westminster Gazette*, No. 7069, 6 *a*). 'He is *none* the worse for his fall.' 'The baby is dying slowly but *none* the less surely.' 'He is resting *all* the better for it.' 'Is he resting *any* the better for it?' 'Is he resting *any* better today?' 'I began to think that it was of no use crying *any* more.' 'She is not *any* less beautiful today than she has ever been.' 'Isn't it *any* later than that?' or in American colloquial speech also: 'Is that *all* the later it is?' '*Nothing* daunted, he began again.' 'He is *a little* better.' 'He is *much* better, *much* taller.' *Much* and *little* are often used outside of the comparative: 'I don't care *much* about it.' 'I care *little* about it.' *Much* is often used sarcastically: '*Much* (= *not at all*) you care about my feelings!'

In general, *any, some, none,* except with *too* and the comparative, are now not so common in England as earlier in the period, but in American colloquial speech there is still a great fondness for these forms: 'I slept *none* that night,' or 'I didn't sleep *any* that night.' 'If our readers are *any* like ourselves, we think they cannot help laughing' (*Analetic Magazine* [Phila.], IX, 437, A.D. 1817). 'A tall fellow . . . stammers *some* in his speech' (runaway advertisement in *Mass. Spy*, Apr. 28, 1785). 'I walk *some* every day.' This usage survives also in Scotland: 'You will quarrel *nane* with Captain Cleveland' (Scott, *Pirate*, Ch. XVIII). 'Having slept scarcely *any* all the night' (Hugh Miller, *Scenes and Legends*, XXX, 450). Scotch influence has strengthened the conservative American tendency here. It occasionally occurs in English writers after verbs: 'He may walk *some*, perhaps — not much' (Dickens in Forster's *Life*, III, IV). In American slang *some* often assumes strong intensive force: 'The papers will make it *some* hot for you' (Robert Herrick, *Memoirs of an American Citizen*, p. 310).

Similarly, the accusative of the comparatives *more, less,* and the superlatives *most, the most, least, the least* are much used adverbially: 'If indiscretion be a sign of love, you are *the most* a lover of anybody that I know' (Congreve, *Love for Love*, I, II, 354, A.D. 1695); now more commonly '*the most* a lover of all that I know,' or '*more* a lover than any other person that I know.'

The old adverbial accusative of goal (*Syntax*, **11** 2) after verbs of motion is preserved in *home:* 'He went *home.*' 'They brought the charge *home* to him.' 'I was *home* by six.' In the last example the verb of motion is not expressed, but the idea of motion is implied. In colloquial and popular speech *home* is improperly used where there is no idea of motion implied: 'I won't live *home* (for literary *at home*) — even if the old gent would let me' (Eugene O'Neill, *Dynamo*, p. 99). In compounds, however, *home* is used also in the literary language where there is no idea of motion implied: *home*-made, *home*-grown, *home*-brewed, etc. *Home* is here an old uninflected locative (*Syntax*, **62,** next to last par.) meaning *at home*. This type of expression has come down to us from the prehistoric period.

The accusative of definite and indefinite time is common: 'I go to Europe *every two years*.' 'The money was paid *the following day*.' '*First thing* in the morning he smokes a cigarette' (Krapp, *A Comprehensive Guide to Good English*). 'He often goes round *the last thing* to make sure that all is right' (*Routledge's Every Boy's Annual*). 'I met him *one day* on the street.' Also the accusative of way: 'Step *this way*, please!' 'I will take you *another way*.' Also the accusative of price: 'This hat cost *five dollars*.'

The adverbial accusative construction has replaced others less common and even some once common, since we now feel that the accusative is the natural case form of a noun that completes the meaning of the verb. It is now much used to denote manner: 'He came *full speed*.' 'The blindfolded man ran *full tilt* into the fence.' 'Have it *your own way*.' 'The windows of the tower face *both ways*.' 'Having sampled America [*in*] *that way*, Europe believes and trusts America' (Woodrow Wilson, July 4, 1919). 'She ran her fingers comb *fashion* through her hair.' 'They went at it *hammer and tongs*.' 'Let us go *shares, halves!*' 'I came in and went to bed *the same* as usual.' 'Then why do you come *your frowning high and mighty airs* with me?' (William Heyliger, *American Boy*, Sept., 1927, p. 34). 'You can't come *it* with me.' In colloquial speech *sure thing* is often used as an intensive form of colloquial *sure* (= literary *surely*): 'Now that you boys know what the expedition is going to face are you still anxious to go along?' — '*Sure thing*' (Victor Appleton, *Don Sturdy in Lion Land*, Ch. IV). Also to indicate time, where in more careful language we find a preposition: '*What* (or *at what*) time do you go?' Also to indicate place in certain set expressions, but rarely with a single unmodified noun: 'He struck me *on the head*,' but 'He smote them *hip* and *thigh*.' 'Bind them *hand* and *foot!*' In the concrete language of popular speech the adverbial accusative of a modified noun is often used instead of an adverb: 'I looked *every place* (instead of literary *everywhere*) for it.' '*What place* (instead of literary *where*) would we run?' (Synge, *The Well of the Saints*, Act.III). Compare **27** 2 *b* for the use of the relative pronoun *that* as an adverbial accusative.

In many distributive expressions, the noun following *a* is now construed as an adverbial accusative of extent, but the *a*, though now felt as an indefinite article, is in fact the reduced form of the preposition *on:* 'I visit him twice *a year.*' 'A robin frequently raises two broods *a season.*' This construction was originally confined to expressions of time, as in these examples, but it now has much wider boundaries: 'His terms are a penny *a line.*' 'She asks five dollars *a lesson.*' 'I paid six dollars *a pair* for my shoes.' The definite article is sometimes used here instead of the indefinite: 'She sold her corn at ten shillings *the bushel*' (Winthrop, *Journal*, Apr. 27, 1631). 'Wheat was at twenty shillings *the quarter*' (Macaulay, *History*, I, Ch. III). 'Five cents *the copy*' (*The Saturday Evening Post*, Aug. 8, 1925). 'How much is salmon *the can* now?' (Zona Gale, *Miss Lulu Bett*, Ch. I). We now feel *can* in the last example as an accusative of extent; but perhaps, originally, it was a nominative, an appositive to *salmon*. Most of these expressions, except those indicating time, may have originated in this way.

b. *'This' and 'That' Used Adverbially.* In the fifteenth century the principle of employing the accusative of indefinite pronouns adverbially to indicate extent or degree was extended to the definite pronouns *this* and *that:* '*This* (or *that* or *thus* or *so*) much I hold to be true.' This usage is best established in the case of '*this* much' and '*that* much,' but in colloquial language it has spread much farther: 'I've never been *this* sick before.' 'He didn't get home until after one o'clock, and his mother told him if he ever came home *that* late again she would punish him severely.' On account of the accuracy of expression here adverbial *this* and *that* are sometimes employed in the literary language, in spite of the protests of grammarians: '"Oh, Mimo! how could you let him sit on the grass!" Zara exclaimed reproachfully, when he got *this* far' (Elinor Glyn, *The Reason Why*, Ch. XV). 'I didn't think he was *that* young' (Jack London, *Martin Eden*, I, Ch. II). Also used like *so*, pointing to a following clause of result: 'I'm *that* hungry, I could eat a dog' (Hall Caine, *The Woman Thou Gavest Me*, Ch. IV). Quite commonly in popular speech: 'I was just *that* pleased I set down an' bust out cryin" (Alice Hegan Rice, *Mrs. Wiggs of the Cabbage Patch*, Ch. VII).

The demonstrative *that* is thus often used adverbially, but the demonstrative *such*, which has a somewhat similar meaning, always remains an adjective, although often classed as an adverb. That it is an attributive adjective when it stands before a descriptive adjective is shown by the fact that it can never be used when there is no noun after the descriptive adjective, i.e. when the descriptive adjective is used predicatively: '*such* severe weather,' but not 'The weather is *such* severe.'

c. Adverbial Use of 'The.' The old neuter instrumental case of the determinative and demonstrative *that* still survives in the form of *the* in two common constructions: (1) In clauses of degree expressing proportionate agreement: 'This stone gets *the* harder *the* longer it is exposed to the weather.' See *Syntax*, **29** 1 A *b* for a more detailed description of this construction. (2) As a determinative adverb of cause standing before a comparative, indicating cause, however, in only a formal way, pointing forward to a following clause or phrase of cause which contains the real cause: 'His unkindness hurt me all *the* more *because I had been previously so kind to him*' (or *because of my previous kindness to him*). 'The indications of inward disturbance moved Archer *the* more *that he too felt that the Mingotts* (name) *had gone a little too far*' (Edith Wharton, *The Age of Innocence*, Ch. V). 'I think a little *the* worse of him *on this account*.' 'She clung *the* more fiercely to her father *for having lost her lover*.' The cause is often not thus formally expressed in a clause or phrase of cause but implied in something that has preceded: '*Sir Arthur looked sternly at her.* Her head only dropped *the* lower.' '*If she were silent* there was one listener *the* more.'

2. **Comparison of Adverbs:**

a. Relative Comparison. Adverbs are compared much as adjectives, as described in **43** 2. A few monosyllabic adverbs add *-er* in the comparative and *-est* in the superlative: *fast, faster, fastest*. 'He climbed *higher*.' 'He lives *nearer* us.' 'He lives *nearest* to us.' 'Come up *closer* to the fire.' 'John worked *hardest*.' 'He couldn't speak *finer* if he wanted to borrow' (George Eliot). 'I can't stay *longer*.' 'He stayed *longest*.' 'I would *sooner* die than do it.' Also the dissyllabics, *often* and *early*, are compared by means of endings: 'He is absent *oftener* than is necessary.' 'You ought to have told me *earlier*.' *Easy*, an adverb in certain set expressions, is similarly compared: '*Easier* said than done.' Examples of the use of the comparatives *farther* and *further* are given in **43** 2 A *a*.

Earlier in the period, terminational comparison was often used where we now employ *more* and *most:* 'There is almost no man but he sees *clearlier and sharper* (now *more clearly and sharply*) the vices in a speaker then (now *than*) the vertues' (Ben Jonson, *Discoveries*, p. 19, A.D. 1641).

Most adverbs are now compared by means of *more, most* and *less, least: rapidly, móre rapidly, móst rapidly; rapidly, léss rapidly, léast rapidly*.

aa. Irregularities. A few irregularities in the form occur, corresponding closely to those found in adjectives (**43** 2 A *a*):

well	better	best
ill, illy (obs.), badly	worse	worst
much	more	most
little	less	least
near, nigh	nearer, nigher	nearest, nighest, next
far	farther, further	farthest, furthest
late	later	latest, last
	rather (comparative of obs. *rathe*, 'soon')	

One of the outstanding features of popular speech is the use of *good* for *well:* 'I don't hear *good*' (instead of *well*).

In American colloquial language *worst* often has the force of *most:* 'The thing I need *the worst* is money.' *The worst kind* and *the worst way* are common in popular speech as adverbs with the force of *very much:* 'I wanted to go *the worst kind* or *the worst way.*'

bb. Newer Forms of Expression. Besides the normal usage described in 2 *a* above there is another which is quite common in colloquial speech and occurs sometimes in the literary language. The superlative is formed by employing the adverbial neuter accusative of the noun made from the adjective superlative preceded by the definite article: 'All good and wise Men certainly take care To help themselves and families *the first*' (Robert Rogers, *Ponteach*, I, IV, A.D. 1776). 'I am going . . . to Havre, whence I shall get *the quickest* to Southampton' (Charlotte Smith, *Emmeline*, IV, 55, A.D. 1788). 'Of all my books I like this *the best*' (Dickens, *David Copperfield*, Preface). 'He was the greatest patriot in their eyes who brawled *the loudest* and who cared *the least* for decency' (*id.*, *Martin Chuzzlewit*, Ch. XVI). 'It is impossible to say whose eyes would be *the widest* opened' (Henry Arthur Jones, *The Divine Gift*, Dedication, p. 49). 'My father liked this *the best*' (*Alfred, Lord Tennyson, A Memoir by His Son*, 3, 245). 'We are sure that those who have known Somerset *the longest* will thoroughly enjoy Mr. Hutton's pages' (*Athenæum*, Dec. 28, 1912). 'Great souls are they who love *the most*, who breathe *the deepest* of heaven's air, and give of themselves most freely' (William Allen White, *A Certain Rich Man*, Ch. XXII). 'Of all the orders of men they fascinate me *the most*' (H. L. Mencken, *Prejudices*, Series III, p. 217).

This form is now spreading also to the comparative: 'He runs *the faster*' (instead of the simple *faster*). 'This led him to consider which of them could be *the better* spared' (Dickens, *Martin Chuzzlewit*, Ch. XXXIII). 'I hardly know who was *the more* to blame for it' (L. M. Montgomery, *Anne of Avonlea*, Ch. XXIII). 'Ruth could not tell which she liked *the better*' (Lucy Fitch Perkins, *The Children's Yearbook*, p. 17).

In the case of the analytic form with *most, least, more, less,* this adverbial neuter accusative cannot be used at all. We often, however, add the adverbial ending *-ly* to the analytic adjective, superlative or comparative, preceded by the definite article, thus marking the form clearly as an adverb: 'If it be true that such meat as is *the most dangerously* earned is the sweetest' (Goldsmith, *Natural History*, VI, 82, A.D. 1774). 'It was difficult to say which of the young men seemed to regard her *the most tenderly*' (Thackeray, *Pendennis*, II, Ch. XX). 'Standing here between you the Englishman, so clever in your foolishness, and this Irishman, so foolish in his cleverness, I cannot in my ignorance be sure which of you is *the more deeply* damned' (George Bernard Shaw, *John Bull's Other Island*, Act IV).

In the relation of sentence adverb the adverbial neuter accusative form of the superlative is replaced by an adverbial phrase, consisting of the preposition *at* and the noun made from the adjective superlative preceded by the definite article: 'I cannot hear from Dick *at the earliest* before Tuesday' (Mrs. Alexander, *A Life Interest*, II, Ch. XVIII), or '*At the earliest* I can't hear from Dick before Tuesday.'

When it is not the actions of different persons that are compared but the actions of one and the same person at different times and under different circumstances, we employ the adverbial neuter accusative of the noun made from the adjective superlative preceded by a possessive adjective: 'Two women shrieked *their loudest*' (Thackeray, *Pendennis*, II, Ch. XXXVIII). 'Carver smiled *his pleasantest*' (R. D. Blackmore, *Lorna Doone*, Ch. XXVIII). An adverbial phrase with the preposition *at* is sometimes used instead of the adverbial accusative: 'He led me in a courtly manner, stepping *at his tallest*, to an open place beside the water' (*ib.*, Ch. XXI). In the relation of sentence adverb this prepositional phrase form is quite common and freely used both with the simple and the analytic superlative, especially the latter: 'Even at *his ungainliest and his most wilful*, Mr. Thompson sins still in the grand manner' (*Academy*, Apr. 14, 1894, 303). 'Nature *at her most unadorned* never takes that air of nakedness which a great open unabashed window throws upon the landscape' (*Atlantic Monthly*, Mar. 1887, 324).

b. Absolute Superlative. This superlative of the adverb is formed from the absolute superlative of the adjective (**43** 2 B *a*). 'Mary's mother is *a most béautiful woman*' and 'Mary's mother sings *most béautifully*.'

The absolute superlative is sometimes formed by employing the adverbial neuter accusative of the noun made from the adjective superlative preceded by the definite article: 'I do not *the léast* mind it' (*Alfred, Lord Tennyson, A Memoir by His Son,* 4, 72). 'It does not matter *the léast*' (Florence Montgomery, *Misunderstood,* Ch. IV).

Instead of this form we often use a prepositional phrase containing a simple superlative of an adjective in attributive use, standing before a noun or the simple superlative used as a noun and preceded by the definite article: 'The letter was written *in the kíndest spírit.*' 'That does not concern me *in the léast.*' Compare **43** 2 B *a* (3rd par.).

Instead of a superlative here we more commonly use a positive modified by *very, exceedingly, absolutely,* etc.: 'She sings *véry beautifully.*' In colloquial and popular language, the intensive adverbs, *awfully, dreadfully, terribly,* etc., are common, sometimes without the suffix *-ly* before an adverb: 'The work is moving *awfully slow.*' 'I lived *mighty comfortably.*'

To express an absolutely high degree of activity in connection with a verb, we place *very* before an adverb of degree, such as *much, greatly,* etc.: 'He is suffering *very much.*' To express an absolutely high degree of a quality, we place *very* before the positive of the adjective: '*very sick, very pleasing, a very distressed* look.' But instead of saying 'I was *very much pleased, very greatly distressed,*' many incorrectly say 'I was *very pleased, very distressed,*' feeling *pleased* and *distressed* as adjective rather than as verbal forms, which they are. Similarly, we should use *too much, too greatly* before verbal forms, not simple *too:* 'I was *too much* (or *too greatly*) discouraged by this failure to try again.'

CHAPTER XIV

UNINFLECTED PARTS OF SPEECH

72. Three parts of speech, prepositions, conjunctions, and interjections, have no distinctive forms to indicate their function.

The position of the preposition before a word indicates that it brings this word into relation with another word (**16**). It often has a characteristic position at the end of the sentence or clause: 'What do you write *with?*' 'This is the pen I write *with*' (**16** 2).

The preposition plays a very important rôle in English. Its functions are quite fully described in **16.**

A conjunction links an independent proposition, or a subordinate clause, or parts of a sentence to the rest of the sentence. Its position immediately before a group of words indicates its function: 'He came early, *but* soon went away.' 'Wait *until* I come.'

The functions of conjunctions are described in **18.**

Pure conjunctions are regularly uninflected, but there are certain inflected pronouns which perform the function not only of pronouns but also of conjunctions (**7** IV *a*, *b*, **18** B 6).

Interjections, *Oh! Ouch!*, etc., are recognized by the peculiar tone which accompanies the spoken words (*Syntax*, **17** 1).

INDEXES

WORD INDEX

The references are to sections and subsections. The abbreviation *p.p.* after verbs stands for 'principal parts.'

A

B

C

D

E

F

G

H

I

J

K

L

N

O

P

Q

R

S

T

Y

Z

SUBJECT INDEX

The references are to sections and subsections. The abbreviation *p.p.* after verbs stands for 'principal parts.'

A

B

C

D

E

F

G

P